Praise for *Men of Tomorrow*

"*Men of Tomorrow* is a briskly written, yet thoughtful, exploration of a commercial empire built on the creation of new mythologies. Jones weaves in threads of biography and social history to illuminate the all-too-human characters behind the super-human icons of American pop culture."

—CNN.com

"With profound appreciation for the unsavory, the shady and the tortured, Jones tells the surprisingly rich tale behind the origins of comic books, revealing the sometimes tormented souls who invented this splashy art form and the unscrupulous operators who sold it. In microcosm, he tells a broader, roiling story of 20th-century America."

—*Baltimore Sun*

"In short, *Men of Tomorrow* is a dream for comics fans; it's also an engaging and worthwhile read for anyone interested in the history of Jews, journalism, New York, intellectual property—heck, in all the convolutions of the American way itself."

—*Ruminator Review*

"It is a well-researched, absorbing, first-rate history of the birth and enduring life of comic-book culture—a serious, readable book with enough thrills, perils, weird twists, heartache and sudden rescues as any classic issue of Captain America. . . . It passes a reader's test for any especially good work, be it novel or comic book: As soon as you finish it, you want to read it again."

—*San Francisco Chronicle*

"In his new book *Men of Tomorrow* Gerard Jones has peeled back the cover of the comic book, and he's discovered an unusual story of how geeks and gangsters in New York crafted a parallel reality better than their own and one that still sells today."

—NPR's Marketplace

"Before there was Michael Chabon's *The Amazing Adventures of Kavalier & Clay*, there was the early comics industry that inspired it—a chaotic, lawless, backstabbing mess of a business that Gerard Jones documents in *Men of Tomorrow: Geeks, Gangsters, and the Birth of the Comic Book*. A former comics writer . . . Jones has drawn on industry lore and long-buried documents, and dug up some remarkably juicy stories about the creators of Superman, Batman, Captain America and Wonder Woman as well as the men who published the first comic books."

—*The Los Angeles Times*

"For anyone who ever craved (or still does) the next issue of *Superman* or *Mad* Magazine or the *Fantastic Four*, Jones will remind you what that thrill felt like. And why."

—*Houston Chronicle*

"Bold and brassy, with a solid grasp of its material."

—*Kirkus Reviews*

"Jones provides a lively portrait of the talent, energy, and chutzpah that gave birth to the comic book industry."

—*Business Week*

"Jones' experience as a comic-book scripter . . . gives him the advantage over most previous writers on the comics milieu, and his vivid writing suits the subject. But it is his impressively thorough research that makes this one of the most valuable books on a distinctively American storytelling form."

—*Booklist*

"Gerard Jones's book tells the ultimate origin story—that of comics themselves. . . . He also charts the small but momentous cultural shifts that allowed comics to happen."
—*The New York Times Book Review*

"Faster than a speeding bullet, more powerful than a locomotive, this story is one that belongs on the bookshelf of anyone with an interest in comics, pop culture or plain ol' American history. This isn't just a good book, it's a necessary one."

—Scripps Howard News Service

"[A] fast-paced and informative retelling of the origins of modern comic-book culture."
—A. O. Scott, *The New York Times*

"Riveting, revealing, and heartbreaking. This is Gerard Jones's true story of the American comic book; dreams of nerds who were financed by bullies and consumed by the powerless. The authorities may have called superheroes a 'National Disgrace' but America's children knew they were gods in colored undies."

—KAZ, author/artist of *Underworld*

"*Men of Tomorrow* is the vivid tale of the daring young men who drew their dreams and made America believe them. Jones excels at digging up new facts. His story is largely untold and utterly fascinating."
—Lawrence J. Epstein, author of *Mixed Nuts: America's Love Affair with Comedy Teams*

"This book has brought me immense pleasure. Jones offers amazing new insights into how girlie pulp publishers and mob-related printers got to the top of the comics business. *Men of Tomorrow* is an extraordinary read."

—Bud Plant, publisher of *Images*

"Bold and colorful. Jones's history of the industry players is as compelling as the adventures of the superheroes. His tales of comic book heroines—'girl reporter' Lois Lane, or the original (and surprisingly feminist-sounding) Wonder Woman—are as enlightening as they are unexpected. *Men of Tomorrow* is for anyone (male or female) who wonders where heroes and heroines come from."
—Catherine Orenstein, author of *Little Red Riding Hood Uncloaked:*
Sex, Morality, and the Evolution of a Fairy Tale

Gerard Jones's books include *Killing Monsters*, *Honey I'm Home*, and *The Beaver Papers*. His articles have appeared in periodicals ranging from *Harper's* to the *National Lampoon*. He sits on the advisory board of the MIT Comparative Media Studies Program, created the Art & Story Workshops for children, and serves as a tutor at the 826 Valencia Writing Center in San Francisco. Once he was a comic book writer, too, and contributed to the adventures of Superman, Batman, Spider-Man, the Shadow, and many other creations of the "Men of Tomorrow."

ALSO BY GERARD JONES

Killing Monsters: Why Children Need Fantasy,
Super Heroes, and Make-Believe Violence

Honey I'm Home: Sitcoms Selling the American Dream

The Comic Book Heroes (with Will Jacobs)

The Beaver Papers (with Will Jacobs)

MEN <u>OF</u> TOMORROW

Geeks, Gangsters, and the Birth of the Comic Book

GERARD JONES

A Member of the Perseus Books Group
New York

For my father,

RUSSELL JONES

Who taught me what a hunk of ink-stained pulp
can mean to a young man in the hardest times

Books published by Basic Books are available at special discounts for bulk
purchases in the United States by corporations, institutions, and other
organizations. For more information, please contact the Special Markets
Department at the Perseus Books Group, 11 Cambridge Center, Cambridge,
MA 02142, or call (617) 252-5298 or (800) 255-1514, or e-mail
special.markets@perseusbooks.com.

Designed by Brent Wilcox
Set in 11.5 point Minion

Library of Congress Cataloging-in-Publication Data
Jones, Gerard, 1957–
    Men of tomorrow : geeks, gangsters and the birth of the comic book /
Gerard Jones.
       p.   cm.
    HC: ISBN-13 978-0-465-03656-1; ISBN 0-465-03656-2
    1. Comic books, strips, etc.—History and criticism.   2. Cartoonists—
United States—Biography.   I. Title.

PN6725.J664   2004
741.5'0973—dc22

                                                            2004009031

PBK: ISBN-13 978-0-465-03657-8; ISBN 0-465-03657-0

05 06 07 / 10 9 8 7 6 5 4 3

TABLE OF CONTENTS

AUTHOR'S NOTE

One of the challenges of this book has been to dig through the tall tales, drunken misunderstandings, and self-protective fudgings that have shaped the accepted history of this oddest of American art forms and arrive at some kind of truth. My interviews and conversations with many of the survivors of the industry's early days and their families proved to be the most important tool in that digging. It was over scrod and beer at the Westport Marina with Irwin Donenfeld that the stories of Harry Donenfeld and Jack Liebowitz first came clear to me, and over doughnuts and coffee in the Property Development offices in Beachwood with Irv and Jerry Fine that I first saw the shape of the Jerry Siegel story as I've told it here. Many other members of the Donenfeld, Siegel, and Liebowitz clans helped me, as well, as did some friends and former business associates of the men I've written about. Some have asked to remain anonymous, either for the sake of decorum or out of respect for the ongoing litigation involving the ownership of Superman, but one I can and must thank is Harry's loyal friend, Jack Adams.

My twenty years of involvement with the comic book industry have blessed me with the opportunity to meet many of the men who created the form. On two occasions in the 1980s, I was fortunate enough to chat with Jerry Siegel and Joe Shuster at the San Diego Comic Con; insights they gave me then have turned out to be important, and previously unpublished, pieces of the book I would write nearly two decades later. During those same years I interviewed or spoke at length with Jack Schiff, Julius Schwartz, Vin Sullivan, Murray Boltinoff, Jack Kirby, and

other pioneers who are no longer with us. I also owe a huge debt to the
men who so graciously submitted to my interviews and sometimes dis-
concerting questions for this project in particular: the late Will Eisner,
Stan Lee, Jack Williamson, Alvin Schwartz, and the very generous Jerry
Robinson.

I've depended not only on the people who lived the history of
comics but on those who've studied it as connoisseurs and collectors
and who were able to lead me through the forest of contradictions and
deceptions to the most plausible path of real events. My Virgil, my Ten-
zing, my Sacagawea was Michael Feldman, who has spent many years
tracking bits of the "big picture" and speaks wisely and knowledgeably
of the place of comics in the larger context of alternative cultures and
Jewish enterprise in a largely buried American past. Others without
whom the book would not have been complete include Will Murray,
Denis Kitchen, Tom Andrae, Mike Catron, Michael Uslan, Mark
Evanier, Anthony Tollin, Richard Halegua, Bob Beerbohm, Mark Waid,
and Paul Levitz. My research in Cleveland was made delightful and pro-
ductive by the hospitality of Mike Sangiacomo of the Plain Dealer and
Carolyn Johnson of Glenville High School. For vital moments of encouragement and correction I'm grateful to Art Spiegelman, Jules Feiffer, Paul Buhle, and Michael Chabon. I'm also very grateful to those who
caught errors in the first edition of this book and so enabled me to cor-
rect this one, including Roy Thomas, Larry Miller, Alan Light, and, especially, Michael Siegel and Douglas Nicholson, sons, respectively, of
Jerry Siegel and Malcolm Wheeler-Nicholson.

If this book's substance was the gift of those thanked above, then its
form was given by the friends who listened to me fret and patted my
head and read the chapters as I felt bold enough to expose them: Allen
Weinberg, Charlie Goldberg, Henry Jenkins, Heidi Anderson, Joe Filice,
Joel Millner, Andrea Rundgren, Helene Manheim, and Erika Silver,
whose inexplicable gift of an ancient copy of Jerry Siegel's *G. I. Joe* un-
locked the door to so much. Then there were the two who read every
damned page of the unrevised draft and too many rewrites: Melissa
McAvoy, who can catch a lazy adverb even while drowning in a vortex of

swirling dogs and children; and Carla Seal-Wanner, who turned her profound indifference to superheroes into a critical weapon to force me repeatedly into reluctant clarity.

My gratitude, finally, to Jennie, who became a single parent for months to enable me to finish the manuscript; to Nicky, who endured so little daddy time with such generosity; to my eternally encouraging agent, Carol Mann; and to everyone with Perseus Books who worked so hard on the countless little details, especially Ellen Garrison, Rich Lane, that prince of copyeditors Steven Baker, and most of all, Jo Ann Miller, the editor whose Solomonic wisdom, Herculean efforts, Atlas-like steadiness, Zeusian authority, Achillean passion, and Mercurial swiftness snatched me from the clutches of chaos and despair at the last possible second. *Suh-HAZ-am.*

Gerard Jones
June 2005

Secret Identity

JERRY PUSHED THE paper across the table. "Read that," he said. He watched her as she read the details. The Mario Puzo script. The plans to cast Paul Newman or Clint Eastwood or Dustin Hoffman in the title role. The images of the hero—*his* hero—laser-beamed onto giant balloons in Battery Park that "created mucho pre-pic talk." When her eyes flashed with rage he knew she'd hit the part about the 3 million dollars. A fortune dished out by Warner Brothers for the rights to make a *Superman* movie, and not a penny to Jerry or Joe or their families.

"You can't let them get away with this," said Joanne. "What more can I do?" he asked. Twice Jerry had fought them in court, twice he had ruined his career and left himself scrambling as they'd gotten richer. "Write to *Variety* yourself," she said. "Tell them the real story." But he was afraid. They'd told him they might do something for him financially if he'd drop his plans to appeal to the Supreme Court. Anything he did now would kill that hope. "They're never going to do anything for you," snapped Joanne. "Not unless you shame them into it. Not unless you tell the world what Jack Liebowitz did to you."

"I couldn't stand that," said Jerry, and he left for work. All his life he'd hidden his pain and loss—the first loss that had shattered his childhood and this other loss he kept reliving, these thirty years of feeling his one great creation torn from him. He'd always tried to seem stronger than his pain. But on the long ride to work, the words began to form. Since his heart attack he'd been riding the bus more than driving, and there are few journeys more dismal or interminable than a bus ride through the Los Angeles Basin in the summer. From Westwood along the underside of Beverly Hills, through the tattered remnants of the Miracle Mile and into the cratered ruins of downtown, he and the retired people on fixed incomes and the Mexicans going to clean houses crawled hardly faster than a young man could walk. He had time to think of what he could tell the world about Jack Liebowitz. The double-dealer, the backstabber, the crook.

At last the bus brought him to the state office building where he worked. There he had more time to think, eight hours as a mail clerk, sorting and delivering and thinking about Jack Liebowitz pocketing his piece of that $3 million. Some of the secretaries in the building had heard who Jerry was, and he could see the skepticism in their eyes as he brought the mail into their offices, see them trying to match this timid little man with the hero of TV shows and movies. "You didn't *really* create Superman, did you?" they'd ask. He'd force a grin and say, "Oh, yes I did!" And he'd remember thirty years before, when his name was in three hundred newspapers every day, when he was on Fred Allen's radio show coast to coast, being listened to by secretaries and elderly mail clerks who wondered what it would be like to create something that everyone in the world knew.

That night Joanne urged him again. What if he had another heart attack, a worse one, while he waited for those liars to make good? What would happen to Laura? Jerry knew what it was like to lose his father. And what good did it do to keep quiet? This wasn't the old days when you weren't supposed to show your dirty laundry. This was 1975, when everyone disclosed everything. Disclosures brought down presidents, filled the news, changed people's thinking.

"At least people would know," said Jerry. Because in his heart that burned as badly as the money: Knowing that his name wouldn't be in the movie credits, just like it had never been on the TV show, just like it had been stripped off the comics three decades before. If he told his story now, people would know, at least, what he'd given them. They'd know how he'd suffered.

So at last Jerry brought out his typewriter—the same old manual that had banged out his first scripts, that he'd ridden to the top and back to the bottom. He rolled in the typing paper and carbon, and he began a press release. The first copy would go to *Variety*, but there would be more. Hundreds more.

He wrote from a lifetime of rage, a rage that had been growing in him since long before his first battles over *Superman*. But he never had learned how to express rage. Always his passion would wheel and tumble into self-parody. "I, Jerry Siegel, the co-originator of SUPERMAN, put a curse on the SUPERMAN movie! I hope it super-bombs." On he raged for ten pages, through misspellings and redundancies, screaming capitals and melodrama. "The publishers of SUPERMAN comic books . . . murdered my days, killed my nights, choked my happiness, strangled my career." "WHAT AN INFERNAL, SICKENING SUPER-STENCH EMANATES FROM NATIONAL PERIODICAL PUBLICA-TIONS." Decades of correspondence and legal battles he wove into a story of villains and innocents. "I consider National's executives economic murderers, money-mad monsters." "Jack Liebowitz, a member of the Board of Directors of Warner Communications, stabbed Joe Shuster and me, Jerry Siegel, in the back. He ruined our lives, deliberately." And beneath that story, unacknowledged but shaping it, lay another: the story of a boy who'd had something even more precious stolen from him, who'd been split violently from his own sense of potency and had spent a lifetime trying to pull it back. Now, by telling his story at last, Jerry Siegel would begin to regain a fragment of what he'd lost.

Some stories are obviously significant when they happen. Others reveal their importance only over time. For thirty years the story of the men who created the American comic book and that peculiar construct now known as the superhero went essentially untold. The men rushed ahead, day after day and month after month, filling their pulp pages with lurid ink, never stopping to consider that what they had done or lived was worth a moment's reflection. When the stories were finally gathered, it was by fans compiling data for self-published journals with no purpose but to gain a deeper understanding of the yellowing comics in their closets. Jerry Siegel was the first to bring the history of the business to public awareness. But the history he told was not the only one.

History is written by the winners—sometimes. But some histories are written by the losers. The history of the comic book has been told by those who got rooked and by those who sympathize with those who got rooked. The men who got rich from them kept their mouths shut. The men who founded the companies, bought the characters, and created the multimedia marketing empires kept their stories to themselves and let the writers and cartoonists write the history.

As Jerry Siegel typed his letters, Jack Liebowitz was chauffeured from his Upper East Side apartment to the Warner Communications offices in Rockefeller Center. He rode the elevator to the top, to the boardroom, where he greeted the other trustees, mostly men much younger than him, men who had never known the New York he knew. As he waited for Steve Ross to arrive for the meeting, he could see out the big windows over Manhattan, south to the end of the island where he'd first arrived from a world now destroyed. Perhaps in his mind he could still see the pushcarts, still smell the ink on the bundles of newspapers, still hear the shouts of the workers at the socialist meetings where he'd learned how America and capitalism work. He could trace his own journey north through the island, to Union Square, where he'd stepped from a mighty labor union to a small printer of girlie magazines—and found the latter in some ways nobler than the former. Then further north to the building on Lexington Avenue where Superman had, in a single bound, made him wealthy and respectable. The respectability mattered to him. He would let Jerry Siegel tell the history of comics—at least the small part he knew. The greater story Jack was content to leave behind the curtain.

Jerry Siegel, Jack Liebowitz, Joe Shuster, Harry Donenfeld, Charlie Ginsberg, Bob Kahn, Stanley Lieber, Jake Kurtzberg, Mort Weisinger: all born in the course of a generation, all acquainted with each other, all Jewish kids, the sons of immigrants, many of them misfits in their own communities. They were all two or three steps removed from the American mainstream but were more poignantly in touch with the desires and ago-nies of that mainstream than those in the middle of it. In the pursuit of a quick buck, a splashy novelty, some relief from their own lonely anxiety, they invented a cultural form that came like a revelation to kids of every class and ethnicity, that would evolve to become part of adolescent and adult fantasy, and that would outlast its initial fad by sixty years and set an entertainment norm in an era vastly different from the one that spawned it.

Many of those young men lacked fathers, either in physical fact or in some emotional dimension. Most had not been permitted to grow as children ideally should grow, having been either forced prematurely into the role of an adult or held in the emotional world of early child-hood, or sometimes both at once. They played at grownup power and independence early while still nurturing the fantasies of the nursery. They dreamed of tomorrow, but it was a fantasy tomorrow, com-pounded of boyish science fiction dreams and wild hopes for their own success. To a degree that shocked even them, however, they saw and shaped America's tomorrow.

Their relationships with masculinity, sexuality, power, individuality, violence, authority, and the modern fluidity of the self were so tangled and so heartfelt that their work spoke to the anxieties of modern life more sympathetically, more completely, more acutely than they could have foreseen in their most inflated summer daydreams. With the pas-sage of time, their creations become only more relevant. They forecast and helped shape geek culture. They laid the template for the modern concept of the entertainment franchise. They created the perfect pack-ageable, marketable fantasy for the culture of consumer narcissism. They spawned artistic subcultures. All without quite knowing what they were doing. All by rushing frantically forward, trying to stay a step ahead of the wolves, snatching at the cultural scraps they found around them on the Lower East Side and in Glenville and the Bronx and shap-ing them into something that could be sold quick and cheap. All by ban-ishing yesterday from conscious thought and dreaming of the score they would make tomorrow.

The Street

IN THE END, Harry was a collection of stories. Of his first thirty-five years there is barely a record, only the stories he told and others told about him, told in bars and casinos, at distributors' meetings, in the box at Yankee Stadium, on the rare, brief visit to his family's dinner's table. He usually said he was born in Romania on October 16, 1893, and came through Ellis Island at age five. But when his son went looking a century later, there were no records of an Itzhak Donenfeld, his wife, or their sons Harry and Irving ever having entered America. Harry said he'd worked his way through New York University to learn business, but there was no record of him there either. There were no birth certificates, no school records, no business papers to track his various careers, his booms and busts, the mysterious origin of the capital on which he built his publishing domain. There were only the stories that he belted out with such glee, such a curbside shill's bravado, that you found yourself working to make them true.

Sometimes the stories soared to the ridiculous. Ask him how he got such juicy paper allotments during wartime rationing, and he'd claim to be in FDR's Brain Trust. Why would the most powerful man in the world want Harry Donenfeld, this runt who went nightclubbing in a Superman T-shirt, in his Brain Trust? "The old man loved me!" Harry would whoop. "I gave him a hotfoot!" (A *hotfoot*? Did he really not know Roosevelt was a cripple, or was that the joke? Harry would be three stories down the road, glad-handing somebody else, before you could think to ask.) But with Harry, sometimes the ridiculous turned out to be the truth. His supposed connections with the top mobsters in America were easy to dismiss as more fiction. But just when you dismissed them, there was the evidence. There was the great fixer himself, Frank Costello.

The unabashed self-promotion, the absurd claims to glory, the refusal to submit to the tyranny of the real or the possible, the understanding that the story is all that matters—all these would be Harry's gift to the industry he helped create, the industry that would ultimately try to erase his memory but would always carry an echo of his laugh, his lies. Harry buried much of his life, but the stories are still there as guides to who he was and how he got where he did: how a man who cared nothing for publishing or entertainment or children became the publisher of DC Comics and brought superheroes to the world.

Harry was tossed into New York by the crest of a wave, for 1899 was the year of the great Romanian diaspora. For nearly twenty years Jews had been pouring from the Russian Empire into New York, but Romania had been a better place to be Jewish. To win French and German support for their war of independence, the Romanians had promised to respect the civil rights of all their citizens. Yiddish speakers had poured into the country from Russia, Poland, and the Ukraine, mingling with centuries-old communities of Turkish-, Romanian-, and Ladino-speaking Jews to create a complex and cosmopolitan Jewish world. By the late nineteenth century, Bucharest and the other big cities of Romania were between a third and a half Jewish. Jews rose in urban government; some were elected mayor in smaller cities. Jews owned big businesses, dominated the textile trade, produced prominent lawyers and doctors. Romania briefly promised to become a Jewish haven without match.

But once the Romanian government felt secure in its footing, it turned. It still promised equal rights to all citizens, but "citizen" was redefined to include only Christians. Then Jews were prohibited from peddling. Finally, in 1896, the Romanians proved that their soaring national pride could be every bit as hateful as the Russians', as they expelled Jews from whole districts of cities and mobilized unemployed young men for the country's first big pogrom. To a people encouraged to expect better it was a galling betrayal. With a swiftness and a unity unknown in any other country, the Jews rose. And they left. It's been estimated that from 1899 to 1904 a third of the Jews of Romania emigrated to other countries, most to America and most of those to New York. Some rich merchants paid the transportation costs for the Jewish communities of entire towns. Thousands of men and women too angry to save for train and ship fare banded together in a spontaneous movement to walk over the Carpathians and out of the country, singing Yiddish songs and sometimes wearing their old Romanian army uniforms in a final *kish mir im tuchus* to the nation that had tricked them. Harry Donenfeld shared with many of his landsmen an anger, an arrogance, an inclination to see the goyim not as long-term oppressors but as tricksters and hypocrites.

So Romanian Jews poured into New York, sweeping the Donenfelds with them. They gravitated toward the First Romanian American Synagogue on Rivington Street, where they packed and packed themselves into the fifteen blocks from Allen to Ludlow and Houston to Grand streets, until even the other immigrants around them began to speak of their blocks with dismay and amazement. The Lower East Side was already the densest neighborhood on earth, the densest in history—half a million people in a square mile—and the Romanian quarter was the densest part of it, with 1,500, even 1,800 people in a single block. They were quick to identify themselves as Romanians, filled the streets with restaurants known for spices and *shmalts,* cracked jokes about the food and clothes of the greenhorns from the Russian shtetls. They became known for their beautiful singing voices, their quick tempers, and their gutsiness in dealing with the goyim.

Just what Itzhak Donenfeld did when he arrived with his wife and children is unknown. We have only the stories from Harry and Irving's childhood, in which he appears as both a peddler and clothes dealer.

Such a lack of documentation was common among the Jewish immigrants of the time. Getting through Ellis Island often meant breaking the law, lying, bribing officials. It could mean a single man paying a family to count him as a brother; it could mean a sudden name change. Once on the new shore, an immigrant might find more reasons to change a name, adjust a birth date. It was a common belief that the military drafted Jewish boys first and sent Jewish boys first to the front—so a little money was slipped to a city clerk and a boy's birth certificate was made to disappear. A twelve-year-old became fourteen so he could work, then six years later he became sixteen to avoid the draft. Harry himself years later would nearly lose his ownership of Batman because a young cartoonist's father had made his birth certificate vanish.

The lack of documents, of fixed names and lineage, of hard facts about the lives left behind in the old country only made it easier and more important to invent a new self in the new world. For a boy like Harry reality was not what you were but what you said you were. Every acquaintance became a new audience and a new collaborator in the authoring of the new Harry Donenfeld. This was the task taken on by an entire generation of immigrant boys: to create a new self, a new kind of Jewish young man, out of the pieces available to them on the Lower East Side. The world that their fathers brought them to was not so very different from the old neighborhoods of Vilna or Warsaw or Bucharest. The sound of the city wasn't that of engines but of hooves and wooden wheels. Goods were moved over the stone streets by pushcart and horse cart; horses pulled streetcars. Only the elevated trains hammering over the shadowed valleys of Chrystie and Allen streets brought the roar of the modern world. Garbage was tossed in the gutters and alleys. Indoor plumbing was occasional, and every morning the contents of chamber pots were poured by hand down backstreet sewers. The air stank. Electric lighting was beginning to take over the public spaces, but shops and homes were lit by kerosene. Outside the classroom, Yiddish was the language, and if you heard a snatch of another tongue on the street, it was more likely to be Russian than English. The adults still dressed as they always had—the beards, the black wool, the wide hats, the babushkas. When Harry Donenfeld was a boy, it was still fashionable on a Sunday for rich Gentiles to ride downtown and look at the funny Jews.

The purpose in coming here, though, had been to find a new world. Pulling roots out of the ancient soil, selling the family possessions and saying goodbye to brothers and parents for the last time, taking on the long terror and punishment of the journey had all been for a future. The only immediate reward of starting life over in America was freedom from the pogrom, and the reports in the Yiddish press about New York's street crime and the mobs of murderous young goyim who prowled the edges of Jewish neighborhoods made that a dubious trade. The money that could be made, the professions that could be entered, the land that could be bought in America were only potential. The messianic passion that had been rolling through the Yiddish world over the past century, the aching for a release that kept the Hasidim wailing and dancing in the shtetl as their more pragmatic neighbors sold the cart and moved away, transmuted into a hungry faith in the promise of a new world.

The kids got the message clearly and constantly: they were living not for today but for tomorrow. Harry said he came to New York at five with no memories of the old country but only of the journey. The new world, however, gave a turn to the message that the parents hadn't intended. The adults had imagined a prosperous new life, the children enjoying that life but still not much different from themselves. The children understood immediately that they would have to become entirely new beings in order to create and enter that tomorrow. And most of the tools for that transformation would be found not in the home or the shul or the American public school but in the street.

The Donenfeld boys rarely spoke of their home life, but we can assume it was as hard for them as it was for most new immigrants in the Lower East Side. When their two older brothers, Charlie and Mike, came across the ocean to join them, six people had to share the family's tiny slice of a tenement on Orchard Street. The four brothers likely slept in a single bed or else, like many kids, in a "hall bedroom"—a roll of bedding unfurled in the building hallway after everyone had gone indoors—to be stepped over and kicked by late arrivals and early risers. The psychological crowding was probably just as intense: parents pushed their sons hard to perfect their schoolwork, learn English and a trade, find a job. Play was discouraged, especially physical play. "Alter, Alter, do you want to kill me?" one writer remembered his mother yelling when he broke his leg playing stickball. "Mom," he yelled back, "whose leg is broken?"

Parents resisted making their sons work and struggled to keep them in school, but when the need for money was desperate they had no choice. By the late nineteenth century, state law prohibited children under fourteen from working in shops and factories, but New York City created a loophole. Whole tenements were designated "work houses," where sewing and other contracted labor could go on without official supervision, where mothers could enlist their own or their neighbors' ten- and eight- and six-year-olds to produce piecework for pay. One block could contain several shops; Orchard Street was once estimated to contain two hundred shops in its five blocks. The Donenfelds apparently took on such subcontracted work occasionally, for Harry's brothers spoke in later years of having to cut bolts of cloth on the kitchen table by kerosene lamps. Even as incomes improved, the pressures didn't ease. Parents who could afford it gave their kids Hebrew lessons; those who could scrape together the payments added piano or violin lessons. And through it all there were the moral lectures: boys caught smoking, gambling, playing ball, talking to strange girls, walking hatless in the street were nagged and scolded without cease.

The shul was an extension of the home—and the young generation pulled further from it even as their fathers drew defensively into it. Lincoln Steffens wrote of the "abyss of generations": "a synagogue where a score or more boys were sitting hatless in their old clothes, smoking cigarettes on the steps outside, and their fathers, all dressed in black . . . were going into the synagogue, tearing their hair and rending their garments. . . . Their sons were rebels against the law of Moses; they were lost souls." Later reminiscences shaped by success, suburbanization, and loss tended to sentimentalize the Lower East Side as a great, thriving, happy experience of Jewishness, but in the moment, for a whole generation of young men the driving hunger was to get *out*—out of the neighborhood, out of the *Yiddishkeit*.

School was a relief for many kids, a reason to get out of the house that no parent could argue with. But it too was suffocating: forty or fifty kids in a room, lined up in rows; ten-hour days for kids who took the extra classes to help them learn English. Nor was it much of an advertisement for its own value. The teachers weren't rabbis honored in their community but young Irish women waiting for husbands to pull them out of poverty. Some immigrant children were rising through school to become lawyers and doctors, but the shortages of time and money made those possibilities remote to boys as poor as the Donenfeld brothers. The "All-rightniks" who bought their way out of the Lower East Side were rarely the best-educated immigrants but rather the slickest salesmen, who opened their own retail stores, or the lucky garment makers who got into that business when it boomed, or the swappers who scored in real estate in one of the new developments in Brooklyn.

For a restless, ambitious, impatient boy, life's great arena was not home, shul, or school but the street, where the kids hung out and shared their own visions of what America was and how to beat it at its own game. The street opened to the world. Immigrant parents knew little but the core of the ghetto and whatever paths they had to follow (quickly, heads down) to get to their factories or places of business, but the kids quickly mastered a larger geography; picked out the safest routes through the wastelands of Irish, Slavs, Germans, and Italians around them; found the harbors where they could smoke under the piers and gaze out to the world beyond the island, learned how to hitch a streetcar or sneak onto a train to get to Coney Island or Central Park.

Few boys were as restless, ambitious, or impatient as Harry Donenfeld. The stories of his childhood are spun around his energy. Tireless mouth, clever tricks, endless appetites. There are no pictures of Harry in childhood, but even from his adult photos an urchin peers out: the lamp eyes looking for a shot at profit or mischief, the voracious grin, and the laugh in the throat. Decades after Harry's death his son would speak with some rue of his long absences from home, his gambling and philandering, his lack of interest in his children's lives. "He just lived his own life," said Irwin. "He always had something else to do." Then, despite himself, Irwin broke into a smile of admiration: "He was a dynamo! A regular little *dynamo!*"

Harry flourished on the street, and the street was where he, the baby of the family, emerged as its driving force. Charlie and Mike had come over in their late teens, never fully mastered English, and never quite lost the awkwardness of greenhorns. Irving and Harry were the Americans of the family, but God had burned different destinies into their tongues: Irving stuttered, while for Harry words flowed like wine. For the rest of his life, Harry told stories about teasing his older brother. He especially liked to tell them when Irving was present. Calling to a pretty girl, "Hey, my brother wants to say something to you!" Playing craps and with the toss of the dice yelling, "Call it, Irving!" Irving would turn red and stomp off, leaving Harry as the star, laughing and eyes twinkling. When it came time for the boys to find jobs, Irving found a way to master words without having to speak: He apprenticed himself to a printer. Harry became a barker, pulling customers into a clothing store with his musical Yiddish keen or buttonholing lonely greenhorns on the street and inviting them up to a dance hall where female warmth could be felt for a nickel a waltz.

Harry's ability to make himself liked served him best in the gangs. It was nearly impossible for a boy not to join a gang on the Lower East Side. They formed in tenements, they waited on stoops, they scared you into joining—unless you were already in a bigger or meaner one. The gangs were creating something new in the world: rough Jewish kids. The ways their parents had learned in the old world, keeping their heads down and avoiding the goyim, didn't hold in the new world. These kids watched their fellow Americans the Irish and the Sicilians and adopted their swaggers. It was not an unconscious process. One tough kid remembered adults arguing in his father's house in Poland, one man saying, "Jews . . . why do you just stand around like stupid sheep and let them come and kill you, steal your money, kill your sons, and rape your daughters? Aren't you ashamed? You must stand up and fight. You are men like other men. . . . Hit them and they'll run. If you're going to die, then die fighting." Years later the former kid said the speech "is burned in my memory. I carried the words with me when I finally traveled with my mother to America and the Lower East Side. I remembered those words when I fought back at the Irish as a boy on the East Side. They were like flaming arrows in my head." But that kid wasn't part of Harry's life yet. Meyer Lansky was still in his future.

In the course of a generation, the Jewish kids proved they could fight and steal with the best of them. In 1890 observers were still asserting that "the Hebrew is the model immigrant, disinclined to delinquency of any kind." But within fifteen years the percentage of Jewish kids dragged before the juvenile courts was as great as the percentage of Jews in the school system. Now the alarmists were calling Jews "congenitally criminal."

As an adult Harry would claim to have been a member of nearly every East Side gang anyone could think of. It's easy to picture him gliding from gang to gang, winning everyone over but never wasting his energy on loyalty. He knew members of the "rough gangs," who'd steal from merchants, extort money from peddlers, commit arson or even murder for cash. They were part of the scene. As Jake Kurtzberg, who grew up in Harry's neighborhood and would later draw comic books for him, would say, "Some of my friends became gangsters. You became a gangster depending on how fast you wanted a suit." But it was never Harry's inclination to suffer, and lifelong he would make an art of avoiding physical fights and jail time. He kept mainly to the run-of-the-mill gangs, devoted to minor turf battles, rustling up beer and cigarettes, playing low-stakes craps and pitching pennies on the stoops, doing some minor scams and pocket picking.

For some scams Harry emerged as a leader. It was he who discovered that the sweetest fruit was in forbidden fields. He would lead his gang out of the neighborhood, across the Bowery to Kenmare and Mulberry streets, deep in Little Italy. The tiny kid with the Yiddish accent found it easy to hold the attention of Sicilian food peddlers. He'd ask what everything was, act like he was bargaining on prices, as they laughed at him and asked him what the hell he was doing out of his neighborhood. While he had their attention, his friends would grab apples and run. Harry was the last to bolt, but he was quick. Once, while trying to get across the Bowery, they all got cut off by a gang of Italian kids. The others got pounded, but Harry slipped away. When they limped home bloody and bruised, they found him on the steps of his tenement eating an apple. In mock outrage he cried, "What happened to you guys? I told you to cut south on Mott!"

It was crime that made anxious parents pull their children off the streets, that made "the street" a watchword among immigrants and teachers and reformers alike. But the streets taught more than crime. They taught kids how to hawk wares, how to buy low and sell high, how to lie with guts and not back down, how to know when to take care of your buddy and when to stick it to him. They taught a kind of self-projection too that would become central to a new American personal style. Eddie Iskovitz was a year older than Harry, lived a few blocks from him on Henry Street, went to PS 160 with him for a few years, and was his friend through the first years of the century. They ran in some of the same gangs, pulled some of the same scams. But Eddie was dirt poor: Orphaned early, he was raised by his widowed grandmother, a door-to-door peddler. Eddie had to pay for much of the food and rent, so he dropped out of school to sing and dance for pennies on street corners. There were a lot of kids singing on corners in the Lower East Side, so Eddie learned to stand out by grinning big, waving his arms, belting loud, and he learned to hold his audiences by winking, rolling his eyes, batting his eyelids, and offering his attentions with a slutty innuendo. By his late teens he was breaking into burlesque, and Harry was already saying, "You gotta see this Eddie Cantor! He's a friend of mine!" The Cantor style became Harry's style: grinning, banjo-eyed, boyish, everybody's naughty friend. But sharp underneath that. Always watching the reaction he provoked. Ready to move on his opportunities.

In and out of school, in and out of jobs, in and out of gangs, Harry created a self of shticks and stories. No one called him smart or tough or very good at anything in particular, but the people he knew found him funny, were flattered by his attention, and found it easy to believe he could someday be the big shot he pretended to be. He showed a knack for losing money at dice and cards but also a knack for making it back in a clever deal or a mysterious errand for a hoodlum or a quick stint as a hawker for a clothing store. Harry was turning himself into a new sort of peddler, one perfectly in keeping with a rapidly changing America about to go on a superheated, advertising-driven economic binge: He was a salesman who sold himself.

THERE WERE OTHER ways to create a new identity. In 1899 in Proskurov, in the Podolia province of the Ukraine, or perhaps in one of the shtetls nearby, a woman in her early twenties named Mindl married a local man. They had a son on October 10, 1900, and named him Yacov. And then the man disappeared. No one would ever know where he went. Mindl would say later only that he must have been too weak to bear the duty of providing for a family and went somewhere, America maybe, where he could make money and keep it himself. She would never tell Yacov his father's name: "That man left us. He isn't your father." All clues to Yacov's paternity, to his original surname, would be left behind in the dirt streets of Proskurov.

Mindl's parents took her in as she learned to stop waiting for her husband's return, sought a divorce through the synagogue, and spread the word that a poor, abandoned woman with a baby was looking for a man who would stand by her. He arrived when Yacov was three in the form of Yulyus Lebovitz. The family had doubts: Lebovitz was a socialist, a fur cutter involved in labor union activity, a risky thing in the czar's empire. But he was a kind and serious man, dedicated to taking care of people, with a special passion for defending women who were exploited by men. He promised Mindl he would always take care of her and her child, and that was more than many women in her situation could ask for. She married him and soon was having children with him: Yacov would have five half-siblings by the time he reached ten.

Socialism was a growing movement among Russian Jews, for it promised not only to free workers from exploitation but to free the world from a set of delusions that usually worked against Jewish welfare. Under socialism the Jewish sense of justice and mutual protection would survive, but the nonsense of religion could be eliminated. This was the same hunger for a better future that fed messianism among the Orthodox and assimilationism among the children of immigrants in America. But socialism also became the flash point of Russian anti-Semitism during Yacov Lebovitz's childhood. Rightists blamed Jewish socialists for the revolution of 1905, which forced the czar to accept a constitution. In the last few months of that year, seven hundred pogroms were launched throughout the empire, nearly forty in the province of Podolia alone. Proskurov itself escaped with little damage, but everyone knew of the five hundred murdered in Odessa and the hundred in Kiev with the acquiescence of the police. Yulyus Lebovitz would later tell his stepson of union meetings broken up by the army, of being hounded by the secret police.

Meanwhile, the streets were full of talk about the new world being made in America. Everything published in Russia was strictly censored, but Yiddish newspapers from abroad were smuggled in and passed around. New York's *Forverts* ("The Forward") was openly socialist and a noisy advocate of Jewish political power. In the winter of 1909 and 1910 Yulyus Lebovitz read of the shirtwaist strike organized by a newly formed group called the International Ladies Garment Workers Union, whose membership was about four-fifths Jewish and four-fifths female. *Forverts* told the story of a "frail young girl" named Clara Lemlich who fought her way to the stage at a union meeting and declared, in Yiddish, "I am a working girl." She described the "intolerable conditions" of her work and called for a general strike. The hall erupted in applause. Within days, 20,000 garment workers had walked off their jobs. "The

Uprising of Twenty Thousand," it was called. "The Great Revolt." In truth, Clara Lemlich was in her twenties, an experienced socialist organizer, and the moment was orchestrated; but the sentimentalized story was a powerful one among leftists and the uncommitted masses alike. It was certainly powerful for Yulyus Lebovitz, protector of women and children. For weeks the news continued of female workers braving cold and cops and strikebreakers. By the beginning of spring, the manufacturers had buckled, agreeing to a fifty-two-hour work week, paid holidays, and union grievance committees. The ILGWU, dominated by socialists, was a major political force.

That same spring, news of a different kind came from Kiev: 1,200 Jewish families had been expelled from the city. Dozens of them found their way to Proskurov, affluent city people begging friends and relatives for attics and hallways to sleep in, bearing dire predictions of worse times to come. For Yulyus the future was obvious: Russia was a deadly place for a Jew to help build an international socialist movement, but in America it could be done, and his family would not have to suffer. In 1910 he brought his family to New York. He became Julius Liebowitz, husband to Minnie, occasional garment worker and full-time organizer for the ILGWU. Little Yacov, now ten years old, became Jacob and then Jack.

Both Julius and Jack discovered the streets of the Lower East Side, but in different ways. To Julius the streets were where socialist newspapers were sold, where union leaflets were passed out, where workers could be rallied and picket lines thrown up. The streets were also where ideas were discussed, where socialists, communists, and anarchists argued with each other and came together to mock the corrupt Democrats and the Orthodox fools.

Jack learned his way among the streets as a newsboy. The tenement garment shops weren't the only loophole that permitted employers to exploit child labor in the new century: A more public one showed itself in the army of news- and delivery boys who scurried on city streets. The newspaper industry depended heavily on nine-, ten-, and eleven-year-olds who were willing to fight their way through the city, hawking the news for a dollar a day. The sentimentalization of the plucky, happy newsboy in the comic strips of the day was largely a calculated effort to keep public sentiment in the industry's corner when reformers tried to extend the child labor laws to include newspaper sales. A newsboy's was not a cheerful life. The hours were long, the money uncertain, the risk of being mugged high, the struggle for turf and sales constant. But Jack was good at it. He was proud of being a newsboy: He worked many other jobs in his youth, but it was only the news hawking that he spoke of in later years.

Jack was a serious kid, dark eyed and intense in his stare. He wasn't especially tall, but he struck people as such because of his leanness, his angular earnestness, his way of standing as straight as he could and taking long strides. He didn't smile much and he didn't joke, apparently not even in boyhood. He worked, he watched, he sold, he learned. He learned how to get his bosses to give him the good corners and how to sell the tired working man his daily dose of crime, corruption, blood, and comic strips. He learned English quickly, worked to throw off his Yiddish accent, modeled himself not on the pimps and hooligans who excited Harry Donenfeld's imagination but on the straight-laced businessmen who bought his papers and the serious socialists who came to his house to argue about the destiny of the working man. He was fiercely loyal to his stepfather, talking of organizing his fellow newsboys, fighting kids in the street who put down the unions, joining the Socialist Labor Party as soon as he was old enough.

But what he would remember most from his childhood was poverty. He remembered the tiny sums his father would bring home for union work, the loans they'd get from other workers to cover the rent, his five little siblings passing down tattered clothes, his mother's constant anxiety about money. "It was always hard for him to make ends meet," Jack would say delicately in later years, "given his ideals." Jack's mother never spoke against his father or his socialism: He had rescued her. But Jack could tell that this was not the life she wanted. Always unspoken in the air was the dream of prosperity that had likely lured her first husband away, that drove the other husbands and sons in the neighborhood. Jack worked as much as he could, and whatever he could save he brought home to the family. When he wasn't working, he was studying. Whatever he did in later life, he knew he wanted to provide.

Jack would always speak of his hard times on the street with a certain satisfaction, much as Harry Donenfeld reveled in his stories of gangs and misadventure. They were of a generation of boys who were never adolescents and yet whose fantasies and emotional lives were caught at the cusp of adolescence forever: children pressed straight into an adult role, tackling it with a ferocity that combined the darkest cynicism with a boyish love of adventure. Harry would act his boyishness out more. Jack was acting like an adult by twelve. But he would always know a good adolescent fantasy when he saw one.

In March 1911, just a few months after the Liebowitzes landed in New York, there occurred an incident that froze the Jewish community in horror and that echoed through the stories of Jack Liebowitz and Harry Donenfeld. The Triangle Shirtwaist Factory caught fire, trapping hundreds of girls and young women nine and ten stories above the street. Girls began jumping from the windows, their dresses billowing in flames, to die on the pavement. In a span of fifteen minutes 146 girls, dozens of them only thirteen or fourteen years old, nearly all of them Jews, were killed. Over the next few days, people learned why some girls had jumped: the owners had chained the exit doors shut to keep them from taking breaks.

For Julius Liebowitz, and for every organizer with the ILGWU, it was a pivotal moment, the beginning of the union's most furious and most successful drive for workplace reform. For ten-year-old Jack it was a demonstration of the brutality of poverty; he knew kids in school whose sisters died at Triangle. Donenfeld family stories conflict as to how the fire touched Harry's life. In one story, he rescued his future wife, Gussie, by proposing to her and urging her to quit her sewing job at Triangle in the days before the fire—but he was still seventeen then and probably didn't even know Gussie yet. In another, he somehow witnessed the fire himself; forever after, he harked back to it when he got drunk and maudlin about how it was people that mattered, not money. Maybe neither story was true, but they both suggest that the fire was a symbol to him of how close at hand disaster could lie, kept at bay only by luck or self-interest. Harry would chase quick money his whole life, but he'd also lose a lot to gambling and sentimentality; the fire could have served to remind him of how essential and how meaningless money could be.

The Triangle fire, however, also taught lessons about the messiness of power and money in the new world. In the Ukraine it was possible to believe that the world was divided into the chosen people and the goyim, that the Jews would do better to always stick up for their own. But Julius Liebowitz had to make the immigrant rank and file understand that the owners of Triangle Shirtwaist, Isaac Harris and Max Blanck, were Jews, as were the owners of 90 percent of the New York garment industry. In the heat of a strike, it was easy to hate Irish cops for their brutality, but the men who called those cops were German and Austrian Jews who lived among the Gentiles on the Upper East Side, and it was Irish firemen who cried over the bodies of the Triangle girls laid out on the sidewalks. The newspapers that Jack Liebowitz sold on the hard streets, especially William Randolph Hearst's *Journal*, exploited the horror of the fire and posed as friends of the working people; but Jack knew the publishers privately fought against unionization and child labor laws.

Father and son Liebowitz learned, too, about the compromises required to survive in the capitalist jungle. Tammany Hall, the crooked, Irish-run machine that controlled the Democratic Party in the city, profited from the whorehouses and gambling dens that fed off workers and stained the Jewish neighborhood. So in the mayoral election of 1896, the Jewish community threw its votes behind a Republican reform candidate. But once elected, Mayor William Strong immediately began prosecuting merchants who opened their stores on Sundays, a deadly blow to observant Jews who closed on Saturdays, and ordered pushcarts driven from the streets, a move ruinous to hundreds of peddlers. From then on, the Lower East Side remained reluctantly in the pocket of a crooked Tammany. To secure police action against brutal employers, leftists like Julius Liebowitz would have to learn to make it worthwhile to the most venal crooks in the city.

And then there were the thugs. Garment manufacturers hired members of the "rough gangs" to break strikes. In the Great Revolt of 1910, the owners hired so many *shlammers* that the unions were forced to outbid them to hire the likes of "Dopey Benny" Fein and Joe "the Greaser" Rosenzweig to protect their workers. Gangsters soon insinuated themselves not only into picket-line battles but into union organizing as well. In 1915 twenty-three union officials, including the treasurer of the ILGWU, were tried for complicity in the murder of a scab. They were acquitted only through the intervention of a crooked Tammany judge.

Young Jack saw the criminals from a different angle. As the gangs grew bigger and rougher, they took control of whole chunks of the neighborhood—first just illegal activity but then, through extortion, legitimate businesses. Running a newsstand or posting newsboys on street corners required working with the gang that ran that street. Jack saw newsboys who tried to invade a rival gang's block beaten, heard about news dealers sliced up by the hook rings used to cut the twine around newspaper bundles. When Hearst formed his own circulation firm to go up against the monopolistic American News Agency, he cut deals directly with the bigger criminal mobs to carve out lucrative territories across America's larger cities. The bloodiest "circulation war" was in Chicago in 1912 and 1913, where twenty-seven news dealers were murdered; a few years later Hearst hired one of his Chicago thugs, Moe Annenberg, to take over his New York circulation. Young Jack didn't know that one day he'd be doing business with Moe Annenberg and probably would have preferred not to know. But he began to understand that he had to learn to cooperate with such men in order to survive.

Jack was raised to believe that the ideals described by socialists, reformers, and teachers had the power to bring more order to the world and advance one's welfare. At the same time, he learned early that everything they argued for existed against a background of savage competition and ethical compromise. He knew from childhood that nothing was quite how anyone represented it. Between the stories America told about itself and the way it actually lived lay a vast gap, sometimes sickeningly and sometimes comically absurd. Nearly everyone Jack knew, including himself, lived in that gap, speaking one reality and living another.

That may be why the world of numbers became such a comforting refuge for him. He considered both law and accountancy in high school, knowing that the socialist movement had need for both skills, but in bookkeeping classes he discovered the satisfaction of balancing a ledger, of entering figures that would not shift and reconciling everything at the bottom of the page. He knew, before he entered adulthood, that what he wanted most was to provide, to make money for his family and ease the daily terror of the bills and debts. He hoped that socialism would someday make that possible, but in the meantime, he would make sure he could take care of his own. He fixed his sights on becoming an accountant.

By the time Jack entered high school, the prospects for a young Jewish man in New York were fairly good. The immigrant Jewish community as a whole was leaving its hardest days behind. The number of new immigrants dropped precipitously with the outbreak of war in Europe in 1914, and growing prosperity was lifting more and more families to the Bronx, Brooklyn, and New Jersey. The old neighborhood, no longer so overcrowded, had been given asphalt streets, electric lights and trolleys, the Manhattan and Williamsburg bridges to open it to the world. Reform movements guided by Jewish leaders had improved housing conditions and routed much gambling, prostitution, and other crime.

The economic boom that accompanied America's entry into the world war was especially good to the garment industry. The business was already growing rapidly as "ready-to-wear" fashions became more accepted and clothing purchases became a larger part of working-class and lower-middle-class budgets. Now with the war, an invigorated American economy, and the halting of European exports, the rag trade exploded. The trade unions were strong and unified, able to push prosperous and confident bosses into significant concessions without resorting to strikes. When Dopey Benny Fein's gang was broken by the police—likely with the help of union insiders—the labor movement shook free of the mobs. Moderate socialists like Julius Liebowitz were firmly in charge of the ILGWU and other Jewish unions. Julius was at his happiest: The family still didn't have much money, but prospects were bright for the ILGWU. He'd proven himself to be not a leader but a solid, hardworking organizer. Among his duties was the production and distribution of leaflets, and somewhere along the way, one of his regular printers was Martin Press, owned by the brothers Charlie, Mike, and Irving Donenfeld.

Printing was a growth industry for Jews in the early century. The field had been dominated in New York by Germans, Irish, and Scots. Businesses passed from printers to their children and apprentices, and there seemed little room for new entrants. But there was something the old-line printers weren't set up to do: the Hebrew characters used in Yiddish. And the Jews were the most literate, most publication-hungry of all the ethnic groups in America. A need for merchants' leaflets and store brochures arrived with the first immigrants, and by the 1890s, a market for Yiddish newspapers was burgeoning. Young workers had an insatiable appetite for books, especially novels of love and adventure, and although Yiddish imports from Europe slaked it for a while, printers in New York were producing cheaper and more Yankee-centric knockoffs by the end of the century. Printers who could keep up with the demand prospered. Irving Donenfeld, working hard and holding his stuttering tongue, earned a reputation as a good printer. His two older brothers pooled funds with him and opened a business. They shifted their emphasis to English printing as the neighborhood changed, and they put together a solid trade in leaflets, brochures, and pages for some of the cheapest of the "cheap books" and "story papers" on the newsstands.

They offered their baby brother Harry a place in the family firm, too, but Harry's passions had led him elsewhere.

JUST WHEN HARRY Donenfeld discovered girls is not recorded, but probably around 1906 or 1907 he awoke to a pleasure even more compelling than talking and gambling. He was an unlikely ladies' man: short, homely, loud, coarse in humor, sloppy in expression, full of himself. But he had that energy, that eye for every angle, that ferocious hunger when he wanted something. And this he wanted. Sex was no mystery to boys who grew up on the Lower East Side. Whatever cloak of shame or delicacy immigrant parents tried to draw around it was shoved violently aside by the neighborhood. Tammany Hall had helped turn the area into the most notorious, possibly the largest, red-light district in the country. Michael Gold wrote that pedestrians on Allen Street "stumbled over a gauntlet of whores' meaty legs." Lincoln Steffens wrote of little girls in a tenement apartment who spent their evenings watching a prostitute who couldn't afford curtains servicing customers. Decades later, when censors shouted that children must be protected from such images as Wonder Woman's skimpy costume in Harry's comic books, it must have seemed just another bit of *goyishe* madness and hypocrisy.

By his teens Harry had learned to dress like a "cadet," as the neighborhood called the pimps who served the brothels and dance halls. He grew a dapper little mustache and wore heeled boots to raise him above his five foot one. He learned to dance and to sweet-talk, to recognize which girls could be talked into a long walk through the night streets with promises of cigarettes and beer and a trip to Coney, and to seize the moment when a kiss could be stolen, an alleyway seized, a skirt lifted. Harry rarely bragged later of the beauty or quality of his women, but of their number and willingness he crooned often.

He learned the power of fashion, too: the way a girl's eyes would light at a gift of the latest hat or jacket, knocked off from a Parisian original by a shop on Second Avenue. Here was the confluence of Harry's desires and his salesmanship. His dapper appearance, his ability to flatter women of all kinds, his eye for what was newest and brightest combined to make him the perfect clothing salesman. No one knows anymore what shops he worked at, but he described them as "classy." Harry would speak fondly of those days, of cultivating the trade of gamblers and high rollers with discounts on snappy suits, of having wholesalers take him out drinking at Chrystie Street taverns or to a casino on Broadway for a game of *stuss* or to one of the classier whorehouses on Houston. It was a low-cost way to look like a big shot.

Harry wanted to be a bigger shot than that, though. He wanted his own shop. To become a businessman, he needed two things: money and a wife. He knew a lot of girls whom an ambitious young man wouldn't marry, but he needed a helpmeet, a money manager, someone to bear him children and give him respectability. He met her in the Seward Park Public Library, which served then as a sort of community center, offering free classes in English, bookkeeping, and useful skills for the new American. Her name was Gussie Weinstein, and she'd arrived from Russia only a few years before. She was hardheaded and practical, intent on moving up in the world; she studied business skills when she could afford the time. She may have worked as a sewing machine girl earlier in her life, long enough to support the tale of her rescue from the Triangle factory, but by the time Harry entered her life, her family had piled up some money. She was just what Harry needed.

Harry was probably in his early twenties when they met; she was five years younger. She would say later that her parents didn't think much of this fast-talking little operator, but he was persistent and she was plain. Somehow he avoided the draft in 1917 (thanks possibly to that lack of documentation), and the war surely reduced the competition for Gussie's hand. Finally he won. They were married in 1918. Soon, with a little loan from Gussie's parents, they crossed the river and opened their own clothing store in Newark, New Jersey.

By the end of the war, all their futures were clear. Julius Liebowitz would go on organizing for a more just, more socialistic world. His stepson, Jack, would work his way through New York University by doing bookkeeping for the union, and when he had his degree, he would become an ILGWU accountant. Three of the Donenfeld brothers would prosper modestly by printing for the union and other cost-conscious clients. Harry and Gussie Donenfeld would get fat and happy selling ladies' ready-to-wear in New Jersey.

Then the Twenties happened.

The Other World

ALL HIS LIFE, in all the interviews he gave, all the talks he had with editors and peers, all the autobiographical sketches he wrote, Jerry Siegel never mentioned what happened to his father. In the story of his life as he told it, his father appears as a mere background detail, the provider of the comfortable middle-class Cleveland home in which Jerry discovered the wonders of science fiction and daydreamed a superhero. Only in the dreams themselves, transmuted into outlandish cartoons, do we see the themes of loss, violence, isolation, invulnerability, and retribution that hint at more.

Michel Sigel arrived in New York around the turn of the twentieth century, adjusted his name to Mitchell Siegel, and found his way to Cleveland. His wife, Sarah, waited for him in Lithuania with their first two children until he'd earned enough money to bring her over. He had an artistic streak and worked as a sign painter. The booming Jewish community of Cleveland provided a good market for him, and soon he was able not only to bring over Sarah and the children but also to help other members of his family and Sarah's five younger siblings come over, too. By 1914 and the end of emigration from Eastern Europe, a large, interwoven Siegel-Fine family was scattered through the Jewish communities along the eastern edge of Cleveland.

Sarah was the matriarch. Stories vary on many details of the family's history, but all agree on Sarah's power. She had commanded her five siblings before her marriage, and as her husband and many of his male cousins and in-laws headed across the sea to find their fortunes, she became the force that held both families together. Once in Cleveland and away from her parents' generation, she became the undisputed head of the whole extended family. "She told everybody what to do," said Jerry Fine, one of her nephews. "Her kids, her sisters, her brothers, their kids. Her husband."

For her, Mitchell left sign painting and put his money into the more reliable world of retail. He opened a haberdashery, did well with it, and bought his family a three-story wood frame house with a deep backyard and a welcoming front porch on a quiet residential street in Glenville, a district booming with an influx of rising Jewish immigrants. Sarah bore enough children to match the size of the family she'd grown up in: Minerva, Rosalyn, Harry, Leo, Isabel, and finally, on October 17, 1914, Jerome. He was the youngest by four years, the child of Sarah's middle years, her baby who remained small and dependent as the others grew up and moved out.

The Cleveland that Jerry was born into was a boomtown. From the 1890s to the 1920s, it grew from a quarter million people to nearly a million, from the tenth largest American city to the fifth. It was a mecca for immigrants: 40 percent of its population was foreign-born or of foreign parentage. It led the country in production of gasoline and electrical devices, was second in steel and cars, third in garments. Cleveland coasted through the industrial depression of 1921 better than any other big American city. Industrial wages were among the highest in the country, and the unions were strong. The deal the ILGWU cut with garment makers in 1921 was the best in the nation, and they got it without a strike. It was a forward-looking city and was conscious of the fact—the first in the nation with public electricity, electric streetlights and trolleys, and an indoor shopping arcade. It set a standard for urban planning and the building of scientifically designed "model factories."

Cleveland's 70,000 Jews were far fewer than New York's million or Chicago's third of a million, but they were enough to sustain a rich culture, complete with a Yiddish press and theater, a few nationally influential synagogues, and dozens of smaller shuls and community organizations. At first the community was packed into the shabby Woodland ghetto near the factories, but around 1910 it reached a size and affluence that allowed its wholesale colonization of Glenville. This was a bucolic district of woods and fields, streams cutting deep gullies on their way to Lake Erie, whose nearby shores were used by rich Protestants for their summer cottages and horse farms. But as the city grew and the automobile increased their mobility, the rich climbed up the hill to Shaker Heights and left the glens to upwardly mobile immigrants. Glenville was 20 percent Jewish when Jerry Siegel was born, over 70 percent Jewish by the time he was ten.

The aorta of Glenville in the early 1920s was East 105th Street. "Almost every block from Superior to St. Clair," wrote one observer, "had its own *shul* and its own kosher meat market—and fruit and vegetable markets, drug stores, creameries, bakeries, and grocery stores abounded." Residents "shared experiences of shopping and dating and discussing in an atmosphere that took Jewishness and *Yiddishkeit* for granted." Kimberly Avenue, where Jerry grew up, was a quiet street only a block long, stopping on one end at a tree-filled ravine and on the other at 105th Street near the Crown Theater, Spector's Creamery, and Solomon's Delicatessen ("Open All Night"). A few blocks north, at St. Clair, were chain stores and old-world restaurants and more theaters and a café with live music. A few blocks the other way was the grand Jewish Center of Anshe Emeth, with its Stars of David looming high above the street, its basketball courts and swimming pools, its dances and classes in everything from Zionism to "Americanization."

Though there was crime in decaying Woodland, where Mitchell Siegel's store still stood, and in blue-collar Mount Pleasant, there seemed to be almost none in Glenville. People who grew up there would later describe the neighborhood with a fondness bordering on reverence: "The long streets were always full of kids playing baseball . . . and large front porches held gobs of kids every night sitting on the swing and on the railings to joke around, exchange ideas and neck—after the grown-ups disappeared." This was the American dream that had pulled so many thousands across the sea from Russia, Romania, Poland, Lithuania.

Kids like the Siegels faced the stresses of a boom. A crisis in school overcrowding found forty-five to fifty students in every class, under-qualified teachers, elementary classes held in basements, synagogues, and borrowed cottages. And yet the Jewish kids thrived, their schools soon outstripping all others in the city in academic honors. When Cleveland, always striving for modernity, became one of the first cities in the United States to institute intelligence tests, Glenville High School scored at the top. One Cleveland educator concluded, "Judaism is less a dogma than a progressive education." Nor were the successes only academic. In 1923, when Jerry Siegel's eldest siblings were students there, Glenville High won the city football championship behind a dazzling halfback named Benny Friedman. A special game was then arranged with Oak Park High School in Chicago, Ernest Hemingway's alma mater, which had what was considered the best high school team in the country. Benny and his skinny Glen Hi "Tar-Blooders" won. In the ethic of the early Twenties, when individual triumph and flash were valued as never before, the Glenville generation shone bright.

Hopes and demands were high for children like the Siegels. The elder five did well, all reasonably popular and successful in school. The boys went out for school sports and were among those playing ball in the streets and hanging out on the porches. As teenagers they worked in their father's store, learning something about business, growing away from their powerful mother and toward their father. Each would go on to a stable career, Harry in real estate and Leo in civil service. The two older girls, old enough to remember the Woodland ghetto, were pragmatic and hardworking like their mother and married solid men with decent jobs.

Jerry was the different one. He was small and myopic and didn't much like roughneck play. Descriptions of him emphasize his "energy," but this wasn't the social energy of Harry Donenfeld. Young Jerry sounds like a fidgeter, more anxious than active. He was bright but more inclined to daydream than study. His mother encouraged him to stay in the house and keep her company, help her with her chores, rather than run with the other kids outside. He would often withdraw to the room he shared with Harry. He especially liked it there when Harry was out playing ball or working at his father's shop, and he could give himself to reading, daydreaming, or drawing pictures.

When Jerry was six, one of his brothers took him to a movie palace to see Douglas Fairbanks in *The Mark of Zorro.* Little Jerry fell in love. The vast darkness, the ceiling soaring above like the dome of heaven and the orchestra swelling like the voice of God, and then the white blaze of the screen and the hugeness of Fairbanks: his mass and swagger, the voiceless bellow of his laugh, and the comedic arrogance that turned combat into slapstick and physics into a joke. And Fairbanks as Zorro, at first holding himself down to play the timid man in a hostile world until he transforms himself in secret into his hidden truth, metamorphoses by will and a costume into a whirl of joyous violence and super-human skill who sends the bullies and bosses of the world sprawling across the floor with a flick of his hand. And the roars of other children in the dark, each alive in Fairbanks's body, set free.

From then on Jerry wheedled and schemed to go as often as he could to the movies, and as soon as he could get permission, he'd go alone, begging a dime and walking to the modest Crown Theater two blocks away. After a few more years he was allowed to trek all the way up to St. Clair Avenue, to cross at the new electric signal light and pay his way into the Uptown, the Doan, or the rococo Savoy, to vanish into their vast gleaming screens. For the rest of his life, when Jerry spoke of his early childhood, he would mention almost nothing but the movies he saw. He loved every movie, any movie, but best of all he loved outlandish action, men transcending physical reality to perform breathtaking absurdities. He loved Harold Lloyd, running at superspeed in *The Freshman* and dangling off the skyscraper in *Safety Last.* He loved Buster Keaton being blown through the air and slammed to the ground and popping up unfazed in *Steamboat Bill Jr.* Mostly, though, he loved Fairbanks: *The Three Musketeers, Robin Hood, The Thief of Baghdad*—every model of manly heroism transformed into hey-look-at-me boy-ishness. Fairbanks the giant boy suddenly taking flight as he swung off a yardarm in *The Black Pirate.* Jerry loved him, and became him, in a way that more athletic, more daring boys could never understand.

Jerry liked to draw pictures of the movies he'd seen or cartoons in the style of the comic strips he liked: the slapstick of *Mutt and Jeff* and *The Katzenjammer Kids*, the impossible adventures of the young boy in *Little Nemo.* According to one cousin, Mitchell Siegel encouraged his son's art. He had been a painter once himself, after all, and had given up the craft to sell hats and support a family in middle-class comfort. Jerry was the first of the Siegel boys to know that comfort from the beginning, the first not to be pressed to find a job before he'd entered adolescence, and Mitchell probably enjoyed encouraging his drawing and fantasizing. Art seems also to have been Jerry's main source of attention from his father. Busy with the store and the older boys, Mitchell left the raising and disciplining of the baby son to the powerful Sarah, but art gave Jerry a tool to catch his father's eye.

Jerry seems the sort of youngest son likely to have found a niche as the artist of the family, the son permitted to find his own way in life, the one who would have gone to college or art school and perhaps then into publishing or advertising. There's no reason to think he had any great promise as an artist or writer, but he might have built a respectable creative career, been able to grow somewhat beyond his mother's control, win his father's approval, and find his way into the male world. If everything had gone the way it should have.

REAL LIFE BECAME harder for Jerry as he neared adolescence. He didn't concentrate well in school and was held back a year; he watched his peers moving beyond and away from him. A cousin remembers him having no friends at the time. Jerry himself would later say that from the moment he discovered girls, he was terrified of them. More and more, he began to seek out worlds other than his own. He had already been drawn to the lurid pulp magazines that beckoned from the newsstands along St. Clair Avenue for years, but now they pulled him in.

They were cheap and fat, hundreds of brown-tinged pages of fiction a month, enclosed in painted covers contrived to inspire dread, excitement, desire, and desperate curiosity. The plots were crowded with thugs and sinister Orientals and underdressed molls, but the ones Jerry liked best were built around he-men: great square-jawed goyim who wrestled beasts and stared down gunmen. There were war pulps, Western pulps, crime pulps, jungle pulps. Some were aimed at adults but many at eight-to-fourteen-year-old boys—"the age of hero-worship," as one pulp editor called it. School libraries didn't carry them and few parents bought them. Many parents, in fact, actively wrenched them from their children's hands and threw them onto their trash incinerators. But boys of the Twenties and Thirties hungered for them. Old men who now sell pulps for small fortunes on the Internet swap stories of pooling their pennies with other kids to buy the magazines, then passing them around until the cheap binding cracked and the ragged-edged pages skittered away. Will Eisner, the son of a furniture painter in the Bronx, remembers a boarder in his parents' home who'd let him sneak back issues of *Black Mask Detective* out of his room. When his father caught him, the magazines went out the window with a cry of, "This is trash!" Only later would Will realize that that trash included stories by Dashiell Hammett, Raymond Chandler, and Horace McCoy.

Sarah Siegel never tried to control what Jerry read and managed to provide him enough allowance to buy his own pulps. Jerry liked detective stories and *Tarzan* and that particular favorite of young men desperate to escape their daily reality, *Weird Tales.* Then, in the summer before he turned fourteen, Jerry saw the flying man.

In the archaeology of popular culture, the August 1928 issue of *Amazing Stories* appears again and again as a pivotal memory of a generation of moviemakers, science fiction writers, cartoonists, astronomers, futurists, and rocket engineers. Against a lucid yellow background floats a man in a skintight red costume, leather pilot's helmet, and sleek black boots, his body prone but angling upward in an attitude of nascent flight. He holds the dynamic ease of a warrior from a Parthenon frieze, his musculature defined by crisp lines and solid colors in a manner both classical and industrial. He wears electrical devices and holds a glowing rod that seems to help him fly. The huge red "A" of "Amazing Stories" floats just above his heel, the other letters arching over him like half a protective dome. He hovers just a few yards above a broad lawn, from which a pretty girl waves her handkerchief at him. A row of trees, a garage laboratory, and a pleasant house on a wooded knoll stretch low and safe and horizontal across the background, the knoll curving up to match the arc of his torso and the title letters above him. In contrast to the monster-filled labs and devastated planets of most *Amazing* covers, this is a world of sun and security, defined by architecture, science, and supremely economical illustration. And in contrast to the terror and grimacing of nearly every face on the covers of the pulps, this man is smiling. In newsstands filled with dread, here suddenly was joy, a safe but unbounded future. Here in the hearts of children who saw that cover was a soft, exhaustless lift into the open, golden sky.

Jerry ran home with it and read it immediately. And after plowing through the whole thing, he read it again. The cover story was the first half of a novel called "The Skylark of Space" by Edward Elmer Smith, about a young tinkerer who develops a device to fly him into space, where he discovers warring interplanetary empires, joins a galactic police force, and has to rescue his fiancé from a star-spanning criminal gang. It was told with the breathless, untutored invention of a boy pacing in his room, and the fact that it was a serial made it all the more perfect for insulating Jerry from reality through the end of summer and the renewed agony of school. In addition to "Skylark" the issue included another story, "Armageddon 2419," by Philip Francis Nowlan, the adventures of a ray gun–wielding soldier named Anthony Rogers in a futuristic war. Though Nowlan's world was darker than Smith's, the two stories fit well with each other, for both presented universes of violence containable by gadgetry and American know-how. They left behind the barbarian nostalgia of Edgar Rice Burroughs and the apocalyptic fears of H. G. Wells and reassured American boys that the future would be theirs and would be wonderful. Together, Smith and Nowlan and the cover artist, Frank R. Paul, had made a new world for Jerry Siegel, more compelling and more plausible than any he'd entered before.

Amazing Stories was an odd magazine. It had been on the stands for a couple of years, mixing articles on radios and rocketry with reprinted fiction by H. G. Wells and Jules Verne. Unlike most pulps, it named its editor on the cover, and that editor, with the intriguing name of Hugo Gernsback, led off each issue with an essay on the power of technology to transform the world for good. Gernsback also edited *Science and Invention, Radio-Craft, All About Television* (in 1927), and—although *Amazing Stories* was the most sexless of all fiction pulps, shunning even damsels in distress on its covers—a magazine called *Your Body*, with some of the most explicit sex advice articles on the newsstands. Gernsback was a utopian popularizer of a pure Twenties vintage, pitching the gospel of science and reason through cheap magazines aimed at the masses.

Jerry haunted the newsstands waiting for the next installment of "Skylark," and when it finally appeared, he found himself confronted by the Gernsback gospel in a most explicit form. The September issue of *Amazing* sported a cover as bizarre as the August issue's was liberating. It bore no images of humans or monsters or spaceships but only a crude heraldic device on a plain white background: a triangular shield with an engineer's compass on a planet-filled background. Two gears read "Fact" and "Theory," and the compass was writing a strange word in florid cursive: "Scientifiction." There had never been such a pulp cover, and even a boy not yet fourteen could have sensed that it sprang from a mission nobler than separating kids from their dimes. Inside, Gernsback expressed his zeal to promote this new kind of literature, this "scientific fiction," that would wage war against superstition and ignorance and illuminate the technological paradise that awaited mankind. Instantly Jerry Siegel was born again as a scientifiction fan.

Other pulps included letters from readers, but the letters pages of *Amazing* had a special electricity, as adolescent boys from all over came together to pledge their energies to spreading the word: Forrest J. Ackerman from Los Angeles, Raymond Palmer from Milwaukee, Jack Williamson from rural New Mexico, A. Bertram Chandler all the way from England, and several from New York, including one Mortimer Weisinger, who would loom large in Jerry's future. Gernsback also ingeniously included not just the name and state of his correspondents but their entire addresses, so they could contact one another directly. Around scientifiction began to grow a community of readers held together by a cause and a worldview. They taught each other about the new kind of fiction, formulated critical standards, and soon began to write crude stories themselves, hoping to see them in the pages of *Amazing* but usually happy just to have them read by their fellow believers. Groups of aficionados had grown up around popular fiction in the past; *Weird Tales* had inspired an especially communicative body of followers. But in scope and fervor there had never been anything like this.

The fans followed Gernsback faithfully: When he lost control of *Amazing Stories* in a financial dispute in 1929, they urged each other to go with him to his new magazine, *Science Wonder Stories*. When, to distinguish the new pulp from the old, he abandoned the world "scientifiction" in favor of "science fiction," the fans immediately followed suit. "Science fiction" would be the name of their passion forevermore. When the first science fiction club met in New York that same year, its members were required to tell "what I have done for science fiction in the past month." Within a few years the fans had coined the word "fandom" to describe their community. When enthusiasts of other fields began to pick up the term, the science fiction fans spoke, only half jokingly, of "the One True Fandom." They were a race apart, and wanted to be. Jerry Siegel began to write to the people named in the letters pages, and those people wrote back. He had found another world to enter, one that would respond to him.

Science fiction was a perfect invention for America in the late 1920s. The horrors of nineteenth-century industrialism and the technological hell of the world war were fading from memory. Radios, cars, and mail planes were connecting people to one another as never before and giving industrial development a new and humane face. A production economy valuing thrift and the accumulation of capital was being replaced by a consumption economy based on spending and credit, self-gratification, and the marketing of the new. In 1927 Charles Lindbergh was deified for using a modern machine to conquer space all alone, and there are surely echoes of his grace and self-satisfaction in the flying man on the cover of *Amazing* a year later. Politicians, advertisers, and popular storytellers all sang the praises of business, invention, America, the self-indulgent individual, and the future. For the first time, Americans were beginning to view the pursuit of novelty as an act of social duty and individual heroism.

At the same time, science fiction ran sharply counter to the pragmatic character of bourgeois America, its distrust of unfettered imagination and scorn of anything overtly childish. Readers who could appreciate a futuristic device described in Hugo Gernsback's other magazine, *Science and Invention*, would scoff at the same device if it defeated a Venusian machine-man in *Amazing Stories*. So science fiction remained a marginal form, if not unnoticed then sneered at by those immune to its thrall—particularly the athletic, social, realistic boys who saw their more oddball classmates reading these spaceman-spangled magazines alone at lunch hour. The fans responded with the arrogance of the outcast: A real debate raged through fandom in the early 1930s as to whether the fan was simply a person of specific tastes or "a superior order of human," marked as a higher rung on the evolutionary ladder by "his vast imagination and openness to possibility." But the outcast's arrogance, of course, is entwined with his agony.

The early fans were overwhelmingly male, mostly middle class, mostly Anglo or Germanic or Jewish, and mostly isolated, whether by geography, personality, or physical disability, until they discovered fandom. Looking at pictures of the early fan clubs, one sees a lot of eyeglasses and few athletic physiques. Like Jerry Siegel, few spoke of their families, but what they said hinted at absent parents, troubled relationships, and loneliness. "I weighed my life up to that time," wrote one fan about the end of his college years, "decided that it had been largely dross, and insofar as I could, cast it from me." Like Jerry Siegel also, most had little to do with girls until after high school. When they found partners, they spoke with a restrained romanticism of the confluence of minds or reading tastes that had drawn them together. The stories they loved and wrote were locked in boyish latency, often lacking females entirely; even the occasional damsel in distress tended to be, like the wholesome fiancé of Smith's "Skylark" series, fairly sexless and unthreatening. They distrusted passion, mystery, and the messiness of grown-up reality. They valued memorized detail and mechanical efficiency. They wrote with the optimism of boys but usually only by denying how much pain and anxiety they negotiated every day.

In their correspondence they strutted with florid self-advertisement masked as self-parody, held onto each other with in-jokes and acerbic wit, like fifth-graders with collegiate vocabularies. They craved clearly marked categories. They argued endlessly, obsessively, about whether science fiction must be based on proven concepts or could stray into speculation, whether the purpose of a story was the imparting of scientific understanding or simply adventure in scientific form. Was time travel "science," or should it be dismissed as "fantasy" like sorcery and gods? They labeled and listed and ranked and included and excluded and collected with passionate exactitude—such hyperrational ordering being the most entertaining way to keep the disorder of life and emotion in check.

They recorded their own histories obsessively, but only their activities as fans and the stories that inspired them, never what they lived or felt. In that way, Siegel's silence about his own family history was typical. Fans would follow that code for generations. When it came time to unearth the history of Jerry Siegel's own creation, they would scour the pulp magazines for the word "superman," comb the comic strips for heroes in tights and capes. They saw themselves in terms of bibliography, not biography: They asked endlessly about Superman's printed fathers but never about Jerry Siegel's father.

The extent of this resistance to human messiness is suggested by the first story Jerry Siegel sent to his peers. By 1929 Jack Williamson was one young fan who was getting his stories into print in *Amazing*. So Jerry typed a story and asked for advice. "He sent me a manuscript in which the characters were geometric solids: cubes and spheres and cones," remembered Williamson. "I pointed out that it had no human values, no human emotion. . . . His story needed human interest." That story is long gone, but a few years later a shorter, humorous variant called "Death of a Parallelogram" appeared in Jerry's high school newspaper. He was still a long way from tackling human interest.

But it was in those years that Jerry found his place. He still liked comic strips, but he gave up drawing, turning all his efforts to writing science fiction stories and letters about others' science fiction stories. He taught himself to type. The frantic energy he'd been known for all his life he now channeled to words. While the other Glenville kids played ball on the streets and necked on the porches, Jerry Siegel sat at the window of the front attic room, tap-tap-tapping to make himself a world.

Seven decades later, his cousins Jerry and Irv Fine sat in Irv's real estate office in the Cleveland suburb of Beachwood discussing the Jerry Siegel they knew. "He always hung around with the younger kids like me at family gatherings," said Irv, "because the kids his own age wouldn't have anything to do with him. He was a nerd."

"Oh, I wouldn't say that," said Jerry, who had been one of those kids Siegel's own age. "He just had a very quiet demeanor. He was very involved in his own interests. He used to take us to his room to see his collection of pulp magazines and all the letters he'd had published in them, but there wasn't much more he was interested in talking about."

"He was a *nerd,*" said Irv.

"Well," said Jerry more quietly. "We didn't have the word 'nerd' then."

Indeed, there was no word for Jerry's kind of boy yet, because there weren't many of them. But their numbers were growing. Of course there had always been boys lost in private thoughts and passions, boys dominated by their mothers and inclined to fantasize about the male world instead of tackling it realistically, boys who held pain at bay with elaborate imaginings. But this was the first generation to grow up with access to an alternate universe provided by commercial entertainment. It was the first to grow up understanding that the very nature of experience and perception could be transformed by machines and artifice, rendering the "make-believe" as palpable and dignified as the "real." Movies, pulps, radio, the phonograph, comic strips—all combined to give the new generation an inexhaustible supply of emotional and imaginative experiences that required no participation in reality. And through fandom, there was now a community—others to encourage keeping one's core in that other world even when school or work demanded the presence of one's outer self. This generation also came of age in a culture that rejected God and tradition and certainty, and so encouraged the relativism of the self-created world. It was a generation of misfits who were given a choice other than complete withdrawal from the world or indentured service to it. They were given another place to go.

This Twenties generation was also the first to grow up in a developed consumer culture that encouraged people to define their identities by what they bought. In an increasingly mobile and fluid society, Americans no longer wanted to be identified by class, ethnicity, or region. But to be a Cadillac driver or a Valentino worshipper or a science fiction reader gave a sense of self and community, especially to young people trying to draw black-ink borders around themselves in a world of runaway change. The early science fiction fans were not a counterculture espousing values radically different from the mainstream. They believed in scientific progress and competitive individualism. Perhaps their only real critique of the greater society was their reverence for brains over emotion and brawn—but they liked spacemen who could fist-fight, too. What set them apart was a passion for a particular packaging of mainstream anxieties and aspirations and an openness to one another's peculiarities so long as the unifying passion was there.

Setting them apart too was the loneliness and the pointlessness of modern childhood. For the modern middle class, daily life was cut off from what had always been the essentials of human existence: growing food, making clothes, children working beside their parents. For people from the already straitlaced cultures of northern Europe, the anomie of modern life, its mobility and anonymity and essential loneliness, was exaggerated. And their kids were growing up in small nuclear families with unprecedented amounts of time alone and indoors. An ever growing number of young people were driven to seek connections and meanings that life had once provided more automatically. So a particular set of personality characteristics and individual agonies became the basis of a subculture. Once in the subculture, the boys fine-tuned one another's identities around the self-definition "science fiction fan"—an indifference to clothes and appearance, a manic but unsentimental bonhomie in their meetings, an amused disdain for the drones who didn't understand them. There was no word for it yet, but now we can see this as the birth of geek culture. And from it every subsequent geek culture—comics, computers, video games, collectible figurines—has either grown directly or taken much of its form.

At the age of fourteen, Jerry Siegel was already becoming a prominent member of early fandom. In 1929 he even brought something new to it. He seems to have wanted to prove that his fascination with the imaginary had a real-world value. He was a retailer's son, after all, and the only son of Mitchell Siegel who didn't help in the store or hold a job. What better way to show his father that he wasn't just a mama's boy playing in his bedroom than to make his hobby turn a profit? So he gathered together the stories he'd been writing, the ones *Amazing* had been rejecting, and he made his own magazine. He asked for hectograph sheets from the librarian at his junior high school; assigned his stories a variety of pseudonyms, hoping he could fool readers into thinking they weren't all the work of the same fourteen-year-old; wrote a grandiloquent Gernsbackian editorial trumpeting the arrival of a new magazine to expand the frontiers of the literature of tomorrow; and called it *Cosmic Stories*. He typed his pages up as neatly as a bad typist with a manual typewriter could—the pages smudged by razor scraping and overtyping—and ran ten copies off at school. Then he spent nearly all the money he'd saved to advertise it in the tiny classifieds at the back of *Science Wonder Stories*.

In later years Siegel couldn't remember if he'd sold a single copy. But he had created the first science fiction fan magazine—soon to be called "fanzines" and later "zines"—a central organ for many future geekdoms. For all his love of science fiction, his heart was ultimately not in advancing the cause but in finding an idea he could sell. He wanted to be noticed. He wanted to believe that an idea was out there somewhere that would make him suddenly significant, suddenly potent, suddenly adult.

Jerry's writing brought him nothing, but he kept dreaming and typing, all the way through junior high. He continued to pursue his friendships-by-mail, which really weren't so much friendships as exchanges of professional advice. In October of his final year in junior high, the American business world suffered its greatest convulsion, the crash of the stock market, but its repercussions weren't felt at first in Jerry's private world. The culture of the Depression would shape him eventually, but not yet. The event that shattered Jerry's world came a few months later.

Jerry was home with his mother when it happened. Mitchell was downtown, closing the haberdashery alone. A neighboring merchant saw the door ajar and the light on after closing time but saw no sign of Mitchell among the shelves. He poked in, called Mitchell's name, and then saw the blood on the floor. He followed it behind the counter, and there was Mitchell on the floor, already dead, with two bullet holes in him. The money was gone from the cash register. The police never found the thief who shot him. Just another hophead or desperate drunk out of work, or would-be gangster in his teens, or Jew-envying thug who vanished with someone else's cash and dreams back into the hard heart of Cleveland.

AFTER MITCHELL SIEGEL'S murder the family hardened in its ways. No one spoke of what happened; younger relatives were told that Uncle Mitchell had died of a heart attack. The relatives rallied financially. Sarah's siblings and older children kicked in a part of their earnings every month to make sure she could keep the house. College was now out of the question for the kids, daily survival more important than the future. And Sarah tightened her grip. In response to the loss, she became more controlling of her siblings and her children. Younger cousins remember the house on Kimberly Avenue as the nerve center of the family, a great tense place where family celebrations were held and family business decided, where the adults would gather on the main floor while the kids retreated to the yard or porch or upstairs bedrooms to avoid the agonized displeasure of Aunt Sarah.

Jerry could have found a job, too, could have taken on the hard, scary work of the newsboy or delivery boy, but Sarah didn't want him to. Jerry alone was allowed to go on being her baby. His siblings spent less and less time in the house, leaving Jerry there with her more and more, leaving him alone during the long stretches when she would vanish into cold grief. How powerful were his daydreams then of freedom and invulnerability and secret identity? How sharp were his self-told tales of loss and exile?

All those tales Jerry brought with him silently into Glenville High School. He was already a year behind his peers and a long step outside the flow of adolescent life. Glen Hi was crowded, competitive, and demanding both academically and socially. It would have been a hard place for Jerry even if life had been more merciful. Now he could never hope to succeed on its terms, never hope to be just another Glen Hi kid. He began to dream of leaping past school and adolescence, of winning instant fame and wealth. If he could somehow hit the big time, he could end the shame of being the only family member who didn't bring anything in, he could win back a little of what that thug had stolen from his family, he could become a man.

At the same time, he retreated deeper into the other world made by writers and cartoonists. He began to dream of men who waged war on crime and of heroes who were above need and above pain.

The Long Party

HARRY DONENFELD HAD a very different Twenties from Jerry Siegel's. Instead of finding other worlds to retreat into, he found himself plunging into the real world in ways he never could have imagined. Like Jerry Siegel, he got there largely through magazines, and like him, he would find his way ultimately to the comic books. But Harry's entry wasn't through spaceships and fandom. It was through printing presses and naked girls.

The passage of the Eighteenth Amendment in 1919 changed Harry's life, although a few years passed before he knew it. Prohibition must have alarmed him at first, because he loved his beer—his friends used to joke that he kept Heineken in business all by himself—and he liked to drink when he gambled and knew that booze was still the quickest route to a girl's drawers. But Harry learned quickly that New York had no intention of playing along with any constitutional amendment just because it pleased the legislatures of Ohio or Mississippi; in fact, New York was one of only two states that never passed a statewide Prohibition enforcement act. In New York City the business of ending alcohol sales was left to a Tammany-run government and an Irish police force, with predictable results. Saloons were closed, but as a young congressman named Fiorello H. LaGuardia complained, "Now we have delicatessen stores, pool rooms, drug stores, millinery shops, private parlors, and 57 other varieties of speak-easies selling liquor and flourishing."

The only immediate effect of Prohibition in Harry's world was to re-inforce the New Yorker's belief in the plasticity of the law. So many laws competed for the immigrant's allegiance: the laws of Washington, of Tammany, of Moses, of the neighborhood, of economics. Lobster was what you bought your most important client at Delmonico's, but you both knew it was *treyf,* forbidden in your mother's kitchen. To have a so-cial life meant gambling, to have a sex life often meant some economic exchange, and both required breaking the laws on the books. Harry grew up viewing such things simply as facts of life in his adopted land; that al-cohol would suddenly join the list was only another stone tossed in his path by the horde of absurd Protestants beyond the Hudson.

The great shock to Harry was the postwar retraction of the American economy. He never would be a sensible business manager. He was superb at making new connections, getting people to take a chance on him, and seizing opportunities. But he had no patience for balancing ledgers or planning ahead, no self-control to keep himself out of poker games or Manhattan casinos. When consumer spending dropped in late 1920 and early 1921, his New Jersey clothing store fell quickly into debt. His wife took over the books, wrestling with costs and credit at night while Harry played cards with wholesalers. But Gussie was young and still learning, and despite all her work and her angry nagging, the store went broke.

Harry was suddenly under pressure to make a living. We don't know how much pressure Gussie applied, but considering that her son, Irwin, would later describe his mother as "the Dragon Lady," we can imagine that it was unrelenting and unpleasant. Apparently Gussie's family re-fused to stake the young couple's welfare to another garment business, because the next thing we know, Harry appears as the salesman and fourth partner in his brothers' Martin Press.

Printing was not a field that cultivated salesmanship, and Harry seems to have brought a new ambition to the family firm. Among his brothers—two greenhorns with thick Yiddish accents and one stut-terer—Harry shone like a star. It was apparently Harry who pursued higher-end jobs requiring slick paper and two-color registration. It was probably Harry who figured out how to work the consignment game: He'd sell Martin Press's services to produce a brochure that required more advanced photolithographic technology than the firm possessed, then subcontract a printer who had the right presses but not the sales force to land the account. Harry also brought his style of humor to what had been a rather grim little company. Once a client entered the office and stuttered, "Is M-M-Mr. D-Donenfeld here?" "Just a second," said Harry, "I'll get him." Going into the back, he yelled, "Hey, Irving, there's a man here to see you." He sat in the back and waited as Irving went out front—and then stormed back in, screaming, "Th-th-that guy th-thinks I'm m-making fun of him! Are you trying to g-get me *k-k-killed?!*" Harry told that one with a laugh for the rest of his life.

But the most valuable commodity that Harry brought to the family business had little to do with printing and everything to do with Prohibition. The generation of street crooks and gamblers Harry had grown up with was transformed by the staggering amount of money suddenly available to men who could provide illegal alcohol to Americans. Young men who had been content to make a small killing running secret casinos or owning a few race horses or fixing an occasional boxing match almost overnight found themselves raking in millions of dollars, buying judges and cops, and organizing rag-tag street gangs into armies of booze runners, hijackers, and turf warriors. One of those young men, Francesco Castiglia, saw a role for Harry Donenfeld to play in the new racket.

Castiglia prided himself on being a modern American, free of the archaic tribal loyalties that had pitted Italian against Jewish street gangs in the neighborhoods. His wife was Jewish, and he was the eldest member of a quartet of ambitious thugs that included one fellow Sicilian, Salvatore Lucania, and two violent Jewish kids, Benjamin Siegel and Maier Suchowljanski. To become more of a modern American, he chose a new name that would be easy to remember and sound less old world to non-Italians: Frank Costello. Two of his partners did the same, Lucania becoming Charles "Lucky" Luciano and Suchowljanski becoming Meyer Lansky. They rose as lieutenants of Arnold Rothstein, the well-born, elegantly dressed Upper East Side gambler who bankrolled and organized New York bootlegging in its earliest days. When Rothstein removed himself from what was becoming an increasingly violent and risky business in 1921, the Judeo-Italian quartet of Lansky, Siegel, Luciano, and Costello quickly became leaders in crime.

At the time, Lansky and Siegel were still in their teens, Luciano only twenty-four; all three were eager to prove how tough and brutal they could be in turf wars. At thirty Costello was the most cautious and pragmatic of them, and he quickly moved himself off the streets and into the safest part of the business: running liquor from Canada to the American coast, where the others could handle the riskier work of unloading and transporting, selling, and riding shotgun. For that he needed respectable-seeming middlemen who could bring in booze under the guise of legitimate purchases. Like printers who bought Canadian paper.

How Harry Donenfeld met Frank Costello is not known. During his heyday in the late 1930s and early 1940s, Harry bragged of his friendships with gangsters, but when comic books came under attack in the late 1940s, he shut up. Decades later, as comic fans tried to sniff out the truth, Harry's son, Irwin, played a cat-and-mouse game with them. In one interview, he told of the day the phone rang and his mother answered to hear a gravelly voice ask, "Is Harry there?" When she said no, the voice said, "Tell him Frank Costello called." Gussie trembled as she told him about it, Irwin said. In a later interview, Irwin said the doorbell rang at their home one day and he opened it to find a dark, chunky man asking, in that same gravelly voice, "Is Harry home?" When Irwin shook his head, the man turned away, saying, "Tell him Frank Costello dropped by." Irwin turned to his mother and they trembled together. Finally, one fan-historian buttonholed Irwin and asked him for the truth off the record. Irwin half smiled and paused and said, "Let me put it to you this way. Frank Costello was my godfather."

Donenfeld family stories, anecdotes passed down through the comics culture, and the business history of the brothers sketch the outlines of a relationship. Harry's contacts among gamblers were extensive, and before Prohibition Costello's business had been gambling. Theirs was an easy match. The Donenfeld brothers regularly bought pulp paper from Canada, and with the right payoff or pressure, customs agents could easily have been persuaded not to look hard enough at their shipments to spot crates filled with Molson ale or Canadian whiskey. The Martin Press warehouse space could be used to store the goods. Printers did business directly with magazine distributors who moved goods to newsstands, smoke shops, drug stores, and candy stores, all common outlets for under-the-counter liquor. And since newspaper and magazine distribution was already under the control of street mobs, the whole business was safely insulated. The result for Martin Press was a sudden infusion of capital and a rapid expansion of contacts among distributors.

It may have been through his new associates that Harry scored his biggest coup as a salesman. While they were expanding their booze-running operations, the Luciano-Lansky team also joined the payroll of the newspaper circulation *macher* Moe Annenberg. Moe had so impressed his boss in Chicago and Milwaukee's circulation wars that Hearst put him in charge of New York circulation for all his newspapers and magazines and in 1922 made him the publisher of his new launch the *New York Daily Mirror*. Moe went for a public appearance of legitimacy, calling himself "M. L. Annenberg" in emulation of "W. R. Hearst," but privately turned to thuggery. He brought Dion O'Banion out from Chicago to handle the Mick neighborhoods and hired Luciano and Lansky for the Wops and Yids. "I used to think of the *Mirror* as my paper," Luciano said later. "I always thought of Annenberg as my sort of guy."

In 1923 Harry Donenfeld landed the job of printing 6 million subscription inserts for *Cosmopolitan*, *Good Housekeeping*, and the rest of the Hearst magazines. The family business moved into a beautiful new twelve-story building in the Chelsea district, invested in a three-color rotogravure, and poised itself to become a major printing firm. It wouldn't be the same family business, however. By some stratagem—no one knows just what anymore—he drove his two oldest brothers out of the business, leaving him as the majority owner. Charlie and Mike Donenfeld went back to the rag trade and never spoke warmly to Harry again. Irving remained as the minority partner and head printer. Harry changed the company's name to Donny Press, after one of his nicknames on the street.

Personally, Harry was rocketed by his new business contacts to a social level far beyond what the ready-to-wear business could have made possible. He lived a nightlife of gambling, drinking, and womanizing impossible on the income of a printing salesman. He had his picture taken with mobsters and hangers-on in the ritziest speakeasies—photos that would later disappear but that young editors would remember hanging in his office as late as the 1940s. This was the long party of Twenties New York, made possible by the cash and social dissolution of Prohibition, when thugs and cops and bankers and movie stars and newspapermen came together over whiskey and green felt, when lowlifes who would once have been stars only in dives like Segal's Café on Second Avenue were being panted after by debutantes and novelists. And Harry Donenfeld was there with them. To a man like Harry the glamour of gangsters was not just the danger of their lives or the smell of blood around them but the fact that they crossed class lines that had been firmly held by the old-time American elite. As a New York detective named Ralph Salerno noted, "Gangsters who never graduated high school broke barriers thirty years before anyone else got near them." While a law-abiding Jewish bookkeeper like Jack Liebowitz would be stuck on the slow road to assimilation, working for Jewish clients and unable to break into a college where the Jewish quota was filled, Harry Donenfeld—homely, small, loud, accented, obnoxiously Lower East Side—could buy a drink for a Tammany judge and slip a note to a chorus girl at Texas Guinan's.

Harry's model was always Frank Costello. To Costello Harry was probably just another minor business operative, a gear in the machine to be occasionally greased (easy enough to agree to be another baby's godfather), but Harry wanted to count him as a friend. Costello was the master of the social connection and the mutual obligation. He made sure the police captains and judges who visited his casinos went home winners, and he let them know who was looking out for them. He knew how to reach the center of information and power: He befriended Walter Winchell when he was first making his mark as a mudslinging gossip columnist, and for years they traded, Winchell getting underworld dirt and Costello introductions to the rich and powerful. Costello became so adept at the bloodless deal, the fix in high places, that his fellow gangsters called him "the Prime Minister." Rumors held that it was he who had neutralized the gangs' greatest potential threat, the FBI. Whenever he heard that a major horse race had been fixed, he'd pass on the name of the sure thing to Winchell, who would pass it on to his friend J. Edgar Hoover, who loved to play the ponies. So it was, at least in the Costello legend, that Hoover denied the existence of organized crime for decades while everyone in America knew otherwise.

Harry dressed like Costello, dropping the loud jackets of the cheap drummer in favor of dark expensive suits just a little too sporty for a Republican businessman. He apparently didn't conduct himself with Costello's self-control, for the hints emerge from Harry's stories that when he got drunk, he could be sloppily sentimental or belligerent, even aggressive with women. He did, nonetheless, cultivate social connections like Costello, and like him, brought diverse parties together. But where Costello used his social maneuverings calculatedly for power and profit, for Harry they appear to have been a reward in themselves. The explosive bonhomie that he brought to every new encounter, whether or not he was meeting anyone of any financial value to him, reveal a man who loved being noticed and accepted.

When Irwin Donenfeld was young, his father always impressed him as a man who was "friends with a lot of judges." To a former street urchin this was the height of power and social acceptance. The dread of every young pickpocket and sneak thief was facing the judge. The judge was the highest public authority a kid would ever see in person, for in juvenile court, from his elevated seat and in his hellish black robes he could remand a boy to a reformatory for months, even a year, without benefit of jury. But in the Tammany system, a judge was only a flunky chosen for the job of rigging trials, and during Prohibition that system was smoothly sold to the bootlegging gangs. Frank Costello took personal charge of selecting and guaranteeing the election of judges throughout New York and New Jersey. Harry Donenfeld would have been useful as a legitimate-seeming middleman between the system's public and secret limbs. More specifically, he was willing to cut deals on the printing and distribution of campaign literature, and by mid-decade he was helping create magazines and flyers for the gubernatorial campaigns of Al Smith, the greatest politician in Tammany's orbit. He seems even to have been part of some sort of campaign strategy group in 1928, when Smith ran for president and Franklin D. Roosevelt for governor— maybe the kernel of truth in his claim to have been in FDR's Brain Trust. The urchin had beaten the game, had put the judges and politicians in his debt.

During those same years another door opened for Harry. It was less likely to lead to money and influence than his connections with Frank Costello or the Democratic machine, but it was an even more compelling opportunity to him. He did business with a magazine distributor called Eastern News, founded by a pair of idealistic young men with their families' rag trade money, Charles Dreyfus and Paul Sampliner. Through their odd assortment of periodicals he discovered another region of Twenties America, a world of fitness fanatics and nude photographers, of sex law reformers and pornographers, of contraband distributors and social visionaries, of Hugo Gernsback and Margaret Sanger. It was by walking through that door that Harry would ultimately, accidentally, make his one great contribution to American culture.

A MEASURE OF HARRY'S peculiar charm is the variety of people who continued to like him in all his incarnations. Even as he befriended gangsters and crooked Democrats, he continued to enjoy the loyalty of that dedicated organizer for the International Ladies Garment Workers Union, Julius Liebowitz.

The years that were so good to bootleggers were not good to radicals and labor unions. In the wake of the world war and the Russian Revolution, the attorney general of the United States orchestrated a vast

purge that put 16,000 suspected leftists in jail for months without trial
and deported hundreds to Russia. (The case made J. Edgar Hoover a
star; his belief that the anarchist writings of Emma Goldman were a
greater threat to American life than the murderous dealings of the
liquor gangs sat well with the national mood.) And this was under a
progressive Democratic administration. When the Republicans took
control of the government in 1921, they winked as laws were ignored,
treasuries were looted, and unions trampled by business trusts. Over the
next few years, the economy lurched onto the credit-driven roller
coaster of the final decade of early American capitalism, and the unions
lost membership and power.

Nationally, control of the ILGWU lay with moderate socialists who
wanted to preserve the accords they'd reached with management during
the war years. But in New York a belligerent phalanx of communists
blamed those accords for the union's decline, broke with the national executive board, and pushed for a major confrontation with the factory
owners. The socialists in the New York locals, led by the young David Dubinsky and including Julius Liebowitz, tried to help the national union in
purging the communists, but the manufacturers seized on the split and
pushed the union to roll back benefits. The rank and file began favoring a
strike. The union was heading for battles with manufacturers and within
its own ranks—just as Julius's son Jack was about to enter its service.

While working to support himself and help his family, Jack earned
his accounting degree from NYU at the age of twenty-four. He'd met and
wooed a girl named Rose but wouldn't marry her until he had his degree
and could start a career. He took a small office near ILGWU headquarters in Union Square and set himself up in business with the union as his
one client. In pictures from the era, he looks older than his years—small
mustache, thinning hair swept back from a slight widow's peak, sensible
suits—already the sort of man you'd trust with your money.

Within a year, Jack was put in charge of the union's strike fund, just
in time for his baptism of fire. In the summer of 1926, 50,000 workers
walked off the job for what would turn out to be a six-month disaster.
The union spent nearly $4 million of the strike fund to keep them fed

and housed, requiring a phenomenal amount of number juggling by young Jack, and when the strike finally ended with the fund still solvent, he found himself in good standing with union leadership.

Other men, unfortunately, found themselves mixed up with leadership, as well. When the strike turned ugly, factory owners hired a murderous thug named Jack "Legs" Diamond to break the picket lines. In response the communists who led the locals called on the street boss of the Lower East Side, "Little Augie" Orgen. The strike began to devolve into a gang war between Legs and Augie. The ugliness of it, the public's pro-business sentiments, the quiet resistance of Dubinsky's socialists, all worked against the strikers, and finally the communists agreed to negotiate. Negotiations went nowhere, however, until Arnold Rothstein, the gambler who mentored nearly every crime boss in New York, agreed to broker a cease-fire between Legs and Little Augie. In the process, he cut the gangs in on both the union and management's action. From that point on, the mob would be an invisible partner in every local, every negotiation, every financial dealing of either the ILGWU or the Manufacturers' Association. Less than a year later, Little Augie's and Legs Diamond's bodies were found riddled with bullets—Augie's dead, Legs's almost—in their Delancey Street safe house. The man behind their shootings, the Rothstein protégé Lepke Buchalter, took over their mob and expanded ruthlessly into other unions and other industries, becoming the most powerful man in American crime, and American labor.

The communists of the ILGWU were forced to settle for such a dismal deal that they were swept from office. David Dubinsky, the hard-nosed, pragmatic escaped convict who valued results more than ideology, was soon running the union as a whole, but it was a union deeply compromised. For many—apparently including Julius Liebowitz—it was a compromise worth making for the sake of the cause. For his son Jack, trying to balance the books of corruption and ideals, it was another lesson in an unsentimental education. It was while he was balancing ledgers to conceal the millions of dollars skimmed from the union by Lepke Buchalter that he apparently began to question socialism. If capitalism conquered every conscience and every ideal so ruthlessly, then perhaps the only truly honest course was to master capitalism itself.

As THE NOBLE experiment of Prohibition went on, the party of the Twenties got rougher. The full-time mobsters consciously drove out the dilettante bootleggers and compelled anyone who wanted to keep making serious money off booze to play by their rules. In 1925 another gangster whom Harry claimed to know, Irving "Waxey Gordon" Wexler, ran into some trouble when a ship's captain running Canadian liquor for him got angry about Waxey's distribution of funds and ran to the police. The affair ended with the captain dead in a hotel room (in police custody, no less) and Waxey having to flee his glamorous Manhattan territory for New Jersey. Harry, wanting neither a hole in his head nor a move back to New Jersey, seems to have reduced his involvement in bootlegging about the same time.

Harry was also taking on new obligations. He'd moved into a middle-class neighborhood on Merriam Avenue in the Bronx, where Gussie gave birth to their son, Irwin, in 1926. Two years later she bore a daughter, given the poetic name "Sonia" but destined to grow up under the nickname "Peachy." Harry would never be a family man; he kept an apartment in Manhattan for himself, leaving Gussie and the hired help to run his respectable household to the north. But he provided financially, and so, under the pressures of practical reality and his wife, he looked for ways to expand the family business.

But Harry wanted not just to be prosperous; he also wanted to be noticed. To the ambitious son of Jewish immigrants in New York in the 1920s, the air, the newsstands, and the marquees were filled with success stories that beckoned and tormented. When a fur merchant named Adolph Zukor first saw a two-bit New York peep-show parlor in 1903, his comment was "A Jew could make a lot of money at this." In barely over a decade Zukor and a small army of other hustlers and outsiders with the same thought—Laemmle, Lasky, Warner, Loew, Cohn—had toppled the Protestant insiders, giants like Thomas Edison and George

Eastman, who ran the film industry. Meanwhile Al Jolson, the Marx Brothers, Jack Benny, George Burns, George Jessel, and Harry's old friend Eddie Cantor were transforming stage and radio entertainment. Irving Berlin, another Lower East Side street kid just a few years older than Harry, had not only changed American pop music and made himself rich but made headlines in 1925 by stealing a beautiful seventeen-year-old heiress from her father and marrying her. A homely, badly educated gutter yodeler from The Bowery could look at fine-nosed shiksa beauties on the society pages and wonder if such creatures really walked the same pavement as he did, but to be thirty-eight years old, still homely, still badly educated, and get one of those girls not only onto the front page of the paper with him but into his bed too—that was a modern American triumph. "God bless America," wrote Irving Berlin, but it wasn't the oceans topped with foam he'd conquered.

For Jews in the early twentieth century, the quickest route to fame was along the edges of mass entertainment, through fields that the scruples, snobbery, or provinciality of old-time Americans kept them from fully exploiting. There the old street-hawker skills paid off: snap quickly, sell cheaply, rebound instantly, watch every change in fashion, and chase customers' appetites without a care for whether anyone thought they were dignified enough. The field most available to Harry was magazine publishing, the one that would shape his life from his early thirties until he died.

In the 1920s, Americans bought magazines as never before or since. Cheap printing technology, automobile-age distribution, high disposable incomes, and the hunger for information about a changing world conspired to make the newsstand a central arena of national culture. There were over 2,000 magazines on the stands early in the decade. Americans spent more time reading fiction magazines—pulps and "slicks"—than in any other leisure activity. Every fringe group and subculture had its own periodicals, and the lucky publisher who tapped into a previously unsuspected public appetite could make a fortune on the smallest investment. No one in 1919 would have expected *True Story* or *Ranch Romances* to sell millions, but so they did. The magazine business was a magnet for visionaries, oddball hobbyists, exploitationists, and racketeers—and sometimes one man was all four at once.

The great object of admiration for would-be magazine magnates was William Randolph Hearst, who had defied the once-monopolistic American News Company to forge his own independent distribution company. But Hearst seemed almost beyond emulation, coming as he did from family wealth and success in newspapers. When Harry Donenfeld and other men like him thought of launching their own magazines, it was Bernarr MacFadden they wanted to be.

MacFadden made his own life story the foundation of his empire: the scrawny boy from Missouri who discovered the virtues of physical fitness when he was sent to work on his uncle's farm, developed a new method of bodybuilding he called "kinestherapy," and moved to New York in the 1890s to found the first of his "physical culture" clubs. He proved to be a master at attracting attention. He changed his name from "Bernard" to "Bernarr" to make it sound like a lion's roar. He grew his hair long like Heracles' and appeared in public in a leopard-skin loincloth over his flesh-colored tights. In 1899 he launched *Physical Culture* magazine to promote his plan of diet, weight lifting, and rational living, and when no established distributor would gamble on it, he used his network of physical culture clubs and sanitariums to build a distribution system of his own. Soon he was penetrating drug stores, cigar stores, and other small magazine venues in cities across America.

In the name of honesty and health MacFadden defied the decorum of his day. He was convicted on an obscenity charge for a frank discussion of venereal disease in *Physical Culture,* then pardoned by President Taft himself. He was harassed by police and churches for the pageants he organized to show off the bodies of his disciples in swimsuits and tights. And people bought his magazines. When the world war ended and paper prices dropped, he tried a new kind of magazine, comprising inspirational stories sent in by *Physical Culture* readers. *True Story*, a monthly compendium of average folk's victories over crises in health, finances, family, and love, was selling 2 million copies within a couple of years. He struck quickly by offering more magazines based on true stories. Month by month he swung further from health and inspiration, plunging deeper into scandal, thrills, and only slightly veiled sex: *True Confessions*, *Photoplay*, *True Ghost Stories*. By 1924, with *True Crime* and that pioneer of what would be called "tabloid journalism," the *New York Graphic*, he reversed his original mission, selling stories of mankind's greatest disease and depravity. But those too sold in the millions.

One of MacFadden's most reliable selling points became the human body: Taking advantage of the cheap rotogravure printing becoming available after the war, he slapped bodybuilders, movie starlets, and beauty pageant contestants across his covers. A well-muscled body in tights became the signature of a MacFadden magazine. His publications were attacked by reformers and postal authorities as pornography, but he always managed to steer just inside the law's line. He continued to promote his ideas of physical culture, often drawing criticism from the medical community, but now more to keep himself in the headlines than to improve mankind. Publicly he played the fool, bursting into his company offices wearing only his loincloth, roaring like a lion, and leading his staff in calisthenics. In fact, he was a shrewd and predatory businessman, devouring other distributors. In 1926 he bragged that his magazine empire outsold Hearst's. His critics called him a kook, a quack, and a pornographer. But he was a rich kook, quack, and pornographer.

Many of the men who emulated MacFadden were businessmen, pure and simple. George T. Delacorte had entered the field with some money in 1921, and by cleverly buying magazines on the way up and selling them as they peaked, he was already rich by the late Twenties. The Fawcett brothers in Minneapolis had some luck with a joke magazine called *Captain Billy's Whiz-Bang* and parlayed it into a mock-MacFadden empire. The Delacortes and Fawcetts of the business would sell a lot of magazines and, later, a lot of comic books, but they brought little original content to either field. The ones who stretched the limits of what the magazine could be were more often those whose original interests weren't in business or even publishing but who, like Bernarr MacFadden, had first come to New York to promote their peculiar passions and saw magazines as a vehicle for disseminating their ideas.

One MacFadden imitator, one who would cross the paths of Harry Donenfeld and Jerry Siegel, was Hugo Gernsbacher. He was a European Jew, but from a Europe and a Jewry unknown to the Donenfelds, Siegels, and Liebowitzes: The son of a Luxembourgian wine merchant, he was raised in a German- and French-speaking cultural aristocracy and was confident that he could create whatever future he wanted. While still in his teens, he fell in love with electrical technology and developed a new kind of battery but was unable to patent it in Europe's restrictive legal environment. He'd grown up reading cheap novels about American cowboys, heroic mechanics, and Twainian river rats, so at age twenty, in 1904, he packed up his battery and took himself to the open range of Manhattan. When he arrived—barely speaking English, dressed like a French dandy, screwing a monocle into his eye—he introduced himself as "Huck Gernsback." Failing to find anyone to fund him as an inventor, he started selling electrical equipment by mail order. He had too much to say about the dawning age of technology and reason to let his catalog remain just a catalog, however; his editorials and descriptions of new products became so compelling to him and his customers that in 1908 he launched *Modern Electrics*, later *Science and Invention*, a sort of futuro-utopian version of *Popular Mechanics*. In it in 1911 he ran his own strange novel, "Ralph 124C 41+," in which he forecast television, radar, fluorescent lights, tape recording, and even jukeboxes, and first demonstrated an idea for fiction that would excite the masses about technology and the future.

In the magazine boom of the 1920s, Gernsback turned that idea into the *Amazing Stories* that meant so much to Jerry Siegel and his fellow fans. He also entered the MacFadden health niche with *Your Body*, dabbled in humor magazines, and even experimented with newsstand reprints of a comic strip, *S'Matter Pop?* Although the history of his distribution arrangements remains foggy, by the end of the decade, he had become a major client for Charles Dreyfus and Paul Sampliner of Eastern News, one of whose favorite printers was Harry Donenfeld. Reportedly, Gernsback was one man who was immune to Harry's charm, finding him crude and mercenary, and Harry apparently didn't like Gernsback's condescending style—not an uncommon result of encounters between educated Germanic Jews and their East European brethren. But their interests overlapped enough in the strange family of Eastern News to make allies of them for a while.

Michael Feldman, a publisher and journalist who has traced some of the mysterious lines of magazine distribution, maintains that Eastern News was "a major nexus for an important, undocumented alternative culture in early 20th Century America." In addition to Gernsback's vehicles, Eastern handled feminist journals, spiritualist magazines, and *Psychology* and *Sex Monthly*, twin guides to mental and erotic health edited by a progressive Christian minister named Henry Knight Miller. And its product line was apparently not restricted to publications.

Gernsback himself was an investor with wide interests. His great passion was radio, in which he saw the hope of the world, an instrument to lift mankind out of provinciality and primitivity. He put his money and expertise into building one of America's first commercial radio stations, WRNY, and as soon as it turned a profit, he dedicated the station to research in the broadcasting of images. Gernsback had been writing about "television" since 1910, and he was the main reason the word became the standard description for the medium that did not yet exist. In 1928 the first scheduled television broadcasts in the world came out of his station.

Gernsback also, according to Michael Feldman, probably continued to sell electrical gadgets and other small consumer goods long after he entered publishing and may have introduced Eastern News to the business of distributing other products to drug stores and smoke shops along with their magazines. It was in that business, Feldman has concluded, that Gernsback, Eastern, and Harry Donenfeld overlapped with a mysterious but ubiquitous figure of the magazine boom named Harold Hersey and his lover, Margaret Sanger.

By the second decade of the century, Sanger had established herself as a leader of Greenwich Village radical politics. It was her work as a nurse on the Lower East Side among the young women Harry Donenfeld knew, women whose lives had been shattered by ignorance and lack of contraceptive devices, that drove her to spearhead the birth control movement. She needed an editor and writer to help her launch her journal, *The Woman Rebel,* and hired Harold Hersey, a young man who had moved from Montana to Greenwich Village to pursue a career as a poet. Sanger was a believer in sexual freedom known for her open affairs with such icons of the day as H. G. Wells and Havelock Ellis. Hersey was a lesser light among her lovers but an important one, for he quickly mastered the business of publishing and distribution and helped her build part of the apparatus of her birth control movement. "We didn't only sell magazines," Hersey would say later, "but also razor blades and other items." The "other items" were contraceptives. Sanger was not only a proponent of birth control but a mail-order dealer, with her own line of condoms, diaphragms, and douche kits.

Eastern News, according to Feldman, seems to have been one of the companies that distributed Sanger's publications and contraceptives in the Twenties. Harry Donenfeld may have been one of the printers of her *Birth Control Review* and other journals. It was in distribution, however, that Harry was most valuable, for it was illegal to send contraceptives and even pro-contraceptive literature by mail. In her early days Sanger got herself arrested more than once for such uses of the mails, and although the arrests earned her some useful publicity, by the Twenties, she was more interested in getting the goods to women and winning mainstream support for her cause than in being a martyr to repressive laws. Eastern News, like all magazine distributors, depended on the postal service to reach most of its territory. But Harry Donenfeld had connections with other distribution systems: those that moved Canadian liquor into the American heartland. So Margaret Sanger's condoms, Hugo Gernsback's science fiction, and Frank Costello's whiskey could ride together in trucks and on trains and through post offices where the inspectors were on the take. And in 1928 those goods were joined by Al Smith's campaign literature.

Harold Hersey, meanwhile, was applying his understanding of publishing to a new career as a magazine editor. It was he who created *Ranch Romances,* one of the most successful of pulps, and *The Thrill Book,* an antecedent to *Weird Tales* and *Amazing Stories.* He worked on several projects for Bernarr MacFadden, including the *New York*

Graphic, and he may have had a hand in giving Walter Winchell and Ed Sullivan some of their first jobs in journalism. Among his creations were some of the weirdest special-audience magazines ever: *Strange Suicides, Medical Horrors, Speakeasy Stories.* He also picked up income as an uncredited consultant for numerous publishers; he was much in demand just for sauntering into a neophyte editor's office and drawling, "Well, this is what we do at MacFadden . . ." He was popular at Eastern News and left his fingerprints on the magazines of one of their most daring publishers, a California bohemian named Frank Armer—and thus on the magazines that made Harry Donenfeld a publisher.

Little is known of Armer's early life, although he was apparently a man of artistic inclination who came of age in Hollywood in the years when Adolph Zukor and his cohorts were transforming it from a sleepy Protestant paradise into a strange world of money, ambition, artistry, and beautiful young bodies. Enamored of the business, especially of its starlets, Armer helped launch *Screenland,* in emulation of MacFadden's *Photoplay,* in 1922. His business manager was Paul Sampliner, soon to found Eastern News; his cover printer was Harry Donenfeld. Somewhere along the way, Armer married a wealthy Jewish woman with garment industry connections, and by 1925 he was in New York, affiliated with Eastern News and starting a little magazine that embraced some of the most energetic contradictions of Twenties America: *Artists and Models.* Its covers featured glamour photos of Ziegfeld Follies showgirls, among them Joan Crawford and Louise Brooks. Opening to the contents page, however, might reveal a monochrome print of a dowager's portrait by Thomas Gainsborough, an article on "The Art of Goya," and a poem by Dante Gabriel Rossetti. Mixed in with those were gossip columns ("Broadway Flashes"), titillating fiction ("Challenge, the Story of a Model"), and illustrations by Erté, a rising star of stage and costume design.

Most prominently of all, every issue profiled a contemporary artist whom Armer felt deserved more attention—and who always photographed or painted female nudes. "The Art of Alfred Barnard" displayed several photos of sleek young women with breasts and buttocks proudly cocked, beside which ran the assertion, "That this type of figure study is especially valuable to the student is attested by the many appreciative letters Mr. Barnard has received from principals of colleges and academies of art." *Artists and Models* was sophisticated, pretentious, cheesy, and disingenuous. It was, most of all, a clever way to get pictures of naked women past censors and postal authorities and onto the magazine racks (or at least under the counters) of cigar stores and newsstands.

Harry Donenfeld printed Armer's covers and photo pages, and he relished the job. Armer must have been an irresistible figure for him. He lived on both coasts, keeping his magazine offices a block from Times Square, where he hobnobbed with theater artists and personally scouted chorus girls for his pages, but spending much of his time in San Francisco, where he consorted with poets and nudists and "Pictorialist" photographers whose nudes were sold to collectors as art but were often impounded by the police as pornography. Harry courted him, personally and professionally. When Armer added *Art and Beauty, Modern Art,* and other "nudies" to his slate, Harry carried much of the cost. Soon he was not only Armer's regular printer but a silent partner in his magazines.

In 1926 Armer plunged into a new genre and struck gold. Magazines featuring risqué humor and stories were a staple of Twenties publishing: *Laughter, La Paree, Snappy Stories*, Hugo Gernsback's *French Humor*. They kept their illustrations titillating but discreet, until one, *Paris Nights*, began stitching twelve-page photo inserts into its issues. At first it stayed with underwear and chorus girl shots but gradually, as the law kept its distance, it added nudes. Armer's *Pep!* started in the same vein, bragging of its "New, Snappy, Spicy Stories and ART," risking ever more daring graphics, even putting a photo of a bare-breasted woman on its December 1926 cover. But soon word came in from newsstands and readers that its snappy, spicy stories were at least as popular as its art. *Pep!*'s writers were a stable of relatively witty and graceful hacks, including most notably the tirelessly prolific and charismatic Robert Leslie Bellem. "Mimi L'Enclos," he wrote in one story, "had a penchant for black, lacy underthings—and a husband who thoroughly approved of her taste in such matters." But she is given a diamond by another man, "and afterward Mimi forgot all about her conscience. She forgot all about Henri, too. In fact, she nearly forgot everything except the gaiety of the moment and the fact that she was glad the black underthings seemed to please Raoul so well."

Story magazines were both cheaper and safer to produce than nudies, and within a few years Armer and Donenfeld had eliminated the photo inserts, returned to painted covers, and unleashed a flurry of imitations: *Artists and Models Stories, Broadway Nights, Real Story, Ginger Stories,* and *Spicy Stories.* In the spring of 1929, Harry and Irving Donenfeld formed a new company, with Gussie Donenfeld as business manager, to publish their own knockoffs, *Juicy Tales* and *Hot Tales.* Armer and the Donenfelds were leading the way into a new genre, the sex pulp—"smooshes" they called them in the business. The editor of most of those magazines was a Methodist minister's daughter named Mrs. Merle W. Hersey. ("Mrs." for that touch of respectability.) She and Harold Hersey always denied that they were related, but the names raise suspicions.

The contours of that "undocumented alternative culture" are traced by these business and social relationships. Booze, gambling, and prostitution on one extreme; feminism, reproductive rights, and scientific utopianism on the other; and in between them nude photography, pornographic humor, chorus girls and movie starlets, businessmen, hucksters, and politicians who opposed Prohibition and favored contraception but couldn't say so out loud. The long party of the Twenties got wilder as the decade rushed to a close, and right in the middle of it danced Harry Donenfeld—salesman, printer, smuggler, loyal Democrat, and smoosh publisher.

Then the lights began to dim. The first blow came from the biggest carnivore in the cheap-magazine jungle, Bernarr MacFadden. He understood as few men did the value of Hugo Gernsback's radio holdings. Within weeks of Gernsback's first television broadcasts MacFadden was colluding with Gernsback's creditors to squeeze him out of business. "Huck" was not the most careful businessman, and although his enterprises made money, he didn't always have enough cash on hand to cover all his debts. By orchestrating a simultaneous demand for payment from his printer, paper supplier, and others, MacFadden forced him into bankruptcy court in 1929 and snapped up his properties, the magazines and the radio station. When fourteen-year-old Jerry Siegel in Cleveland noted the great Gernsback's disappearance from *Amazing Stories,* he had no idea what business practices shaped the magazines he loved.

Gernsback rallied with new magazines and survived as a publisher, but he would never become the communications magnate he wanted to be. Eastern News was shaken and was especially vulnerable to the economic shock waves that followed the stock market crash. The month of the crash, October 1929, was the same month that *Juicy Tales* and *Hot Tales,* marking Harry Donenfeld's debut as a publisher, hit the stands. The long party was ending—but Harry had one more important contact to make in its final moments.

JACK LIEBOWITZ'S FALL out of socialist idealism seems to have occurred slowly but steadily through the late 1920s. For many socialists the watershed proved to be the execution of Nicola Sacco and Bartolomeo Vanzetti in the summer of 1927. The battle to save the two anarchists from the death penalty had galvanized progressives worldwide and reignited the utopian hopes of American leftists after years of social and political reversals. The battle's conclusion in the men's deaths left bitterness and exhaustion: "All right you have won," wrote John Dos Passos. "America our nation has been beaten by strangers who have turned our language inside out . . . they have built the electric chair and hired the executioner to throw the switch . . . all right we are two nations." The most passionate revolutionaries closed ranks. Those having doubts drifted away. Jack was among the latter.

He was also taking on responsibilities. He'd married Rose and taken an apartment in the Bronx where they planned to raise a family. Jack was determined to be the ideal husband and father, to make sure that his family was comfortable and secure. In the last years of the decade, he took on work for clients other than the union. He also began to study the stock market. The acumen that he had once expected to bring to the cause of labor he now turned toward understanding capital. At first his efforts worked to the union's benefit as well, as he invested the strike fund in stocks to good effect. But with the crash, his strategy backfired. The value of the union's holdings plummeted. Stories conflict as to whether Jack was let go by the union leaders or walked away in disgust at their anger; either way, by the end of 1929, he was looking actively for a new client.

At the same time, Harry Donenfeld was looking for a new business manager for his publishing company. As shrewd and strong as Gussie was, she couldn't raise two kids and run a company. That's when his old client Julius Liebowitz at the ILGWU, hearing of Harry's growing fortune, asked, "Can you find work for my boy Jack?" Harry was generous and sentimental when it came to throwing work and money around. He was always glad to hire an old friend or a friend's son from the neighborhood. Jack took the job, not intending to keep it for long. Neither the socialist idealist he had been nor the respectable breadwinner he wanted to be could make peace easily with the idea of being an accountant to a pornographer.

Neither man could see how perfect their pairing was. Harry Donenfeld and Jack Liebowitz had come of age in the jungle of early-twentieth-century American business and had developed different skills for mastering that jungle: Harry's quickness and cleverness and boundless power to make people like him; Jack's self-control and hardheadedness and genius for balancing countless variables. Together they would make a complete entity, one that would survive and prosper in the hard years ahead. One that would emerge from the Great Depression as something no one could have imagined.

This was the bed in which the comic book was conceived: countercultural, lowbrow, idealistic, prurient, pretentious, mercenary, forward-looking, and ephemeral, all in the same instant.

The Perfect Man

FROM HIS MOTHER'S house on Kimberly Avenue Jerry Siegel would walk past half a block of identical wood frame houses, turn right on Parkwood, and continue another block to Everton, sometimes crossing the street to walk beside the long stand of trees that lined the gully that had once been a river. On weekday mornings Parkwood would fill with Glenville High School's 1,600 students, coming by bus, by bike, or on foot. Jerry might scan the faces for the few kids he trusted well enough to greet, but most mornings he would walk quickly with his head down, in private pain. Up the steps, past the two great columns where the ivy was growing in thickly, into the noisy, horny, competitive hive of Glen Hi he would plunge too quickly to be caught or distracted or teased.

The few photos of Jerry from his high school years show that combination of watchfulness and distance: his face immobile but betraying distrust in the slight too-wideness of the eyes, the eyes fixed on us, not in communion but looking to see what new threat the camera brings. Jerry's writings reveal a teenager always too young, but the camera captured a boy already too old.

Glen Hi was not an easy place for Jerry Siegel. He didn't stand out academically, didn't mix well, and didn't go much for extracurriculars. His one enthusiasm was *The Torch*, the school's weekly newspaper. He spoke often of wanting to be a reporter when he grew up, as a lot of kids did then, for that was the high point of America's romance with the big-city newsman. Jerry's new Hollywood heroes were the fast-talking, fedora-cocking newshounds who could bring down any crook or millionaire or beautiful dame with their wits. Jerry, unfortunately, was no Pat O'Brien. His peers with *The Torch* would remember him as a nervous kid, somehow self-important and shy at the same time, inclined to disappear into the background. And those peers were intimidating.

Seymour Heller, the class entertainment director and a junior rabbi at the Jewish Center, bought a Hupmobile coupe with the money he made as a clarinet player and band manager and wrote a cocky gossip column, "Subtleville Slander" ("Many of Glenville's newly decided blondes tell us that the color of their hair was changed by the sun. Some sun, eh, kid?"). Jerry Schwartz whipped out articles with precocious poise and breezy self-aggrandizement and was voted "Most Popular" in his senior class. Willie Gomberg cracked everybody up as he banged out bits for the humor page, "The Blowtorch." Hal Lebowitz covered sports and hung around with the school's star athletes. William Herman, entering essay contests and taking assignments from technical magazines as a sophomore, was making nearly a grand a year as a freelance writer before he graduated. Nathan Zahm was getting news stories published in the *Cleveland News*. Wilson Hirschfeld, a kid as shy as Jerry Siegel on the surface, found editorial work with the biggest paper in town, the *Plain Dealer*, in his senior year. The talent in those kids can be guessed by their later careers: Jerry Schwartz and Willie Gomberg would become successful Broadway playwrights as "Jerome Lawrence" and "Willie Gilbert"; Hal Lebowitz, Cleveland's most popular sportswriter; and Sy Heller, one of America's richest talent agents. Wilson Hirschfeld would go on to become the *Plain Dealer*'s managing editor and a nationally recognized journalist.

And then there were the girls. Martha Yablonsky, cute and dimpled, two years younger than Jerry but serious about journalism, became the most prolific writer on staff and the editor of the paper. Charlotte Fingerhut used her "Thimble Thoughts" to flatter her peers: "Reubie Schrank actually thinks that the reason Louis XVIII was a good king . . .

was because he was fat and had the gout. Honest, he said so in history class." As Charlotte Plimmer, she would later edit *Seventeen* magazine for the Annenbergs. Lois Amster was another "Most Popular" winner, a bundle of teasing and school spirit. "Petite Lois" *The Torch* called her. "Little Angel," joked the yearbook staff. "She was beautiful," remembered one classmate; "she had boys lined up." The girls kibitzed with the boys, shared sodas and sandwiches with them at Bernice's Confections and Barney's Deli, joined the long evening talks on their front porches. But Jerry Siegel seems to have been a dim memory for all of them. He never joined the club's social life and didn't make an impression in the paper's classroom "office." Lois Amster later claimed that Jerry and Joe both had crushes on her and named one of their most famous characters after her. Jerry insisted irritably that he and Joe had barely even known her. Lois was a girl who expected boys to have crushes on her but didn't leave them feeling happy about it.

"I had certain inhibitions," Jerry said later. "I had crushes on several attractive girls who either didn't know I existed or didn't care I existed. As a matter of fact, some of them looked like they *hoped* I didn't exist." He began to daydream about ways to get girls' attention. "What if I had something special going for me, like jumping over buildings or throwing cars around . . . ? Then maybe they would notice me." Instead he began to write about guys who had something special going for them.

He belonged to the Torch Club for most of his high school tenure but never made the paper's regular staff. He wasn't interested in gathering profiles of impressive students or describing the new graduation procedures. Jerry Siegel lived in ink: He spent every evening and weekend in pulps, magazines, comic strips—and at his typewriter. When he finally took a job to help his family through the hard times after his father's killing, he found it at a printing plant, delivering bundles to clients four days a week after school. His schoolwork suffered, and he fell behind on his class credits, but his reading of science fiction, detective stories, swashbucklers, and gothic horror did not abate. He wrote occasional book reviews for *The Torch*, breathless advertisements for the most socially acceptable of the books he loved. "The Reign of Terror—

the guillotine descending swiftly on innocent and guilty alike. The only hope lies in the aid of the 'Scarlet Pimpernel,' a mysterious Englishman who risks his life to save . . . the unjustly condemned." Surely no one else on the wise-ass *Torch* staff would have gushed so over Baroness Orczy's *Child of the Revolution*, but Jerry loved the Pimpernel and Zorro and all those secret heroes who masquerade as mild-mannered citizens.

Mostly, though, Jerry wanted to make up his own stories and drop his own name. He found a way to do it, and please his peers, by making fun of his own passions. Late in his first year at Glenville, he created a Tarzan parody called Goober the Mighty. The other *Torch* kids thought it was funny, and early the next year, they asked him for a sequel. "Goober, adopted son of Oolala, the lion, lifted his tousled head and drew in a mighty breath. 'If I take breathing exercises one hundred times a day for one hundred years,' he informed himself, 'I'll have the greatest chest in existence.'" Of course, when Goober pounds his chest, he sends himself into a coughing fit.

Goober was Jerry's first public success. Decades later, when most of his early writing was a blur to him, he still laughed at memories of Goober and his wild stunts: "I used to have him running along telephone wires, jumping over trees, every crazy thing I could think of." He would follow with more genre parodies for *The Torch*, absurd riffs on his beloved detective fiction and *Weird Tales*. Some were humorously self-promoting, starring Jerry Siegel, "master of deduction." Some jabbed at the mental inferiority of others: "'Say, aren't those guys dead?' he asked. 'Sure,' Siegel replied, 'from the neck up.'" But every boast and jab was directed through a self-mocking reference. Through parody Jerry revealed that he loved superhuman heroes but also that he knew what made them ridiculous. He'd found a niche at Glenville: the odd-ball you had to like because he made you laugh before you could laugh at him. He'd turn that to great profit in the next few years—using humor to get readers to drop their defenses, then letting them indulge their most absurd fantasies.

Through the nonsense of Goober, Jerry Siegel was making fun of more than his beloved pulps. He was making fun of real-life musclemen too, of the fitness promoters who peddled "breathing exercises" in the ads at the backs of pulp magazines. That "tousled head" was a jab not just at Tarzan but, as any high school kid in 1931 would have realized, the maven of "physical culture," Bernarr MacFadden. To some extent, Goober was also a jab at Jerry's new friend, Joe Shuster.

JOE WAS SHORT and scrawny as a boy, badly nearsighted, cripplingly timid. His family had been moving for generations: His grandparents had been born in Russia, his father in Holland, Joe himself in Toronto. When Joe was nine years old, his father pulled up stakes again, seeking work in the booming Cleveland rag trade. His younger siblings, Frank and Jeanette, adjusted to their new world fairly quickly, but Joe had trouble, falling behind in school and failing to make friends. Their father was a tailor, and while other men in the Shuster family did well and remained in Canada, Julius struggled. He dreamed of opening his own tailor shop, but he made do instead as a piece worker and presser. Their mother, Ida, is a vague figure in family stories, apparently inclined to stay indoors and unable or unwilling to work outside the home. When he was nine, Joe had had to work as a newsboy on the streets of Toronto to help the family, and now he had to do it again on Kinsman Avenue in Cleveland. Joe was a gentle boy, fragile, where Jerry Siegel was hard-edged, and quiet, where Jerry was frenetic. Selling papers was a brutal job for him. Every night, once he was off the street and out of the rushing crowds, he went into his room to draw. Sometimes his father could afford to buy him paper, but when money was short, Joe drew on the scraps of tissue and wrapping paper he cadged from his father's work.

Joe had a touch for humorous faces, and he liked to draw cartoons that made his siblings laugh. As he entered adolescence, though, what he came to love most were dreams of heroism, movement, flight, and freedom. He'd just turned fourteen when he saw the flying man—the same cover of *Amazing Stories* that was changing Jerry Siegel's life just a couple of miles to the north. He loved the graceful male figures, the wondrous devices, and the gleaming future cities that Frank R. Paul drew for every cover of *Amazing*. Most of the time, he didn't have the money to buy the pulps, so he'd try to memorize the images on the newsstands and go home and draw his own versions.

The one source of artistic inspiration Joe could always get his hands on were the comics in the newspapers. Comics then were printed nearly twice their current size, allowing an astonishing variety of detailed and idiosyncratic art. Sunday sections ran typically to sixteen pages, and a single strip could fill an entire newspaper page, its visual intricacies laid down with a richness of color and precision of printing inconceivable in our age of degraded newspapers. Reading the funnies was one of the great unifying rituals of American life. To compare someone to Happy Hooligan, Mutt or Jeff, or Andy Gump was to call upon a universal shorthand that transcended class, region, and ethnicity. At the same time, the comics offered honest looks at social classes—the race-track lowlifes of *Barney Google*, the social-climbing Micks of *Bringing Up Father*, the fussy townsfolk of *Gasoline Alley*—unavailable in any other popular medium. They provided visual wonders: the metamorphosing linear fantasies of Winsor McCay in *Little Nemo*, Rube Goldberg's time-taxing complexities, the dreamlike surprises of George Herriman in *Krazy Kat*. While Joe Shuster was young and was learning what cartooning could be, the ability to outdraw and outdesign the competition was becoming a point of pride for the top tier of comics artists.

In 1927 and 1928, when Joe was in junior high school, something new began to enter the comics. A new generation of cartoonists, weaned on movies and adventure fiction, began to take the funnies seriously as a place to tell long stories. Little Orphan Annie bolted from her mansion and took up with a circus where she fell into real jeopardy in every final panel. E. C. Segar's *Thimble Theater* became far more than a series of Hollywood satires when the Oyl family set off in search of the legendary Whiffle Hen and took up with a violent sailor named Popeye. Washington Tubbs, for years just a flapper-chasing wastrel, found himself thrust onto the throne of a Ruritanian kingdom and teaming up with a soldier of fortune named Captain Easy. *Wash Tubbs* was Joe Shuster's particular favorite, the creation of a genial Indiana artist named Roy Crane who combined energetic figures and silly humor into warm, rhythmic, seemingly effortless narratives. Joe copied Crane's work and embraced his aesthetic; he would never be one for visual gymnastics that tried to impress an audience, preferring an easy charm that asked to be liked.

Joe's art lifted him out of anonymity in junior high school. The editor of the school paper took a look at one of Joe's sweeping drawings of pretty girls and flying machines and gushed, "Say, you can really draw!" Joe was touched by his attention and drew a comic strip in his honor called *Jerry the Journalist*; for the editor was Jerry Fine, the cousin of Jerry Siegel who would one day be so loath to call him a nerd. When Joe told him he hoped to go to Glenville High, Fine said, "You should look up my cousin when you get there. He loves the comics, too."

Most comics were intended for all readers, adults and kids, but soon some of the smaller syndicates began to experiment with strips devoted entirely to juvenile adventure. The first two, *Tarzan* and *Buck Rogers*, saw print on the same day in January 1929, although they found their way only gradually to the Cleveland papers. Both were awkwardly drawn by advertising artists pressed into duty by ambitious syndicators, for there was no such thing yet as "serious" comic strip art. But one featured a he-man battling animals in the jungle and the other an air ace fighting a war against evil Orientals in the future. Even a young artist like Joe Shuster had to forgive their clunkiness. For Joe and a whole cohort of kids born around 1914, the onset of adolescence coincided with a revolution in the comic strip that aimed the medium straight at their hearts. They began to view the comics as their own world.

Joe Shuster, though, had another world to call his own. His daily, solitary efforts to shape and perfect a physical reality did not stop with the work of his pencil on paper. Joe was a bodybuilder. He hated sports—the competition and unpredictability and painful social negotiations of playing games with other boys—but he loved to withdraw into the gym at school and work his body with weights and pulleys and batons. Bodybuilding was a fad in the 1920s, but to most young men a suspect one. "I'd try to get him to come out and play ball," said Joe's cousin Frank from Toronto, "because I was a much more active and physical kind of guy. I'll admit that Joe believed in lifting weights and making himself strong, but he was never one for actual activity." Body-building was the turf of health nuts, Muscle Beach fairies, and most of all, Bernarr MacFadden.

In New York, men like Harry Donenfeld took MacFadden as their model for getting rich in the field of shabby magazines. A thousand miles away, a meek boy like Joe Shuster could take him as the model of what a man could be. MacFadden's *Physical Culture* was central to bodybuilding culture and so as much a part of Joe's consciousness as *Amazing Stories* and *Tarzan*. In fact, MacFadden helped shape that make-believe world: Tarzan wore a full lion skin on his early book covers, but switched to a loincloth as Bernarr made it his trademark.

MacFadden promised power and success to those who would follow him, and he created stories to back up the promises. In 1922 he publicized a physical culture follower in Brooklyn named Angelo Siciliano as Charles Atlas, "the World's Most Perfectly Developed Man." After a few years on the pageant circuit, Atlas hooked up with an advertising man and started his own mail-order fitness business. He was the first body-builder to use a comic strip in his ad and the first to sell fitness with violence: The ninety-seven-pound weakling could beat up thugs through isometrics. His ads first appeared in magazines in 1929, and the mean mood of the early Depression made him a success. Joe Shuster turned fifteen that summer. It's easy to imagine him at Euclid Beach or Edgewater Park, a timid, skinny tailor's boy submerged among the brawny sons of German and Slovakian steelworkers. It must have seemed as though Charles Atlas was speaking directly to him.

Such promises of perfection flourished in the 1920s. The breakdown of old orders and the wonders of technology came together to make any imaginable future seem realizable, if only the right system or device could be found: scientific socialism, fascism, positive thinking, technological progress, spiritualism, or health regimens. Others spoke of natural aristocracies that would take command if only they could realize their own superiority: capitalists, scientists, white Protestants. Edgar Rice Burroughs believed in the innate virtue of the "Anglo-Saxon race." His Tarzan was a romantic daydream on the idea that a high-born English baby dropped into the jungle would naturally come to master not only the beasts but black men as well. Thanks to the plasticity of fiction, however, to a MacFadden follower like Joe Shuster the ape man could also be a demonstration of the virtue of physical fitness.

The living realities in which these dreams were bought usually fell far below the peaks of Burroughs's or MacFadden's promises. The Shuster family was doing just well enough by the end of the decade to dare to move into the more expensive Glenville neighborhood. They rented half a duplex on Amor Street right off 105th, just a few blocks from the Siegels' house but significantly cheaper because it sat next to the Glenville Garage. No sooner had they moved than the economic freeze of 1930 spread over their fortunes. They hung on in Glenville, but as Joe's father had trouble finding work, it became a struggle. Joe scrounged for whatever work he could find. There were months when he had to continue his drawing on scraps of butcher paper wet with blood and strips of wallpaper plucked from trash bins. But nothing stopped him from drawing.

Such was the odd amalgam of dreams and realities that Joe Shuster brought into Glenville High in the fall of 1930: a sweet, quiet boy, more pretty than handsome with his huge doe eyes; given to sketching beautiful girls but never speaking to them; later remembered fondly but not clearly by his peers; devoted to drawing comics like a little boy and lifting weights like a he-man. He liked to do things at school. He joined the Tumbling Club, designed scenery for school plays, and served as president of the Art Club for a while. He joined the Torch Club, too, where he began submitting visual gags and editorial cartoons. Unfortunately, Joe had as much trouble shining on that talented staff as Jerry Siegel did. The paper's regular cartoonists had more confident lines and better instincts for what made their peers laugh. If Joe hoped to use his gift for the fantastical and adventurous to attract attention, he had to outdraw Bernard Schmittke, a pulp fan who could afford real art instruction and would within a few years be drawing for the science fiction magazines. In four years of high school Joe got only one cartoon published in *The Torch*.

It was on *The Torch*, though, that he and Jerry Siegel became friends. It seems not to have been a quick process—Jerry's angry edges and nervous self-absorption probably didn't sit easily with Joe's self-protective sweetness—but they found passions in common, and in the way of shy pop culture fans, they discovered that they could talk joyfully for hours without ever having to enter the painful places. They both loved Douglas Fairbanks movies, comic strips, and pulp science fiction. But where Joe could only dip into the pulps sporadically, Jerry had dozens of them stuffed in his attic bedroom. Jerry knew that *Buck Rogers* was based on a novel from *Amazing Stories*—and not just any novel but *Armageddon 2499 AD* by Philip Nowlan, which had run in that same August 1928 issue that had seized them both. Jerry had a sharp enough critical eye to know that it wasn't a very good comic strip, but he understood what a validation it was of science fiction that the whole world was exposed every day to this step-child of Hugo Gernsback. He also knew that the art for the color Sunday *Buck Rogers* looked so much better than the dailies because they were being ghosted by a twenty-year-old in Chicago named Russell Keaton, a kid only four years older than Jerry and Joe. Jerry had even written to Keaton and discovered he was a fellow science fiction fan. Jerry must have impressed Joe mightily.

Joe loved Jerry's humor writing, especially "Goober the Mighty." Jerry made cracks about Joe's exercising, but he also appreciated it. "I used to go to the school gym and watch Joe in action," he said. "He was pretty good." A few classmates remembered Jerry himself falling in love with bodybuilding schemes for a while (but the line between reality and self-mockery could be confusingly thin in Jerry's case). A real friendship grew up between them, an understanding that whatever excited them could be shared. In all their reminiscences, neither spoke of any other friendship. At sixteen they'd each finally found someone to trust.

As THE BOYS built their lives around comics, pulps, and movies, a shift was occurring in the way the business of junk entertainment ran. For one thing, publishers and manufacturers were becoming more aware of the juvenile market. Even though adults still did nearly all the buying, kids were being given more voice in family decision making. A *Tarzan*-loving ten-year-old could make the difference when a father had to choose between the *Plain Dealer* and the *Press*. At the same time, as collections of comic strips sold well off the newsstands and movies were spun out of *The Katzenjammer Kids* and *Tarzan*, an increasing number of entrepreneurs were catching on to the value of selling a character to more than one medium. When a minor-league Chicago syndicator spotted the flying man on the August 1928 *Amazing Stories*, he saw an image that he thought could sell newspapers and lunch boxes. He ended up licensing a different character in that pulp, Anthony "Buck" Rogers, but one embracing the same boyish fantasies, and so Jerry and Joe's beloved science fiction began to come to them through a new medium.

This is one of the small wonders of consumer capitalism: As the business turned more mercenary and seedy, it was able to provide a more complete fantasy world for its most devoted fans. A genuine zeal had been needed to bring Philip Nowlan's odd vision of the twenty-fifth century to print in the first place, but the investors who stretched it into the daily papers, the silver screen, the radio waves, the book pages, and the toy shelves examined and sold it like a bolt of cloth. To the kids who could now immerse themselves in that simplistic, vibrant reality at any time and through nearly every sense, it didn't matter. The cheesiness was a price worth paying for immersion.

In early 1931, just as Jerry and Joe were becoming friends, the same process transformed the pulps. The fiction magazines had generally lacked regular starring characters since 1915, when Street and Smith converted *Nick Carter Weekly* into *Detective Story Magazine*. But in 1930 Street and Smith decided to bankroll a weekly radio drama to promote that same *Detective Story*. One of its producers decided the show needed a recurring host, a creepy voice to narrate and introduce the stories, and came up with an all-knowing mystery man called "the Shadow." Soon magazine dealers were reporting that customers were asking for "that Shadow magazine." Since there was no "Shadow magazine," the editors created one in a hurry. They cobbled together some notes, grabbed an old cover painting off the stacks, and collared Walter B. Gibson—a crossword puzzle designer, stage magician, and article hack who ghost-wrote for the likes of Harry Houdini—and told him to make a character out of the Shadow that would keep bringing readers back.

Gibson was no fiction writer. His lunging narrative was almost impossible to read: "He was cloaked entirely in black, that being, except for his head, on which was a dark slouch hat. The headpiece was quite effective as the cloak, for both hid his face, but neither concealed his hands." But he understood, as a fiction writer might not have, how much young Americans loved theatrical flamboyance, Victorian excess, and the shock of the unbelievable. His Shadow was a mystery man who masquerades as a wealthy playboy and commands a secret network of operatives, a sort of blending of the Scarlet Pimpernel and the Phantom of the Opera. Except that he fights the most brutal gangsters with a pair of blazing .45 automatics. After a few issues, a cover artist gave him visual form—hat and swirling cape concealing all but the nose and eyes of a raptor—and someone at Street and Smith coined a slogan that spoke to every young man's hunger for power over an inscrutable and uncontrollable world: "The Shadow. He Knows."

The first issue of *The Shadow* sold out. In the economic free fall of 1931, very few magazines were selling out. It began as a quarterly, but by late that year it was coming out twice a month. Through a hasty series of commercial moves, Street and Smith had given American boys with angry dreams another idol as vivid as Buck Rogers or Edward G. Robinson's Little Caesar. By 1932 the company was already preparing more pulps starring crime fighters of superhuman prowess and distinct appearance. Soon its editors had developed an in-house word for the type of character: "superhero."

Jerry Siegel was a Shadow fan. He already liked heroes who masqueraded as milquetoasts, but here was one not bound by the gentleman's code of a Zorro or Pimpernel. Here was one who rained death mercilessly on the urban thugs who killed innocent men. These pulps gave form to a darker, less optimistic set of fantasies than Gernsback's science fiction did—fantasies that must have shot straight at Jerry's heart.

Six months after the Shadow premiered, the same darkness came to the comic strips. In October 1931 the Chicago Tribune Syndicate launched *Dick Tracy*, Chester Gould's angry, nightmarish reworking of hard-boiled pulps and gangster movies. Its instant success guaranteed that comics would turn grimmer. More crime comics would follow (*Secret Agent X-9*), and social melodramas (*Apple Mary*), and westerns (*Little Joe*). *Popeye* and *Little Orphan Annie* turned dark and scary. Even *Mickey Mouse* turned to crime busting and adventures.

The comics pages were becoming an extension of the world of pulps and adventure movies. And yet they remained the most free and most idiosyncratic of mass media. Movies and radio shows were group products, pulp fiction was shaped by each magazine's editorial philosophy, but the best comics flew off cartoonists' drawing boards with little time for editorial interference. They defied and invented genres. Their characters blazed like fever dreams: the Sea Hag, Daddy Warbucks, Mandrake, Ming the Merciless, Flattop, Pruneface. The comics became the place where the great American popular dramas took place: the craziest dreams, the most talked-about cliff-hangers, the most famous heroes, the most elemental fantasies, the rawest communication between storyteller and audience.

Joe Shuster was a member of a whole generation of young artists shaped by the comics of the Thirties, but there was one strip that he, and most of his peers, mentioned more than any other. The same month *Dick Tracy* began, the same month Jerry Siegel's second Goober story appeared in *The Torch*, a new artist took over *Tarzan*. Harold Foster was a classical draftsman who understood that the real power of a story about an ape man lay not in its cliff-hangers or its jungle proscenia or its naturalistic beasts but in the beauty of the male human body. No male figure ever printed on cheap paper, not even the musclemen in Bernarr MacFadden's health magazines, had ever shown such grace and dynamism.

Tarzan's power embraced sex. The first naked body a pubescent boy sees, after all, is his own, and the male body contains all the first terrors and joys of sex for him. Harvey Kurtzman, a cartoonist ten years younger than Joe Shuster, said that the ape man's near nudity fascinated him as a boy, and some of his first ventures into masturbation transpired over Foster's panels. But Tarzan embraced more than sex; he embraced all the wishes a boy holds about his body, his identity, and his future. Foster's Tarzan was supremely self-contained, an invincible male who wore none of the costumes of male power but only his own perfect form. When a powerless boy yearns to be a man but cannot understand how he will ever get there, a symbol like Tarzan can come to him as a revelation. If he doesn't have a father, or not enough of a father, then the revelation burns that much brighter. *Tarzan* became the talk of every kid who loved to draw: "Foster's so *good!*" He was good, though not better than the other great cartoonists on the pages around him. He was simply the best there'd ever been at what boys needed to see.

Girls liked Foster's *Tarzan,* too. They might claim they were just reading over their brothers' shoulders, but they were reading. They had their own curiosities about the naked male body, their own reasons to engage with idealized symbols of male potency—and because the Ape Man lacked the accoutrements of the real-life men they knew, girls found it easier to identify with him than with most male heroes. As masculine as he was, Tarzan was so unencumbered by social roles and familiar reality that he served as a far more pliable vessel for girls' own dreams of individual power than the soldiers and cowboys who usually dominated juvenile adventure. It didn't take long for boys like Joe Shuster to realize that girls took notice of a well-drawn romantic hero. So misfit boys discovered a new function for junk-culture fantasies: They could catch the eyes of the other sex if they could render those fantasies simply and beautifully and innocently.

In the swirl of fantasies and images brought by the Shadow, Tarzan, Buck Rogers, Dick Tracy, Popeye, and Wash Tubbs, Jerry and Joe began collaborating on comic strips. They started with *Goober the Mighty,* but they began to play with less humorous ideas: a futuristic police force, a band of interplanetary adventurers, a cave man, a Gernsbackian group of scientific crime fighters with gadgets that see through walls and amplify sound. Joe seemed to enjoy the drawing for its sake, but Jerry sent them out to newspaper syndicates. They were all rejected, but Jerry began to believe he and Joe might have a career in the comics.

As HE IMMERSED himself in ink, Jerry came to identify himself more and more with his writing, even to the point of obnoxiousness. Jerry Fine remembered him trying to impress his cousins at one family gathering. "I can write a story about anything. You see that Coke bottle? I could write a story about that Coke bottle if I wanted to." But then, he didn't have much else in his life. He lived alone now in the big Kimberly Avenue house with his mother, and every night he'd hole himself up in his attic bedroom and write. He continued to send short stories to the pulps with no success. Those stories are now lost, not because Jerry didn't keep his own work—he was becoming something of a pack rat, in fact—but because he was usually too impatient and impulsive to remember to include return postage with his submissions.

For all his energy, though, Jerry's writing lacked a focus—until, in the late spring of 1932, the third issue of *The Time Traveller* arrived in the mail. He'd spent a dollar for a subscription to the new fanzine from Mortimer Weisinger, Julius Schwartz, Allen Glasser, and Forrest J. Ackerman, four of his peers in the first wave of Gernsback fandom. Many young men had tried to sell their assorted mimeographed and dittoed fanzines in the two and a half years since Jerry produced his own *Cosmic Stories*, but none had come from such a pantheon of prominent, witty, in-the-know fans. *The Time Traveller* sold a hundred subscriptions right off the bat, and with its third issue it was professionally typeset and printed. The moment Jerry Siegel pulled it from its envelope, he knew he was going to create his own magazine.

That fall, Jerry Siegel would turn eighteen. The new school year was his third at Glenville High and should have been his last; except that he, like his buddy Joe, had fallen so far behind in his class requirements that he wouldn't be able to graduate with his class. It was a circumstance he would never speak of publicly. His first appearance in *The Torch* that year was a breathlessly self-aggrandizing press release for the birth of

Science Fiction: The Advance Guard of Future Civilization. He promised that it would include the work of "several prominent Glenvillites" as well as "well known" writers and that "a great deal of capital is being used for advertising which is expected to bring staggering results." The ads, in "practically every other pulp paper magazine on the newsstands," would be seen by 5 million people. "A few thousand subscriptions are hoped to be secured from this resort." The magazine would be mimeographed only "until a large enough circulation warrants printing." He was bold enough to charge fifteen cents an issue, half again the price of *The Time Traveller.*

In fact *Science Fiction* was written almost entirely by Siegel under various pseudonyms and illustrated by Joe Shuster. The ad budget took Jerry no further than tiny notices in *Amazing* and *Wonder*, and to sell subscriptions he had to arrange with Mort Weisinger to piggyback *Science Fiction* on *The Time Traveller*'s order form. (Mort was supposed to send Jerry his share of the subscription money—but Jerry never saw it.) The Glenville *Torch*'s Bernard Schmittke contributed a sophisticated industrial moderne cover, and Forry Ackerman, fandom's leading proponent of monster movies, provided pictures from the upcoming *King Kong.* It was the book-review column that brought Jerry his greatest gift, however, for it was while researching it that he seems to have collided with the product of a literary world very different from the one he'd known, a novel that sent his fantasies spinning in a significant new direction: Philip Wylie's *Gladiator.*

Wylie represented a late-Twenties America very different from the one Jerry knew. The son of a Presbyterian minister who broke angrily with his father's God, he had studied theater at Princeton, dropped out to become a successful advertising writer, lost his career to a dubious paternity suit, decided to write fiction, and sold his first novel, a bombastic indictment of repressed Presbyterians, to Alfred A. Knopf—all before his twenty-sixth birthday. His second novel, the juicily titled *Babes and Sucklings,* was a ravaging of his own angry first marriage and a screed against modern morals, and he welcomed the cries of "indecency" from small-town librarians. His writing tilted and pitched, as from one page to the next he'd strain to be Sinclair Lewis or H. L. Mencken or Havelock Ellis or Elinor Glyn. A *New York Times* reviewer said he wrote "in a manner reminiscent of the vaudeville man who plays an entire orchestra single-handed."

The next year, 1929, Wylie decided it was time to tackle a grand social allegory. He wanted to show how a truly superior man would be loathed and destroyed by our mediocre society: "Great deeds were always imminent and none of them could be accomplished because they involved humanity, humanity protecting its diseases, its pettiness, its miserable convictions and conventions, with the essence of itself—life. Life not misty and fecund for the future, but life clawing at the dollar in the hour, the security of platitudes . . . the needs of skin, belly, and womb."

His plot was a scientific conceit: A biologist turns his son into "a super-child, an invulnerable man," who grows into a being of incomparable strength and vitality and innate moral superiority. "There, in the forest, beyond the eye of man, he learned that he was superhuman. . . . 'I'm like a man made out of iron instead of meat.'" He tries to use his strength to uplift the world, but mankind is too small for him. Bullies pick fights with him, the military presses him into a venal war, women give themselves to him and then run from his power, a little Jew cons him into the boxing racket, a money-grubbing communist calls him "Fool! Dreamer! Impossible idealist!" He imagines tearing down the Capitol like Samson but knows it will accomplish nothing.

Wylie's use of biological fantasy would later lead science fiction fans to claim *Gladiator* as a product of their beloved genre, but his models were not Gernsback's pulp stories. Wylie mocked junk culture, mocked yellow journalism and Bernarr MacFadden and narcissistic bodybuilders, and he'd surely have mocked *Amazing Stories* if he'd bothered to notice it. He lifted tricks from the satirical parades of Henry Fielding and William Thackeray, pulled themes from the intellectual allegories of H. G. Wells and Friedrich Nietzsche. Then he fell in love with his hero, his man of "breathtaking symmetry . . . a man vehemently alive, a man with the promise of a young god," and hurled him into scenes of sexual awakening and combat and political melodrama as clotted and super-heated as anything on the pages of *Cosmopolitan* or *Collier's*.

The result was a drunken disaster of a novel, dumbest at its most in-tellectually ambitious and emptiest at its most passionate, in the end lurching wildly into a lamppost of self-pitying nonsense: "'Now—God—oh, God—if there be a God—tell me! Can I defy You? Can I defy Your world? Is this Your will? Or are You, like all mankind, impotent? Oh, God!' He put his hand to his mouth and called God like a name into the tumult above. Madness was upon him and the bitter irony with which his blood ran black was within him.

"A bolt of lighting stabbed earthward. It struck Hugo, outlining him in fire. His hand slipped away from his mouth. His voice was quenched."

Hugo Danner wasn't the only one struck by lightning. So was Jerry Siegel.

When other fans called Jerry's attention to *Gladiator* in 1932, it had already been on the shelves for two years. Wiley had had two more books published and was deep in his first big novel, *Finnley Wren*. He'd have cared nothing for a young science fiction fan's love of *Gladiator* (and would no doubt have been shocked to learn that eight years later he'd be preparing to sue that fan for plagiarism). It was, however, the perfect moment for Jerry. Eighteen years old and still in the middle of high school, still locked in silent grief for his murdered father, still with-out a girlfriend or a plausible career but launching a magazine and dreaming of beauties and riches—*Gladiator* must have touched upon everything he wanted and feared to be.

The "superman" was scarcely a new idea and was in fact a common motif of both high and low culture by the early Thirties, the inevitable product of those doctrines of perfectability promoted by everyone from Bernarr MacFadden to Leon Trotsky. The word had descended from Ni-etzsche's *Ubermensch* through Bernard Shaw's *Man and Superman*, but it was easily wedded to ideas neither Nietzschean nor Shavian. In Ger-many Adolf Hitler was claiming that a whole nation of supermen could be forged through institutionalized racism and militarism, and his popularity was rising steadily. In America the idea of eugenics was being actively explored at Ivy League universities. Eugenics inspired Wylie's pseudoscientific plot device in *Gladiator*, and his hero explicitly considered its use to improve mankind.

Even leftists could use the word: a Cleveland radical named Joseph Pirincin argued in his lectures that socialist production methods would create a "superabundance" of goods and opportunities, would make the citizen of a socialist future a "veritable superman" by our current standards. He claimed he once gave this lecture at a community center in the early 1930s and in the audience were *two young Jewish men who later* . . . We can complete the anecdote and surely dismiss it as wishful thinking, but it's a measure of the ubiquity of the symbolic superman.

The idea of the superman was explored in much of the more romantic pulp culture, even if the term wasn't used: Edgar Rice Burroughs's Tarzan and John Carter of Mars were not simply the strongest and noblest of their breed, but were clearly described as of an order apart, beings of such innate and apparent superiority that they rose to command every world they entered. Their ties to the English nobility and the old Confederacy explained their potential for superiority, but that potential was realized only through a miracle that lifted them outside history: Tarzan's return to the evolutionary Eden of the apes, John Carter's unexplained, almost mystical longevity. In 1929 Jerry Siegel's old pen pal Jack Williamson wrote a novel, published by Hugo Gernsback, that explained the superbeing in a science-fictional way. Called *The Girl from Mars*, it featured a strange visitor from another planet with powers far beyond those of normal men.

Until he encountered Wylie's Hugo Danner, however, Jerry had never seen a superman whose feats were set so vividly against a familiar and constraining reality: "I can do things, Dad. It kind of scares me. I can jump higher'n a house. I can run faster'n a train." Hugo transforms cliché scenes of trench warfare in France when he learns that a bullet can't pierce his skin and even a bursting shell only knocks him down. And Jerry had never seen a human portrait of the superman that encompassed his flounderings, his frustrations, his isolation, his pain. Hugo Danner displays his superstrength as a child and frightens the townsfolk. His father draws him aside to explain that he must use his strength for "a good and noble purpose" to keep people from hating him; indeed, when men first see his full strength they call him "a demon." Hugo withdraws from the world "to become acquainted with his powers" and builds a solitary fortress in the woods. When he brings his greatness to the world, he knows moments of triumph, but each one only deepens his isolation. He's taken to bed by an Ivy League beauty: "Half goddess, half animal . . . the vanguard of emancipated American womanhood." But only once, for "she learned something, too, so that she never came back to Hugo, and kept the longing for him as a sort of memory which she made hallowed in a shorn soul."

The capsule review of *Gladiator* in Siegel's fanzine hints at none of the impact it must have had on a lonely, angry boy. But his story in the next issue of *Science Fiction*, dated January 1933, suggested that it had changed his ideas about the purposes of fantasy.

"The Reign of the Superman" by "Herbert S. Fine" (a nod to his cousins) is framed by Joe Shuster's illustrations. Joe's work was coming along: The snarling villain and the futuristic city of skyscrapers, drawn in a clear-line style based on the cylinders and circles of industrial design, show that he was well attuned to the iconography of his moment. Then the nine densely typed pages of Jerry's story begin:

The bread-line! Its row of downcast, disillusioned men; unlucky creatures who have found that life holds nothing but bitterness for them. The bread-line! Last resort of the starving vagrant.

With a contemptuous sneer on his face, Professor Smalley watched the wretched unfortunates file past him. To him, who had come of rich parents and had never been forced to face the rigors of life, the miserableness of these men seemed deserved. It appeared to him that if they had the slightest ambition at all, they could lift themselves from their terrible rut.

Professor Smalley selects a vagrant as a human guinea pig and injects him with a mysterious element he's discovered in a meteor from another planet. His subject escapes and discovers that the element has given him superhuman powers. He can hear the thoughts of strangers like words in the air: "Brains is what this gang needs and brains is what it ain't got." "I gotta have that dough, Ma. I gotta have it!" "He's just a kid, Mame. Why don't you let him alone?" "To hell with the anarchists!" "I wish he'd keep on his own feet. A helluva nerve he has askin' a swell dancer like me to fox trot with a palooka like him." "Look here, punk, you may be the star reporter on this rag but unless you turn in your copy by three o'clock you'll be out in the street peddling shoelaces."

Late 1932 was a politically electrical moment, and most bright eighteen-year-olds, especially in a left-leaning Jewish milieu, could have waxed fairly eloquent about unemployment and class agendas; but Jerry went not an inch beyond the most common Hollywood tropes. The people of his world thought in bad Warner Brothers dialogue. And he obviously had no more interest in science than he had in social reality or character: The "Superman" goes to the library to read "Einstein's Expanding Universe." "Trash! Bosh!" he cries. When the librarian tells him to be quiet, the Superman hisses, "If I had a ray-tube within reach, I'd blast you out of existence!" Jerry raced impatiently past every detail that would have made his story more convincing to get to the one long sequence that seemed to excite his passion: the angry struggle for control between the Superman and his maker.

One passage leaps out to the reader who knows about Jerry Siegel's later life:

[Smalley] secured pencil and paper and began to write a long, heated letter. He told how he had taken Dunn from the breadline to make him the noble subject of the greatest experiment of the century. He told of how the chemical had been administered and Dunn's subsequent vanishing. "And," he concluded, "unless this creature is snared and shot dead like a beast, he will grow, his powers will strengthen, increase, until he will hold the fate of the world in the palm of his hand!" When the letter was completed he placed it in an envelope, addressed it to the City Editor of the largest newspaper, then left the laboratory and mailed it.

Maybe it's only an accidental foreshadowing of the long, heated letters that Siegel would later use in his fight to regain control of Superman; but it is the one moment when a character steps out of the strictures of plot and behaves in an oddly small and human way. It may be that even before he had a real property to fight over, Jerry was already waging wars of entitlement in his head.

Smalley tries to partake of the meteorite himself, but the Superman murders him first. He's now learned to master others with his mind and plans to achieve world domination by sending "the armies of the earth to total annihilation against each other." "The International Conciliatory Council was in session. . . . Chinaman and Jap, Frenchman and Englishman, American and Mexican, all smiled genially at each other." The Superman broadcasts "thoughts of hate," and the delegates begin "attacking each other like mad hate-filled wolves."

But a reporter reads Smalley's letter and confronts the Superman. (The reporter's name is Forrest Ackerman; for the fan, the in-joke is always more real than the drama.) The end comes in a scene of religiosity and shouting echoing the lightning-bolt finish of *Gladiator:* "In this moment of dread and terror the reporter sent a silent prayer up to the Creator of the threatened world. He beseeched the Omnipotent One to blot out this blaspheming devil. Was it true that Forrest saw the look of hate swept from the Superman's face and terror replace it, or was it mere fancy?" "No!" shouts the Superman to the empty air. He realizes that the drug is wearing off. "The arrogant, confident figure had departed. Instead, there now stood, a drooping, disillusioned man. . . . 'I see, now, how wrong I was. If I had worked for the good of humanity, my name would have gone down in history with a blessing—instead of a curse.'"

Jerry Siegel was not a religious kid. "I don't think he ever went to the synagogue in his life," said Jerry Fine. The Omnipotent One entered via Wylie. Jerry was uninterested in grappling with Wylie's idea that a man could be good and yet still be unable to make a difference, preferring the reassurance of genre fiction that we can all choose whether history will bless us or curse us, but he was playing with the question raised by *Gladiator*: What can and should a superman do in a world of real violence and pain?

Just a few weeks after he'd mailed out that issue of *Science Fiction*, the world of pulps sent him a signal that his imagination was moving in the right direction. He was flipping through the latest issue of *The Shadow* when the boldface word jumped out at him: "SUPERMAN." Beneath it was a picture of a he-man wrestling with a gunman, with the legend "Doc Savage—man of Master Mind and Body." It was the first ad for Street and Smith's new "superhero."

Doc Savage may also have owed something to Wylie. Like Hugo Danner, Doc had been cultivated to human perfection by science, and he had a Fortress of Solitude where he went to think. His name and appearance—a muscular giant with mahogany skin, bronze hair, and gemlike eyes—may have come from a more recent Wylie novel, *The Savage Gentleman*. He shared the Shadow's network of operatives, but instead of an urban crime fighter he was a globe-trotting rescuer of innocents in peril. Before the issue hit the stands, Jerry and Joe knew they would be fans.

Then there appeared, in March 1933, an odd product of the cheap magazine trade that united Jerry's passions for fiction and comics. As spring melted the Cleveland snows and the nation waited to see what Franklin D. Roosevelt could do against the Depression, and as Jerry and Joe waited to see what Doc Savage would be like, a cheesy, tabloid-sized, cardboard-covered magazine called *Detective Dan* appeared on the newsstands. In the wake of *Dick Tracy*, hundreds of young cartoonists had whipped out their own tough-cop comic strips to peddle to the syndicates. One of those, Norman Marsh, experimented with having his unsold samples printed in black and white and placed on the newsstands. Released under the company name "Humor Publications," they weren't distributed well—barely beyond Chicago, in fact—and probably didn't pay back even their printing costs. *Detective Ace King* and *Bob Scully, Two-Fisted*

Hick Detective disappeared almost without trace, but *Detective Dan* found its way to Cleveland. They were what future comic book historians, always in quest of origin stories, would come to call the "first modern single-character original-content comic books." Jerry Siegel, with those quivering pop culture antennae that enabled him to be the first creator of a science fiction fanzine and one of the original subscribers to *The Time Traveller*, was one of the few people who would ever recall having actually seen one on the stands—and apparently the only one who made an important career decision because of it.

Jerry bought *Detective Dan* and brought it to Joe. Joe thought it wasn't *Dick Tracy* by a long shot but it was pretty good. Jerry said that wasn't the point. The point was that it wasn't much better than what he and Joe could do—but it was in print. And its publication didn't depend on the distant and indifferent world of newspaper syndication but on what was, in Jerry's mind at least, the far more familiar world of cheap magazines. "We can *do* this!" he said.

In his mind it may already have been real: They'd write and draw a comic strip based on an action hero of their own creation and sell it to Humor Publishing. To make it stand out, they wouldn't copy *Dick Tracy* or any other strip but take their inspiration, like *Buck Rogers* and *Tarzan,* from the pulps. They'd draw on *Gladiator* and the ads for *Doc Savage* to create a pulp adventure about a brawling do-gooder of extraordinary strength.

He even had a title: *The Superman.*

New Fun

D URING THE HIGH times of the 1920s, Harry Donenfeld had been content to follow the market. Using his charm and business wits to stitch together connections among distributors, publishers, and racketeers was enough to keep the money flowing in. But the hard times of the 1930s didn't allow coasting. As magazine sales dropped through 1930 and 1931, Harry either had to fall by the wayside or move to the front.

Small publishers typically folded up when the debts got too high and resurfaced later with new products. Distributors didn't have that luxury. There was room in the business for only a handful of them, and a furious war was fought over "rack space" and geographic territory, a war that intensified as sales dropped. A distributor's business depended on relationships with local jobbers and retailers, the reliable weekly delivery of product. It involved warehouse space, truck leases, mailing permits, delivery routes. A successful distributor had the deep pockets to cover printers' bills and keep small publishers afloat, but it also had a mechanism that would grind to a halt when the cash stopped flowing. When that happened, the jobbers and retailers had to jump quickly to another distributor. Hard times were especially hard on smaller distributors, since news dealers with tight cash flows had to favor those who offered quantity discounts. For a company like Eastern News, cutting back to save costs could mean spiraling toward oblivion.

By the end of 1930, Harry Donenfeld was publishing four "smooshes" (*Joy Stories, Hot Stories, LaParee Stories,* and *Gay Parisienne*) and a line of "art nudies." He also seems to have taken over Frank Armer's line, including *Pep* and *Spicy Stories,* because Armer's editorial address was no longer on 42nd Street but on 20th, in the Donny Press building. The "captive publisher" was a common entity in the Depression, as publishers gave up shares of their companies to cover debts to printers and distributors that they couldn't pay. This would become Harry's favorite method of expansion during the next few years, the one that led him into unexpected fields.

Then, sometime early in 1931, Eastern News announced it couldn't pay its publishers what it owed them. Harry did the only thing a prudent publisher could do: screw his creditors. He'd already developed a reputation for delaying payments to writers and artists to cover cash flow shortages, incurring the warning in the trade magazine *Author and Journalist* that he "shows no ability to pay for accepted material." This time he had to pull a bolder stunt. He declared his magazine company, Irwin Publishing, bankrupt, then sold the titles of his magazines to another company he'd created, Merwil. He still had his magazines, but as *Author and Publisher* noted, "Writers who had money due them from the Irwin Publishing Company are left holding the sack, and it is the contention of Mr. Donenfeld that his new company is not obligated to pay the same."

The next crisis was legal. This was a time of great scandals in New York. A Republican Party pulled under by the vortex of its own hopeless policies blamed everything it could on Democratic corruption. Judge Samuel Seabury, a man of such sterling Episcopal lineage that people called him "the Bishop," had launched an inquiry into Tammany Hall that was about to bring down the immensely popular but lavishly corrupt mayor, Jimmy Walker. Now other mugwumps joined the hunt. The New York Citizens' Committee on Civic Decency made their target the girlie magazines, and in the spring of 1932, it pressed the DA's office into ordering the arrest of four newsdealers for selling smutty pulps. Charges were dropped only after a number of publishers, including

Harry and Armer, agreed to meet with the committee and collaborate with them in terminating the most offensive magazines and "pay closer heed to the proprieties" with others.

In the meeting with the Decency Committee in July, Harry consented to cancel *LaParee* and tone things down in the others. Hands were shaken, fine words were spoken between the uptown Protestants and the downtown pornographer. Then Harry went off and quietly continued publishing *LaParee*. If he told his editor to tone down its content, one would never know it by the blazing pink nipples on its December cover. Harry was learning how to shrug off the angry screams of creditors and censors alike. His chutzpah made for great stories around the gin rummy table. He didn't yet know just how angry he had made the decent citizens of New York.

Three months later, in October 1932, Paul Sampliner and Charles Dreyfus of Eastern News filed for bankruptcy. They had tried to hang on until the corner to prosperity was turned, but the economy only got worse. A few weeks before the Democrats swept the national elections, Eastern scattered its publishers and salesmen to the four winds. Sampliner and Dreyfus owed Harry Donenfeld nearly $30,000.

Other publishers survived by finding distributors who'd cover their debts in exchange for control, but Harry did not want to be a captive publisher. He needed cash and distribution that would respect his ownership. So he took Paul Sampliner out drinking and sketched out his idea for the Independent News Company. He would function as head salesman. His brother Irving would stay in printing and publishing. Jack Liebowitz would juggle the numbers. And to fund it, Sampliner could borrow money from his mother.

Harry loved to tell that story in later years, especially when Sampliner was in the room, with affectionate contempt for the mama's boy who'd seeded his fortune. In Harry's world the street kid would always run the show and make the big score, and it was a lucky rich boy who hitched his wagon to him. From then on, indeed, Sampliner seemed content to follow Harry's lead and grow quietly rich. Personally, he became a prominent member of the Jewish community and a leader of the

Anti-Defamation League. But Independent News avoided the highfalutin psychology and politics that Sampliner had supported at Eastern and focused on what Harry knew he could sell: sex and thrills.

Independent was ready to move goods within weeks after Eastern's collapse. The first, easiest venues for the nudies and smooshes were burlesque theaters and former speakeasies like the Onyx that featured "dancers" along with jazz bands and dirty comedians. Between the Depression and Repeal plenty of frantic bar owners and small-time racketeers were willing to gamble on sex to keep the cash flowing in, and Harry knew how to talk to them. His happy patter and willingness to sit down and bend an elbow for a while must have made him far more appealing than the bottom-rung thugs who usually pushed pornography. He may have kept moving Margaret Sanger's products, too, or her competitors'—rubbers for the guys who could afford a stripper's after-hours attention, *Spicy Stories* for the ones who couldn't. Publishing historian Michael Feldman has said, "It may not be a coincidence that Armer and Donenfeld called one of their magazine companies Trojan Publishing. They may have wanted retailers to know that they were buying their girlie mags from the same reliable folks who sold them their latex novelties."

To survive, though, Independent had to win back the magazine jobbers, news dealers, drug and cigar and candy store owners Eastern had lost. Its most effective weapon was the consignment system: Instead of risking his money by buying publications outright from the distributor, a dealer would take a shipment "on consignment," return the magazines he hadn't sold, and pay only for those he had. Since unsold past-date magazines were of no value to the distributor, the dealer could save shipping costs by tearing off the top of the cover and sending it back as a proof of return; the rest he was contractually bound to throw away, so he couldn't compete against his own distributor with a secondhand copy of the same magazine. The number of old magazines and comics that still show up for sale with the title strip torn off suggests that plenty of retailers broke that compact by reselling the returned goods anyway. But then, Harry Donenfeld matched them by slapping new covers around the guts of returned pulps and reselling them as new issues. Readers might have felt cheated when they realized they'd already read the magazine they'd just bought, but the guys in the business laughed. They were street kids like Harry, and the hard times just gave the slickest chiselers an excuse to show how good they were.

The problem with consignment was the financial pressure it put on the distributor. Print runs had to be determined long before orders were placed and so were based on predictions made months in advance. The trick was to print enough copies to satisfy dealers, guarantee rack space, and maximize sales but not so many that returns outnumbered sales and ate up all the income. Optimism was punished by dealer refunds, pessimism by a loss of rack space and potential income. The need to expand one's line of goods battled constantly with the need to be cheap. This made for a strange sort of madness among distributors, making them wildly daring when they saw a new market opening or a new fad kicking in, but then suddenly, self-defeatingly conservative.

Distributors had been using the consignment system for a long time for some products and some retailers, but during the Depression, it became the only system dealers would accept. Independent News had no choice but to lead with the most generous plans it could sustain. That meant Jack Liebowitz would have to manage the cash flow and balance the financial risks with extraordinary precision, anticipating sales patterns months in advance, running profit and loss estimations that took into account rapidly fluctuating production costs (including the strength of the Canadian dollar, which had everything to do with paper prices), and calculating print runs with an eye on that narrow, elusive band of security in which retailers could sell all they could but returns weren't crippling. Liebowitz had been a solid functionary of Donenfeld's publishing business for three years. He'd handled Harry's nonpayment shenanigans deftly. Now he was being asked to conduct an orchestra without a score.

No one in the cheap-magazine field had Liebowitz's understanding of modern cost accounting or passion for making the numbers work.

He and Rose had two daughters now, Linda and Joan, and he wanted to buy his family a house of their own. Donenfeld's companies teetered at the brink of disaster, but there weren't many other jobs available. Harry was also promising to take good care of him if things worked out; Jack didn't have a piece of the company yet, but Harry was known to be generous with bonuses when he could afford to be. And Jack understood the potential: As a publisher, Harry made twice as much money per copy as his competitors because he handled his own distribution and cover printing. As a printer and distributor, he could count on his own publications to keep the system running, and he could shift debts and cash flow freely from one business to another to stay afloat. If Harry could pick up new, reliable clients and properties, Jack might be able to set himself and his family up forever.

Liebowitz understood that a large distribution firm couldn't survive the unpaid bills and bankruptcy stunts that Harry had used as a publisher. He made sure that bills were paid on time and clients' trust was earned. At the same time, he built a reputation for controlling expenses with an iron fist and pushing debtors ruthlessly. He started looking for properties and opportunities too. If the early Depression made Harry Donenfeld a leader, then it made Jack Liebowitz a boss. Irwin Donenfeld would say that everything he knew about business he learned by being barked at by "Uncle Jack." Within a few years, no one spoke of Donenfeld and Sampliner, even though theirs was the partnership that owned Independent. They spoke of Donenfeld and Liebowitz.

They were a strange pair: Harry, small and quick, drinking, laughing, and pouring on the banana oil; Jack, stiff and grim, looking almost WASPy in his dull suits and little mustache. At first glance he almost looked like Thomas Dewey, that rising young Republican vice buster who represented everything Harry's crowd feared. But the contrast worked. Donenfeld blew bubbles, made promises, took clients out drinking and whoring, closed the sale; and then Liebowitz stepped in and fought over the numbers, drew the bottom line, gave the bad news, had the shouting matches, and made the books balance. Jack got along well with Harry, enjoying their gin rummy games at the end of every workday before Harry went out to carouse and he went home to his family or back to the office for more work. But he also became very good at watching what Harry did and cleaning up his messes.

HARRY SAW HIMSELF as the class of the girlie pulps. He paid sixty bucks for cover paintings—twice what the competition paid—and kept a stable of art school graduates with old American names—R. A. Burley, Enoch Bolles, Earle K. Bergey, H. J. Ward—who might have found work with the "slick" magazines if that market hadn't collapsed with the economy. Their sinuous, translucent dames and witty designs still gleam across the decades. He paid a whole cent a word for scripts, where others paid only half, so he kept his best writers: Robert Leslie Bellem, master of slangy dialogue; Bob Maxwell, who also wrote patter for radio shows; and the wry Jack Woodford, who once described his story formula as "Boy meets girl, girl gets boy into pickle, boy gets pickle into girl."

The stories got raunchier: "The thin silk of the dress tore easily as he split it to the hem. . . . Her beautiful breasts, free and untrammeled, stood out like cocoanuts, and Phil's eyes dilated. . . . Phil lowered his head, and Helen watched the top of it as it slowly receded. She began to shake and when she felt fingers fumbling with the cord of her waist, she groaned and lay back on the pillow." Sales rose.

But Harry's eyes were on bigger markets, especially on the hottest topic of all in Depression America: crime. For thirteen years Prohibition had been turning average citizens into criminals and funding racketeering empires that co-opted whole cities, and now those citizens were being bankrupted and thrown out of work by a system that had been gimmicked by crooked millionaires. The head of the New York Stock Exchange was being prosecuted about the same time as the mayor of New York and Al Capone. J. Edgar Hoover and his G-men became national heroes for machine-gunning bank robbers. Vigilante justice, an

American staple that had begun to fade, was reasserting itself in small cities and towns. Some crimes, especially ransom kidnappings, set off a public bloodlust. A vast majority of Americans were happy to see a jobless German immigrant die for the murder of Charles Lindbergh's baby despite a shaky case. A lynch mob in San Jose, California, strung up two accused kidnappers before they could go to trial, and the governor of the state called it "the best lesson that California has ever given the country." Not surprisingly, the national hunger for crime stories of every kind, true and fictional, polite and brutal, was bottomless.

America's fascination with crime had the fervor that comes only with profound ambivalence. The meaner, the angrier, the more morally tangled crime stories became, the better they sold. *Little Caesar* and *The Public Enemy* sold so many tickets that the movie studios were flying into the face of outraged citizens' groups to grind out more gangster melodramas. *Dick Tracy* was filling the daily pages with lunatic murderers dying horrible deaths—Flattop getting trapped beneath a pier and drowning slowly was as sickeningly satisfying as the photos of the cops over the bullet-riddled bodies of Bonnie and Clyde—and selling more papers all the time. Every writer, editor, and publisher in the business watched Dashiell Hammett soar on the strength of the hard-boiled stories he'd sold to a pulp called *Black Mask*; one minute another cheapmagazine hack, the next a best-selling author, literary lion, and Hollywood golden boy.

Harry acquired the rights to a moribund Victorian rag called *The Police Gazette* and assigned Merle Hersey to make it over for the modern age. "We are going to give the barbers of the nation a *Police Gazette* that will bring men in to have their hair cut regularly once a week," announced that minister's daughter, "[with] lots of sex, underworld stuff with a sex angle, and plenty of pictures of semi-nude night-club girls." Harry and Armer started developing a crime fiction pulp called *Super-Detective* (that prefix "super" was everywhere in 1933) and assigned their usual pool of freelancers to keep it fast, racy, a little sexy. Then Armer had another idea: combine the crime pulps and the smooshes. Private dicks were already tangling with ravenous molls and half-naked heiresses all the time, so why not let them untrammel a few cocoanut breasts on the page? So Harry created a new company, named it "Culture Publications" in a whimsical moment, and prepared *Spicy Detective Stories* for publication in February 1934.

The first issue's cover was adorned by a nearly naked blonde backing away in terror from a brutish rapist while a gun pokes in from a window. It was an instant hit. American men had made do for so long with smiling chorines and sweet titillation in their sleazy magazines that no one realized how hungry they were to have their sex mixed with terror and blood. Based on the first dealer reactions alone, Harry ordered the magazine immediately cranked up from bimonthly to monthly.

Then New York City threw its first punch. At the beginning of March, the commissioner of business licenses said he would pull the permit of any newsstand on city streets that sold indecent publications. Art nudies and smooshes were yanked by over 3,000 dealers and immediately returned to their distributors. Donenfeld and one of his competitors, Henry Marcus, filed an injunction, but until the court made a decision, they were helpless.

Only three weeks later the second punch landed. A couple of months earlier Harry and Frank had decided to test the law's limits by running some frontal nudity in *Pep* without airbrushing out all the pubic hair. It was only the tiniest glimpse of fuzz, but it was enough for the district attorney's office. On March 21 Harry was indicted for publishing obscene materials, and the DA was talking about jail time.

Harry had caught on too late that the long party of Prohibition was over. After the fall of Tammany's Jimmy Walker, the mayor's office had been won by the oddest one-man band in American politics: a half-Italian, half-Jewish Republican from East Harlem named Fiorello LaGuardia who hated racketeers as much as he hated Prohibition. His pro-labor, pro-welfare, anti-crime "fusion" of liberal and conservative positions seized the imaginations of New Yorkers and gave him a mandate to roust out the people he portrayed as enemies of the common weal. Vice charges weren't going to be dropped with a call to Tammany or a modest exchange of funds anymore.

Nor was it just the obscenity charge that scared Harry. This was a bad time for him to be under government scrutiny. He was rumored to be still in business with Frank Costello. All the smarter bootleggers had been preparing for the end of Prohibition for years, and Costello had been one of the most inventive of them. Anticipating the urgency of speakeasy owners to find new income streams in order to survive as legal bars and restaurants, he created a firm called the Mills Novelty Company to distribute jukeboxes and mechanical games of chance, made ostensibly as "amusements" but easily used as gambling devices. That distribution racket was also a convenient adjunct to the numbers game and illegal bookmaking. The gambling machines proved to be very popular in candy stores, cigar stores, and newsstands, and one of the distributors most helpful in placing them there was Independent News. Pornography might attract a prosecutor, but there were worse things to be found once he started looking.

The racketeers were scared, too. Thomas Dewey, that fire-breathing federal attorney, had just put Harry's old acquaintance Waxey Gordon in jail for tax evasion. And not just jailed him but humiliated him on the stand, made him a laughing stock. That didn't kill the New Jersey mob—Abner "Longy" Zwillman stepped up to take Waxey's place—but it showed that the big bosses were no longer safe. Now Dewey was going after Arthur Flegenheimer, "Dutch Schultz." Every crook in New York was checking his tracks.

Harry was forty years old. He was struggling to keep a roof over Gussie and the kids' heads, he was still digging out from under Eastern News's collapse, and he'd just had his first glimpse of big money as a publisher. He needed somebody to feed the wolves. He picked Herbie Siegel. Herbie was a dimwit Harry had given an editorial job to as a favor to a relative. He didn't have a lot going for him in the work world, and he was grateful for whatever he could get. Harry took him to dinner, probably someplace beyond Herbie's dreams, the Stork Club or 21, bought him drinks, maybe introduced him to a couple of girls, made his pitch. If Herbie would swear to the court that he was the editor of that issue of *Pep* and that he slipped in the bush shots without poor innocent

Harry's knowledge, then he'd be guaranteed a job for life. Even if Harry went out of business, he had plenty of friends who'd pay off the debt in exchange for Herbie taking the heat.

It was a good deal all around. Herbie probably only served sixty or ninety days, and he got the job he was promised. Thirty years later new employees at DC Comics and Independent News would see the old guy carrying parcels, pouring coffee, but mostly just sitting and reading the racing form. "Who's this Herbie?" they'd ask after a while, and they'd get the story, everyone's first introduction to the Donenfeld legend.

Harry promptly dissolved Merwil, *Pep*'s publisher of record, selling all their assets to a new company, D. M. Publishing, with its address in Wilmington, Delaware. That meant someone had to drive to Delaware and back every day to collect and drop mail, but it also meant Harry couldn't be prosecuted by LaGuardia's government.

In May the license commissioner's right to forbid indecent material on newsstands was upheld in court. That hurt sales in the short term, but it also helped Harry expand his little empire: His rival Henry Marcus decided to get out of the smoosh racket and sold Harry his best-selling titles, *Tattle Tales* and *Bedtime Stories*. Then Harry ordered his editors to impose a bit more decorum on their covers—or at least a bit more satin on the knockers—to minimize future trouble.

That same month, Harry unleashed his first follow-up to *Spicy Detective, Spicy Adventure Stories*. Its cover, sumptuously executed by H. J. Ward, managed to follow the letter of public decency laws while selling the most obscenely racist and sadistic sexual fantasies. A voluptuous pink maiden is tied to a stake, her bee-stung lips parted and her mascaraed eyes wide in inviting terror, her body twisting to escape so that her lush breasts spill toward us. Her clothes have been torn down to a shred of white over each nipple and the smallest swath of khaki between her legs, the lovingly tinted curves of her belly and inner thighs offered to us, her breasts lifted by the rope that holds her to the stake behind. Fire burns in the background. And into the foreground steps a snarling black man, his mere darkness violent against her rosy softness. He holds in one hand a spear dripping blood and in the other the severed head of a white man, its eyes rolled horribly back into its sockets, blood pouring over lips open in almost sexual slackness. It was Harry's big, wet Bronx cheer for the censors. It was also his entry into the market for a special sort of rageful male fantasy. It would prove to be a much larger market than anyone could have guessed.

The "Spicies" were Harry's first big successes. He added two more, *Spicy Mystery* and *Spicy Western*. *Spicy Detective* broke out of the ghetto of sleaze and into the fiction mainstream, mostly because of Robert Leslie Bellem's "Dan Turner, Hollywood Detective" stories, wild romps through a hard-boiled slang of his own invention: "I jammed the roscoe in his button and said, 'Close your yap, bo, or I squirt metal.'" S. J. Perelman called Turner "the apotheosis of all private detectives" in a piece for *The New Yorker,* "Somewhere a Roscoe." "I hope nobody minds my making love in public," Perelman wrote, "but if Culture Publications of 900 Market Street, Wilmington, Delaware, will have me, I'd like to marry them."

Harry was thrilled. Jack Liebowitz was less so. To him, 1934 was another disaster narrowly averted. The Spicies hadn't yet attracted the ire of the censors, but they might. He wanted some means of building for the future and avoiding disaster, but there was none at hand. Until the United States Cavalry finally rode to his rescue. One disgraced former member of it, anyway: Major Malcolm Wheeler-Nicholson.

COMIC STRIPS IN magazine form were nothing new. Cheap books telling stories with sequences of drawings were being sold in New York by the middle of the nineteenth century. No sooner had Joseph Pulitzer and William Randolph Hearst published the first color comic strips in the 1890s than publishers were finding ways to collect *Little Nemo* and *Buster Brown* for bookstores and magazine racks. One publisher was using the phrase "comic book" by 1917. When newspaper comics with long-running story lines became a craze in the late 1920s, reprint collections were everywhere.

In 1929 the enterprising George T. Delacorte, wanting to move into that niche with a low-budget entry as he'd done with every other niche, set up a new project for the company that printed most of the major Sunday newspaper comics sections of the northeast, Eastern Color Printing. *The Funnies* was a weekly tabloid imitating the Sunday newspaper comics sections but comprising strips that no syndicate or newspaper would buy. Delacorte believed in it enough to keep it going through price and format changes for months, but nothing would stop it from losing money—one of the few publishing gambles he lost. No one touched the idea for a few years after that. When Humor Publishing in Chicago tried a similar strategy in 1933 with *Detective Dan* and its fellows, it didn't do any better.

Another way to make money off cheap comics reprints was the giveaway. Retailers had already discovered how to bring the power of juvenile whining to bear in their favor by giving away cheap kid's books and other premiums. In 1932 Eastern Color had produced color comics magazines in half-tabloid size—"standard size," as the pulp publishers called it—as subscription premiums for the Philadelphia *Ledger*. The Eastern Color sales staff, which included a couple of men who would soon loom large in the comic book industry, Harry Wildenberg and Lev Gleason, tried to sell the idea to advertisers and manufacturers but had little success. Then, in the cold early months of 1933, when banks were being closed and the American economy hit its rocky bottom, a hungry pitchman named Charlie Gaines limped through the door.

He'd been a teacher and a school principal under the name Maxwell Charles Ginsberg until sometime in the Twenties, when he found he could no longer support his wife and two children. He changed his name and tackled whatever advertising and merchandising schemes he could think up or find. At one point he sold painted neckties. He was a smart man but an angry one, limping from a childhood injury, grimacing through constant pain in his leg and lower back, inclined to take out his bilious frustration on his son, Bill. At the bottom of the Depression, he found himself jobless and in his forties. He offered himself to his friend Harry Wildenberg at Eastern Color as a commission-only sales-man. If he could find clients for comics giveaways, he'd get a cut. If not, nothing.

The legends of the industry, shaped by Charlie's son, have made him into the creator of the comic book. Charlie, says one story, looked at Eastern Color's idle printing presses and realized suddenly that comics art could be printed half size and the pages stapled into a con-venient pamphlet. He alone peddled the idea to advertisers and he alone realized that the pamphlets could be sold on the newsstand. It's another of the superheroic origin stories that comic book people crave—but it is not true. What Charlie Gaines did was line up cus-tomers for a thirty-two page comics giveaway called *Funnies on Pa-rade*. Wildenberg cut deals to use *Joe Palooka, Mutt and Jeff*, and some other popular comics; Procter and Gamble ordered ten thousand copies; and America's kids sent in coupons snipped out of soap pack-ages until every one of them was gone. Gaines and Wildenberg sold the same deal to Kinney Shoes, Canada Dry, Wheatena, and others, and Eastern found itself with orders for 100,000 copies of its second effort, *Famous Funnies*. It did even better with *A Century of Comics*, at a hundred pages. By the end of 1933, Eastern may have sold as many as 30 million pages of comics in just those three premiums.

Now George Delacorte reentered. He arranged for 35,000 copies of *Famous Funnies* to be sold in the children's departments of a few chain department stores. This edition was sixty-four pages, with a wrap-around cover, and cost a dime—it was a comic book, as millions of kids would come to understand it in just a few years. It entered the stores in February 1934 and sold out in a matter of weeks. Delacorte pitched the idea of a newsstand comic book to the American News Company, the biggest and oldest magazine distributor in the country, the establishment against which MacFadden, Donenfeld, and all the rest defined themselves as "independents." American News was doubtful that kids would spend money on comics they'd already read in the pa-pers, but Delacorte had just become their favorite client with a series of crossword puzzle magazines that were outselling nearly everything on the newsstands. *Famous Funnies* reached the newsstands in June 1934, and it sold. Delacorte promptly left it to create his own line of Dell Comics, packaged by Charlie Gaines. Other distributors began looking for comic-strip magazines; Major Malcolm Wheeler-Nicholson's moment had come.

The major swept through the world of low-rent publishing in a Panama hat and ice-cream suit, his jacket draped on his shoulders like a cape and a cigarette holder angling up from his jaw. The tales he told about himself were extraordinary. As the youngest major in the U.S. Cavalry he fought Pancho Villa, the Moros, and the Bolsheviks. He served at Versailles in 1919, where he wooed and wed a Swedish countess. Then, frustrated by the Army's tradition of rewarding longevity over merit, he wrote a public letter of complaint to President Harding and was rewarded with a court martial and an assassination attempt (he enjoyed showing off the bullet scar on his head). So he wrote a book—*Modern Cavalry*—and began selling war stories to *Argosy* and other magazines. Most extraordinary of all, the tales were true. Unfortunately, the ambitious major was inclined to overreach himself, erecting business ventures on bad checks and seducing investors with assets he didn't yet have. Some associates came to believe that the only skill he'd really learned in the cavalry was shoveling horse manure.

The major had barely begun to learn how the world of magazines and newspapers worked when he made his first attempt to conquer it. In 1925 he set up a company to syndicate his own fiction, miscellaneous filler articles, and comic strips by various cartoonists. Most of the comics were standard gag stuff, but he took a chance on adaptations of *Treasure Island* and *Ivanhoe*. He was preparing to publish a newspaper-format brochure of his material, *The Syndicator,* when the money ran out.

The major returned to pulp writing for another eight years, but with the collapse of the magazine business early in the Depression, he turned again to the dream of publishing. This was the peak of kids' love affair with newspaper comics. While most papers cut back on their Sunday comics sections, William Randolph Hearst aggressively boosted his to an unprecedented thirty-two pages, and circulation and advertising revenues went up. So the major talked the distributing arm of *McCall's* magazine into letting him take over a moribund rag that reprinted comic strips from England and convert it into *New Fun*, specializing in brand-new comics. Wheeler-Nicholson was open about his business plan: "I see these magazines more or less as brochures to interest the newspaper syndicates in an idea. It's much easier to sell a comic strip if you can show it in already published form." But in a cleverly jury-built piece of Depression-era commerce, it would appear on newsstands to make it valuable to advertisers and sell ad space to cover its costs. One of those advertisers was Charles Atlas, beginning his long association with the comic books.

New Fun featured swashbucklers, westerns, and *Oswald the Lucky Rabbit*. It was a cheaper package than *Famous Funnies*: tabloid sized, black-and-white interior pages, original strips that hadn't sold to any newspaper. Some of those the major had left over from the Twenties. The rest were easy to come by with small ads in artists' trade magazines. The major was a master at impressing young artists. "He always bowed when he shook hands with you," said Craig Flessel. He was also a master at dodging the people he owed money. His first two editors, Lloyd Jacquet and Sheldon Stark, quit after months of nonpayment. They were replaced by a pair of cartoonists, Vin Sullivan and Whitney Ellsworth. A couple of months later Ellsworth was gone, too.

New Fun lasted six issues. Sales were bad, the debts ran too high, and in the summer of 1935, *McCall's* booted it. A couple of investors the major had taken on now grabbed half his inventory, hooked up with his former editor Lloyd Jacquet, and went looking for backing to create their own Comics Magazine Company. The major spent the fall looking for someone to carry him. In the end, the only one he could find was Independent News.

THE SUN WAS shining on Harry Donenfeld. He was adding new magazines in every genre and outselling his competitors in most of them. Gussie was turning their new home in the north Bronx into a showplace for entertaining and card games. She was popular with Harry's friends and associates; "G" they called her (or "Gea" in writing). To make sure the kids got wherever they had to go, Harry deployed his chauffeur, Frank Moschello. Frank was another case of Harry taking care of someone who'd taken care of him. He was a street kid, a boxer, a former cabbie and minor-league booze runner during Prohibition who'd taken some kind of fall for one of the rackets Harry was involved with and had been promised a job for life. All of Harry's friends knew him, talked to him, bought him drinks. In a joking tribute to Harry, someone gave this line to Frank: "I really admire Mr. Donenfeld most because he has raised the level of my intellectual life. I have worked for many people before, but they were mainly interested in one round of pleasure after another. However, I find my present employment much more elevating and I have learned to know my way around all the city's leading educational institutions, art exhibits, etc."

At night he would drive Harry to his nightclubs, his casinos, and his brothels, but during the day, Frank was there for Irwin and Peachy. "Frank Moschello was more of a father to me than Harry Donenfeld ever was," Irwin said. "He went to every baseball game I was in. He'd sit there and watch, and on the drive back he'd talk to me about it. My father went to one of my games. And after a couple of innings he just stood up and left. Frank stayed." Irwin turned ten in 1936. He never had any interest in money or business. He wanted to play ball and box. No matter how nice their neighborhood in the north Bronx, no matter what school Harry's money put him in, Irwin always wanted to be a street kid.

Harry had no time for kids' games. His life was an adventure. As the nation's premier publisher of girlie magazines and a friend of gangsters, he had a cachet at every poker table, nightclub, and sporting event. Through *The Police Gazette* he could arrange to meet anybody eager for blue-collar exposure: boxers, jockeys, police brass, showgirls, producers. Jack Dempsey, long past his boxing championship, even got a magazine published in his own name. Make friends with Harry and anything could happen. But what took Harry away from his family was something more: He was in love.

Every businessman of Harry's generation and level of success kept a mistress. The manufacturers and the racketeers would go to 21 on Friday night with their wives and kids, come back Saturday with their sleek young things. The maitre d' knew all their names. But Sunny Paley was more than a trophy for Harry. She was younger than him by at least ten years and prettier than his wife; but she was no shiksa showgirl with skyscraper legs. She was a Jewish girl with manners and an education. How she entered Harry's life is unclear, as is her connection, if any, to the Paley family that sold cigars and owned the Columbia Broadcasting System. But she quickly became more than his girl-on-the-side. She began to join him at the evening gin rummy games in the Independent offices. She traveled with him and even served as his companion at business conferences. A distribution executive who often went out drinking with him remembers him gushing about her as he got drunk. He spent as many nights in her Manhattan apartment as he could, and he missed her when they were apart. He began to talk about marrying her.

Gussie knew. Irwin remembers ferocious battles at home, then his father storming out to go back to Manhattan. Back to Sunny. When Irwin was thirteen or fourteen, doing odd jobs at Independent, he once lingered after hours so he could sneak down to his father's office and peak in at the gin rummy game. He wanted to see "that woman," whose never-spoken name haunted their house. He saw her, slightly overdressed, slightly taller than his dad. Playing cards and joking with Jack Liebowitz and Paul Sampliner and the rest of them like she was part of the family. Irwin knew she was more a part of his father's real family than he was.

With every expansion of his personal life Harry's need for money grew. And with boundless energy he expanded his business. Harry became Independent News's traveling ambassador, stretching its connections far beyond New York. Irwin, who would try to play the same role years later, said the essence of the work was making friends out of dealers. "He'd get drunk with the dealer in Pittsburgh, go on a moose hunting trip with the guy in Detroit, go out and get laid with the guy in Baltimore. A wholesaler's not going to give the same kind of breaks to Dell or Fawcett if he just got laid with you the night before."

Harry began to go where Eastern News had never gone, into that other America, the one he'd roll past on the train to Miami: Richmond, Charlotte, Charleston, Savannah, Atlanta. Then inward to a country he'd only heard about from horse races and football games: Tallahassee, Chattanooga, Birmingham, Biloxi. The Deep South wasn't known to be friendly to New York Jews selling dirty books. Harry was old enough to remember the case of Leo Frank, the Brooklyn accountant railroaded for rape and murder, lynched by a mob that stormed the prison as "Kill the Jew" rallies sprang up all over Georgia. There were still towns in Georgia where you could buy postcards of Frank dangling from the tree, over the legend "The Lynching of the Jew."

But Harry went to those towns. He glad-handed the tobacco dealers, the book jobbers, the local racketeers, the barbers' suppliers, whoever moved sleazy magazines. He learned to joke and find common ground with Baptists and Episcopalians and French Catholics. In the smaller towns, he shook hands with men who'd never touched a Jew, men who expected him to show up in skullcap and beard with a peddler's sack. By train and car he crisscrossed the South, bellowing in his faintly Yiddish lilt, making himself the lovable clown, winning over whomever he needed to get *Pep* and *Spicy Detective* onto the same rack as the latest issue of *The Fiery Cross*.

And he brought people together. When Harry first entered the South, he found magazine distribution broken up into regional fiefdoms that made it hard for anyone to carry a large slate of publications. He encouraged local distributors and jobbers to pool their common interests. Gradually he made Independent the center point in the formation of a Southern Distributors' Federation.

Harry was rising in distribution circles. Once in Miami he was invited to play poker with Moe Annenberg, one-time leg breaker for William Randolph Hearst, now publisher of the *Racing Form*, head of the nation's biggest betting wire, fixer of countless races, and new owner of the *Miami Tribune* and the *Philadelphia Inquirer.* Harry played at Moe's table, where he ribbed and razzed and winked like an old friend. When he left, Moe asked another player, "Who *was* that little guy?" But Harry was invited back and so joined the circle of one of the great *machers* of distribution.

There were storm clouds building, though. The censors' modest victories over the girlie magazines in 1934 had satisfied them for a while. But by 1937 public sentiment had reignited the crusade. America's reaction against the license that Prohibition had inspired was gaining strength. Racketeers were being arrested on narcotics charges as never before. The pulp-paper industry had been trying for years to use marijuana as an excuse to destroy its biggest rival, the hemp business, but the public didn't have much interest. The sudden national fear of narcotics tipped the balance, and in 1937 public support, aided by William Randolph Hearst and others with huge lumber holdings, sent anti-cannabis laws sweeping through state legislatures.

The country was in love with mob busters, especially now that the mob no longer supplied the country with its liquor. New Yorkers still loved to gossip about the big-time gangsters, but they didn't like them running their labor unions, fixing their boxing matches, or moving brothels into their neighborhoods. In the fall of 1936, Thomas Dewey, now the district attorney of New York, pulled the most brazen stunt anyone could remember a lawman pulling. He sent his forces out to arrest every prostitute they could find, literally thousands of them in a single night, and held every one of them until she ratted out at least one gangster. Then, with the hookers' words as a basis for arrest, he locked up dozens of pimps and low-level mobsters, pushing them to tell what they knew. When he had enough testimony, he went for the big fish: Lucky Luciano.

It was a tremendous shock to the racketeers. Income tax evasion and narcotics convictions were one thing, but prostitution had been such an accepted part of New York commerce and politics for as long as anyone could remember, no one thought you could get nailed for that. Most of those guys had grown up around whorehouses, had made money as lookouts and pimps even when they were kids. The more cautious mobsters, like Luciano's friend Frank Costello, had stayed out of that racket, if only because it got messy and sleazy, but even they got the message that nothing was safe anymore. Dewey did his usual star turn in the courtroom, painting Luciano as a fool, as a low-class immigrant pretender to American society. Then the jury found the defendant guilty of three counts of forced prostitution. He was sentenced to thirty to fifty years in prison.

The racketeers began to retract. Those who could move their money into legal assets did so with more energy than they'd shown since the months before Repeal. Investment in Nevada, Miami, and Cuba speeded up. The Jewish racketeers in particular began to look at other ways to use their capital, connections, and expertise.

Harry knew Luciano. He'd done business with Frank Costello for fifteen or sixteen years, and Luciano had been Costello's partner from his first days in crime. Harry felt the heat. When Mayor LaGuardia began to complain about indecent publications again in early 1937, Harry must have known that this had the potential to be a lot more than a bump in the road. It was an election year. LaGuardia was a heavy favorite for a second term, and he knew the voters were behind him in his war on corruption. *Pep, LaParee,* and the rest of the smooshes and nudies were probably doomed. *Spicy Detective* and its imitators would have to be toned down, and there was no telling what that might do to sales. Even *The Police Gazette* and its ilk would have to be cleaned up—no more cover photos of men about to be executed. It's what Jack Liebowitz had been telling him: They needed safer moneymakers.

What neither Harry nor Jack may have seen yet was that the answer to all their problems was already coming together right under their noses. For in late 1935 Major Malcolm Wheeler-Nicholson had washed up on Independent News's doorstep, seeking a distributor. We don't know who he talked to or who made the decision, but he was told that Independent would carry him and advance him production money on a set of conditions: switch to the "standard size" of the pulps; add color;

launch a second comic book to increase rack space; and use Donny Press as his cover printer. It must have been a difficult choice to accept. For one thing, Donenfeld and his people were obviously interested in calling the shots. For another, the Tennessee-born major of the cavalry didn't like Jews. But he made the only choice he could.

So Harry Donenfeld and Jack Liebowitz got into the comic book business. It was a minor concern in 1936 and 1937. But their futures were being set in motion by a series of small decisions made by the major, his editors, and a couple of young guys in Cleveland.

Action

JERRY SIEGEL ALWAYS told Superman's origin as a simple story of inspiration and belief. And the world was always eager to believe it.

One hot summer night he lay awake in his attic room on Kimberly Avenue, and the ideas began to come. "I hop out of bed and write this down, and then I go back and think some more for about two hours and get up again and write that down. This goes on all night at two hour intervals." When the sun came up, he'd written weeks' worth of a *Superman* comic strip. "I dashed over to Joe's place and showed it to him." Joe was excited. "We just sat down," he said, "and I worked straight through. I think I had brought in some sandwiches to eat, and we worked all day long." When night came again, they had pages of samples.

Then they began sending the strip out. And editors began sending it back. On Fred Allen's radio show Jerry would say, "It took us six years to sell *Superman*. Just about every comics editor in the country turned us down." That was his standard line for years, and he had a few choice quotes from rejection letters. "A rather immature piece of work," declared United Features Syndicate. "Pay a little attention to actual drawing," said Esquire Features. Until, the story goes, almost by a fluke, *Superman* found a berth. It became an instant sensation, and then those editors realized what fools they'd been. They hadn't taken Jerry Siegel seriously, but he knew what he had, and in the end, he showed them all. He became a hero to young dreamers everywhere.

But there are problems with the story. "Six years to sell Superman" would put that sleepless night in 1931 or 1932. But then fans tracked down the *Detective Dan* connection from 1933. Siegel's story shifted. Someone at Humor Publishing in Chicago, he said, expressed casual interest in sketches for *The Superman*. Jerry and Joe, in heedless enthusiasm, took it for a sale in hand and rushed off to draw the whole comic. Then, after months of silence and several pestering letters, the publisher finally sent the pages back with a note explaining that he didn't plan on releasing any more comic books. The boys were devastated. "I'm a perfectionist," said Joe, "and I think the fact that the drawings had been turned down made me want to tear them up. I simply destroyed them." He and Jerry remembered little of that lost *Superman,* except that he was "just a man of action," not yet a costumed superbeing. The only clues they kept were one pencil sketch and the cover. The former shows a he-man in a sleeveless undershirt hoisting a thug over his head as another blasts him with a machine gun. The latter is a stark ink drawing of a bare-chested hero breaking up a kidnapping, beneath the slogan "A science fiction story in cartoons."

Now Jerry moved the memory of that hot night when the ideas wouldn't stop to the summer of 1934, a little more than three years before *Superman* finally sold. That night, he said, was when he thought of the Superman we know today and wrote the scripts that would eventually see print, when the unbroken run of rejections began. But new problems emerge with that story: What about the 1934 correspondence with someone in the office of *Super-Detective Stories,* one of Harry Donenfeld's pulps, who apparently expressed interest in *Superman?* What about Major Wheeler-Nicholson's promise of a syndicate deal in 1935? And why was that cover from 1933, supposedly the only piece remaining from the original *Superman* that Joe destroyed, found decades later in the desk of Charlie Gaines, salesman for *Famous Funnies?* Jerry said he submitted his samples to *Famous Funnies* in 1934 but that the package was returned unopened. So how did Charlie get that cover?

When the various pieces of information are lined up, the portrait of the twenty-year-old Jerry Siegel that emerges is far more complicated, and far more interesting, than that of the naïf he would always play.

In June 1934 Jerry Siegel and Joe Shuster graduated from Glenville High School. Their peers had all moved on a year before. Even some younger kids, like the terribly popular Lois Amster, had already graduated that January. Joe was a month shy of his twentieth birthday, Jerry four months. They were expected to be fully in the workforce now; no more *Torch,* no more built-in audience for their daydreams, no more free mimeographing. They still lived at home, still scrambled for part-time work, still talked about fame and riches in pulps and comics. They were trying to be more commercial, developing a strip based on Laurel and Hardy and a spin on P. G. Wodehouse called *Reggie van Twerp.* That's when Jerry discovered his ability to talk his way to a deal.

The existing recordings of the young Siegel's voice do not suggest a commanding figure: His voice is thin and adenoidal, shyness chokes him high in the throat, his tones are flat, and he rushes impatiently past small talk. But when he speaks of an idea that excites him, there's a sudden quaver. You hear his belief in what he has. It's not hard to imagine him talking the publisher of a local advertiser, the *Cleveland Shopping News,* into believing that he could actually put together a comics tabloid that would boost circulation and advertising. And it's not hard to imagine Jerry's optimism when he closed the deal. Instead of just selling to a syndicate or publisher, he could *be* one, selling his *Popular Comics* to advertisers in other cities, then maybe to real newspapers, moving it up from monthly to weekly by hiring other writers and artists to ghost for him. He had the passion and the ideas, and through science fiction fandom he had the contacts.

The work Siegel and Shuster completed for *Popular Comics* shows how much they were learning. *Gloria Glamour* opens with a stunning interior of a High Deco movie set that displays Joe's love of monumentalism and modernism. Suddenly in jaunts a press agent sketched in fluid, minimal lines to accost a neatly, iconically rendered beauty queen, and Joe shows a humane and generous art for body language: the press agent's slouching, lurching, forward-leaning intensity, the movie star's languorous indifference. Siegel's Hollywood dialogue is now tight and lively: "What's the joke?" "This fan letter from Lone Peak, Montana . . . an honorable proposal of matrimony!" "Matrimony . . . marriage! Say, that would make a swell press release!"

By the end of the strip's one and only page, Gloria finds herself engaged and the poor rube from Montana is being seen off at the train station by a deftly drawn mob of well-wishers. The style is taken mostly from Roy Crane's *Wash Tubbs,* and at moments it nearly equals his vivacity and propulsive narrative. The story is a riff on *Bombshell,* a movie released the year before, and in a medium not always amenable to character subtlety, Jerry and Joe have managed to catch a bit of the fire of Lee Tracy and Jean Harlow. They were showing a gift for bringing material from the pulps and the movies to the comics page.

But again Jerry and Joe were disappointed. The *Shopping News* pulled the plug before the first tabloid could see print. Some of the material was sold to a local department store as a Christmas giveaway—Siegel and Shuster's first paying comics work—but nothing followed.

The surviving pages of *Popular Comics* show Jerry and Joe trying to conquer every genre: slapstick gags, supernatural suspense, blue-color melodrama, science fiction, Jewish humor, and even a reworking of *Jerry the Journalist* from Joe's junior high years. But there is one creation conspicuously absent. For even as they were preparing their tabloid, Jerry had taken *Superman* from Joe and was trying to launch it with another artist.

Nearly every Superman story for decades would refer to "the two teenagers from Cleveland" who created him. It's one of the most charming pieces of the legend: the two lonely boys who found each other and between them made a dream complete. And it's true—but with a missing piece. Jerry Siegel was a young man of commercial instincts, and when he saw that Superman was going nowhere with Joe, he went looking for another collaborator.

Tony Strobl was a year younger than Siegel and still in the Cleveland Art Institute; he wasn't the type to take a flier on a new idea and became one of Disney's best house artists after he graduated. Mel Graff was a few years older and already working in the art department at NEA, the syndicate that handled *Wash Tubbs* and *Alley Oop*. Graff said later that he had some interest in this idea of Jerry Siegel's, but before the end of 1934, he moved to New York to launch a new strip for the Associated Press, a children's fantasy called *Patsy*. In the spring of 1935, Graff introduced Patsy's friend, the Phantom Magician, a caped and costumed hero who used magic to save the day. Comics historian Will Murray wondered if Graff had gotten the idea from his talks with Siegel, or if Siegel got the idea for the cape and costume from Graff.

After he lost Graff to New York and success, Siegel turned to Russell Keaton, the anonymous artist on the *Buck Rogers* Sunday pages. Keaton's buoyant, fluid style was not unlike Joe Shuster's, but Keaton was a graduate of the Chicago Academy of Fine Art and a respected professional with a realistic shot at launching his own strip with a major syndicate. He and Jerry bounced ideas for Superman back and forth for a few months. Jerry's hopes soared, as they always did, and when Keaton finally decided not to gamble on such a young and inexperienced writer, Siegel wrote back to him in anger. If Keaton backed out on him now, he said, he'd be "stuck with an amateur." By early 1935 Jerry and Joe were right back where they had been.

Now the cavalry arrived in Cleveland. Major Malcolm Wheeler-Nicholson's *New Fun* reached the newsstands, and Jerry Siegel promptly wrote in with a list of comic strip ideas. The major solicited two, and the boys turned them around quickly: *Henri Duval of France, Famed Soldier of Fortune*, and *Dr. Occult, the Ghost Detective*. Again they drew on Hollywood more than other comics. *Henri Duval* is a swashbuckling adventure with an absurdism straight out of Douglas Fairbanks: Siegel makes his hero a dandy who draws swords on men who insult his clothes. *Dr. Occult* is lifted from Dr. van Helsing of the Dracula movies. Joe's art is richly textured as he tries to capture the atmosphere of a horror movie—although his figures turn stiff as he tries to be too serious, and his one truly lively image is of an unintentionally comical vampire.

The major liked what he saw. He bought a page of each, for $6 apiece, to run in his sixth issue. And in the late summer of 1935, the issue saw print. Nothing fell through; no one reneged. Siegel and Shuster were published. They were still poor: The major apologized in one letter because a Shuster submission was "lost in the shuffle here, as it appeared to be simply a piece of wrapping paper." And they'd stay poor for a while. Cartoonists in New York had a hard enough time getting a check out of the major by collaring him in his office; no doubt much of Siegel and Shuster's appeal for him lay in the fact that they were a thousand miles away. Still, before they turned twenty-one, they had something to show for all their crazy dreams.

The major had already commissioned more from them, and they'd responded. All the frenetic energy that Jerry had poured into spinning big dreams and creating self-publishing gimmicks he now turned toward cranking out comic strips. Joe drew in tireless absorption, sitting for hours on a hard kitchen chair, using his mother's breadboard as a drawing surface, his weak eyes close to the page, his mother or Jerry bringing him sandwiches. The two always seemed to do their collaborative work at Joe's place, even though it was smaller and more crowded; Jerry's mother never appears in their reminiscences; perhaps Sarah Siegel's controlling presence was too much for them. Sometimes Joe's brother, Frank, helped, and sometimes Jerry pitched in with the lettering and inking. Joe still delivered groceries, and Jerry still delivered for a printing company as they waited for those first checks from the major, but they gave every night to making comics. Among the projects they sent him was *Superman*.

WHAT FORM THEIR hero had by then we cannot know. We have only a letter from the major to Jerry Siegel in October 1935: "The Superman strip is being held for an order now pending from a national syndicate. . . . This is for a sixteen-page tabloid in four colors in which we could include Superman around the first of the year. . . . I think myself that Superman stands a very good chance."

Now we trip on another odd wrinkle in the legend of Siegel and Shuster. Supposedly they felt that Superman was too valuable a property to risk on the major's "pending" order, and so they turned him down. But everything Jerry and Joe had ever done shows their willingness to plunge ahead at the slightest encouragement, and nothing could have excited them more than syndicate interest in a color comic strip. Indeed, the one piece of surviving evidence suggests that they took that pending order very much to heart.

It's a piece of cast-off paper on which Joe had drawn a woman in an evening gown, possibly from a life drawing class. Apparently it's what he grabbed, or all he had, when he and Jerry began brainstorming slogans to promote Superman as "the smash hit strip of 1936." They called it "a strip which we sincerely believe will SWEEP THE NATION! The Super-Strip of Them All! The greatest single event since the birth of comic-strips! The greatest super-hero strip of all time!" They promised "Speed—Action—Laughs—Thrills—Surprises. The most unusual humor-adventure strip ever created! A new personality greets the world! You'll chuckle! You'll gasp! It must be seen to be believed!" And in words that must be Jerry's, they made themselves the heroes of their own imaginations: "Once in a great while a strip appears that sweeps into the life-blood of the nation by sheer rugged narrative power."

Among the slogans, there are sketches of boxes for cereal and whole wheat crackers with Superman's likeness. Siegel knew how to pitch, and he knew that the real money for a syndicate was in licensing. The Superman Shuster drew is rough, but he looks like the Superman we know. He wears a cape and tights with a triangular symbol on his chest, although there's no big "S." The style is antic. The hero is grinning. Clearly Siegel and Shuster had taken the character far from that combination of Doc Savage and *Gladiator* that we can infer from the surviving scraps of 1933. This looks like the Superman that America would fall in love with at the beginning of the 1940s.

Superman was an evolving hero, as he would continue to be forever. As simple as he looked from the outside, he contained a great, contradictory jumble of inspirations, from Philip Wylie to Douglas Fairbanks, from Edgar Rice Burroughs to Bernarr MacFadden. In the early going, Jerry Siegel later said, "the *Popeye* animated cartoons were one of the strongest influences." Those cartoons were the offspring of a pair of rough-edged Jewish immigrants from New York, Max and Dave Fleischer, and there had never been cinematic violence so frenetic and fantastical. "The super-strength and action," Jerry said, "were absolutely sensational. I thought, this is really great, but . . . what if it featured a straight adventure character?" So the "humor-adventure strip" they hoped would sweep the nation fused elements from the most self-important men's fiction and the most ludicrous slapstick. And into that fusion Jerry and Joe injected bits borrowed from period comedy. In 1934 Leslie Howard and Merle Oberon starred in a Hollywood adaptation of *The Scarlet Pimpernel*, one of Jerry's favorite novels of dual identity. Howard's sniveling submission to Oberon's disdain (all in the interest of preserving the secret of his identity as the Pimpernel, of course) proved to be the perfect model for Clark Kent's twisted relationship with Lois Lane—and Oberon's high-cheeked loveliness does seem to peer out from Joe's early drawings of his girl reporter.

In trying to pull together their many passions, Jerry and Joe had created a character who transcended and redefined genre: Superman was both a primary-colored cipher of the purest fantasies and a cartoon that could comment on nearly every strain of mass entertainment. They knew they had something special on their hands, and in late 1935 they were riding a wave of optimism that buoyed their "new personality" as he prepared to greet the world. It helped *them* greet the world in new ways, too. Joe decided to hire a model for Lois Lane. To an extent, this was a professional move: Magazine illustrators were famous for using real models, and art directors took pride in spotting the low-income poseurs who swiped all their drawings of women from photos and other illustrations. But there had to be personal motives, too. The inhibitions that Jerry and Joe so often spoke of continued after high school; in fact, with the daily population of female classmates gone, their distance from the other sex seems only to have grown. Over the decades, a number of Cleveland women emerged saying they'd known one or both of them "back when," but all spoke of encounters after *Superman* had become a hit. In the years before, Joe at least, seems never to have had a single date.

So when he saw the classified ad placed by a Jolan Kovacs offering her services as a model, he called her. Jerry reportedly protested Joe's waste of money, but he also managed to be there when the girl arrived. Jolan was a short, skinny teenager with narrow eyes and a sharp nose, cute but no glamour girl. "My father was out of work," she said, "so in order to have any spending money, I had to earn my own money. I found that no one would hire me because I had no skills or training. . . . I had read an article about modeling, and I thought maybe I could get away with that. So I practiced various poses in front of a mirror, and I put an ad in the *Cleveland Plain Dealer*." She rode the bus from West Cleveland to Glenville with her mother and knocked on the door; "it opened a little bit, and I saw a young boy on the other side, and I said, 'I'm the model that Mr. Shuster is expecting.'" The boy let her in and started chatting her up. "Finally I said, 'Does Mr. Shuster know that I'm here?' And he said, 'I'm Mr. Shuster.'" The date of the meeting is uncertain, but Joe, who seemed such a young boy, was at least twenty-one and at least five years older than Jolan.

When Joe led her into the living room, she met Jerry Siegel. "I was absolutely astounded with his energy—talk about superenergy! He was sitting in a chair and his feet were going, he was flipping through magazines, anxiously waiting to meet me." Jerry started explaining the character to her. He told her how hard Superman could punch a bad guy, and he jabbed his fist in the air and hollered "Pow!" Then he told her how far Superman could leap, and he jumped across the room and crashed into the couch. "Wow," said Jolan. Decades later she would say, "We were all kids playing at being grown-up, trying desperately to be grown-up." And yet the two older men straining to impress her were not kids, but men half-trapped in childhood, trying to bluff their way past the hardest parts of growing up.

Jolan posed for Joe several times. The drawings that survive look nothing like her. In fact, they look like a lonely boy's fantasy of Merle Oberon. Hiring Jolan was a search for an emotional experience. "She was a great inspiration for me," Joe said. "She encouraged me; she was very enthusiastic about the strip." They had a few soda dates, although they never went beyond conversation. She left Cleveland, found jobs as an artist's model under the name "Joanne Carter," got married and divorced. Joe exchanged letters with her for years, until he finally met her again a decade later. He would always speak sweetly of her, even when he lost her to Jerry Siegel. There is no Jolan in his drawings of Lois, not literally. But the passions that she touched are there, turned as he would turn them all his life, into a nimbus of lines on paper.

THE OPTIMISM OF late 1935 did not last. Whatever syndicate deal the major was working on never came to pass. For a few months, in fact, before Independent News rescued him, he failed even to bring out *New Fun*, and Jerry and Joe thought they'd been burned by another fly-by-night. Then, at the beginning of 1936, the major's second magazine, *New Adventure*, and the seventh issue of his first came courtesy of their new distributor. They'd stay on schedule from then on, and the checks began to arrive on time, now that Jack Liebowitz was guaranteeing the major's debts. Jerry and Joe shelved Superman and focused on the work they were getting into print.

Calling All Cars was a cop series, *Federal Men* an energetic *Gangbusters* pastiche. The latter became popular enough for the major to attempt a Junior Federal Men of America fan club. The major lengthened their stories to four pages, allowing Joe to stretch out into some larger panels and graphic experiments. Jerry and Joe grew bolder with success and began to make all their series more fantastical. The Federal Men battled giant robots who invaded New York, giving Joe a chance to draw wondrous, apocalyptic science fiction scenes straight from the covers of *Amazing* and *Wonder*. Dr. Occult took a tip from Flash Gordon and shed his business suit in favor of tights, boots, a red cape, and a sword. Joe loved the drama of a scarlet cape.

Then Superman reappears in the story, this time in the company of Charlie Gaines. Since helping launch *Famous Funnies* for Eastern Color

Printing, Charlie had been making his way as a comic book packager for George Delacorte and a freelance procurer (as "M.C. Gaines") for the McClure newspaper syndicate. Whether *Superman* came to him directly from Jerry Siegel or he picked it up somehow from another source is disputed, but sometime in 1936 he tried unsuccessfully to place it in Delacorte's *Popular Comics*. Around the beginning of 1937, we find Superman being rejected by *Tip Top Comics*, an Eastern Color client edited by an old friend of Charlie's, Lev Gleason. *Tip Top* was produced by United Features Syndicate, and it was then that Jerry got his beloved "immature piece of work" letter.

It may also be that sometime during this period Siegel and Shuster reconceived Superman for a different market. Worth Carnahan, one of Donenfeld's cover artists and editors, remembered Siegel and Shuster coming to his office to pitch *Superman* for the men's pulps. We know that Siegel, at least, began to take train trips to New York after the major's checks began to arrive. We know that the lines between the major's business and Donenfeld's were thin by 1936, and we know that some Donenfeld pulps included comic strips. We know that Joe liked to draw sexy girls and that Jerry's work could have a rough edge. They might have felt that Superman could be adjusted to fit the naughtiness of *Pep* or the luridness of *Spicy Detective*. Carnahan didn't see a future in it, and Superman was back on the slush pile. In fact, by then he may have been in several slush piles—the major's, Donenfeld's, Gaines's, and Siegel's—and in several different forms.

Again the paying work took precedence in Siegel and Shuster's lives. Their big concern at the beginning of 1937 was the major's launch of a new title: *Detective Comics*.

JACK LIEBOWITZ AND Harry Donenfeld watched the market for comic books grow through 1936. The major's two titles were doing better for them. His erstwhile partners had gotten *The Comics Magazine* off the ground and started a comic book based on crime pulps, *Detective Picture Stories*. *Famous Funnies*, *Tip Top*, and Delacorte's *Popular Comics* were all doing well with their reprints of newspaper strips. There wasn't big money in comics yet, but they brought something valuable to Independent News. Being a girlie mag distributor put a lot of dealers off, but if a sales rep could go into a grocery store in Toledo or Lubbock or Butte and say, "Look at these funnies—they're great for the kids," he'd be listened to. Then he could say, "If you like those, why don't you take a flyer on a *Super Detective* or maybe a few *Spicy Detectives* for the men?" So Jack and Harry advanced the major more money and told him to increase his magazine line to four.

The major's most loyal editor, Vin Sullivan, put together *Detective Comics*. The other launch, *Thrilling Comics,* seems to have somehow involved Charlie Gaines. The major had hired a new editor, a teenager named Sheldon Mayer who also did work for Gaines. Mayer quit in a rage when the major wouldn't pay him and went to work exclusively for Gaines at the McClure Syndicate. In the chaos, *Thrilling* fell apart and *Detective* debuted alone in the spring of 1937. Gaines and Mayer had entered the orbit of Independent News, however, and they wouldn't leave it until they'd transformed the comics field more than once.

Vin Sullivan conceived *Detective Comics* not as a brochure for newspaper syndicates but as a comic book equivalent to pulps, with self-contained stories in a single genre. For his main features he wanted thirteen-page-a-month series—two or three times the usual length—and to do one, he turned to his favorite team: Siegel and Shuster. They turned to their beloved Roy Crane's *Wash Tubbs and Captain Easy* for inspiration, with a little of Milton Caniff's *Terry and the Pirates* thrown in, and produced the globe-trotting fisticuffs of *Slam Bradley.*

Slam's first adventure threw him straight into Terry's country, as he waded mitts first into a horde of evil Chinese. "His thundering fists seem to be everywhere!" reads the caption. "Fui Onyui haplessly gets in Slam's way and the next moment he is soaring thru space by the end of his pigtail. The Chinamen are demoralized by Slam's indomitable courage, surprising strength, and laughter in the face of overwhelming odds!" "Who wants the next ride?" yells Slam. Siegel's writing was courageously stupid. Shuster's art was sketchy but brash. There is such absurd glee in the image of Slam whipping identical, ball-headed Chinese stereotypes through the air by their preposterously long queues that not even modern sensibilities can make it revolting.

Siegel and Shuster did a second series in that same comic, the four-page *Spy*. Seventeen of the comic's sixty-four pages were theirs. Soon they were selling nearly thirty pages a month to the major, and their price increased to $10 a page. Splitting almost $300 a month wasn't bad for a couple of young guys in the Depression. Joe wasn't drawing on wallpaper anymore; in fact he was starting to use Craftint, an expensive, chemically treated paper that enabled rich texturing with little effort. Jerry, for the first time in his life, was a man to his family. He still lived in his mother's house, but now he could buy things for her, he could give her back some of what she'd lost when his father had been killed. He still sat typing in that same attic bedroom, looking down at the kids playing ball on Kimberly Avenue, watching the pretty girl across the street walk home from high school every afternoon. But now he could walk out there without such shame, carrying the secret knowledge of his worth. He could even ask the girl out.

Success, unfortunately, was also hurting the quality of the pair's work. Those thirty pages a month meant a page a day, written, penciled, lettered, and inked. Even by the time of the first issue of *Detective*, the strain was showing in the sparseness of backgrounds and the roughness of some of Joe's ink lines. Already in the first installment of *Spy* appear figures too clunky for Joe to have drawn even in a rush. He was getting help, possibly farming out work. Some of Jerry's acquaintances in science fiction fandom remember him offering to pay for story springboards.

Then came the new comic book. The major was deep in debt to Harry Donenfeld and needed a success in a hurry; in November 1937, he and Vin Sullivan began pulling together the fragments of that fourth entry they'd failed to bring out months before. Now they were calling it *Action Comics*. There was no time to go soliciting material—the Independent News sales crew was ready to push it hard if it could hit the racks the following spring—so they had to go to the slush-pile. He collected a decent set of adventure strips, but no catchy central character that he could splash on the cover. Sullivan asked his friend and former coworker Sheldon Mayer if Charlie Gaines had anything knocking around that he hadn't been able to set up with the McClure Syndicate.

Shelly Mayer was short, slight, and nearsighted. He was smart and funny and a talented cartoonist, but never taken very seriously. He'd been working as an assistant to assorted newspaper cartoonists since he was fifteen, and before he turned eighteen, he was selling his own strips to Major Wheeler-Nicholson. His gift was for busy, energetic absurdity: *The Strange Adventures of Mr. Weed.* He'd grown up in a turbulent household with an angry father, and he had an explosive rage of his own, but the rage tended to break down into tantrums and screaming. He blew up when the major tried to shine off his demands for payment. He worked better with the cantankerous Charlie Gaines, maybe because they both felt too smart for the world around them and they didn't mind the yelling.

Shelly found samples for a *Superman* newspaper strip in Gaines's stacks. The version he saw was a hard-boiled one. It begins with Superman saving a man from a lynch mob, then learning from him that a woman sentenced to die in the electric chair for murder that night is innocent. Superman bursts in on the real murderess, a bottle-blond chanteuse, in her dressing room. She shoots him. The bullet bounces off. He grabs the gun and crushes it, then he grabs her arm. "Are you ready to sign a confession? Or shall I give you a taste of how that gun felt when I applied the pressure?" She writes a confession, knowing it will mean her death. He binds and gags her and carries her to the governor's mansion. The governor's butler attacks him with a knife, but the blade bends. Superman rips down the metal door to the governor's bedroom and demands that the old man listen to what he has to say. The governor pardons the innocent woman. The next day he calls a secret meeting of his advisers to tell them about the terrifying being who visited him last night: "He isn't human!"

This was a grim, almost cruel Superman. His feats had no flamboyance, nothing to suggest the verve of Siegel and Shuster in the *Slam*

Bradley era. The whole strip had the metallic odor of the early Depression. It may be that the samples Shelly Mayer found were from some version of *Superman* closer to the original concept of 1933, or one intended for the Donenfeld men's magazines.

Shelly liked what he saw. While older eyes found that combination of fantastic feats and sweaty realism jarring, the twenty-year-old Shelly understood. He knew how a young man could graft the superheroic fantasies that adults thought were sweet and silly onto a real rage. How a science fiction–loving nebbish could want to be strong enough to frighten and hurt. When his friend Vin asked him if he had anything for a lead feature in *Action Comics,* Shelly knew what to suggest.

Vin was excited. He was a young cartoonist, too, and attuned to the market. By late 1937 Superman looked more salable than he would have just two years before, for kids' entertainment as a whole was being shaped by the same success stories that had excited Jerry and Joe. The Shadow had inspired a flurry of dual-identity crime fighters on radio and in the funny pages. *Tarzan* had made the male body a popular comic strip subject; now Alex Raymond's *Flash Gordon* had become a sensation on the strength of its sweeping draftsmanship, romantic heroes, and beautifully rendered bodies in tights. In early 1936 the creator of *Mandrake the Magician*, Lee Falk, combined the two trends with a new strip called *The Phantom*. Its hero was a bored New York playboy who dons a mask to fight crime (although a copyright dispute soon forced him to move to the jungles of India), and Falk dressed him in tights like a Douglas Fairbanks swashbuckler. Superman was still uniquely fantastical, but he no longer looked quite so peculiar.

So Vin wrote a letter to Jerry and Joe, telling them that their *Superman* samples were heading for Cleveland by parcel post and that if they could cut and paste them into thirteen comic book pages in a matter of days, he'd buy them. When the pages arrived, the two collared Joe's brother to help and hunkered down at the Shusters' apartment to work. They whipped out an introductory page: a single panel showing an infant's escape by rocket from a dying planet, then a summary of his powers and "a scientific explanation of Clark Kent's amazing strength." Then they plunged into their old samples—although, for reasons now lost, the first eight days of strips didn't make the cut. There is no lynch mob or evil chanteuse, only Superman inexplicably racing to the governor's mansion with a woman in his arms. From there the action hurtles forward: Superman saves an innocent woman from execution, tangles briefly with a wife beater, rescues Lois Lane from gangsters, goes after a crooked munitions dealer, and leaps into a cliff-hanger ending on page thirteen. Along the way, he has time to become Clark Kent and be humiliated in front of Lois, in an obvious parody of a Charles Atlas ad.

The pages went back to New York and into the first issue of *Action Comics*. They were rough. The narrative was choppy, as if chunks had been dropped. Rough rewrites intruded, as if Joe and Jerry were scrambling to reconcile an older version of *Superman* with a later conception. In the end, it didn't matter. The pieces were there.

On the cover, Superman lifts a car above his head and terrifies the tough guys around him. Immediately there is the destruction of a planet, the sense of apocalypse. Then, disjointed as though in a dream, there are those moments: Superman sneering as bullets bounce off him, Superman tearing things down, Clark being mortified in Lois's presence. At the very end comes the one glimpse of humor. It's an old gag Jerry saved from *Goober the Mighty* in the Glenville High *Torch*. Superman runs along a power line carrying a terrified crook. Don't worry, he says; "birds sit on telephone wires and they aren't electrocuted—not unless they touch a telephone pole and are grounded! Oops! Almost touched that pole!"

The Superman as practical joker was something new. Doc Savage, the Shadow, the Phantom, Tarzan, Flash Gordon—none of them would have run along a power line to terrify a dumb thug and had so much fun with it. Philip Wylie's Hugo Danner would have been aghast. Douglas Fairbanks would have done it, but who would have imagined him in such coarse pulp adventure? This may have been the most important gift Jerry and Joe could bring, the moment when their unbreakable boyishness lifted them above all the self-important hero makers of the adult world: the sheer delight in having all the power a kid could wish for.

Jerry and Joe got a check for $130. They signed a release surrendering all rights to the publisher. They knew that was how the business worked—that's how they'd sold every creation from *Henri Duval* to *Slam Bradley*. Joe said he'd be willing to give up other series to make room for *Superman*. Wild action, after all, was more fun to draw than *Federal Men* or *Radio Squad*. They got back quickly to the business of meeting their deadlines.

Malcolm Wheeler-Nicholson didn't earn much more off *Action* than they did. In early 1938, Harry Donenfeld sent him and his wife on a cruise to Cuba to "work up new ideas." When they came home, the major found the lock to his office door changed. In his absence, Harry had sued him for nonpayment and pushed Detective Comics, Inc. into bankruptcy court. There a judge named Abe Mennen, one of Harry's old Tammany buddies, had been appointed interim president of the firm and arranged the quick sale of its assets to Independent News. Harry gave the major a percentage of *More Fun Comics* as a shut-up token and wished him well. The major gave up on the world of commerce thereafter and went back to writing war stories and critiques of the American military.

Vin Sullivan went on editing the comics. Jack Liebowitz kept running the company. Battling the censors, Harry probably paid no attention to *Action* or *Superman*. None of them knew how everything would begin to change when that first issue of *Action Comics* came out. None of them could have foreseen how they would change the popular culture of America. None of them could have imagined how different their own lives would become, how huge the money and the fame and the ruination would be.

American Boys

A T THE END of his iconographic history of midcentury America, *The Glory and the Dream,* William Manchester conjures a snapshot of average people at the bottom of the Depression: "It is summer, yet the adults look very formal. The men are wearing stiff collars, the women vast hats and shapeless cotton dresses. But it is the children who seem oddest. Like their parents they are quaintly dressed. There is something else, though. It takes a moment to realize why they look so peculiar. Then you see it. There is an intensity in their expressions. They are leaning slightly forward, as though trying to see into the future. And they are smiling."

That Depression smile is hard to understand across the intervening generations, but it's impossible to deny. For all the stories of growing up in hard times, the voices that tell those stories crackle with a humor and optimism that somehow never buckled. The generation born around 1915—those kids who spent their childhoods in times of wild promise and entered the workforce just after it all fell apart—attacked the hustle and shuffle of the Thirties with an astonishing lack of self-pity and despair. The texture of American life after the world war may hold part of the answer. They were raised in an atmosphere of daily revolution and constant novelty, led to believe that their own futures must coincide with the great Future of mankind. They were the first generation raised in the age of popular psychology, their childhoods examined and designed for the furtherance of their happiness. They were sheltered from hard work and adult knowledge like no generation before, allowed to play past an age when their parents would have already slipped on the yokes of realism. They were given the inexhaustible fantasies of a juvenile culture industry such as the world had never known. Whatever the reasons, in the worst of times, they proved themselves capable of the most acrid pragmatism, the biggest dreams, the most exuberant resiliency, and the grittiest laughs.

The dreams, laughs, wisecracks, and schemes came loudest from the throats of Jewish kids. It was a breathtaking moment for Jewish possibilities. Roosevelt had Jews in his Brain Trust and cabinet. Every intellectual and pseudointellectual in the world was citing Marx, Freud, and Einstein. The Jew haters were getting noisy again, but no one thought they could stand against the rising tide. Irving Thalberg of MGM, after visiting Germany in 1934, said, "A lot of Jews will lose their lives . . . [but] Hitler and Hitlerism will pass, and the Jews will still be there." There was even something faintly ridiculous about crazy Adolf. Jewish teenagers hooted at him in the newsreels. Anti-fascist movements were growing quickly, becoming downright fashionable over the war in Spain. The Nazis would probably come crashing gloriously down before they did any real harm.

Nowhere was Jewish influence greater than in American popular culture. Jews ran the movie studios and wrote the songs—and not the pampered children of rich German families but old shtetl fur peddlers and Delancey Street spielers. Benny Goodman was the sound of sex. There were Jewish movie stars, not only clowns like Eddie Cantor but Paul Muni, Sylvia Sydney, even Ricardo Cortez. Jewish dads made sure their gangster-crazy kids knew who Edward G. Robinson and John Garfield were behind their goyish screen names. "Did you read Walter Winchell today?" they'd say. "He's Jewish, you know." Those dads had grown up viewing American culture through the eyes of outsiders, but the kids knew it was their culture, theirs to take and theirs to remake.

These pop culture kids were mostly an urban, middle-class generation. The garment trade, still the Jewish community's greatest source of income, muscled through the Depression, while such Twenties bonanzas as cars and construction collapsed. The immigrants and their kids kept moving out of the Lower East Side, Williamsburg, and Greenpoint, out to the newly built comforts of Bayside, Bensonhurst, and the Bronx. Critics called the Bronx sterile and mechanistic, built too quickly with too little thought, but the kids who lived in its intellectual and cultural life, its edgy insolence and electric competitiveness, knew they were in the middle of something that mattered. Queens was quiet. Brooklyn was Brooklyn. The Bronx was a cheer, a clanking elevated train, the arrogance of Yankee fans. It was a bedroom community, emptied of men every morning and given over to the schoolboys who ran the streets. Compared to the Lower East Side, it was spacious and peaceful. The buildings were new and regular, the parks large, the sidewalks free of whores and hustlers. It was also an abrasive, hastily settled ethnic patchwork. Alex Singer, a movie director who grew up in the Bronx during the Depression, has said that when he wasn't reading violent pulp magazines he was "working out routes to get to school and back every day with the lowest likelihood of getting beaten up." "The Italian and Irish kids hated Jewish kids," he said. "Our only saving grace was that they hated each other more."

A lot of families moved to the Bronx just to get their sons into De-Witt Clinton High, an all-boys school, overwhelmingly Jewish, with tough entrance requirements. It was the most competitive school in the city, and it had turned out a staggering number of successful intellectuals and artists: the reputations of Mortimer Adler, Edward Bernays, Lionel Trilling, Richard Rodgers, and even Fats Waller loomed over the kids who climbed its wide steps. Bronx kids came of age with armor on their feelings and razors in their brains. They rode the trains south to Manhattan hot with expectations. When the comic book burst suddenly upon New York, they were ready to make it their own.

Mort Weisinger, Julie Schwartz, Bob Kahn, Will Eisner, and Bill Finger were only five of the hundreds of Bronx kids who loved comic strips and pulp magazines and wanted to make their futures somehow in the worlds of writing and art. They were all born between 1914 and early 1917, within about two years of Jerry Siegel and Joe Shuster. Like Jerry and Joe, they all grew up speaking English in the home, none had much use for religion or tradition, and all defined themselves clearly as Americans. "I knew I was Jewish in the same sense that any American knows he's Irish-American or Italian-American," Eisner has said. "It influenced me in that the stories I grew up hearing were the stories told in Jewish families, but I never thought about being Jewish when I did my work." Like Jerry and Joe, these kids believed in their power and right to create their own futures. Some of them would go on to attain the very futures those boys in Cleveland reached for but couldn't hold.

Mort Weisinger was a great slab of a kid. Early descriptions call him genial, later ones domineering. He loved to laugh and greet his friends loudly, and he loved controlling conversations with his booming voice and big waving hands and forward-thrusting torso. Mostly he used laughter, wild anecdotes, and chest-swelling confidence to dominate a room, but he had anger in him, too, and he knew how to use it. His father was a successful footwear manufacturer who wanted his son to be a doctor. Mort didn't want to be a doctor. He loved magazines. He was another of those isolated, frustrated twelve-year-olds who fell in love with Gernsback's *Amazing Stories* in the late Twenties. He quickly moved to the fore of New York fandom, offering a room in his parents' big house as the monthly meeting place of the club that called themselves the Scienceers, launching *The Time Traveller* with his friends Julius Schwartz, Alan Glasser, and Forrest Ackerman.

Mort felt a power in the science fiction world that he never found in academic competition or under his father's roof. As he entered his teens, he fought bitterly with the old man over his refusal to throw out his cheap magazines and concentrate on his grades and over his stubborn insistence that he wasn't going to medical school. His father told him he'd never amount to anything. For the rest of his life, Mort would fight angrily, bitterly, to prove his father was wrong. He even attempted a fan club putsch, resulting in a two-year schism that left two groups calling themselves Scienceers. Commanding loyalty mattered a great deal to Mort.

His most loyal follower was Julie Schwartz, an epically homely boy with a great convex nose, buck teeth, a soaring dome of a forehead, and bottomless watery eyeglasses. He and Mort formed a sort of Mutt and Jeff team, Mort always pouncing first on a conversation, Julie's disarming baritone drawling dreadful puns and calming the nerves of those who found Mort unnerving. They'd ride down to Manhattan together to the rare audiences that Hugo Gernsback and other mavens allowed their most loyal fans. They served as gossip columnists for *The Time Traveller*, a sort of Walter Winchell and Ed Sullivan of fandom. They even supplied gossip to Jerry Siegel's *Science Fiction*.

While Julie seemed content to be a funny kid having a good time, Mort was hungry to get somewhere. He saw writing as his route. He'd write anything: essay contests in newspapers, brain twisters for puzzle books, phony inspirational stories, hobby hints, detective stories. He lived according to *Writer's Digest* and *Author and Journalist*. When the writing itself wasn't enough, he found other ways of building his reputation. He'd point to a piece in a magazine with a phony-sounding byline and claim he'd written it under a pseudonym. Then he'd use that to talk an editor into assigning him a short piece, retype something from another magazine, and submit it as his own. Once he had a track record, he started telling friends he'd split the money with them if they'd let him sell their stories under his name. Once those were in print, he'd tell anyone but the authors that he'd written them himself. His buddy Julie used to say his headstone should read "Here Lies Mort Weisinger—As Usual."

When Mort was only eighteen, he pulled off a dazzling gambit. Few writers allowed themselves the luxury of literary agents in the depressed pulp market, and no science fiction writers did. There were three magazines in the genre, everyone knew everyone's name, and the established writers, more fans than businessmen, mostly felt grateful to be doing as well as they were. But Mort saw money and influence to be won and talked Julie into joining him in the "Solar Sales Service." They'd already corresponded with writers who lived far from New York: Edmond Hamilton in Ohio, Stanley Weinbaum in Wisconsin, the team of Earl and Otto Binder in Michigan. Now they offered them their services, promising they'd take no commission until they proved their value. Then Mort went to T. O'Connor Sloane, the elderly retired scientist who had been placed in charge of *Amazing Stories* by an uncomprehending publisher, and convinced him that he represented the cream of science fiction writers and could get them to deliver whatever the market wanted. Next he told Charles Hornig, Hugo Gernsback's new teenaged editor of *Wonder Stories*, that he was going to take his whole stable of writers to *Amazing* unless *Wonder* bought just as much from them. Then he told F. Orlin Tremaine at *Astounding* that he had the other two magazines in his pocket. Finally he went back to his writers with story suggestions and promised sales. Mort and Julie had made themselves the first literary agents in a field that didn't even know it needed agents.

When a better deal presented itself, though, Mort didn't hesitate to dump the agency and run. He heard that Gernsback had run into money trouble and decided to sell *Wonder Stories* to Ned Pines's publishing company, and immediately he called Pines's chief editor to ask who the editor of the new *Wonder* would be. The editor said he wanted to keep Charles Hornig in the job. Mort snorted. What did that milquetoast know about running a magazine? Hornig was just a fan who lucked into a job. His heart was still in the fanzines—that's why *Wonder* went broke. But Mort was a pro. So Charlie Hornig was out of the job; Mort Weisinger was in. It wouldn't be the last time Mort showed that he wasn't intimidated by more established men or scrupulous about other people's careers; Jerry Siegel would come to know those qualities well. He left Solar Sales to Julie Schwartz. Mort, at twenty years of age, was editing the most respected magazine in his field.

Not that it would be so well respected by the time he was done with it. His fellow fans were thrilled at first that one of their own had taken the torch that Gernsback could no longer carry, but they would learn quickly that Mort no longer had any use for being one of them. Ned Pines published *Thrilling Mystery, Thrilling Love, Thrilling Adventure,* and other energetic schlock, and from the moment he walked in the door, Mort Weisinger made himself Ned's kind of guy. He let his writers know that he wanted less science, less futurism, less thought, and more hideous creatures, beautiful girls, and blazing ray guns. There would be no more gracious Frank R. Paul cityscapes on his covers. Mort knew what scared little boys and agitated their older brothers; he gave the world the "bug-eyed monster" and the space opera damsel in bustier and shorts. The motto of the new *Thrilling Wonder Stories* was "Stranger Than Truth," and every cover-featured story came with an ad line: "A Novelette of Mad Catastrophe," "A Novelette of Universal Destruction," "A Story of Throttled Life Forces." The titles of the stories in the first few issues left little doubt of the new tone: "The Brain Stealers of Mars," "The Revenge of the Robot," and from Earl and Otto Binder, "The Hormone Menace." Mort even added comic strips to the pages.

Older fans screamed, but sales climbed. In 1938 Mort was asked to launch a second magazine, *Startling Stories*. He was climbing toward the top of the pulp heap, when comic books struck.

Robert Kahn was born in the Bronx in 1916, a year after Mort and Julie. He was famous at DeWitt Clinton as a mama's boy. His mother would sometimes walk him to school or show up to walk him home. If he had the sniffles, at least so his classmates said, his mother would keep him home. Rumors ran wild that he was a bed wetter, but maybe that was just an easy slur to slap on a slight, sensitive, big-eyed boy who liked girls better than the fellas. His father was an engraver and printer with the *New York Daily News* and encouraged Bob's love of drawing. As an artist, Bob was a talented mimic, better at pleasing adults than depicting any inner reality; at fifteen he won a prize for his imitation of the newspaper strip *Just Kids,* an event he took as a sign that he was meant to be a comic strip star. His father would bring home the Sunday funnies still smelling of ink, before any other kids in the neighborhood saw them, and Bob would sit down and copy them. "I could copy them exactly," he said. "I impressed everybody."

As he grew up, Bob realized he had another way to attract attention: He was handsome. Skinny as a hose but with a long, fine nose, a dimpled smirk, brushstroke brows, and eyes that crinkled when he smiled. He compared himself to Robert Young, that favored young male of MGM who always played the insouciant son of the stuffy plutocrat, and he cultivated the style. If girls giggled when he crinkled his eyes, then he'd polish his crinkling in the mirror. Word spread quickly at that all-boys school that Kahn was the fellow to know if you wanted to meet girls, assuming you could endure his boasting and preening and flagrant lies. "We were supposedly friends because we were both artists," said one classmate, Will Eisner. "But really, it was so we could double-date and he could set me up with the most beautiful girls. Then it started to dawn on me that I wasn't getting anywhere with these girls—and neither was Bob. You couldn't get all the way with the beautiful girls. I decided I'd rather date the average girls who'd actually let you get somewhere." So it would always be with them: Eisner wanted action, Kahn the appearance of action.

Their families helped pay their ways to art school in Manhattan, Bob to the Commercial Art Studio in the Flatiron Building, Will to the Art Students League at the top of the Times Square triangle. Like Bob's, Will's father was an artisan working below his aspirations, a Viennese painter who had apprenticed to masters working in Catholic churches, who'd come to America to work in theater painting, only to be forced by the Depression to make his living in furniture decoration. He took little Willie to the Metropolitan Museum, encouraged his love of H. Rider Haggard and O. Henry, threw away his pulp magazines to save him from the debasement of junk. He loved Willie's experiments in woodcut and drypoint and bought him expensive books illustrated by Rockwell Kent.

Willie's mother, though, was a peddler's daughter from Romania who spent her life concealing the fact that she was illiterate. "She had peasant smarts," said her son, "but no sophistication, no understanding of culture." She complained about her husband's trouble keeping a job and pushed Willie to work. Sixty years later, in an autobiographical graphic novel, *To the Heart of the Storm,* he had her saying, "If your father wasn't such a big shot, he'd do house painting where he really belongs." How they had come to marry Will never quite understood, but he carried the duality of art and money inside him all his life.

The Art Students League crackled with artistic fire: A battle raged between the faculty's leftists, who wanted to hire the acidic German caricaturist George Grosz, and the old guard, who found him too dangerous; and the students chose sides. Will Eisner, though, stuck to the business of learning to draw cartoons. That was part honest passion—he loved the adventure comics of Hal Foster and Alex Raymond—but it was part hard pragmatism too. Rough-edged Jewish kids knew they had a steep hill to climb if they wanted to become "high-class" illustrators, not only because of editors' prejudices but also because of the costs of the training, studio lighting, and live models needed for that perfect sheen. "The comics were still viewed as trash," Eisner said, "so they were an easier business to enter, the way peddling or the rag trade had been."

Bob Kahn saw things similarly. He loved the gag cartoonists of *Judge* and *College Humor* but felt he couldn't sell his work with an obviously Jewish name, so he took the name "Bob Kane," not only in print but in his private life as well. He worked hard on a signature that couldn't be missed, a big box holding the bold letters of his new name with a voluptuous "O" riding high. Sometimes he and Will would run into each other on the cartoonists' track, carrying their portfolios to editors' and art directors' offices, Will picking his way through crowds of tourists and touts, Bob hiking up 5th Avenue past the men in suits to the magazine publishers, syndicates, and ad agencies that littered Midtown. They'd sit in offices for hours waiting to have their stuff looked at, passing portfolios around to the other kids waiting with them, discreetly studying the older cartoonists who came in after them and were shown in first. They must have been a striking pair: Will broad shouldered and straight backed, hair rolling in waves back from a high brow above an aquiline nose; Bob dimpling and grinning, flirting with the receptionists. Neither got much but rejection.

Bob had to take a job in his uncle's garment factory. "It's difficult to put into words the loathing I felt for this type of operation," he said, "for I knew in my heart that it was not meant to be my destiny." Finally he picked up some work at Max Fleischer's animation studio, cleaning up drawings and "in-betweening" the cell-by-cell movement.

Will found a job cleaning presses at a printer's in the far south of Manhattan. He grabbed every drawing gig he could find—almost. One of the printer's sidelines turned out to be "eight pagers," cheap comic books showing celebrities and comic strip characters making whoopee in pornographic, and illegal, detail. The mobster who distributed them offered to pay Will to draw a few. "It was one of the toughest moral conflicts of my youth," Will said. But he passed.

Then one day when they were both nineteen, Will and Bob ran into each other on a Midtown street. Bob announced he was organizing a cartoonist's union and invited Will to the meeting. Will scoffed at the idea of freelance cartoonists ever unionizing; more than likely Bob just wanted himself known to editors as a potential troublemaker so they'd raise him from five to six bucks per cartoon to keep him quiet. What Will wanted was work, any work, drawing. Bob said he'd sold a few "Hiram Hick" cartoons to something called *Wow, What a Magazine!* Will hiked straight down to 4th Avenue to show his stuff.

The garment industry was still the source of much of the investment capital that launched Jewish publishing enterprises in the 1930s, and the piecework and sweatshop models of the trade were employed by many small publishers. Nothing, however, blurred the line between *shmattes* and magazines quite so literally as *Wow*. It was made in a shirt factory. A failed cartoonist named Samuel "Jerry" Iger had talked a shirtmaker into bankrolling a boys' magazine and giving up some space at the front of his factory for the editorial office. One artist who worked for Iger called him "a promoter and operator." He was another of those would-be syndicators like Major Malcolm Wheeler-Nicholson who thought if he could just connect the right cheap talent to the right hungry publisher, he'd strike it rich. He was short, cigar stinking, in his thirties and still hustling for his break, talking like a big shot and a ladies man.

Will Eisner did not have high hopes when he rode the elevator through the shirt factory to *Wow*'s offices, but as he put it, "I was hungry. I was real hungry." He walked in the door with his portfolio. Iger immediately brushed him off. He had to go solve a problem at his engraver's. Will wouldn't be brushed. He walked out of the office with Iger, stuck to him along 4th Avenue, saying, "Why don't you just look at my portfolio while we walk?" He ended up walking into the engraver's with him. The engraving company must have been cheap, a fly-by-night, because the problem that was stumping them was one Will had already learned to solve at his printing job. "Does anyone have a burnishing tool?" he asked. The engravers stood around stunned while this teenager burnished down the plates that had been tearing up the mattes. "Who is this kid?" one asked. "He's my new production man," said Iger.

In fact Will got only a few comics jobs out of *Wow*. One was a story about a two-fisted treasure hunter inspired by H. Rider Haggard, another a swashbuckling adventure aspiring to the romance of Rafael Sabatini and the illustrative sweep of N. C. Wyeth. It was elegant work for a kid, more mature in its use of page design and the multipage format than anything coming simultaneously from Major Wheeler-Nicholson's *More Fun* or *New Adventure*. Will thought he was on his way—until the shirtmaker decided he'd lost enough money on *Wow* and turned off the spigot. He and Iger were both out of work again.

That's when the businessman in Will Eisner stirred. He knew the comic book business was growing, and he knew that comic strips were becoming increasingly popular as cheap filler in magazines but that publishers often couldn't afford the staff to find the talent or do the production work. Will called Jerry Iger. "I'd like to meet with you," he said. "I've got an idea."

They had lunch across from the *Daily News,* where Bob Kane's father worked. Will pitched. Surely publishers would appreciate the partnership of a cartoonist and a salesman-editor who could deliver camera-ready comics pages of reliable quality. It was simple piecework, the lifeblood of the New York garment industry. Iger said it would cost money to start up, and that's what he didn't have. "My second wife's divorcing me and she's taking me for everything I've got." Then Will played the big shot. He had $15 to his name, money he'd just earned off a one-shot advertising job. He still lived with his parents and didn't have to pay rent. Midtown was full of half-vacant office buildings, erected on Twenties expectations and emptied by Thirties realities. Will found one on 41st Street and Madison that rented small offices for $5 a month, no questions asked, and so they moved in among the bookies and con men. Iger began to peddle their services to publishers, calling himself "S. M. Iger" in the manner of W. R. Hearst. He claimed to have a five-man art staff, but it was all Will under pseudonyms. Will insisted they call the company "Eisner & Iger," because the money man's name should always come first, even for $15.

Iger came in with one major contact in his pocket. Through that invisible network of barterers and favor traders that spread through New York in the 1930s, he'd hooked up with a man named Joshua Powers who claimed to be a former secret agent now making his fortune from the contacts he'd made overseas. Powers bought up the foreign rights of comic strips ranging from *Mutt and Jeff* to *Dick Tracy* and packaged them for export to Britain, Australia, and South America. But in that global depression, foreign newspapers couldn't pay for comics, so Powers traded them for column inches in the papers, which he then resold to American advertisers. It worked well until one of Powers's partners broke with him and made off with the British rights to his comics. Powers had to scramble to come up with cheap original comic strips—and that's where the Eisner and Iger shop suddenly came in handy.

With cash coming in, Eisner and Iger jury rigged their own variation. They hired a couple of salesmen—"fast-talking hotshots," in Eisner's words—who visited small-town newspapers all over the Northeast and sold them a page of comics with a blank space for ads at the bottom; then they'd go personally to local merchants and find someone to buy that ad space for the same price as the comics page. The newspapers got comics for nothing and Eisner and Iger got the money minus sales commission.

Now they put an ad in the paper calling for young artists who were willing to sit in a studio drawing comic strips all day for $15 a week. Sixty a month was just barely enough for a young man to survive on if he lived at home or with other young guys; in a good month, Jerry Siegel and Joe Shuster split five times that. The number of responses showed just how many young artists were out there, inspired to draw by the comics, yearning to be the next Hal Foster or Milton Caniff, desperate for an open door. Eisner was able to pick only the best of them, kids who'd gone to Pratt Institute or the School of Industrial Art. When Siegel and Shuster sent him a couple of strips called *Spy* and *Superman,* he sent them back with the note, "You're not ready yet." (So Eisner joined the club of men who could look back on that great missed opportunity and laugh at themselves.)

The names of the young men he hired over the next two years read like the roll call in one of those war movies celebrating the melting pot: Klaus Nordling, Stanley Pulowski, Chuck Cuidera, Chuck Mazoujian, Reed Crandall, Nick Viscardi, Bob Fujitani, "Tex" Blaisdell. There were no women among the artists. Like science fiction fandom, the world of adventure comics was a boy's club in which women figured only as mothers and girlfriends. It was a bit more blue-collar and socially normal, though: At least these guys actually *had* girlfriends.

In the early going, Eisner would develop the ideas, design the characters, sometimes do a few pages, then turn them over to the studio hands. Often one artist would draw in pencil, then hand it over to others to finish it in ink, rule the panel borders, do the hand lettering. The boys would work all day and deep into the night if the jobs were there, cheek by jowl at their drawing boards, kibitzing and wise-assing, sharing brushes, pooling their change for beer and smokes. From one another they learned how to draw and how to work with people. They learned that Mort Meskin would stare at his drawing board for hours in blank-page anxiety until somebody else walked up and scribbled random lines on it. With lines to connect, Meskin's hands could start moving, could start carving those square, craggy, expressive figures of his. They learned to put up with Stan Pulowski's griping about "kikes," telling each other a Polack didn't know any better (and it was Pulowski, not Meskin or Fine, who signed his work "Bob Powell"). And they gathered around Lou Fine just to watch him draw, to watch those wonderfully liquid lines flow from his brush and bring to life men of a sinuous grace and weightless agility that his polio-crippled body would never know.

At twenty Eisner was younger than half the boys he hired but was already the picture of the shop boss: demanding and decisive, pushing his young workers hard but able to inspire their loyalty. They called the studio a "sweatshop," not always in jest, but usually. They did nice work too, in almost every genre: cops, spies, spacemen, buccaneers, magicians, and a female version of Tarzan they called Sheena, Queen of the Jungle. And

Eisner was making money off them. He moved out of his parents' house and rented an apartment in Tudor City, a modern, middle-class development within walking distance of the studio.

By early 1938 comic books were still a modest but obviously growing field. Harry Donenfeld was giving the big push to his comics, and sales were rising past 100,000 copies a month, up there with reasonably successful pulps. The publishers of *The Comics Magazine* and *Detective Picture Stories* were expanding their line. Now Jerry Iger cut a deal with Fiction House, one of the smaller pulp publishers, to produce *Jumbo Comics*. It was tabloid sized, black-and-white, featuring mostly material Eisner and his studio had already created. Sheena and her leopard skin swimsuit got no more space on the cover than Peter Pupp; the comic book makers didn't know their market yet, but they knew a market was there.

The creator of Peter Pupp, and a provider of regular humor pages to Eisner, was Bob Kane. But Kane didn't work in the studio with the rest of the artists. He wasn't a man to play on a team, especially if he weren't the captain. By now he was telling his friends that he reminded himself of Tyrone Power: less jollity, more dash. He'd had just enough success getting his name in print and just enough failure lining up a regular berth that he was hungry for a high-profile strip of his own. He started selling humorous private-eye fillers to Vin Sullivan at Major Wheeler-Nicholson's comics, and he wanted to develop ideas for stories longer than a page or two. But stories were Bob's weak spot. As Eisner would say, "Bob wasn't an intellectual."

Then he met Bill Finger. Bob said it was at a "cocktail party"; one imagines a kid's parents gone to the Catskills and his pals showing up with beer and gin. Whatever the case, Bill was a drinker. He was another DeWitt Clinton graduate, a couple of years ahead of Bob, smart, articulate, well-read, depressive. He wanted to be a writer, a real one, known for his short fiction and novels, although he enjoyed the better pulps too and was willing to write potboilers if that's what it took to make a living by writing. But he'd gotten married early, and at twenty-four he already had a son to support. When he met Bob, he was selling shoes. When Bob said he was a successful cartoonist who needed help with the writing end of things and was willing to pay for it, Bill jumped at the chance. Bob was likable, the work sounded like fun, and it was money for writing. Finger agreed to help brainstorm the ideas and do the writing for a portion of the income while Kane dealt with the editors and took all the credit. Bill was an agreeable guy, and for the rest of his life, he would suffer terribly for it.

With Finger doing his writing, Kane began to sell regularly to Vin Sullivan. *Rusty and His Pals* and *Clip Carson* were pastiches of *Terry and the Pirates* for *New Adventure* and *Action Comics*. A partnership was born—although everything the partnership produced was still signed just "Bob Kane."

In the spring of 1938, these five Bronx kids were between twenty-one and twenty-four years old. They were making decent livings in the comics and magazine trades. They were building a community too, a geek's community: some geeks handsomer or better at business than others, but all deeply invested in wild, printed fantasies, all smugly uninterested in the things that occupied most boys in high school and the years right after. Already they'd all climbed a rung above their fathers on the American ladder, in self-satisfaction and glamour if not necessarily in money.

Then the man in the blue tights changed everything.

THE CONSIGNMENT SYSTEM prevented publishers from knowing how well their magazines had sold until months after they'd been shipped. When Vin Sullivan put Superman on the covers of the first and seventh issues of *Action Comics* and gave the others to elegant renderings of parachutists, Mounties, and jungle explorers, he was only guessing at what would attract kids' attention. What publishers did have was word of mouth from local dealers. By the time the fourth and fifth issues hit the stands, in the late summer of 1938, word was coming in that *Action* was selling through quicker than the other comics. Harry Donenfeld sent his sales staff out to run an informal survey of news dealers and their customers, and they came back with the word that kids were asking for "the comic with Superman in it."

This was just about the time Superman first truly emerged as a character on the printed page. The cut-and-paste quality of his adventures continued after his first appearance. *Action* number 2 featured a story strangely similar to one used in *Detective Comics* the year before; some panels seem to have been pasted in from another source, and in some of them Superman's cape has obviously been drawn onto a different character. The next month brought a story about a crooked mine owner, starring not Superman but Clark Kent in disguise, as if a strip about a crusading newspaper reporter had been cobbled together with another effort in order to buy time for Superman. The fourth story was more polished, but it also contained few glimpses of Superman in costume; its centerpiece was a football sequence that echoed a chapter of Philip Wylie's *Gladiator* and may have been a survivor of some earlier version of "the Superman."

Then, suddenly, in the fifth issue, Superman appears. "Telegraph lines broadcast to the world news of a terrible disaster! The Valleyho Dam is cracking under the strain of a huge downpour!" "Kent! Get me Clark Kent!" "He isn't in his office!" "Well, look for him, Lois!" "But why not have *me* handle the assignment?" "Can't! It's too important! This is no job for a girl!" "No job for a woman, eh? I've half a mind to . . . " "Clark Kent! Just the man I'm looking for!" "You mean you're actually *glad* to see me?" "I should say I am! Would you do me a favor and cover an assignment for me? . . . Go to the city hospital's maternity ward. A Mrs. Mahoney is expecting septuplets!" "What a story! Thanks, Lois! You're a peach to let me handle this!" "Somebody's been spoofing you, pal! There's no Mrs. Mahoney registered here." "That's strange! Say! I wonder if Lois is by any chance pulling a double-cross?" "You brainless idiot! The greatest news story in months on the fire, and you waste your time at a hospital! Kent! Report to the cashier! *You're fired!*" "But Kent has other plans! When alone, he strips off his outer garments and stands revealed in the Superman costume!" "Now, to *get that story!*"

He leaps into the night, bounding over the city, outracing the train on which Lois rides. "If Lois thinks she's going to outscoop me, she's badly mistaken!" But he finds the trestle about to give out, so he drops to the base and holds it up as the train hammers across it. Arriving in Valleyho, Lois takes over an abandoned taxi and drives it to the dam, where Superman is holding the concrete together by sheer strength. "Suddenly, with a great roar, the huge dam collapses . . . Superman leaps above the water's turbulent fury . . . but Lois finds herself directly in the path of the great, irresistible flood of onrushing water." He plunges in, tears the car open, and bears Lois's limp form back to the air. Now he outraces the flood on its rush to the town, "springs to a high pinnacle . . . then pits his tremendous strength against a great projection of rock! . . . The avalanche of rock crams shut the mountain-gap below—cutting off, diverting the flood to another direction, away from Valleyho Town!"

"You did it! You saved all those people! Oh, I could kiss you! As a matter of fact, I *will!*" "Lady! PLEASE!" "WOW! What a kiss!" "A super-kiss for a Super-man!" "Enough of that! I've got to bring you back to safety—where I'll be safe from you!" Lois tells him she loves him, but he's off with a wave. Then he calls the chief and scoops her. "Lois! That wasn't a nice stunt you pulled on me! But I still like you." "Who cares! (The spineless worm! I can hardly bear looking at him, after having been in the arms of a *real* he man—)."

Shuster's Superman is suddenly exploding through space, his cape flowing behind him as he leaps and races over cities, over water, across the moon in a desert sky. His figures are simple but alive, their faces rich with cartooned expression. The sly Lois, the gibbering Clark, and the arrogant Superman come to life. Shuster's trains and dams and bridges are bold icons of Thirties modernism. He defines vast spaces with sweeping curves and open fields, then places his tiny people against them. His Superman is thrilling not because he's a monumental hero out of *Flash Gordon* or *Tarzan* but because he's as small and colorful and cute as a little boy's drawing, and yet by some miracle of unglimpsable power he's able to hold up the trestle and save the train.

This is still not quite the Superman we would come to know. He can't fly, only jump, he has no X-ray vision, and he can hold a dam together only by "battling like mad." But the cataclysmic drama, élan, and winking humor of Superman at his apex are in place. This was something new in entertainment. Whatever antecedents for Superman's powers, costume, or origin we can find in Edgar Rice Burroughs or Doc Savage or the Phantom or Zorro or Philip Wylie or Popeye, nothing had ever read like this before. The racy mix of slapstick, caricature, and danger is familiar from Roy Crane's *Wash Tubbs,* but Crane never leapt into such pure fantasy. Hollywood had made breathtaking moments out of natural disaster, and Douglas Fairbanks had let us feel the same joy in physical liberation, but they had nothing to equal the immediate pleasure of these bright, flat colors and fiercely simplified forms. This was a distillation of the highest thrills in the purest junk.

It's surprising, then, to realize that even this was built up from panels photostated from an earlier version. The letters and line thicknesses grow and shrink from panel to panel; connective sentences have been written in a different hand; the dam sequence, at least, seems to come from samples for a proposed Sunday comic strip, although the Lois and Clark material may be new. We may be looking here at that "humor-adventure character" Jerry and Joe scribbled notes about in the high hopes of late 1935. This may be the "rugged, narrative drive" that they dreamed would sweep the nation. Belatedly, it seemed to be happening.

The great missing piece in any archaeology of kid culture is what the kids themselves were saying. Were there ten- and eleven-year-olds who discovered Superman in the summer of 1938 and ran to tell their friends, "You gotta read this"? Did the word spread through school playgrounds in the fall? Or was it still mostly isolated kids, each discovering it on his own? All we have now are sales figures and editorial decisions. Over a nine-month period *Action* more than doubled its monthly sales. But other comics started selling better, too. It seems that Superman was selling comic books to kids who didn't normally buy them, and then those kids were trying other comics. Somewhere in the 1938–1939 school year a comic book fad was born.

It was a good time for Superman to arrive. The kids born in the late Twenties and early Thirties had never known the thrill of taking a new medium or genre for their own: The kids a decade older had been pioneer audiences for radio, talkies, adventure comic strips, hard-boiled pulps, and science fiction, but a depressed economy had supported little that was new. Now something had come along that adults and older siblings didn't know about, something cheap and colorful and exotic. This was a skeptical generation, too, raised on lower expectations and hard realities. The comics, cartoons, and radio shows had increased the American appetite for fantastic heroes, but at the same time, plenty of adolescents and precocious kids found Flash Gordon and his ilk fairly ludicrous. The humor and excess of *Superman* made it possible to laugh along with the creators while still thrilling to the fantasy of power. That had always been Jerry and Joe's special insight: You could want the invulnerability and the power, but you had to laugh to keep people from knowing how badly you wanted it. The hero who dressed like a Bernarr MacFadden bodybuilder and bounced bullets off his chest contained that laugh almost by nature.

In their sixth published *Superman* story, perhaps their first conceived for comic books, Jerry and Joe showed that they shared their readers' conflicting cynicism and dreams. They threw their hero up against a would-be manager who sells Superman's name to a car company, has a nightclub singer wail a Superman torch song, and sponsors a Superman radio show. "Why, I've even made provisions for him to appear in the comics." They were parodying the genre before the genre existed. The comic book superhero first sold himself to a suspicious public through humor, then dared them to follow him into earnest power fantasies. After all the gags, it was satisfying to see the manager's hired stand-in for Superman break his fist on the real hero's steely chest.

In September 1938 Jerry and Joe took the train to New York, this time not to hustle samples but to be feted by Vin Sullivan. Even Jack Liebowitz and Harry Donenfeld greeted "the boys" who were selling so many comics (although they didn't take them to the Stork Club). Jerry hooked up with some of his pen pals from science fiction fandom, Mort Weisinger and Julie Schwartz among them, finally able to play the role of a fellow success story.

The big news, though, was from Charlie Gaines. He was thrilled by Superman's success. For one thing, he got a cut from everything printed by the McClure Syndicate, and McClure had the printing contract for *Action Comics*. For another, he was still selling McClure items for syndication. He'd failed repeatedly to set Superman up with the syndicate, but now he had evidence that kids liked the thing. He told Jerry and Joe to prepare new samples, insisting that these be more polished than anything they'd sent him before. Presumably, too, he planned to link it with Buck Rogers and Flash Gordon, because the first two weeks of the version finally accepted by McClure were taken up by a grand space opera of Krypton's destruction and baby Superman's exodus. Harry Donenfeld held the rights, of course, but he was eager to make it happen and cut Jerry and Joe a generous deal to do the strip themselves: 50 percent of the take. Harry hadn't made so much money so easily since the Hearst printing deal in 1923. He was in an expansive mood.

Jerry and Joe rode back to Cleveland knowing they were at the brink of hitting the big time. A newspaper strip is what they'd wanted all along. They knew they'd need help. Back in June they'd already hired a couple of young artists to drop by Joe's apartment sometimes and help them handle the growing workload. They'd need more to do this. They'd need to create a studio. Jerry apparently didn't trust his skills as a science fiction writer, because he hired a friend from fandom, Harold Gold, to write the initial origin sequence for the comic strips. He began asking other friends to sell him ideas for stories and help him script.

McClure placed *Superman* with *The Houston Chronicle*, then the *Milwaukee Journal*, then the *San Antonio Express*. The first strip, a stunning sequence of a man racing at superspeed through a futuristic city beneath an alien sky to see his newborn son, would appear in newspapers scattered across America in January 1939. Jerry and Joe celebrated in the final panel of the tenth issue of *Action* with an evocation of dreams once deferred: "Superman, the Strip Sensation of 1939."

But Jerry had already begun to wonder if he'd cut a smart enough deal with his publisher. He looked at the cost of a studio and thought about the $10 a page he and Joe were being paid. In the moment he saw his dreams about to be realized, he began to feel them being stolen. He'd hardly come home from that triumphal trip to New York when he began his first angry letter to Jack Liebowitz.

CHARLIE GAINES WAS the first to look for other ways to capitalize on the new hit. He immediately began packaging *Superman*, the first magazine devoted entirely to a character born in a comic book. He pushed Jerry and Joe to pull it together quickly, ahead of the glut of competition that he knew would be coming. Then he started assembling a *New York World's Fair Comics* with Superman on the cover, to be distributed at the highly touted "World of Tomorrow" opening in the summer of 1939. Someone involved even gave the hero a new sobriquet: "The Man of Tomorrow." And while those comics were still in production, Charlie went to Harry Donenfeld and asked him for the capital to start his own publishing company, All American Comics.

By the beginning of 1939, the word was spreading through the printing and pulp business: There was money to be made in comics. Lev Gleason, once a salesman for Eastern Color Printing alongside Charlie Gaines, found an investor named Arthur Bernhardt and launched *Silver Streak* comics; it was named after the model of Pontiac Bernhardt owned. Lloyd Jacquet, that former partner and rival of the major's, organized his own packaging shop called Funnies, Incorporated. Everett "Busy" Arnold, a printer who had worked with Jacquet, announced he was now Quality Comics. Jacquet, meanwhile, connected with a pulp publisher and former employee of Hugo Gernsback named Martin Goodman; because one of Goodman's pulps was called *Marvel Science Stories,* they would end up calling their product *Marvel Comics.* One of Goodman's fellow Gernsback protégés, Louis Silberkleit, found a couple of partners and created MLJ Comics.

A gold rush was beginning, and it spawned gold rush legends. One story passed among creators for years, now presented as fact in nearly every history of comics, concerned a Detective Comics bookkeeper named Victor Fox who saw the sales figures for the first issue of *Action Comics,* closed his ledger, said he was going to lunch, rented an office in the same building, and that same afternoon announced that he was a comic book publisher. The story isn't true. Fox never worked for Detective Comics. He was probably never a bookkeeper. He was an English-born Jew who had come to America at the end of the world war and for twenty years hustled from one financial scam, racket, and dubious investment to another. How he heard about the comic book bonanza is unknown, but in late 1938 he appeared to the Eisner & Iger studio and said, "I want another Superman." The bookkeeper story was made up because it had to be: Things were happening so quickly, so many entrepreneurs coming from God knows where, that the field needed a story to symbolize its absurdity.

As it turned out, Victor Fox supplied plenty of real absurdity. Eisner and Iger pulled in all their artists and in less than a week cranked out the first issue of *Wonder Comics,* starring Wonder Man, a golden-haired muscleman in red tights with a yellow "W" on his chest. He might have worn blue, too, had Fox spent the money for four-color printing, but he wanted this on the cheap. The moment the issue saw print, Harry Donenfeld sued Fox for copyright infringement, but by then Fox had moved on to getting more hasty heroes into print: Yarko the Magnificent, the Flame, the Blue Beetle, the Green Mask. The cover of *Wonder Comics* promised "1000 Prizes Given Away Free," but apparently not one ever was. Later Fox promoted a product called Kooba Cola in his pages that may never have existed; his competitors said he wanted to see if he could line up enough advance orders before he ordered it bottled. He wanted the fastest, cheapest art he could get. The only real money he spent was on the covers—lurid, pulpy things that steadily displayed more and more female flesh, revealing that boys deeper into adolescence than Superman's readers were drawn to comics for their own reasons.

He was a tiny man with big cigars and a bald dome who'd pace by his artists as they worked, muttering, "I'm the king of comics! I'm the king of comics!" The artists snickered, but Fox was getting rich. No matter how bad the comics, sales kept rising. Soon he was publishing three hundred, then four hundred, pages a month. The comic book fad was becoming a craze, and in 1939 it seemed impossible to produce enough material to keep it fed.

IN LATE 1938, with a hit on his hands in Superman, Vin Sullivan started asking all his contributors to bring in ideas for costumed heroes. He particularly wanted one as a cover feature for *Detective Comics,* some sort of crime solver who would fit the theme but tap into the fantastical appeal of Superman. Among those he talked to was Bob Kane, who was now selling him two series a month but still looking for something to attract real attention. Sullivan told him about the *Superman* newspaper strip and said Siegel and Shuster could be making thousands of dollars a month soon. It was Friday. Kane said he'd be back with a new hero on Monday.

Kane and Finger told different versions of what happened next. Kane, in fact, told several versions himself, the earlier ones excluding Bill Finger entirely, the later ones, under pressure from fans who kept finding more evidence of Finger's involvement, acknowledging a small contribution from a friend. Kane would even go so far as to forge sketches that he supposedly drew in January 1934 "at the age of thirteen," showing a "bat-man," a "hawk-man," and an "eagle-man" inspired by Leonardo da Vinci's sketches of a winglike flying machine; so he tried to prove not only that Finger hadn't helped him but that he couldn't even have been inspired by the Birdmen in *Flash Gordon*, which he'd already cited as an influence in interviews. In one absurdly pat document, Kane lied about his age, stole Finger's credit, placed himself in the Renaissance tradition, and nicked a bit of glamour from the men who created Hawkman. Even for Bob this was a masterstroke of brazenness.

It's likely that Kane did first go off and work on ideas by himself. The only recent cover of *Action* featuring Superman was the seventh issue, which showed the smugly smiling hero leaping over a city street in apparent flight, towing a crook by his ankle. That billowing cape and exuberant sense of flight may have impressed itself on Kane as the feature to imitate. He dug into his *Flash Gordon* clippings, where he knew another red-caped hero could be found, and considered Alex Raymond's beautifully drawn Birdmen. He may have remembered da Vinci's artificial wings from art school or thought of the frame-and-canvas wings of early gliders. That night or the next day he got together with his friend Bill Finger and showed him what may have been the last thing created by Bob Kane alone: a red-garbed crime fighter with mechanical wings called "Bird-Man."

Finger didn't think it was good for a detective comic. He suggested they think more along the lines of the Shadow in the pulps: nocturnal, secretive, dark cloaked. How about "the Bat-Man"? Bats were a common pulp image: One of Harry Donenfeld's own pulps, in fact, had featured a villain called "Batman" and there were pulp crime fighters named "the Bat" and "the Black Bat." Kane and Finger worked out a spooky figure in gray and black, with a cape ribbed and scalloped, an eared cowl, and eyes appearing only as sharp white slits. Like Jerry Siegel and Joe Shuster, they'd both loved Douglas Fairbanks in *The Mark of Zorro* when they were young, and it showed in the design of the cowl. They put the outline of a bat on his chest in imitation of Superman's "S" and gave him a "utility belt" just like Doc Savage's. Like the Green Hornet and the Shadow of radio and the original Phantom of the newspapers, he was secretly a "bored young socialite." He had no known origin. He was simply "a mysterious and adventurous figure fighting for righteousness and apprehending the wrongdoer."

Kane took the sketches to Vin Sullivan on Monday morning, and Sullivan approved the strip as a monthly six-page feature. Kane, however, didn't settle for selling his pages outright as Siegel and Shuster and most other young cartoonists did. His father, who engraved comic strips for a living, knew something about the business of publishing, so he asked around and got his son some free legal advice. Kane would never talk about the deal he signed, but it apparently guaranteed him some security and control of the material. Considering that no one who knew him spoke well of Bob's intellect, he would show a remarkable canniness at cutting deals with his publisher over the years ahead.

Kane brought the good news to Bill Finger, without mentioning whatever long-term deal he'd signed, and Finger went to work for a piece of the page rate. He was an exacting and conscientious craftsman, and it shows in the tight efficiency of his story, so different from the hurtling action of a Siegel and Shuster plot. He began with a boilerplate mystery, added some rooftop action to keep the Bat-Man busy, and then tossed in a wonderfully absurd death trap: An evil lab assistant decides to kill a snooper by lowering a huge glass gas chamber on him from the ceiling. The Bat-Man leaps through the transom, grabs a wrench, slips into the descending chamber, plugs the gas jet with a handkerchief, and smashes his way out through the glass. As the Bat-Man explains the crime like a sleuth in a drawing room mystery, the villain goes for his gun. The Bat-Man belts him, sending him over a railing and into a conveniently placed open tank of acid—and then vanishes suddenly through a skylight. In a coda, Commissioner Gordon of the police relates all this to bored socialite Bruce Wayne. Bruce only simpers, "A very lovely fairy-tale, Commissioner, indeed." In the final panel, our mysterious hero emerges again, and the narrator tells us, "If the Commissioner could see his young friend now . . . he'd be amazed to learn that he is the 'Bat-Man'!"

From Finger's first script, *Bat-Man* was a perfect formula. The art was flat and stiff, and faces changed from panel to panel, as though Kane were swiping from different sources or someone else were touching up the art. But what Bob Kane did well was the most important thing: He made the figure of the Bat-Man fascinating. Although he showed no gift for cityscapes or interesting angles, he placed his hero repeatedly against a full moon, drew him in full silhouette for his dramatic entrances and exits, and made something truly spooky of his slit-eyed, tight-lipped stare. He worked on the action scenes too, swiping from the best of the fistfight artists, Milton Caniff and his ghosts on *Terry and the Pirates*.

What was lacking in Kane's pages was provided by the cover. Against a nocturnal skyline, the Bat-Man, a crook in his grasp, swoops through the air by a rope. The image is too elegant to have been executed by Kane. Perhaps Kane conceived the design, perhaps not; but whoever did so clearly understood the romance implicit in the Bat-Man. The hero swinging on a rope was a swashbuckling staple. A pulp cover had already shown the Shadow swinging over New York. But on this cover the hero floats against an empty sky, his rope stretching off the page to an imaginary point where no building can possibly stand. He is flying, symbolically, as surely as Superman is flying when he leaps over tall buildings, bursting free of the cage of reality, carrying us with him into superhuman fantasy. Although no rope swinging occurred in the first story, that image echoes in our minds as we read, shaping the scenes that we imagine between the panels.

No one ever took credit for the art in the second Bat-Man story, but the quickest glance shows that someone with a mastery of perspective far beyond Kane's drew the strip's first vertiginous rope-swinging shots, that someone with far more experience with the human figure drew that long, lithe Bat-Man in the fight scenes. Many artists hired assistants to fill in backgrounds and ink the pencil drawings, but Kane had brought someone in to draw his hero in the most crucial scenes. He knew the kind of art Bat-Man required and how far short his own abilities fell. Kane's vanity may have led him to deceive everyone else, but he never tried to fool himself.

With the third issue, we know who did the finished art: a seventeen-year-old named Jerry Robinson, just starting journalism school and not even thinking of being a professional artist. In early 1939 he showed up on the tennis court of a New Jersey resort wearing a jacket decorated with his own drawings. Bob Kane was there, too, and wanted to know who this talented cartoonist was; he'd just gotten Vin Sullivan to increase Batman's page length, and he needed help. Robinson found himself almost immediately inking an entire ten-page story over Kane's rough pencils. Suddenly *Bat-Man* looks like *Batman:* The rich ink lines turning every interior into a sculpture of shadows, Bruce Wayne's supercilious grin, the clouds scudding across the moon and the moonlight slanting across floors, the tilted camera angles, buildings pitching back against the hero as he climbs a sheer wall. Kane wanted the kid to keep his mouth shut and let him take the glory, but Robinson was too sharp and too talented to play that game. Soon enough, just as Kane had no doubt feared, the company was luring him away to work directly for them, creating *Batman* stories that Kane didn't profit from. From then on, Kane would hire less impressive and less headstrong ghosts.

That third issue also marked a change in the stories. Bill Finger was already behind on his deadlines, and Kane told Vin Sullivan he needed a script in a hurry. Vin commissioned one from a friend named Gardner Fox. From the first scene of Dr. Death and his turbaned assistant, Jabah, we know we have entered a realm of Victorian fantasy far removed from the usual pulp realism of crime comics. "The Batman" (no hyphen now) shows off his miraculous utility belt by whipping out suction cups and a gas pellet. Then, as if to bring us down sharply from the realm of dreams, Batman is shot. He bleeds and has to change back to Bruce Wayne and drive himself to a doctor. It was a Dick Tracy moment, and it established Batman instantly as the opposite number to Superman, whose favorite gimmick was letting bullets bounce off him. Then Fox found the perfect note of gruesome, almost self-mocking melodrama, as Dr. Death's lab explodes into flame in his climactic battle with Batman. "Ha! Ha! Oh—ha-ha-ha—you—you fool!" cackles the doctor from the flames. "You are the poor fool," says the Batman. "He has gone mad. Death . . . to Dr. Death."

Finger immediately incorporated Fox's florid touches into his own scripts and improved upon them. Jerry Robinson would commend Finger's "visual imagination"—high praise from an artist to a writer. Finger would take the younger kid to the Metropolitan Museum and to art movie theaters, where he exposed him to German Expressionist films. Within a few months it was becoming apparent that Robinson was taking over more of the design work from Kane and that Fritz Lang was on his mind. When Batman needed an archvillain for the first issue of his own comic book, Robinson supplied one: the Joker. When Finger felt Batman could use a sidekick to talk to, he and Robinson created Robin the Boy Wonder, talking Kane out of his idea for a myth-based kid called Mercury.

For decades fans and even other professionals thought Robinson was the one ghost Kane hired—until Sheldon Moldoff, Jim Mooney, and others began to come forward. Jerry Siegel and Joe Shuster formed a studio to do their work under their byline, but they talked openly about it and let everyone work in the same room and socialize with each other. It's what all the big cartoonists did: Al Capp, Ham Fisher, and Milton Caniff made fortunes, traveled the country getting their pictures in the paper, dated beautiful women, and were becoming notorious for giving all the tedious work to anonymous assistants. That was the life Kane wanted, but he would never admit that anyone but him was drawing his comics, even when they *were* being drawn by anyone but him. Kane never even told his ghost artists about each other. It kept the prices down.

Detective Comics number 27, starring the Batman, came out in the spring of 1939. It looked good on the stands, and dealers said kids liked it. Soon the stories were given more pages, and the hero's likeness was put on every cover. Kane and Finger began to sense that they were onto something. Now someone at DC signaled his seriousness about Batman's future by asking Kane to provide an origin story for him. Superman had demonstrated the power of a dramatic, traumatic episode that set the hero apart from the rest of humanity. The origin story that Finger wrote for Batman's sixth issue, was a twist on Superman's—the loss of parents and the vow to fight evil—but it was also a turning point in the development of the mass-market hero.

Thomas Wayne, his wife, and his son are walking home from a movie when a stickup man demands his wife's necklace. Thomas tries to defend her and is shot to death. His wife screams for the police, and the thug shoots her too. Little Bruce Wayne watches both his parents die. Days later, praying by his bedside, he says, "And I swear by the spirits of my parents to avenge their deaths by spending the rest of my life warring on all criminals." For fifteen years he trains himself to be a master scientist and athlete. But he needs a disguise. "Criminals are a superstitious and cowardly lot. So my disguise must be able to strike terror into their hearts. I must be a creature of the night, black, terrible . . . a . . . a . . . " "As if in answer a huge bat flies in the open window." "A bat! That's it! It's an omen. I shall become a *BAT!*"

The shooting of the father and the son's pain evoke the story of Jerry Siegel. But Jerry had never told anyone in comics about his father's violent death. He would never refer to it even when asked again and again what made him think of an invulnerable man who laughed at bullets and crushed the guns in thugs' hands. He and every other creator of superheroes, from the dime novels, to the pulps, to the comic strips and radio, had avoided psychology in favor of ethics and allegory, seeming to be content with the idea that a man would devote his life to fighting crime simply because his father had told him to or because he was so inherently good. Bill Finger was the first to bring a novelist's questions to bear on a superhero. Why would a man choose such a life? He found the answer in pain. Bill Finger the dark, boozing, overburdened young writer saw how the pain of loss could harden into a rage that made a man unlike other men. And perhaps Bill Finger the father could see a child's pain in a way his childless peers in the comics business couldn't.

And as the one real writer in the business, Finger could see the cores of stories instead of just the pieces they were made of. A Jerry Siegel might read *The Count of Monte Christo* and see sword fights. Bill Finger saw rage leashed by a vow of revenge. He transferred that to Batman and turned just another Superman knockoff into a character with a soul. Accidentally, he had shined a light on a hidden piece of Superman's own origin. He had found, through a storyteller's logic, the secret heart of the superhero.

IF ANYONE IN publishing missed the building comics craze in the first half of 1939, he would have been slapped in the face with it by the first issue of *Superman*. In three printings it sold 900,000 copies.

Will Eisner found himself producing comics for Fiction House, Victor Fox, and "Busy" Arnold all at once. He increased his staff to fifteen artists, still sent many of them off with extra work for nights and weekends, still bought pages from freelancers. He'd buy scripts from any artist or artist's wife who could turn them out. He'd buy pages from freelance artists and have his own staff cut up each page, paste the panels over two or three blank pages, and then extend the backgrounds to fill the space. Thus one page could be resold as three. The result was bad composition and a mess of line work that must have offended Eisner's visual sensibilities, but it fed the maw. And it paid. Jerry Iger and Will Eisner cleared $100,000 in profit in the first year of the boom. It was a staggering sum for a frayed promoter and a twenty-two-year-old cartoonist.

Another young man was watching the comic book from a little further way. Mort Weisinger was still the star editor of Ned Pines's pulp line. Pines was now getting into comics himself. Mort wasn't involved in Pines's comics, but he knew people who were: Jack Binder, whose brothers Otto and Earl were among his steadiest writers, was the art director for a comics shop producing material for Pines. It was a still a small community. In late 1939 Mort launched his own superhero pulp: *Captain Future*. The captain was a science fiction equivalent to Doc Savage, a cousin to Flash Gordon. But he had Superman in his blood, too, with his tight red and gold space suit and his remarkable feats. For his first few issues the covers called him "Wizard of Science," but within a few months that became "Man of Tomorrow." That byname had appeared in *Superman* months before.

Weisinger's regular writer on *Captain Future* was Edmond Hamilton. This was good news for Mort's erstwhile partner, Julie Schwartz. He was Hamilton's agent, and this meant a steady commission without having to sell new material. But it didn't bode well. The captain was a young boy's superhero, and the pulps were already losing that readership. Mort was a man of tomorrow himself. He knew that pulps were fading and comics were rising. With *Captain Future* as his calling card, Mort was going to get a job at Detective Comics. He was going to ride Superman and Batman to new heights.

Five Bronx boys: two artists, one writer, one agent, one editor. One was rich, one was about to be; one was being screwed, one was about to lose his livelihood; and one wanted to be the boss of them all. Wherever their lives went now, they had turned forever because of the odd man in the blue tights.

High Times

WHAT A GLORIOUS boozy dream they must have been, those years of Superman's rise. The Waldorf and Great Neck, the studio and the Heights, Fred Allen and Charles Atlas and Walter Winchell, mistresses and country clubs and high school girls with glowing eyes. And all because, in Harry Donenfeld's words, of "a fluke." "Pure luck," Jack Liebowitz called it. Neither pretended to have had the slightest knowledge of what they had in Superman. But when it came into their grasp, they seized it.

There had been other bountiful children's franchises, Mickey Mouse and Tarzan and the Lone Ranger, but none that had caught fire so quickly. In early 1939 Harry hired a press agent named Allen Ducovny, "Duke," who showed a genius for getting the hero written up in newspapers and magazines. Suddenly cameramen and reporters from the *Saturday Evening Post* were showing up at Joe Shuster's bedroom "studio" in Glenville. Ducovny then teamed up with one of Harry's favorite smoosh writers, Robert Joffe (who wrote as "Bob Maxwell"), to create sample episodes of a radio series. Together they typed out an opening that captured the exuberance of Siegel and Shuster's fantasy at its best: "Faster than an airplane, more powerful than a locomotive, impervious to bullets! Up in the sky, look! It's a bird! It's a plane! It's Superman!" Harry bankrolled a high-class production, including Agnes Moorehead as Superman's Kryptonian mother and one of the busiest actors in radio, Bud Collyer, as the hero. Collyer thought Superman was such a ridiculous character that he refused to do it at first, and Maxwell had to trick him into recording lines "just to help with the audition." Then Maxwell cut his lines into the demo recordings, lined up a small-time oatmeal maker as a sponsor, and told him, "You're Superman." Collyer sighed and went along for the ride.

All the networks rejected the samples, but Hecker Oats bought time on ten individual stations and put *The Adventures of Superman* on the air in February 1940. Ratings soared and eventually the Mutual Network and Kellogg's came on board. With the radio show driving it, the comic strip sold to nearly three hundred newspapers by 1941, and Duke Ducovny was claiming that 35 million people were following *Superman* in at least one medium. By then Harry was in negotiations with Republic Pictures for a matinee serial, but suddenly little Republic found itself being outbid by Paramount, one of the two giants of the business. Paramount paid Fleischer Studios to make a series of *Superman* cartoons, spending $50,000 on the pilot, quadruple the usual budget for an animated short. The result was the most stunning cartoon action ever on screen.

With Superman's fame came hundreds of thousands of dollars in licensing for toys, costumes, puzzles, Big Little Books, watches, and cereal. Harry formed a separate company—Superman, Incorporated—to handle it all, with Duke Ducovny in charge. Foreign sales were stupendous as Superman's simplicity made him an easy sell to Europe and Latin America. Sales of the comic books kept climbing, *Action Comics* at nearly a million per issue, *Superman* at half again as much. Advertising rates soared. Harry's comic book business brought in $2.6 million in the fiscal year that ended in 1941, and he was still publishing pulps and printing covers and had interests in paper and ink suppliers and the presses that printed his interior pages. And with Superman to get him in the door, he was expanding rapidly in distribution. Soon Independent News was carrying several other comics publishers, producing millions more comics every month—publishers that might have looked like competitors from the outside but were in fact another source of Harry's wealth.

Harry Donenfeld was suddenly rich, and off a racket that was not only legal but downright cute. Harry's friends started greeting him with "Hey, Superman!" Harry would strike the pose: "Up, up, and away!" All the drinkers at the Stork Club or El Morocco would look and laugh, and then the buzz would go around: "That's the guy who publishes Superman!" Winchell himself would nod and half smile: "Hiya, Superman." Harry took to wearing a Superman T-shirt under his shirt. He'd wait for the right moment—a spilled drink or a beautiful woman alone at the bar—then throw open the tuxedo jacket, jerk open the shirt (pearl studs flying), and yell (Yiddish rhythms pounding on the consonants, stretching the vowels), "This looks like a job for *Superman!*" Big laughs, more scotch all around.

In 1939 he and "Gea" celebrated their twentieth anniversary with a party for hundreds and a ten-foot-tall cake. A few months later he moved his mistress into a suite at the Waldorf-Astoria. That two-towered palace on Park Avenue was the pinnacle, the twin peaks of the hustler made big, the great tits of the bitch goddess of Manhattan herself. Everything about her, from her gold-lettered facade to her mile-wide lobby to the naked bodies in the mosaics on her floors and the spindly limbs of her Empire divans, spelled the Class of all Class to every gambler and peddler who'd shot from the gutter to the top. It was at the Waldorf that Johnny Torrio had run the legendary meeting at the end of Prohibition that carved up the nation's rackets into the "crime syndicate." It was at the Waldorf that Lucky Luciano kept his love nest and entertained the high-dollar hookers who finally sent him to the can. It was at the Waldorf that Frank Costello himself now ruled. He kept his wife and family on Central Park West, his mistress in a suite at the top of the Waldorf, and every morning he would travel from one or the other to the flashing gilt of the Waldorf barber shop to get his shave and manicure and to take his first meetings. And if unfriendly cops or reporters came sniffing around, the entire hotel staff—bellmen, switchboard operators, house detectives—knew how to spread the word and keep their most valued guests from being bothered.

Now Harry put Sunny in a room there. Now Harry could saunter through the lobby, take the greetings from the staff, joke with the big shots, drop in to the barber shop to toss a wave at Costello or talk boxing or horses with whatever boosters or punks wanted to hang around. It was like being on the corner in the neighborhood again, part of the gang, but this was the corner of all corners, the gang of all gangs. This was Superman's gang.

Harry continued traveling to meet with his regional distributors and buyers, but now he traveled by Pullman, springing for a few cronies to come along and drink and play gin rummy from city to city, coast to coast. One was a disbarred lawyer with a shady past named Ben Sangor; he was also the father-in-law of Ned Pines, the publisher, and got into the comics-packaging business to supply Pines with material. After enough drink and gin playing, Harry set Sangor up in his own publishing company, the American Comics Group. Harry liked to do favors.

He would stay at the best hotels in every city. One of his favorites was the Ambassador in LA, where he could drink under the fake palms in the Cocoanut Grove with a famous gambling buddy or two, maybe Eddie Cantor or the Ritz Brothers, and wait for movie stars and directors to be shown to his table for a quick handshake and a photo and a few "Look, up in the sky" gags. Then there was the Wofford in Miami, where Costello and Meyer Lansky ran their high-class, cop-protected casino. Harry was always welcome there because his bets would increase as the comics' sales rose and the scotch went down. Sometimes Harry brought Frank Moschello, his chauffeur, to Miami to drive him around. Maybe sometimes they cruised by the Deauville Hotel, the resort Bernarr MacFadden had built when he was the king of the cheap magazines. Now it was in the courts' hands, as the Depression savaged the MacFadden empire and the great bodybuilder was kicked out of his own company and sued by his stockholders for financial malfeasance. Harry Donenfeld had outlasted the king of pulp.

The Fleischer brothers' new cartoon studios were in Miami, too, and during 1941 Harry would visit there to see how the cartoons were coming. The Fleischers were tough New York kids of Harry's vintage and he liked them, more than he ever could have liked Disney or most of his imitators in Hollywood. That August, when the first *Superman* cartoon was ready for its first full screening, Harry heard that his old friend David Dubinsky of the International Ladies Garment Workers Union was in town for a labor conference. Harry tracked him down. "Dubinsky," he said, "you gotta see something. It's a movie cartoon of my Superman." These were high times for Dubinsky too. In nine years as president he had led his union through a tremendous expansion, become the toughest anti-communist in the labor movement, and made himself a major force in the American Federation of Labor. He had Roosevelt's ear, and he didn't give him hotfoots. But he went with Harry and watched the cartoon, those seven minutes of nonstop action and swinging camera angles and stylized figures zooming across a world of looming menace.

When the lights came on, Harry was glowing. "So what do you think, Dubinsky?" he crowed. "Ah," growled Dubinsky with a fat-handed wave. "It's got no social significance!" Two little scrappers at the top of the heap, playing their roles.

Then there was Cuba. A ninety-mile cruise through the warm night, booze and open gambling all the way across, then the glittering harbor and the Hotel Nacional, where Lansky and Costello had built the most modern casino in the world, from which Lansky forged his alliance with Fulgencio Batista and made Havana a subsidiary of the New York mob. Harry seems to have invested in some of Costello's developments there and gotten involved in some sort of Spanish publishing for the boxing and horse-racing communities. Sometimes with a crony or two, he would go to Cuba to do business, gamble, and make time with the most beautiful whores in the world. Sometimes he'd bring Sunny and hit the open dance halls by the beach, the rumba bands and conga lines. Harry was never a great dancer, but he liked being on the floor, and when he was drunk enough, he made it entertaining.

The impossible suddenness of the money must have seemed even less real in that apocalyptic moment. As Superman soared, England rolled over before Hitler in Czechoslovakia, and Hitler answered with the cruel laugh of *Kristallnacht*. Then Stalin joined him to slice Poland open at the belly, and the British and French declared war and did nothing for a long winter until the Germans swept like a storm through

Holland, Belgium, and France. One month and Western Europe was gone. Then the air war in England, the dispatches over the radio night after night all through the summer, Edward R. Murrow hollering from the rooftops over the sounds of bombs in every living room in America. And still Americans were afraid to fight, or afraid to admit that they knew they would have to. Roosevelt shot a lightning bolt through American politics by running for a third term, and everyone knew it was partly to get America into that war, but still he had to campaign as a peace president. Most Jews were thrilled. Retrospection asks whether Roosevelt did enough as the Holocaust began, but no world leader had ever gone to war for the Jews, not even indirectly. No leader had ever before made the Jews feel like such a part of a nation, such a part of a global cause. Just twenty years before, the United States had fought the Bolsheviks on behalf of the hated czar. Maybe this was the strangest thing of all: that the Jews were eager for battle, the Jews who had never trusted governments or militaries and had always tried to keep their sons away from the front were rooting for Roosevelt to get us over there and spit in Hitler's eye.

Plus, for Harry, there were foreign markets to be lost. Hitler had already denounced Superman as a Jew and banned him, and Mussolini had followed suit. Now all of Europe was falling. If the Nazis kept winning, would the Superman bubble pop, would this all turn out to be just the last good hand at the start of a long, hard night at the tables?

Harry was drinking more than ever. Not just beer but beer with a shot of scotch. Maybe it was the giddiness of the moment or just knowing that he could get away with it, that all he had to be now was a fun guy to do business with and the money would keep pouring in. But he could also turn terribly melancholy and sentimental, and rumors cropped up of his anger, of him belting someone in a bar, of a woman threatening to sue him for getting her drunk and taking advantage of her. He'd come into Detective Comics' offices loaded. He'd grab secretaries' breasts and walk off laughing. Jack Liebowitz was writing checks, said the rumors, to buy people's silence and paying Frank Moschello to keep an eye on him and steer him away from trouble.

Irwin Donenfeld turned thirteen in 1939 and was trying to understand the life his father lived all those days and nights away from the house. He was working after school at Independent News, getting gruff business lessons from Jack Liebowitz, and keeping his ears open. He thought his father wanted to leave his wife for Sunny, but Gussie was determined to fight. The "Dragon Lady" could endure the existence of a mistress, but she would not go through a public abandonment graciously, and she would not relinquish her shares in the Harry Donenfeld empire without a fight. Business associates thought it was Jack Liebowitz who kept talking Harry out of going through with it. Harry would tell Jack he had to be with Sunny, he'd yell and swear and sob about what a witch Gussie was and how much in love he was with Sunny, but Jack didn't want to hear it. This was a company issue. He didn't want a vengeful Gussie Weinstein Donenfeld as a shareholder. So he'd let Harry yell himself out, and then he'd bark at him not to be a stupid prick. Just take care of Sunny and let Gea keep the title.

It may be that Sunny was pressuring Harry, too, either to leave his wife or give her more that she could count on if things went bad in the future. Harry began seeing more women during those years, not just hookers, not just secretaries who'd let him *shtup* them on a desk, but contenders. "He had a wife and a mistress," Irwin would say, "and he was cheating on both of them." It may be that Harry was just taking what the money and fame made possible. Or it may be that he was trying to escape. What other pressures were on Harry? Michael Feldman, who pieced together so much about the contraband distribution industries that Harry was involved in, asked, "What made Harry run?" Harry had been enmeshed with some of the toughest racketeers in the country for a long time. Those men were never content just to have their loans paid back. When someone in their circle struck gold, they wanted a piece. "Harry was suddenly the Godfather of a new racket," said Feldman. "Along with its legit revenues, the volume of product and cash opened up new opportunities for many of the standby residual benefits—money laundering, cash skimming, smuggling from Canada. In his own company, Harry might have been the boss. But he would have found himself with a lot of new silent partners to answer to."

While Harry unfurled with the winds, Jack Liebowitz held the rudder. His gambling was of a different sort: He played the stock market, played it with aggression, diligence, and research. He was also a publisher now himself. When Charlie Gaines had asked Harry for distribution and financing to start his own publishing company, Harry had agreed on one condition: that he take Jack Liebowitz as his partner. Then Harry gave the money to Jack for his share. It wasn't a loan; it was a gift. In part that was no doubt a payoff for Liebowitz's heroic services to the company during its hardest years, when he had nothing to gain but a salary. But Harry must also have known that Jack would be tempted to leave and form a competing company if there was nothing to hold him. And it may well have been a way for Harry to keep Gaines under control; since Jack was still drawing a salary and significant bonuses from Detective Comics and Independent News, he wouldn't let Gaines take off on his own or act against the interests of the other companies. In any case, at the end of 1938, Charlie Gaines became the principal and Jack Liebowitz the minority owner of All American Comics. Soon All American was bringing out Flash, Green Lantern, Hawkman, and other profitable superheroes.

Liebowitz was mostly content to let Gaines and his young editor Sheldon Mayer run All American, but he applied a firmer hand to Detective's "DC" line. New magazines were being added and more pages given to Superman, Batman, and a flurry of new costumed heroes. He agreed with Harry that the acquisition of Superman was luck, but he didn't see this as just another racket to suck dry and discard. He saw something that could be built and sustained here, a kind of entertainment that kids liked better than pulps and would continue to if given reason to keep coming back.

In 1940 Liebowitz found himself in a position to build a new editorial staff. Vin Sullivan had been hired away by a new publisher who hoped that his editorial magic was the key to Superman's success. No one yet knew, after all, what made a comic book successful; Will Eisner once found himself in the DC elevator with Harry Donenfeld, who announced loudly, "If a title's not selling, I just fire the editor and get a new one—that's how this business works!" In hiring Whitney Ellsworth, a thirty-one-year-old newspaper cartoonist and former associate of Major Malcolm Wheeler-Nicholson, Liebowitz chose polish, experience, and a gentlemanly style over the young adventurousness of a Shelly Mayer.

Liebowitz and Ellsworth sat down immediately to develop a code of acceptable behavior for superheroes, the first of its kind. The censorship that had killed the girlie pulps and hurt the Spicies was barely a year in the past, and Liebowitz knew that as soon as the protectors of public decency realized Harry Donenfeld was responsible for Superman, they'd be going over the pages with a magnifying glass. Harry might enjoy baiting censors, but that didn't fit the Liebowitz plan for building a children's entertainment empire. In one early episode Superman had torn the wings off the bad guys' plane and let it crash in a fireball. Batman, for his part, had jumped in a fighter plane and machine-gunned a Kong-like monster. Liebowitz and Ellsworth decreed that no DC hero would ever knowingly kill anyone again.

Liebowitz also kept Superman out of the war in Europe. Smaller companies were sending patriotic heroes out against Hitler look-alikes by early 1940, and plenty of writers and artists, Siegel and Shuster among them, were eager to pit DC's heroes against Germanic madmen. Siegel got away with it in a series he wrote for Shelly Mayer at All American, *Red, White, and Blue,* about a trio of American military men with no costumes or superpowers (although even there he was apparently told to make the stories less political after a few months). Liebowitz, however, didn't allow Superman to take even an implicit stance on the subjects of war and fascism. Too many isolationists out there had the power to keep their kids from buying comics. So Jack Liebowitz found himself in the same straitened position as the Hollywood moguls who had ignored their writers' and directors' pleas to make anti-Nazi movies out of fear it would lose them the German and Italian markets. Accountancy breeds complicity.

He was ferocious within the industry, though. As Superman imitations poured from cheap printing presses in 1939 and 1940, it became almost habitual for the company to toss around lawsuits and threatening letters. Most of these were quietly settled or ignored, but when Fawcett

Publishing scored a huge hit with its caped, red-tighted, gold-emblemed Captain Marvel, Liebowitz bore down like a bulldog. He would accept no settlements or compromises, and when the court case first went against DC, he demanded an appeal. He hired Louis Nizer, already making his reputation as a brilliant copyright lawyer and courtroom orator. Liebowitz assigned one editor, Jack Schiff, to work nearly full-time poring over *Superman* and *Captain Marvel* comics to help Nizer prepare his case.

Captain Marvel's success—his comics were soon outselling Superman's—was no doubt much of the reason for Jack's particular ferocity in this one case. But perhaps the nature of Fawcett had something to do with it, too. The Fawcetts were Minnesota Protestants, and they favored comics stories of a neat, passionless charm such as Midwestern Germans and New York WASPs—Otto Binder, C. C. Beck, Bill Woolfolk, Kurt Schaffenberger—produced best. The Marvel Family's adventures had the quality of a parody too, that slightly smarmy tone of adults playing a children's game and winking at each other over the wee ones' heads, as if the customers weren't little Timmy and Joan but their Aunt Trudy from Muncie buying the comics she thought they should like. The other publishers had mostly come up through the stink of the printing presses and the New York rackets. Those guys had territorial rights. The Fawcetts were poaching. (But DC was not above stealing back from Fawcett: Captain Marvel was flying when Superman was still jumping like a flea.)

Liebowitz was known in the office for his straight-backed, word-biting toughness. He didn't yell much, but his tone allowed no argument. He was only forty years old, younger than Harry Donenfeld or Charlie Gaines, just eight years older than Whitney Ellsworth, but he was mastering the manner of a patriarch when he'd bark through his intercom or give orders from behind the big desk in his dark office without looking up from the typewritten reports in front of him. "I only heard him make one joke in his entire life," said Irwin Donenfeld. "One day I looked at his ankles, and I said, 'Uncle Jack, you're wearing one black sock and one brown sock.' He looked down at them for a second, and then he said, 'And I've got another pair just like it at home.'" Irwin laughed at the memory. One soft moment from a man who never softened deserved a laugh.

He was always "Uncle Jack" to Irwin, even when Irwin himself was forty years old and the number-two man in the company. Harry made sure Irwin always had a part-time job at the company and knew he would have an executive position waiting as soon as he finished college, but beyond that he didn't guide him much. When Irwin was about to go off to Bates College, he asked his father, "What should I major in?" and Harry said, "Whatever you want! They don't teach comic books in college!" It was Liebowitz who would take Irwin into his office and tell him how things worked. It was also he who drafted Irwin into the company's nightly ritual when he was old enough. "I'd hear a gruff voice over the intercom around five o'clock," Irwin said. "'Come into my office!' I'd go in, and there was Uncle Jack, and Paul Sampliner, and Paul Chamberlin and Jack Adams with Independent, and they'd be playing gin rummy. Every night they had to play gin. And they were tough games, too. No playing around." Every New York businessman was playing gin in those years, but it was an especially perfect game for Jack Liebowitz, with its mathematical complexity, its quick tallying, its harnessing of chance with lean rationality.

Apart from work, stocks, and gin rummy, Jack lived to take care of his wife and daughters. As soon as he could afford it, he took them to the north shore of Long Island, to a manor house in the village of Kensington in Great Neck. This was a dream home, in a town blessed, in the words of a promotional book from 1936, by

> golf courses, yacht clubs, tennis courts and polo fields practically in our back yards . . . a community made up entirely of incorporated villages, each wisely and properly governed by owner resident officials who make sure that nothing can be built that is not architecturally right or that does not conform to restrictions set down, maintained, defended and protected by every resident; a community made up of residents who have come from all over the world because they were successful and could afford the good things to be had and were smart enough to know good things when they saw them—professional men, merchants, manufacturers, artists, bankers

and a variety of others and their wives and families, all big minded and intelligent—in other words the best of good neighbors.

"Big minded." "From all over the world." Code words meaning that immigrants and Jews were welcome if they had the right standards and the right income. Great Neck was an expanse of forested colonial estates carved into suburbs for the nouveau riche, but this suburb, unlike so many "exclusive communities," was marketed to the new money from Manhattan. It had been the basis for West Egg in *The Great Gatsby,* from which Jay motored to meet the dark-joweled gangster, Meyer Wolfsheim, in Manhattan. Now the young sharpies who would have looked up to Meyer Wolfsheim were middle-aged and moving to Great Neck. They supported the local symphony and the Jewish Community Fund and motored to the synagogue on Old Mill Road.

Kensington had been named after the gardens in London, its entrance secured by replicas of the original's flamboyant Victorian gates, and it had immediately attracted a cosmopolitan Broadway population. Flo Ziegfeld lived there, and his beautiful wife, Billie Burke, was a prominent hostess for Rose Liebowitz to woo and emulate. Shy little Rose of the Lower East Side was now the lady of a grand house, hosting luncheons and teas and fund-raisers for the Anti-Defamation League and refugees from Europe. Moe Annenberg and his son Walter, who'd turned *Racing Form* money into a publishing empire, had houses there, too. The Liebowitzes joined country clubs and attended cocktail parties given by bankers and business leaders, Jack stiff in his black tuxedo and Thomas Dewey mustache, Rose in flowered dresses as expensively frumpy as any on a DAR matron. Their daughters, Joan and Linda, swam at the country club, boated in the harbor, and prepared to live the lives of prep school girls.

Jack worked hard to make himself and his new industry respectable. But all the work must have seemed in vain in May 1940, when Sterling North, the literary editor of the *Chicago Daily News,* wrote a column entitled "A National Disgrace." "The effect of these pulp-paper nightmares is that of a violent stimulant. Their crude blacks and reds spoil a child's natural sense of color; their hypodermic injection of sex and murder make the child impatient with better, though quieter, stories. Unless we want a coming generation even more ferocious than the present one, parents and teachers throughout America must band together to break the 'comic' magazine." The comics were "guilty of a cultural slaughter of the innocent." The column was picked up by newspapers all over America and immediately spawned dozens of similar columns and even hard news stories on this alarming childhood craze.

As is nearly always the case when entertainment sparks widespread fears, generations, regions, ethnic groups, and cultures were in collision. Sterling North came from a world far from Jerry Siegel and Joe Shuster's, not in miles but in culture. He was born in a farmhouse in the Wisconsin woods the son of an amateur historian and grew up fishing and hiking in the endless forest and raising raccoons in his yard. When he was twelve years old, he was crippled by polio and spent his adolescence fighting to learn to walk again. Trailless hikes and ice-skating on frozen lakes were lost to him forever. He moved to Chicago as a young man to be a journalist—the Chicago of Ben Hecht and the Capone gang—and became a hard-drinking, hard-arguing, two-fisted barroom intellectual, physically bent but verbally as straight as a spear. But always in his mind was a lost childhood that he saw as a lost America, when boys stood straight and made their own amusements and settled matters honorably with fistfights under the trees. Years later he would distill that last shining year of his childhood into a delicately heartbreaking novel called *Rascal: A Memoir of a Better Era*. In subsequent editions the publisher would drop the subtitle and market it as a children's book about a boy and his raccoon, but to North it was a portrait of an ideal America, one that many people born before the world war wanted to remember as their own.

So when Sterling North saw newsstands splattered with the underdressed women of Lou Fine's covers and the eyeless stare of Batman and the flying metal of a speeding locomotive smashed by Superman, he didn't see any youthful dreams he recognized but only violent stimulation in crude color. He didn't see any aesthetic that an early-century children's culture in Wisconsin would have produced or a book critic would have understood. He saw, as people who are already certain the world is going to hell always see, another sign that children were being pulled further away from him and into barbarism. Time would not bear him out: The generation that grew up on superhero comics was far less prone to crime than the generation before it, for reasons that had everything to do with prosperity, national unity, and ethnic assimilation and nothing to do with what it read. But what he said struck a deep chord. Confronted in that apocalyptic moment with an alien entertainment form that had come from nowhere to infiltrate the taste of seemingly every child in America, adults reacted with a collective gasp. Even George Orwell, across the Atlantic, expressed dread. He saw Superman as "bully worship," an American version of the same craving for a strongman that had raised Hitler and Mussolini to power.

The sheer numbers of comic books consumed was a shock to most adults. Fifteen million were sold a month, and market studies found that each one was read by four or five kids. Ninety percent of fourth- and fifth-graders described themselves as "regular readers" of comic books. No books or magazines had ever come close to such numbers, and it's doubtful that even radio or the movies could have equaled it. What had been a small corner of the junk culture industry in the summer of 1938, of far less concern than pulps or books or even children's story magazines, had become, in two years, the greatest single unifying element of American childhood. In a time when the whole world could turn upside down in the space of months, it was easy to imagine that someone was stealing the children.

Publishers reacted to the outcry according to their own backgrounds and goals. Dell had initiated a line of comics based on Disney characters and movie personalities, but it carefully avoided superheroes; the decisions on what to publish were mostly in the hands of George Delacorte's editorial right hand, a young editor named Helen Meyer, whose heart was in books, not comics. Fawcett emphasized the innocent humor of their comics all the more. Victor Fox damned the newspaper columns, if he ever bothered to read them, and cranked up the sleaze.

But Jack Liebowitz launched an immediate counterstrike. He called on his staff and partners to help him find accredited experts who would speak well of comics. He hired them for an "Editorial Advisory Board," printed their names and credentials in the comics, and quoted them in press releases. One, a gestalt psychiatrist from Bellevue Hospital named Lauretta Bender, said that superhero stories "would seem to offer the same type of catharsis which Aristotle claimed was an attribute of the drama." Another, Josette Frank, the children's book expert at the progressive Child Study Association, compared Superman to Paul Bunyan and John Henry. And the "consulting psychologist" for *Family Circle* magazine, a loose-cannon theorist with an eye for publicity named William Moulton Marston, said comics "speak to the innermost ears of the wishful self," to "the tender spots of universal human desires and aspirations."

Public criticism settled around the more lurid comics from then on and generally left DC and All American's superheroes alone. Jack Liebowitz had turned a band of masked vigilantes and grandstanding strongmen into solid citizens and models for youth. The sort of neighbors you'd be pleased to have in Great Neck.

THOSE WERE HIGH times for Jerry Siegel and Joe Shuster too, at least compared to what they'd known. They'd signed a ten-year exclusive deal to produce Superman pages for the comic books, and with *Action* and *Superman* being joined by *World's Fair Comics,* that was a lot of pages, often over fifty a month. They were soon producing not just a daily but a color Sunday comic strip as well, with a generous cut. Even after they rented a real studio and hired four full-time artists to keep up with the load, they were still making more money than any other twenty-five-year-olds they knew and were looking forward to a lot more.

From the beginning, however, Jerry was haunted by the fear that he was going to be screwed out of what he deserved. Just a few months after Superman's first appearance, when Jerry returned from the New York trip on which the newspaper syndicate deal was set up, he wrote to Jack Liebowitz demanding a page-rate increase from $10 to $15. We don't know what Jerry wrote, but we do know Jack's reaction:

> Frankly, when I got through reading [your letter], it took my breath
> away. . . . The amount of increase you demand does not hurt me as
> much as your attitude in the entire matter. . . . Is it possible that be-
> cause we treated you like a *human being*—you suddenly got a swell
> head? . . . Don't get the idea that everyone in New York is a '*gyp*' and
> a *highbinder* and because you are treated as a gentleman and an *equal*
> not only by ourselves but by Mr. Gaines and the McClure people, that
> *we are seeking to take advantage of you . . . so come off your high horse.*

Even given Jack's tactic of shouting down opponents in negotiations, a real outrage rings clear. Jerry's way, since his father's death, had
been to show no unhappiness in public but to nurse feelings of betrayal
and violated entitlement in private. This was not the last time those feelings would burst out through his typewriter. Jack gave Jerry his raise,
but the two parties would be wary of one another forever after.

Joe didn't involve himself in any of the arguments about money and
rights, leaving the real world to Jerry. Unfortunately, that world wasn't
Jerry's domain, either. As the battles heated up, Vin Sullivan quietly gave
Jerry the name of a lawyer friend and suggested he give him a call. "I
don't need a lawyer," said Jerry. Family members in Cleveland suggested
the same and got the same response. Jerry had been playing the deal
maker and businessman since high school, and he wasn't going to give
it up. The deal he and Joe signed with DC promised them "a percentage
of net profits accruing from the exploitation of Superman in channels
other than magazines." But the terms were dangerously ill defined.

The disputes subsided in 1939, as Superman's star rose and new opportunities came one after another. Jerry and Joe were too excited to
fight—for a while.

Their work was changing, both for better and worse. The newspaper
strip was their slickest product, with their best assistants contributing their
most polished draftsmanship and Whitney Ellsworth editing it carefully;
but the unpredictability of the early Superman was giving way to formu-
lae. The comic books suffered visually—especially the quarterly *Superman*,
with its sixty-four pages of original stories—as assistants and fill-in artists

were often drawing against the clock, cutting corners, passing panels off to other hands. At the same time, Superman and his world were growing in interesting ways. Jerry and Joe began working characters created by the radio show's writers—blustering Perry White, bumbling Jimmy Olsen—into the comics, organizing a repertory company of likable foils. Lois began her obsessive pursuit of Superman's true identity. X-ray vision, superhearing, and flight were added to his powers, and his strength increased until he was less a caricature of a strongman than a minor deity. As he became more powerful, Jerry and Joe gave him an archvillain, like those the best heroes of the pulps had: a mad scientist named Lex Luthor.

It's startling to see how little fantasy those two science fiction fans brought into the first two years of Superman's adventures. To them a superhuman character was interesting to the extent that he could shake things up in the world we knew. By 1940, though, the excitement of success seemed to dare them to send their fantasies flying further from the earth. The Man of Tomorrow would still go after gangsters and even show up petty bullies, but now he was also meeting science fictional menaces worthy of his powers. Instead of an expression of what a ninety-seven-pound weakling wished he could do, the comic book superhero was becoming a metaphor of release, transformation, and revealed truth. William Slater Brown, one intellectual critic who knew how to read the symbols of fantasy instead of taking it literally, wrote in 1940 that Superman, "besides affording entertainment for the romantic young, seems also to fill some symptomatic desire for a primitive religion."

Jerry and Joe had found their alchemical story formula: Clark Kent playing at cartoony mundanity, then bursting free into hallucinatory grandeur before cloaking himself at the end and winking knowingly to the reader. It was an allegory that echoed for immigrants and Jews: the strange visitor who hides his alien identity so as to be accepted by a homogeneous culture. But it was a more essential symbol too, the acknowledgment that although we may conceal ourselves for others, the uniqueness we keep locked in our hearts is our true power and glory.

Despite the speed and volume, despite the many hands on the art and the many people Jerry hired to help with story ideas and finishing scripts, the creators' personal investment in Superman still shone in the early years. Just as much as Jack Liebowitz, they began to take Superman seriously as a model for children and a force for fairness in the world. Their hero was no longer battling lynch mobs or wife beaters; now he took the time to help young weaklings stand up against bullies, to lead poor boys back from gangdom to their mother's tables, to teach snotty urchins a lesson or two and send them on their way as humbler citizens. Theirs wasn't a coherent political statement, but it was a New Deal Hollywood portrayal of a world where innocent people are hurt by greed and callousness and we could all use a primary-colored conscience to zoom in and knock us to our senses.

Jerry Siegel's confidence and energy soared in that moment. Even as more and more Superman work came his way, he kept taking on new projects. Joe didn't have that luxury, as he never had as much time to do his own artwork as he wanted and had to give up every series but *Superman*. But Jerry produced his scripts quickly, especially now with the help of the studio, and he kept trying to make lightning strike again, this time with another artist. There was *Red, White, and Blue* for Shelly Mayer and Charlie Gaines, his last project before superheroes became the only game in town. Then *The Spectre* in late 1939; a year later *The Star Spangled Kid*, his effort at the new vogue for patriotic superheroes; and then a humorous science fiction spin on heroics in *Robotman*.

The Spectre shows the jump in Jerry's confidence best of all. He cocreated it with a daring and atmospheric artist named Bernard Baily, who pushed him to stretch into new realms. Even more than Superman, this was an idea with no category or antecedents to open its way—the story of a man who is murdered by gangsters and then sent back by God to fight crime with magical powers. It may have been mainly Baily who drove the dream logic of the stories: The Spectre walked through walls and time and parallel universes, turned men's heads invisible to "read your knowledge in the thought impressions on your brain," grew so huge that he could stand in outer space and hurl stars like stones. But the anger that pours out in the smaller moments, not diverted into formula or goofiness this time, looks like Jerry Siegel's. The Spectre's very gaze can kill. In his first story he stares into the eyes of a murderer with white, pupilless hate, and the man dies in terror. Then he turns another into a living skeleton. "Don't leave me this way!" pleads his fleshless victim. Our hero holds up a pitiless hand: "You've robbed—you've killed—and this is your reward!" Under the new DC superhero code, Jerry was asked to pull his punches, but still there were moments. Once, the Spectre grows huge and crushes a getaway car with his foot. We don't see anyone die, but we feel it. The Spectre was also given a central tragedy that no other Siegel character was: He had just become engaged on the night he was murdered, and the loss of his dream fueled his hate.

With fame and money and a triumph in his chosen field, a new Jerry Siegel was emerging. But the old Jerry Siegel did not stop writhing around within him. No comics creator who'd reached his heights went on grinding out comic book material for a page rate. No doubt Jerry hoped one of his new creations would take off, but surely he couldn't have imagined that anything at once as fantastical and as gruesome as the Spectre could have the universal appeal of a Superman. He never tried to parlay his reputation into better writing opportunities, never asked to write a script for the *Superman* radio show, never tried to create a bidding war for his services with DC's rivals, and waited years before trying to sell another newspaper comic strip. He didn't even demand to work with the best artists in the field, but settled for who was available. When his creation took the Donenfeld comics business from anonymous mediocrity to fame and riches in a heartbeat, he took a page-rate increase of 50 percent. He had made it to his years-long goal, writing a national newspaper comic strip, and he seemed content to use it just to pick up a few new assignments from the same old boss, as if he could not imagine himself outside the pulp mills, as if he were afraid to make the jump that might make himself truly different from what he had been.

Whatever fears and self-doubts were hinted at in his professional decisions came clear with the girl across the street. He would watch her from his attic window on Kimberly Avenue as she walked home from Glen Hi, sometimes gabbing with friends but more often alone, books pressed to her breasts and black hair pulled back with a comb, until she vanished into her house with a swirl of skirt. Bella was small and shy and pretty in that way of girls who don't believe they're pretty. Her family always seemed to be in tight straits, and sometimes at night her voice could be heard arguing shrilly with her mother.

Bella was fifteen when the awkward, pudgy twenty-two year old who lived with his mother across the street first asked her out. She went out with him a few times, though he wasn't a great prospect: He had to fish bottles out of garbage cans to pay for their dates. She didn't know what to make of it when he began selling stories to comic books. But suddenly he was asking her, "Say, do your folks take the *Plain Dealer?*" Telling her with a grin that his comic strip was in there every day, then telling her about Superman's write-ups in the newspapers, his ten-year contract, his studio, his coming visit to the New York World's Fair as a guest of his publisher, the plans for a radio show based on his idea. Now when he asked her out, she learned what it was like not to be walked to Solomon's Deli but to be driven in a new car to the grand ballrooms on the lake.

Jerry's mother began to ask him why he was spending so much time with that little girl. Jerry said she was a nice girl and he liked her. Sarah said he could do much better. She was too young, her house was slovenly, and everyone knew the family was lazy. Jerry would stomp up the stairs and slam the door. Sarah would retell these arguments to her sisters, even in the presence of his cousins, waiting for everyone to nod and agree that Jerry could do much better, especially now that he was a success. If Sarah had other girls in mind who were right for her boy, she didn't talk about them. To his cousins' eyes she seemed happy to have him where he was; but now that she was finally able to brag about him, now that he was finally able to buy her nice things, he was leaving her alone in the house more and more, spending his money on a schoolgirl who'd given him nothing. She began to say, "I'll die if he marries that girl." Sarah Siegel did not say such things lightly.

Jerry began to see Bella every night. What he said to her we don't know. Maybe he talked about his years of rejection and determination, maybe his big plans for Superman. Maybe he got to play the go-getter with her, the idea man and boss of the studio, the one who called the shots for Joe and the rest of them. Maybe she gazed big-eyed and nodded or reached through his frantic energy and awkwardness to calm him down with her touch. There's a scene in the first *Spectre* story, a cliché moment but an interesting one from a man who almost never wrote a romantic scene, scripted in the summer of 1939 soon after the consummation of his romance with Bella. "Why a real lady like you should be interested in a mug like me is beyond me," the hero says. "But one thing is certain: There's going to be one boss in our family and that's *me*." With that the lady kisses him, and they're engaged. There are many power fantasies a young man can write into a comic book.

By the spring of 1939, the first issue of *Superman* was on the stands, the comic strip was picking up new papers every week, and Charlie Gaines was telling Jerry and Joe that, no doubt about it, they had a hit on their hands. One night Jerry came to Bella's house, talked nervously for a while about his new success, and then fumbled in his pocket for the box. Bella opened it to find a ring with a bigger diamond than she'd ever seen.

In the screaming that followed, all the older people and all the women in the Siegel and Fine families took Sarah's side. Jerry's brothers and male cousins said Jerry should be able to marry whomever he wanted, and there were some cracks about the miracle that any girl would marry him, but they kept their heads down. Jerry's aunts cornered him one by one and told him what a terrible mistake he was making. This girl was too young. She was eighteen now, Jerry said. She didn't know how to cook or run a household. Jerry didn't want a cook; he wanted a companion. It would kill his mother if he married this girl. His mother, Jerry said, would learn to love her as he did.

They were married in June, a week after Bella's high school graduation. Sarah wept and raged for days. Jerry had taken an apartment not far from home, but when Sarah refused to set foot in any house kept by "that girl," he'd had enough. He announced that he and Bella were moving to New York. For many members of his family that was the last they would see of Jerry for years. Even when he returned to Cleveland, he would keep his distance. Sarah grew quieter after that. She didn't speak much of her youngest son and she began to complain more about her health.

Jerry and Bella found a nice apartment in a colonial-style building on one of the greener streets in Jackson Heights. This seems to have been a good time in Jerry's life. He loved his young bride, he loved his neighborhood (prosperous, lively, Jewish, like a more urbane Glenville), and he loved taking the train to Manhattan to be greeted like a movie star in the DC offices on Lexington Avenue, to go out drinking and talking plots with Whitney Ellsworth, to visit the recording studio with Duke Ducovny and tell the writers and actors on the radio show what was coming up next for Superman. He rarely went out with Bella, though. She didn't like to socialize. She didn't enjoy the loudmouthed young artists and chain-smoking editors Jerry kept company with. Jerry was still a very private man, and now a curtain was drawn across his married life. He didn't show her off and he rarely spoke of her, except for the occasional henpecked husband joke.

JOE WAS LEFT running the Cleveland studio mostly by himself as Jerry kept him posted on publishing and editorial developments by mail. Joe designed characters, did rough pencils on the most important stories, drew the faces of Superman and Lois, and otherwise directed the pleasant young men who worked under him: Paul Cassidy, Leo Nowak, John Sikela, and Wayne Boring. He said he missed doing the whole job of drawing sometimes, but mostly he was enjoying his freedom from the tedious work of illustration. He didn't tell anyone yet, not even Jerry, that he enjoyed it in part because his always weak eyesight was growing steadily worse. The finesse was already slipping from his ink lines, even on the familiar face of Superman. He had to be wondering whether he could, even if he had to, draw a comic book himself anymore.

Personally, Joe's confidence increased to the point that he began asking girls out. His method was to catch their eyes by drawing sketches in a coffee shop or at a soda fountain, then present them with a drawing of Superman and ask if they wanted to get something to eat or visit his studio. The problem was that he couldn't hold their interest after he'd gotten them listening to him. When he was twenty-five, he took out a fifteen-year-old named Eileen Freeman. He talked endlessly about Superman and drew her a picture of him on "brown manila paper like we used to use in art class." "He was showing off," she said years later. "It was a nothing date. I don't remember where we went. I don't remember what we did. But I do remember I never saw him again."

Sometimes Jerry would take the train to Cleveland to brainstorm new plots and kibitz the art being produced. At other times Joe would head into New York. Jerry liked to take visitors from Cleveland out to the best restaurants and most famous bars, dropping a lot of money but not lingering long. Joe preferred hanging around cartoonists' studios, watching them draw and talking shop. For the writers and editors in the comics business, accustomed to working with other men whose business was all hot air and words, the ability of cartoonists to talk for hours about paper surfaces and pen nibs or simply watch one another work was an endless source of mystery and boredom. Joe liked sitting with Jerry Robinson and Mort Meskin in a paper-littered room, forgetting about the bigger world that Jerry Siegel was so restless to conquer. (And when Robinson thought Joe needed to be pulled away from the drawing board, he'd set up a double date.)

The highlight of Joe's New York visits, the moment he really knew he'd arrived, was Superman Day at the second summer of the World's Fair, in 1940. Duke Ducovny had arranged for Macy's to sponsor a big show featuring a parade and celebrity appearances—including one by Charles Atlas himself. When Joe was a little boy, those bodybuilders in tights and trunks in the MacFadden magazines, Atlas chief among them, had given him his first glimpse of the superheroic. In his teens Atlas's ads had first shown him a strongman as an enemy of bullies, and the very first published *Superman* story had included his visual joke on those ads. Superman was a fantasy of Charles Atlas in more ways than one, and here was the World's Most Perfectly Developed Man himself, offering Joe his hand to shake.

Later that year Joe announced he was moving to New York. The artists in the studio could move east, too, he told them, or go on working for him long-distance. He wasn't leaving his family, though. He could afford to rent a ten-room house in Queens, and he moved them all there with him: brother, sister, and parents. Once again the Shusters were pulling up stakes, but this time Joe wasn't suffering for it. Joe was in charge.

As the radio adventures of their hero entered the American consciousness, Jerry and Joe were becoming heroic symbols themselves. In late 1940 Jerry found himself on *Town Hall Tonight* with Fred Allen, one of the most popular and prestigious shows on radio. Allen asked him how he'd come to be the creator of Superman, and Jerry played himself as the regular guy next door who just had a good idea and stuck with it. It was painful to listen to, as Jerry struggled through shyness to keep up with his script while Allen tripped him up with condescending ad libs. But still, it was Jerry Siegel, Goober the Mighty, trading lines with Fred Allen. He mentioned DC comics and "my editor, Mr. Ellsworth," and he made sure to mention Bella too, although only as the wife who gets after him if he's late with his scripts.

A few months later, *Liberty* magazine established the Siegel legend that made the most sense of geekdom and comic book obsessions to the normal American adult. "Jerry, being undersized and undernourished, found himself considerably pushed around by the neighborhood toughs. As he absorbed black eyes and beatings, Siegel lived in a dream world of Muscle Men, lapping up the deeds of Hercules, Samson, Tarzan, Doug Fairbanks, and sundry dime-novel superheroes, dreaming of a day when he could hang one on the eye of a tormentor himself." So he and Joe created "their Man of Tomorrow, one who, according to Siegel, would 'smack down the bullies of the world.'" Jerry was becoming a symbol of the little guy fighting back. It was a role he would begin to take seriously as his relationship with DC began to change.

Meanwhile, he'd discovered a problem with living in New York: he was having deadline trouble, and he didn't like being so available to demanding editors. So he took Bella home, buying a small but elegant Federal-style house in a quiet new tract on Glendon Road in University

Heights. All the time Jerry was growing up, Glenville was the "better" neighborhood than Mount Pleasant or Woodlawn, but the Heights was for the Jews who'd made it. He'd continue to keep apartments or hotel rooms in New York and live there part of every year, but Cleveland was home once again. He liked being the suburban householder. He and Bella spread the word among the neighbors that "Superman" had just moved in, and he enjoyed telling interviewers that little boys and girls would knock on his door and ask, "Is Superman here?" He kept a Superman costume to show them, explaining that the Man of Tomorrow was out right now but would return before his next adventure.

Jerry showed his new house off to his mother, but she complained so bitterly about Bella's housekeeping that he preferred to drive down into the flats and visit her in the old house on Kimberly. He saw little of the rest of the family. His cousin Jerry Fine was surprised to learn years later that Jerry and Bella had a house in Cleveland. "I thought he was off in New York all that time," he said, "just getting rich."

From that house on Glendon Road in August 1940, Jerry wrote the oddest story of his Superman career, one that marked a subtle turning point in that career. It introduced the "K-Metal from Krypton," Jerry's first version of kryptonite, and marked the first time he played with the gimmick of Superman finding his powers stripped from him. The K-Metal, in this case, was an asteroid that swerved past the earth, but it stuck Clark and Lois in a collapsing mine shaft and left our hero unable to save his love from certain death without revealing his true identity. Jerry and Joe had put Superman there plenty of times, as had the radio writers, and so every reader would expect him to find some clever way out. A cloud of coal dust could obscure her vision. Lois could learn the truth but be struck on the head by a falling rock and get amnesia. Instead, "knowing that she cannot live much longer if relief is not given to her tortured lungs, and hating to see her suffer, he comes to a momentous decision." He whips off his outer garments and stands revealed as Superman. He flies her to safety, and this time he makes no effort to trick her again.

"It's AMAZING! It's BEWILDERING!" she cries as they soar into the sky. "Why didn't you ever tell me who you really are?" "Because if people were to learn my true identity," he answers, "it would hamper me in my mission to save humanity. You must keep it a secret, you understand!" "Now I begin to see," says Lois. "Your attitude of cowardliness as Clark Kent—it was just a screen to keep the world from learning who you really are! But there's one thing I must know: was your—er—affection for me, in your role as Clark Kent, also a pretense?" "THAT," he says, "was the genuine article, Lois!" Then comes a Lois Lane we've never seen before: "How foolish you were not to let me in on the secret! You should have known you could trust me! Why—don't you realize—I might even be of great help to you?" "You're right! There were many times I could have used the assistance of a confederate. Why didn't I think of it before?" Lois throws her arms around his neck and exclaims, "Then it's settled! We're to be—partners!" Superman smiles down at her. "Yes—partners!" And in a final scene, they wrap up the plot as a team.

Barely two years into Superman's published life, only six months after his radio debut, Jerry Siegel changed one of the central conceits on which the idea was built. Was this Jerry's marital bliss spilling onto the page? Was it Bella's voice in his ear? She wouldn't have been the last comics industry spouse to ask her husband, "Why does he treat her that way? Why does she put up with it?" In that final scene, where Lois works as Superman's partner, she blows up at him: "I just remembered how long you've been secretly laughing at me! I don't like to be laughed at, Clark Kent—but—I'll assist you . . . only for the good of humanity, however!" One of the assistants at the Siegel and Shuster studio would say later that Jerry never said much about Bella, except to complain sometimes that she didn't like Superman. Maybe Clark's regular humiliation of Lois was a boyish power fantasy that Bella wanted to get rid of.

Whether it came from Bella or from within, the change marked a shift in Jerry's relationship with his fantasy hero. Superpowers were no longer for taking revenge on the girls who sneered at you. Now they were for transforming shallow, shrewish girls into admiring partners. The change, however, was not to happen. And from that moment Jerry Siegel ceased to be the principal guiding force of Superman's development.

"The K-Metal from Krypton" was never published. The very idea of the metal was deep-sixed until the writers of the radio show pulled it off the shelf three years later and called it "kryptonite." Even then, although it figured prominently in radio episodes, kryptonite was kept out of the comics until 1949, after Siegel and Shuster were gone. DC's editors didn't want Superman to have an Achilles' heel, and they certainly didn't want an end to the Clark-Lois tango. A handwritten note in the script's margin by an unknown editor reads simply, "It is not a good idea to let others in on the secret." And so it would be.

DC was changing its philosophy of editing. In the beginning, in the days of Vin Sullivan, an editor bought material, assembled magazines, and told freelancers what the market was favoring. The writers and artists decided what their heroes would do and sent the pages in. Now, with one colossally lucrative property under their control and others with potential, Jack Liebowitz and Whitney Ellsworth agreed they needed more editorial control. Jerry Siegel might have started the Superman industry, but that didn't give him any right to mess it up now that so many people were depending on it.

In early 1941 they hired a second editor, one to work under Ellsworth with a particular responsibility for the story lines and quality of Superman and Batman. They chose for the job not a cartoonist like Ellsworth, Sullivan, or Shelly Mayer, who would be able to talk to the freelancers like one of their own, but a fiction editor from the pulps. A powerful young editor known for generating his own story ideas, increasing sales by targeting kids, and telling his writers what to do: Mort Weisinger, the creator of *Captain Future*.

Weisinger brought a few extras to the job. He'd done some writing himself and had commercial ideas; no sooner had he taken the job than he sat down and created two dull but reliable new heroes, Aquaman and Green Arrow. He could bring good writers with him: As soon as he told Edmond Hamilton, Alfred Bester, Henry Kuttner, and other science fiction writers how easy and lucrative comics work was, he had them producing superhero scripts for Detective and All American. He liked bosses. From the first day, he knew how to schmooze Liebowitz and Donenfeld, how to play the kid eager to learn the business from his elders, and once he broke the ice with them, he learned how to play gin rummy, hold his liquor, and tell dirty jokes as well as they did.

Perhaps best of all, Mort wasn't intimidated by the talent. In the pulps, with the exception of those few with literary aspirations, writers were hired hands and their most valuable work was often anonymous. *The Shadow* was written by several different men under the house pseudonym "Maxwell Grant" in a mode of manufacture standard to dime novels since the 1870s. It was the character and the appearance of creative continuity that mattered, not the writer or artist. This was the understanding that Mort brought from the pulps, in place of the comic strip editor's ingrained respect for the cartoonist. *Flash Gordon*'s fans, at least the older ones, knew who Alex Raymond was, and the syndicate believed in the value of his style and his signature. But Mort knew that when Gardner Fox was brought in to pinch-hit a script because Bill Finger was drunk or procrastinating, *Batman*'s readers didn't even notice. And that they wouldn't notice even if someone else were brought in to replace Jerry Siegel on *Superman*.

After the burying of the K-Metal story, Jerry kept producing fun Superman stories in his usual vein. At first he was amused and delighted to find himself working with his old pal Mort Weisinger, who had contributed to his mimeographed *Science Fiction* nine years before. Then Jerry sent in his Superboy idea. DC trademarked the name in anticipation of a launch, and Jerry developed a concept to go with it. What if the future Superman, before he'd learned adult responsibility, had used his superpowers for practical jokes? Then Jerry and Joe could cut loose with the slapstick and self-mockery of *Goober the Mighty*. Weisinger shot it down. The pranks would set a bad example for America's youth. And the silliness would dilute Superman's value. Jerry kept producing, but he was becoming frustrated. He had thought that success meant freedom and acceptance. In fact it only gave Mort Weisinger and Whitney Ellsworth more reason to keep him under control. It didn't help that *The Spectre* was selling only modestly well and that *The Star Spangled Kid*, despite a big publicity push, wasn't setting the newsstands on fire.

Jerry was becoming painfully aware that the attraction wasn't him but Superman and that his editors must have been realizing the same. The Siegel and Shuster studio didn't help either, because so many *Superman* stories were so obviously not drawn by Joe Shuster that any editor would have had to wonder how essential Joe was. Jerry and Joe were glad for their ten-year contract.

Their frustrations were made worse by the Superman merchandise appearing in every toy section and children's clothing store they entered. At first they were thrilled and would buy the stuff themselves if they didn't get it free from DC. But they kept waiting to hear how much money they were going to get from the licensing, and the radio show, and the flurry of published products like the *Superman* novel from Random House. Acquaintances and relatives would say, "You must be getting rich off that radio show," but they could only grin.

As early as January 1940, when the radio show had just found its sponsor, Jerry had written to Jack Liebowitz to remind him of their deal, and Liebowitz had responded with a dismissal: "Get behind your work with zest and ambition to improve and forget about book rights, movie rights and all other dreams. We'll take care of things in the proper manner." But 1940 passed and 1941 began, and deals came and went (Paramount Pictures guaranteed the company a hundred grand for the animation rights, the radio show's sponsors nearly that much for the first full season), and the money still didn't show up. At the end of fiscal year 1941, after Jerry wrote to ask for the percentage of net profits they had been guaranteed, Liebowitz asserted that their figures "show that we lost money and therefore you are entitled to no royalties. However, in line with our usual generous attitude toward you boys, I am enclosing a check for $500, which is in effect a token of feeling." Donenfeld's companies had grossed a million-and-a-half dollars directly off Superman, and yet Jack's figures showed they'd lost money. The "boys" were up against an accountant.

Jerry could only stew and stomp and rage. Whenever he went to New York, he let it be known that he was unhappy, and word quickly found its way to Harry Donenfeld. Harry liked his people happy. He would tell Jerry, "Don't worry, we'll take care of you boys; you'll get whatever you've got coming!" He promised that Jerry and Joe would have employment for the rest of their lives—and he probably meant it, although with the unspoken implication that they would owe him for this, that they would be expected to repay him with lifelong loyalty. This was the code as Harry had learned it in the streets before the world war; it was the system by which the favor traders and racketeers of his world ran their businesses. But Jerry and Joe had never learned any codes on the street, had never made any real deals, had never known the boozy smoke-blowing world of business. They knew movies and comics and pulp stories, where words meant what they meant and good guys and bad were clearly delineated. And they were too afraid to expose their youth and innocence by asking for help.

Jerry took Harry literally and filed his promises away as part of the deal he thought he had made. He knew that Harry was Jack's boss, at least in title, and became more insistent about what he'd been promised. But Jack was an accountant who had mastered his trade among unions, racketeers, and pornographers. He'd held his companies together through times that destroyed most of the competition. He was fighting a quarterly war against the New Deal's steadily rising tax rates. He'd had to pay Harry Donenfeld's way out from under his own messes too many times before, and now finally he had real success in his grasp. He wasn't going to be beaten by a couple of junior luftmenschen who didn't know what "net profit" implied.

Jerry kept writing. His work remained racy and buoyant. But he was building a righteous anger inside. Some of the most powerful moments of his scripts were dramatizations of that anger. The Spectre's death-dealing gaze. Superman tearing off his shirt with that rageful glower on his brow and saying, "Now to pay Luthor a *personal* call!" But he was about to learn that the world was not a superhero script, and victory does not go to the most injured or most angry.

Harry Donenfeld with his new bride, Gussie, in 1918, probably at Coney Island. Harry looks dapper, intent, and already impatient to put the honeymoon nonsense behind him and get down to business—and real fun.

Jack and Rose Liebowitz in the early 1940s, when everything was breaking right. The Lower East Side was far behind them; they'd become the perfect Great Neck couple. (Photos courtesy of Irwin Donenfeld.)

Jerry Siegel and Joe Shuster both took their glasses off for this Superman publicity shoot circa 1940. This was the peak of their confidence: they could look back on a fearful climb, or forward to a fearful slide.

The magazine cover that turned young men into "scientifiction" geeks all over America—Jerry Siegel among them. Art by Frank R. Paul, the Swiss illustrator who defined the utopian futurism of the 1920s.

Other magazine covers had other effects on young men. Enoch Bolles was Harry Donenfeld and Frank Armer's favorite early cover artist, with his genius for finding the place where cuteness and perversity overlapped. 1930 (Courtesy of Douglas Ellis.)

Still another way to excite young men. The Shadow can claim to be the first "superhero." Not superhuman, but a new combination of romance, violence, and visual trademarks. Cover painting by George Rozen, 1936. (™The Condé Nast Publications, Inc.)

Joe Shuster combines pulp magazine covers, comic strip lines, and the aesthetic of body building magazines to give Superman his first visual form. The muscle-shirt would have evoked weight lifters and acrobats in 1933.

Joe's idealization of Woman to complement his idealization of He Man. He said he was looking at a teenage girl named Jolan Kovacs when the drew this sketch of Lois Lane in 1936; surely his mind's eye was turned inward, to movie memories and lonely dreams. (Superman and Lois Lane™ DC Comics, Inc.)

Jake Kurtzberg before he was Jack Kirby (upper right), with fellow newsmen at the Boys Brotherhood Republic. Looking for a way off the Lower East Side, 1935. (Courtesy Blue Rose Press.)

Harry Donenfeld works distributors Allen and Ivan Ludington, around 1940. Note the smiles trying to break through the frowns: No one could resist Harry long, not even a pair of Protestants from Michigan.

Harry's girlie mags were under siege by the censors when he launched his "serious" line of pulp fiction. This image was less offensive to the Citizens for Decency than the girls in the "nudies"—at least she's wearing pants while she gapes at her fiancé's severed head. Cover by H. J. Ward, 1934. (Courtesy of Douglas Ellis.)

Joe Shuster and Jerry Siegel brought their own racial mayhem to Harry's magazines. This was Joe's peak as a draftsman and story teller; overwork and failing eyes would shortly destroy his art just as he hit the big time. Detective Comics #1 © 1937 DC Comics. (All rights reserved. Used with permission.)

The early Superman had an angry streak; the Mr. Superhuman Nice Guy would arrive when the world embraced him as its favorite hero. These panels from the Superman newspaper strip samples were left out of Action Comics #1 but restored to Superman #1 © 1939 DC Comics. (All Rights Reserved. Used with permission.)

Superman himself expresses the buoyancy of Siegel and Shuster and the comics business as they all took flight. An unpublished piece by Joe Shuster, from the early 1940s, showing the charm he could bring to his figures when his workload allowed. Inked by Wayne Boring (Collection of Bruce Bergstrom. Superman and Lois Lane™ DC Comics.)

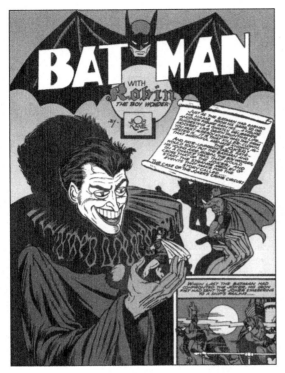

Jerry Robinson was still a teenager when he brought a new beauty and drama to superhero art as Bob Kane's finest "ghost." He'd never studied art, either. The young comics business rewarded great "naturals." Script by Bill Finger. Batman #4 © 1941 DC Comics.

While Robinson and other talented kids drew under Bob Kane's signature, Bob himself was in Miami chasing girls. He probably really did draw this picture himself. Sometime in the 1940s. (Batman and Robin™ DC Comics.)

The little boys don't know, but the publishers understand. This strip commissioned for Harry Donenfeld's 50th birthday card shows that Harry and cronies were not unaware of the complex tangle of imaginings that made superheroes so compelling. Artist unknown, 1943. (Courtesy of Irwin Donenfeld. Superman™ DC Comics.)

"Anger will save your life," said Jack Kirby, and on the comic book page he let anger unleash the male body from the bounds of realism, physics, and panel borders. Joe Simon collaborated on this page with him, but the violent visual poetry is Jack's. Captain America #7, 1942. (Captain America © and ™Marvel Comics Group.)

The reader shouldn't feel too smug for spotting an erotic subtext. Dr. William Moulton Marston, psychologist and promoter of alternative lifestyles, knew exactly what he was doing. Art by Harry G. Peter. Wonder Woman #5 © 1943 DC Comics. (All rights reserved. Used with permission.)

THE LUSTY LIFE OF AN UNINHIBITED SUPERMAN
—by the author of FINNLEY WREN

Gladiator

PHILIP WYLIE

The image of the Muscle Beach body builder runs through the iconography of the superman. The 1930 edition of Gladiator helped inspire Jerry Siegel and Joe Shuster to create Superman. In 1949, Superman's name is helping sell Gladiator to the tawdry new paperback market. (Note the vertical "back pocket" creases; this copy did good service.) Cover artist unknown.

Lev Gleason, Communist Party member, HUAC victim, and purveyor of gory crime comics, was pitting superheroes against real supervillains while Superman was still restricted to pitting his strength against mad scientists. Art by Bob Wood and Charlie Biro (slavering fiend in corner courtesy of Jack Cole). 1941.

The mob profited from comics, but it contributed a bit too. Here Lucky Luciano, acquaintance of Harry Donenfeld, makes a cameo to help sell the goods. Nothing else combined anger, sensationalism, and a left-wing conscience like Crime Does Not Pay. Cover art by Charlie Biro, 1943.

Money, self-disgust, and anger at the censors came together to make crime comics irresistible even to Jack Cole, whose Plastic Man was so bright and joyous. This became Fredric Wertham's favorite example of why comic books must be "legislated off the shelves." 1947.

Enter the next generation, collegiate and hip. Bill Gaines and Al Feldstein with some of the "New Trend" comics that were about to get them into hot water, 1950.

The cover hoisted before the cameras by Sen. Estes Kefauver, future candidate for Vice President of the United States. For the artist, Johnny Craig, it had been just another dark joke. For the comic book industry it became a symbol of freedom and self-destruction. 1953. *Crime SuspenStories* #22 © 1954 EC Comics, Inc. (All Rights reserved.)

Harvey Kurtzman and Wally Wood unmask the dramas of sex and anger in the relationships of "Clark Bent" and "Lois Pain" that had always been kept just slightly out of sight. Mad #4 © EC Publications, Inc. (All rights reserved. Used with permission.)

Zuggy, the Super-Swell Guy, guided Jerry Siegel and Joe Shuster through their lawsuit against DC comics in 1947 and '48. The sentiments might have been less grateful a few years later, when Albert Zugsmith was a big-shot movie producer and Jerry and Joe were scrambling to survive. (Courtesy of Richard Halegua. Superman™ DC Comics.)

Pain and loss were at the heart of the hero, after all. Jerry Siegel and veteran Shuster-studio artist Wayne Boring make something simple but beautiful of superhuman agony. "Superman's Return to Krypton," Superman #141 © 1960 DC Comics.

The real world provided its own sad twists to the Superman story. The Man of Steel was still a major cultural symbol in 1959, representing everything that tabloid journalism and an actor's death did not.

Jerry Robinson, 1974: the cartoonist, writer, and organizer whose piercing gaze cut to the heart of the decades-long dilemma of Siegel and Shuster and forced Warner Communications to act at last.

Jerry Siegel in the 1980s: a California tan, a grin, some security and recognition at last.

Joe Shuster in 1991. In the last year of his life, legally blind, ill from his "years in the wilderness," his proudest memory was still the hero to whom he'd given form.
(© 1991 *Toronto Star*)

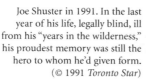

The Whirlwind

SUDDENLY THERE WERE a dozen comics publishers, then two dozen, then more, popping up all through midtown Manhattan. In his attack on comics Sterling North had called them a "mushroom growth." The description applied better to the businesses that made the things—the pulp houses, printing companies, sheet music publishers, small-time distributors, toy makers, and rooms full of art school dropouts who plunged into the business. *Superman* and *Action* stayed on top of the heap for a while, but then *Captain Marvel* and its companion magazine, *Whiz,* slipped ahead, and *Batman* and *Detective* rose quickly behind. New comics—titles like *Flash, Hit, Crack, Pep, Zip, Speed*—came out of nowhere to become hits. Several comics were selling over a million copies an issue by 1941. Pap that hardly anyone in the business noticed was selling 100,000 or 200,000.

Production was limited not by the market but by time on the printers' schedules and the availability of paper. Sometimes a sudden windfall of paper or cash brought a comic book into existence out of nothing. Lev Gleason, former printing salesman newly flung into the ranks of publishers, found himself with a chance to reserve a few million pages of pulp one day in early 1941. The catch was that he had to stake his claim for it *immediately* or someone else would get it and that he had to turn it into something salable *immediately* or the distributor wouldn't advance him the money to pay the bill. So Gleason bought the paper with the promise that he'd have his comic's pages at the printers on the following Monday. Except that it was Friday, and he didn't have a comic to print.

Gleason turned to his favorite cartoonist and packager, Charlie Biro, and said, "Get me sixty-four pages by Monday morning." All he asked was that his one name superhero, Daredevil, have the lead story. How they filled the rest of the pages would be up to them. Biro shared a cheap art studio on 52nd Street, among jazz clubs and strip joints, with his best friend, Bob Wood, and *Batman*'s star artist, Jerry Robinson. Wood brought in his brothers, Dick and Dave, to help. Robinson brought in his roommates, Bernie Klein and Mort Meskin, and a fellow ghost artist for Bob Kane, George Roussos. They were all nineteen or twenty years old and had already been published comics artists for at least a year.

They had two drawing tables in the place, one of them big enough for two guys to squeeze onto. Whoever wasn't at a table worked on the floor or propped a board on his knees. They plunged in with loud jokes and insults, making up stories and characters, breaking down pages in pencil, flying through Friday night smoking and drinking coffee. Robinson created "London," a newsman covering the London blitz who puts on a mask to fight the Nazis. He didn't know it, but it was the first comic book story to tackle the real events of the war. Roussos liked the idea so much that he came up with "Blackout," a Hungarian scientist whose lab is bombed by the Nazis and ends up covered in black fur. Saturday they kept grinding, still calling to each other with problems but saving their words now. Saturday night they kept pushing, lettering when they got sick of drawing, dropping whole captions and shortening sentences when they got sick of lettering.

Then the snow came. The biggest blizzard to hit Manhattan in years. On Sunday morning the cartoonists found a five-foot drift against the door of their building. They drew lots to see which poor bastard had to go find food: Klein lost. The rest of them dug the snow out of the doorway, and Bernie climbed over the banks into the middle of 52nd Street, where the snow was lowest, and trudged off in search of any grocery store or restaurant open on a Sunday in Midtown after a paralyzing blizzard.

He was gone for hours. The others kept drawing, getting hungrier and angrier, increasingly certain that Klein had either abandoned them or frozen to death. Until finally Bernie lurched in, chilled to the bone. He'd had to hike down 6th Avenue to 34th Street before he found a dairy open, and he'd brought back his prize—two bottles of milk and a dozen eggs. "For Christ's sake!" yelled Biro. "What are we gonna do with *raw eggs?*" The studio had no kitchen. There was plenty of paper to light a fire, and a bathtub to light it in, but nothing to cook the eggs on. Then someone pointed to the tiles on the bathroom wall. They pried off the tiles with art knives, heated them with burning scrap paper, and cooked one egg on each tile. It was just enough food to get them through Sunday afternoon and a long Sunday night. When Monday finally dawned, they were whiting out the most egregious gaffes and deciding they could leave the rest. And *Daredevil* was done.

It was a weekend that captured an era. Twenty years later Robinson told the story to Jules Feiffer, who used it as a centerpiece in *The Great Comic Book Heroes.* From there Michael Chabon turned it into a passage in *The Amazing Adventures of Kavalier and Clay.* Commerce, luck, and youth had never come together so perfectly to create a moment so evanescently American. It paid off, too. Oh, the comic book they made that weekend was a mess. But it was loud and colorful and full of fighting heroes. And here and there, from the seediness and haste, emerged those moments of unannounced beauty—a perfect line, a living figure, a composition of nearly accidental grace—that are so heartbreaking and so liberating in junk culture. Gleason ordered more issues of *Daredevil.* Biro, Wood, Robinson, Meskin, Klein, and Roussos kept working.

The good artists, even the just-decent artists, were getting more jobs than they could handle. "The work was relentless," Feiffer would say. "Some men worked in bull pens during the day; free lanced at night—a hard job to quit work at five thirty, go home and free lance till four in the morning, get up at eight and go to a job. . . . Eighteen hours a day of work. Sandwiches for breakfast, lunch, and dinner. An occasional beer, but not too often. And nothing any stronger. One dare not slow up." But even the worst, youngest, rawest artists were getting paid to draw. Some could only finish their pages by copying other artists, so that, as Feiffer said, "you'd find nine pages of swiped Milton Caniff next to nine pages of swiped Alex Raymond." But there were publishers hungry enough to buy anything. "The schlock houses were the art schools of the business. Working blind but furiously, working from swipes, working from the advice of others who drew better because they were in the business two weeks longer, one, suddenly, learned how to draw."

Eli Katz was sixteen years old when he got his first art job from an assistant editor at *Pep* named Sidney Feldman. Life at *Pep* was tough for new kids. "They would take rubber cement," Katz remembered, "and while a guy was working, they would circle him with the rubber cement, pour it on the floor, and drop a match. The fucking rubber cement would ignite, he'd jump up about four feet high, scare the living shit out of the guy, he'd throw himself over the work he'd just done." Katz complained and, because they said he "made too much noise," he was fired. He found himself working at Jack Binder's shop, where fifty or sixty artists were jammed at drawing boards in a Fifth Avenue loft. "It looked like an internment camp," Katz said. He was thrilled when Feldman asked him to come back to *Pep*. (The kids who could survive learned: Eli Katz would become one of the best-known artists in comics under the name "Gil Kane"; Sidney Feldman would take the name "Scott Meredith" and become the biggest literary agent in the junk fiction trade.)

Comics were piecework, just like the rag trade. Who created that superhero? Ask who created that jacket, who finished the sleeves, who attached the lining. But even in the midst of the schlock, from the speed and the freedom and the almost total lack of editorial oversight emerged moments of the freest fantasy and most personal expression.

One of the young men who found himself in the Will Eisner studio was Jack Cole. He was born in 1914, the same year as Siegel, Shuster, and Bill Finger, but in the hard mining town of New Castle, Pennsylvania. His father was a dry goods dealer, musician, and Methodist Sunday school teacher. According to his biographer, Art Spiegelman, the young Jack was "introspective, imaginative, high-spirited, and graced with a pronounced sense of humor." He was also depressive, speaking often of suicide, rarely gratified by worldly accomplishments and most at peace when he was drawing. He was impulsive, too. At seventeen he bicycled across the United States to attend the Los Angeles Olympics, only to discover when he got there that he needed money to attend. He eloped with his high school sweetheart but then went on living at home so his parents wouldn't find out. Then he moved to Greenwich Village with his wife to become an artist with nothing but one correspondence course for training.

Cole started out doing silly humor, but with the superhero boom, he threw himself into heroes, villains, and violence with a strange, wonderful madness. He created the Claw, a fever dream of a pulp Oriental mastermind. Fanged, devil eared, huge eyed, needle clawed, "a god of hate," he shoots lightning, breathes fire, and swells to giant size. He invades America, turns Manhattan into a graveyard of rubble and melted girders, until he meets Daredevil—the same Daredevil of the lost weekend. The Claw tries to throw him into space, but Daredevil bends himself into the shape of a boomerang and arcs back into his eye. The Claw tries to swallow him alive, but Daredevil snatches up a bundle of dynamite and flips it down the villain's throat ahead of him. "If dynamite down his windpipe fails," he exclaims, "I'll be ground meat!" It explodes, and the villain retches him to freedom and escapes in a burst of smoke.

Soon Cole was working with Will Eisner and then being hired by one of Eisner's publishers, Busy Arnold, to do knockoffs of Will Eisner. In early 1941 Arnold needed material for his new *Police Comics* and asked Cole to create a superhero. Cole's mind went where no power-hungry geek or pulp melodramatist or imitator of Siegel and Shuster had ever gone. Instead of a hero tougher and stronger and faster than any normal man, he created one more free and absurd. "India Rubber Man" could bend and bounce and flatten himself like a rug and transform himself into a red-and-yellow divan. What Superman was to bodybuilders, India Rubber Man was to contortionists. The publisher liked him, but his promotional instincts were sharper than Cole's. Make him futuristic, Busy said, name him after a new miracle substance so your readers feel like they're experiencing freedoms yet to come. Call him "Plastic Man."

In freeing his hero from the bounds of physics, Cole freed his own pencil and brushes for the most astonishing art in comics. "Cole's world teems with invention, gags, and an amazing number of hyperactive characters tucked into every nook and cranny of a panel," Spiegelman said. "Plastic Man never stretches exactly the same way twice. . . . What remains most remarkable is [Cole's] ability to be so fully present in his comic-book work from moment to moment, always following his lines of thought with the same curiosity the reader might have—as astonished as any reader by where they take him." Cole also freed the superhero genre from the expectation that it must gratify someone's desire to be Charles Atlas without the hard work. Setting kids loose from reality was enough.

Jack Cole was a friend, neighbor, and coworker of Charlie Biro, but they were from different worlds. Cole was thin, a teetotaler in youth, devoted to his wife, a small-town Methodist. Biro was a Brooklyn Hungarian, six-four and massive, a drinker, a fighter. "He had enormous vitality; he would overwhelm a room," said Gil Kane. He lived in the Village with his friend and collaborator Bob Wood, an even heavier drinker, where they'd write and draw and chase skirts day and night. They bragged incessantly about the women they'd talked into coming to their rooms to be painted nude, only to stay to drink and get screwed. Biro was almost adolescent in his predations, contriving to peek into women's dressing rooms and groping the female elevator operators at the *Pep* offices. Wood beat women when he was drunk. Once Jack Cole had a fight with his wife and spent the night in Wood's spare room. Through the walls, he could hear Wood pounding on his girlfriend. Another time Cole and his wife took a cab with Wood and his date. The Coles got out first. When Jack looked back at the departing cab, Wood was already hitting her.

But Charlie Biro was also a cartoonist with a social conscience and a man who cared about kids. When Biro was walking with friends, he'd stop to talk to gangs of boys in the playgrounds and on the stoops. He'd work himself into a left-wing rage about the savagery of working-class childhood in a capitalist society. When he took over Daredevil, he gave the hero a gang of kid sidekicks called the Little Wise Guys and gradually made them the stars of the stories. He peppered their funny kid antics with political lances straight out of *Dead End* and put them through the kinds of ethical dilemmas poor city kids had to face.

When Lev Gleason asked Biro and Wood for a cover that would really sell *Daredevil*, they responded with one of the great visual icons of the American left. Daredevil and a trio of other heroes launch boomerangs, missiles, blades, and fists at a gigantic Adolf Hitler. Not a drawing of Hitler but a photograph, colored, pasted onto a cartooned body, with eyes redrawn to make him look scared. The title screams across the top: *Daredevil Battles Hitler*. Down in the corner, Jack Cole's evil Claw draws our eyes to a placard promising that "DAREDEVIL deals the ACE OF DEATH to the MAD MERCHANT OF HATE!" It hit the stands in the late spring of 1941, while America was still officially at peace and Superman was still dodging the war.

Biro hit it off well with Gleason, a bona fide communist who also published the liberal *Friday* newsmagazine. While Harry Donenfeld gambled with Moe Annenberg, and Jack Liebowitz shook hands at country club luncheons, Gleason went drinking with his artists and writers. He even cut them a share of the profits on their more successful creations, and he put Charlie Biro and Bob Wood's names on the covers of the comics they edited. When, in the waning days of 1941, he asked Biro and Wood for a new comic book idea, they came back with *Crime Does Not Pay*. It would be all true stories, stuff straight out of Donenfeld's *Police Gazette,* the most gruesome murders and gangland tortures they could find but told in broad, overplayed comics form. Their first cover featured a pair of hands in the foreground, one sticking a switchblade straight through the other into the table beneath. In the background, a man uses a voluptuous woman as a shield as he sprays a barroom with machine gun bullets. The lead stories were mostly about gangsters: Lepke Buchalter, Lucky Luciano, other acquaintances of Harry Donenfeld's. For all its perverse sensationalism, though, *Crime Does Not Pay* also had a distinct political twist. Many of its stories delved into the hard, poor environments that had produced their subjects. The police rarely came off as admirable, a fact that would get Gleason in trouble in years to come.

Biro and Wood's comic was a success, the first nonhumor comic to rival the superheroes in sales, the first to open the comic book market to large numbers of late adolescent and young adult males who thought costumed heroes were stupid. Out of anger, brutality, and booze they had made something powerful that shoved open a door in America's mass culture.

At the same time, Will Eisner was making something powerful out of frustration. He'd set out to be a cartoonist and writer, and for a year he'd done almost nothing but run a factory. Then, in late 1939, Busy Arnold at Quality Comics arranged to print a comic book–style newspaper insert for the Register and Tribune Syndicate of Des Moines, and he offered Eisner the job of producing the pages. Eisner wanted to do more than add it to the shop schedule; he wanted to write and draw his own feature. He asked Jerry Iger to buy out his half of the studio and let him leave with a couple of good artists and the newspaper insert job. Iger told him he was nuts, the shop made too much money, the syndicate game was too shaky. But Eisner saw his chance to do something that he cared about, that would build his reputation, and that would reach a wider readership than what he called the "ten-year-old cretin child" whom comic books were aimed at. He told the syndicate he wouldn't do it unless he retained ownership of the characters and stories. Hardly any newspaper cartoonists owned their own strips—the only big name who did so was Harold Foster with *Prince Valiant*—but even at twenty-two Eisner knew that was where the long-term money and control lay.

The weekly inserts debuted in June 1940. The lead character was a crime fighter in a mask, fedora, and three-piece suit called the Spirit.

These were the first superhero comics aimed at adults as well as kids. The plots were taut little pieces with twist endings in the style of O. Henry and Saki. The art was atmospheric and generous, the storytelling cinematic: An opening in a windswept cemetery lets us follow the characters past scary trees and tombstones for four panels before we're plunged into action. The Spirit himself was rumpled, charming, irritable, sometimes clumsy, always singular. And the series grew, becoming not more streamlined or formulaic like most comics but more complex. Eisner was one of the many young cartoonists who fell in love with *Citizen Kane* the moment it opened in May 1941—Jerry Robinson was another—and he immediately began to emulate its use of framing, depth, juxtaposition, and visual wit to intensify a story. He would chortle decades later to hear himself called "the Orson Welles of comics."

Eisner bridged the newspapers and the comic books, for *The Spirit* appeared also in Quality's *Police Comics,* right behind Jack Cole's *Plastic Man.* Together Cole and Eisner pointed toward the potential of the medium.

A different sort of pioneer was Jake Kurtzberg. Jake did not try to bring superheroes closer to familiar reality but distilled them into their purest form. He passed through the Eisner shop at the same time as Jack Cole, and like Cole, he was an artist of little formal training but powerful imagination and deeply personal passions. Like Cole, he gave the impression of being mostly submerged in his own inner world, of being happiest when he was drawing. But in anger and pugnaciousness he was more like Charlie Biro. "I think anger will save your life," he once said. "I think anger will give you a drive that will save your life and change you in some manner." Jake's anger took him to places very different from the brutish realism of Charlie Biro. It took him to a romance of violence that transformed the superhero, that took Siegel and Shuster's invention to its organic conclusion—that in effect completed what they had begun.

Jake was born on August 18, 1917, a few months after Will Eisner. His father, like Eisner's, was an Austrian Jewish immigrant, but unlike Eisner's, he was no artist. He was a garment worker, and the course of his life placed Jake in a world very different from Eisner's Bronx. Not all the Jews of the Lower East Side had been lifted out by the prosperity of the Teens and Twenties. Many remained stranded there on a shrinking Jewish island surrounded by increasing numbers of poor Sicilians, their community just as poor but less vital and less optimistic than it had been a generation before. Suffolk Street was a violent place. "Each street had its own gang of kids, and we'd fight all the time," Jake said. "We'd cross over the roofs and bombard the Norfolk Street gang with bottles and rocks and mix it up with them." Stepping into the street meant engaging with violence. "Some guy would come up from the next block and you would fight. If you knocked him out, you and the guys would lay him out near his mother's door and vice versa." After a while, Jake said, "fighting became second nature. I began to like it."

His burning desire was to get out of the neighborhood. His first ambition was to be "a crooked politician." But Jake wasn't the type for politics. He was tiny, defensive, unsure of himself socially, and hardest of all, inclined to disappear into daydreams. The ghetto, he said, "made me so fearful . . . that in an immature way, I fantasized a dream world more realistic than the reality around me." He liked to draw pictures and looked for places where he could learn more about art. First he tried the Educational Alliance, that august charity founded by liberal German Jews to help their East European brethren assimilate into American life. "They threw me out," Jake said, "for drawing too fast with charcoal."

Where he found his haven at last was the Boys Brotherhood Republic on East 3rd Street. This was a "miniature city" where street kids ran their own government, cared for their own facilities, and published their own newspaper. Jake played baseball and boxed, but more than anything he loved drawing cartoons for the paper. The other kids on the paper chose him, at fourteen, as their editor, the first time Jake had ever been anything but another tough kid to adults and an oddball who liked to draw pictures to his peers. "In my neighborhood they didn't even know what an artist was," Jake said. "To be something, you had to be a car mechanic, so when I became an artist they couldn't understand; they thought I was mixed up in something illegal."

Ben Kurtzberg understood what art meant to his son, however, and knew that this was Jake's best chance to get away from Suffolk Street. On his factory wages he saved enough money for Jake to attend the Pratt Institute. But then, at the rock bottom of the Depression, Ben lost his job. The money for school went back into helping the family survive. Jake sold newspapers and took delivery jobs. Late at night he practiced drawing, determined now to make money at it. He knew now that everything, even selling cartoons, was a fight.

At eighteen he got a job doing in-betweening at the Fleischer cartoon studios. Bob Kahn, soon to be Batman's Bob Kane, was there at the same time, although they never remembered meeting. Then Jake landed what looked like his dream job, drawing cartoons and comic strips for a small newspaper syndicate just starting out, Lincoln News. He turned out to be so fast and prolific that he produced most of Lincoln's comic strips, playing with a variety of pseudonyms to make himself look like a stable of creators. The one he liked best was a simplification of his real name with an Irish twist that reminded him of Jimmy Cagney, one of his movie heroes: "Jack Kirby." When he called himself "Kirby" he felt more like Cagney, bounced on the balls of his feet, kept his arms poised and liquid like a dancer and a lightweight boxer. Over the years, the name became him. Even his wife would call him "Kirby" in affectionate amusement. When he changed his name legally, his friends ribbed him about "looking more Irish already." Kirby flushed and balled his fist. "I'm not ashamed of being a Jew," he said. "I just like the name."

Lincoln News, unfortunately, was another casualty of the recession of 1937 and 1938. He knocked around various jobs, including the Eisner & Iger shop. Eisner quickly got a glimpse of the Kirby fantasy world. The towel service at their building kept jacking up the prices, and one day Eisner demanded to talk to a representative. A broken-nosed thug with a black shirt and white tie came into his office and said they couldn't lower their rates. Eisner threatened to find another towel service, and the guy said, "We're the only company that services this building." It was a mob arrangement. Just then, five-foot-two Jack Kirby stepped into the office. "Is this guy giving you trouble, Will?" "It's okay,

Jack, get back to work." "Do you want me to beat him up?" The thug turned. "Who's this guy?" Eisner said it was his best artist and nobody'd better hurt him or he wouldn't be able to pay for his towels. The thug said, "We don't want no trouble; we just want to do things business-like." The rate increases stopped for a while. "Let me know if he comes back, Will," Kirby said. "Tell me if you want me to beat him up."

Kirby picked up work from other shops and publishers, including that "king of comics" Victor Fox. That's when he came to the attention of Joe Simon, a cartoonist intent on becoming the next big packager. Simon was only two years older than Kirby, but he was a tall, middle-class kid from Syracuse who'd been a minor celebrity on the paper there, and he had a worldly confidence Kirby lacked. He'd created a couple of superheroes for Funnies, Incorporated, then broken with them and was talking directly to publishers about supplying them with material. He liked Kirby's versatility and asked him out to lunch. Kirby had been mostly living on sandwiches his mother made for him and didn't eat in restaurants much. Dining on Simon's dime, he ordered a dessert called a Brown Betty, not because he knew what it was but because he thought it made him sound like a guy who knew what he was doing. When it came, he saw the raisins slipping out of its apple innards and recoiled. "I can't eat this!" he yelled. "What's the problem?" asked Simon. "It looks like roaches," said Kirby. "It looks like roaches got into it!" Simon could only laugh. Syracuse was a long way from Suffolk Street.

In early 1940 Simon cut a deal with Martin Goodman, publisher of *Marvel Comics,* to create new features. Goodman ran an odd company from his offices in the Empire State Building, neither schlock house nor class outfit. It had no name, for one thing: To manipulate tax laws, Goodman would publish under at least eighty different company names over the years, usually several simultaneously. Insiders usually called his line "Timely," after one of his short-lived magazines. "Marvel" would become the name best identified with him, but he wouldn't adopt it officially for over twenty years. Goodman was younger than all those publishers of Donenfeld's generation, only thirty-two when he went into business with the twenty-five-year-old Simon. He had been a fan of *Weird Tales* as a teenager and learned the business from *Amazing Stories*'s Hugo Gernsback in his twenties. That made him the only pulp publisher to have grown up reading the things.

In his Marvel pulps he showed a predilection for the lurid and outré, and he had a reputation for imposing few editorial controls. The pages he bought from Funnies, Incorporated, for *Marvel Comics* were filled with the market's most idiosyncratic and least heroic variations on the superhero. The Human Torch was an android who burst into flame, escaped his maker, and spread terror through the land. As the stories went on, he came gradually around to fighting crime, but he remained volatile and inhuman, still more of a science-fictional curiosity than a wish fulfillment. The Black Widow was a horrifying woman with magical powers who killed criminals, but only to deliver their souls more quickly to her master, Satan. The Sub-Mariner, by a hard-drinking Irish cartoonist from Massachusetts named Bill Everett, was the cantankerous king of an undersea race who hated surface people for their exploitation of the sea. Supremely neutral in the coming world war, he despised any nation that used submarines, depth charges, and floating mines, and he launched an invasion of New York just to make us leave him alone. It was a romance of superhuman violence without good guys or a hope of a happy ending, a supreme Irish barroom fantasy.

Marvel was doing fine but not spectacularly on the newsstands, and Goodman's efforts to follow it up had flopped. Goodman wanted more product out and he wanted a superhero to sell it. In the beginning, no one had quite known why Superman sold so well, and it seemed reasonable to think that fantastic stories and superhuman feats were enough. With the success of Batman and the new Captain Marvel, however, it became apparent that these costumed characters were not simply outgrowths of the Weird, Thrilling, Amazing, Wonder, Marvel school of the pulps but were a special kind of children's hero, requiring costumes, secret identities, a public appearance of ordinariness, and an absolute commitment to defeating bad guys. Having heard already how litigious Harry Donenfeld could get, Goodman insisted on steering clear of Superman and Batman, but other models for imitation were out there.

Goodman's former boss, Louis Silberkleit, was enjoying significant sales with a red-white-and-blue hero called the Shield. In the fall of 1940, as London endured the blitz and Roosevelt rolled to his third election, Joe Simon got to work. He improved on the design of the Shield, then even dared to play off his model's name by attaching a star-spangled shield to his hero's arm. The name was a cinch, between Captain Easy in the comic strips, Captain Midnight on the radio, and Captain Future in the pulps: Captain America.

Goodman liked it. Simon said not so fast. He was working with Kirby on samples and a cover, and he knew he had something spectacular. He and Kirby shared the work, both contributing to stories, both inking, Simon doing most of the dialogue and the lettering; but the layouts and the figures were mostly Kirby's, and there lay the power of the pages. Simon had known Kirby did energetic figures in motion, dramatic foreshortening and rippling musculature, high-impact punches. But until Jack poured all his rage and exultation into this grinning, granite-fisted embodiment of America vaulting over Berchtesgaden walls, smashing through legions of jackbooted fascists, and belting Hitler himself in the jaw, he had never shown just what he could do. Simon knew there were bigger buyers than Martin Goodman out there. DC and Fawcett could easily outbid Goodman and bring much bigger licensing operations into play.

So Goodman cut an unprecedented deal for Captain America. He would premiere in his own magazine, not buried in an anthology, and Simon and Kirby would get 15 percent of the take and salaried positions as Goodman's comics editor and art director. The deal alone instantly made Simon and Kirby big guns in the industry. When the first *Captain America* hit the stands in February, selling out in days, and when the next print run was set at over a million copies, they were stars.

What Kirby brought to the comic book page was an opera of line and mass. The stories didn't matter, so much drama did his anger bring to the figures bursting out of panels, the bodies hurtling through space as fists and feet drove into them, the faces contorted in passion, the camera angles swinging wildly and the panels stretched and bent by the needs of the action. His hero's anatomy made no sense. Kirby had never been able to afford life drawing lessons; he was making it up. But Captain America came to such life and moved so forcefully through a time and space that existed only because Kirby said they did that he became more real than any of the carefully drawn heroes of the art school graduates. Kirby celebrated the body, the male body, male sweat and muscles, not with the fetishism of bodybuilding but with savage joy. And countless boys at the brink of puberty loved him for it. Within two issues *Captain America* was selling a million copies a month. Suddenly every young artist was drawing action like Jack Kirby.

What Simon and Kirby together brought to the superhero was the passion of the immigrant, of the Jew. Secret identity stories always reverberated with the children of Jewish immigrants, of course, because they were so much about the wearing of the masks that enabled one to be an American, a Modern, a secular consumer, but still part of an ancient society, a link in an old chain, when safely among those who knew one's secret. A Clark Kent in the street and a Superman at home, Moses Mendelsohn might have said. The superheroes brought something to those stories that Zorro and the Scarlet Pimpernel never had, for their *true* identities, the men in colorful tights, were so elemental, so universal, so transcendent of the worlds that made them wear masks that they carried with them an unprecedented optimism about the value of one's inner reality. We all knew that Clark Kent was just a game played by Superman and that the only guy who mattered was that alien who showed up in Metropolis with no history and no parents.

Captain America brought those metaphors of masking to a new poignancy. Steve Rogers shuffles into a secret lab scrawny and slump shouldered, then is given an injection of a supersoldier serum and is transformed into an Adonis. He continues to play the nebbish, however, revealing his power and courage only when he doffs his army fatigues and becomes the embodiment of America itself. The underfed ghetto kid transformed into a roof-rattling power by seizing American opportunities, the weary old-country survivor reborn as the new fighting Jew through the crucible of American freedom and violence. And through that immigrant passion Simon and Kirby captured an entire national awakening: America the provincial stirring itself to become a world power. Captain America, like Superman, became a symbol of a universal boyish fantasy that was, secretly, an adult fantasy as well.

But this is where the dirty roots of the comics business showed themselves. Goodman wore an Ivy League bow tie, played golf, and talked about becoming a real book publisher, but all his working life he'd been in cheap magazines; he'd learned how to run a business from the promoters and peddlers and money jugglers who'd spent the Depression staying one unpaid bill ahead of receivership. So he screwed Simon and Kirby. He didn't pay them that 15 percent he owed them, and when Simon demanded a reckoning, he lied about how much money he'd made. Or at least, so Simon said. Goodman accused Simon of trumping up the whole conflict so he could cut a better deal with Jack Liebowitz. No one would ever know the truth—it was the comics business.

Liebowitz told Simon and Kirby he'd double their pay, live up to their deals, push them in house ads ("These boys are really good!"), and let them create any series they wanted. Goodman had to scramble not only to continue *Captain America* with lesser artists but also to hire an editor and writer. He gave the job to the only person left in the office, a nineteen-year-old office boy named Stan Lieber. Stan didn't read comics. In fact he was embarrassed by them—he wanted to be a journalist or a novelist. He'd taken the job only because his mother was Martin Goodman's cousin and it looked like easy money. But he jumped in the saddle and let it carry him, using a pen name, "Stan Lee." Goodman's company would be a second-rater, all quantity and imitation, for the next twenty years. DC was indisputably the place to strive for now, the Tiffany of trash.

NOT EVERYONE WHO found himself making a living in this mushroom growth of an industry had grown up dreaming of pulps and comic strips. So much material was needed that sometimes just walking through the right door was enough to start a career and just meeting deadlines was enough to sustain it. Stan Lee, new editor for Martin Goodman, was proof of that, but there were plenty of others. The comics business was not a meritocracy. Call it an opportunocracy, a fluke-ocracy, a dumb-ass-luck-ocracy. The truest kind of American enterprise.

Gardner Fox was a lawyer who couldn't find a job in the recession of 1937 and 1938. An old school chum, Vin Sullivan, was editing *Detective Comics* and needed writers to help his artists fill pages, so he asked Gardner to take a stab. The young attorney had never thought of writing professionally, but he could do it well enough for comic books. When Shelly Mayer, editor of All American Comics, needed someone to crank out superheroes in a hurry, Vin put him on to his old friend. Gardner discovered that gimmicky heroes and breakneck action stories flowed out of him like water. Too many words, not enough plot, but always something going on. For Sullivan and Mayer in one venue or another he created the Flash, Hawkman, Skyman, the Face, Sandman, Starman, and Dr. Fate. And he wrote hundreds of stories for characters he didn't create.

Alvin Schwartz was a poet and editor of a literary magazine called *Mosaic* that published William Carlos Williams and Ezra Pound. His agent, Curtis Brown of London, had been trying for months to sell his first novel, but the depressed book market was against him. Alvin was two months late on his Greenwich Village rent that day in 1940 when he ran into an artist friend and asked him for a loan. The artist suggested he try writing for these new "comic books" that Street and Smith was publishing. The scripts Alvin sold were to *Fairy Tale Parade,* but so desperate was Whitney Ellsworth at DC for decent writers who could meet a deadline that he asked Alvin to take a shot at *Batman.* Within a year he was a regular writer not only for DC but for Sheldon Mayer and Charlie Gaines at All American.

Gaines and Mayer were unlike any other editorial team. They followed the DC policy of not hiring shops, working directly with freelancers, and running everyone's work through the editor. But they cared less about superheroes than their peers at DC, partly because they didn't have a property like Superman to protect and partly because they just couldn't take such things seriously.

Mayer was twenty-two in 1939 and was a geek who certainly understood superheroes—he was the one who got Superman sold—but he was also a humor cartoonist who couldn't help finding them ridiculous. Even during his editing tenure he kept his own series going: *Scribbly*, about a comic book–obsessed kid whose rotund mother puts on red underwear and drops a saucepan on her head to become that nemesis of crime, the Red Tornado. As editor, Mayer bought the silliest one-trick ideas from whatever artists walked through the door, as long as they were superheroes. But it worked. An advertising artist named Marty Nodell, who never knew comics existed until he needed a job, took samples to Mayer and was told to "come back with a superhero." Marty walked to the subway trying to think of ideas and saw a workman holding a green lantern. So he threw together a hero clad in green, red, yellow, and black—with a huge *purple* cape—who finds a green railroad lantern, powered by a meteorite from ancient China, that generates a magic ring. It made no sense at all, but Mayer bought it. And then the kids bought it. Green Lantern was a hit.

Gaines was a contrast: a former schoolteacher pushing fifty who wanted to do something better, something more challenging with comics. His pet project was *Picture Stories from the Bible*, which he envisioned as the foundation of a whole educational "Picture Stories" line. At first he rejected Shelly Mayer's urgings to create new superheroes and may finally have given in only after loud fights with his junior partner, Jack Liebowitz. Gaines didn't have Liebowitz's cool devotion to the balance sheet nor Harry Donenfeld's joy at whatever came around the bend. He worked hard, gimping around the offices on his bad leg, yelling at the people around him. Staffers would tell of the screaming matches that rose in volume and diminished in coherence from behind Liebowitz's closed office door (Jack always waited for the other guy to come to his office—he never went there), ending with a slam and the arhythmic thump of Charlie's angry stalk down the hall. On paper, Gaines was the majority partner, but Liebowitz had Donenfeld's ear, and Harry was the real power.

So Charlie would scream at Shelly Mayer, who would scream back. Or he'd scream at his son, Bill, who worked in the office until he turned eighteen and started at NYU. Bill was bright but fragile, a doughy kid, a letdown to a father who liked intellectual toughness. Charlie would call his son fat, stupid, and incompetent. Bill would flush, tremble, and try clumsily to go on doing his job, not looking his father in the eye. When his father was gone, he would turn to Shelly Mayer for protection and reassurance. Shelly was only five years older, but Bill treated him like the father he wished he had. Mayer's daughter would remember Bill coming by their house even years later, when Bill was in his midtwenties and Mayer about thirty, asking Mayer to meet his new girlfriend and tell him if he approved. The consolation that Bill kept repeating to himself was that he was only doing this until he could get through college and become a science teacher. Then the comics industry would never hear the name William M. Gaines again.

Maybe that was part of Charlie Gaines's rage, that his long, hard struggles in junk culture would enable his son to have the teaching career he couldn't afford to keep. Maybe that was why he was so intrigued when a psychologist in *Family Circle* magazine complained about the crude violence of so many comics but also thought they could touch those "tender spots of universal human desires and aspirations." Gaines invited the psychologist, William Moulton Marston, to join the new DC/All American "Editorial Advisory Board," and promptly found himself among the strangest bedfellows any comic book publisher could have imagined.

Marston was another of those middle-class WASPs, like many people in Frank Armer's nudie-magazine crowd and Bernarr MacFadden's self-improvement movement, who developed unconventional ideas about sex and gender as they came of age around the time of the First World War, then plunged feetfirst into the great social experiment of the 1920s only to find themselves high, dry, and rather quaint in the

Depression. Marston was a big man, obese in his middle years, given to loud laughter and overflowing affection. He studied both law and psychology at Harvard and married a brilliant, hardheaded woman named Elizabeth who had studied the same subjects at Boston and Radcliffe. While still a graduate student, he explored the relationship between increased blood pressure and emotional distress, which made him a key player in the development of the modern lie detector. With a bright reputation by the time he earned his doctorate in 1921, he promptly landed a position at Tufts University. Unfortunately, he just as promptly began to display the three cravings that would undo his career: for panaceas, for publicity, and for the domination of a good woman.

His continuing interest in human emotion, persuasion, and power led him to observe a "baby party," a weird sorority initiation at a women's college in which new pledges dressed like babies and were tied up, poked with sticks, and wrestled into submission by other girls. His research assistant was a graduate student named Olive Byrne, with whom he was also having an affair. Not long after that he revealed his affair to his wife, Elizabeth, but rather than ending either relationship, that only drew them tighter. Olive moved in with the Marstons in a ménage à trois. Eventually each woman had two children by Marston, all of whom were raised mainly by Olive as Elizabeth supported the family with a series of academic and editorial jobs.

In 1928 Marston cited the "baby party" and other adventures in his most popular book, *The Emotions of Ordinary People,* in which he argued that we can all be understood in terms of four "elementary behavior units," dominance, influence, steadiness, and compliance. It was an easily applicable look at the social power games of daily life, and if there was any doubt that he intended it to make him a popular pundit rather than a respected researcher, he even gave his system an acronym: DISC. All this was perfect for a tale of the Twenties, but not so perfect for academia, and that was the end of Marston's professorial career.

For the next decade, he rolled from coast to coast exploiting his reputation for DISC and the lie detector. He did public relations at Universal Studios for a year and appeared in magazine ads for Gillette razors (a lie detector test showed that men *really* thought Gillette shaved closest). Much of the time, he couldn't find work at all. One year the whole family—Marston, four children, and mistress—moved in with his wife's parents in Massachusetts while Elizabeth herself lived in New York, working at Metropolitan Life and mailing home checks. Finally, at the end of the decade, he made his arrangement with *Family Circle*. Psychologists weren't yet a standard component of the child-rearing industry, and his modest fame was enough to overcome his peculiar reputation. He cleverly boosted his apparent value by making his contributions not through articles under his name but through worshipful interviews by a journalist named "Olive Richard"—who was, of course, Olive Byrne.

This is where Charlie Gaines found him in 1940. The two hit it off well, the former teacher resentfully selling junk and the fallen intellectual trying to survive on sales pitches. They saw value in each other too, as money and academic credentials usually do. Gaines needed ammunition in his power struggles with Jack Liebowitz, something that would put him across as the idea man who ought to be listened to. Marston needed income. So Gaines listened when Marston said that "comics' greatest offense was their blood-curdling masculinity." There were a few minor heroines scattered through the comics, but none who had a chance against the supermen who were giving the industry such a rough reputation. Marston offered his psychological expertise in creating a superheroine who would appeal to children and reassure parents. He believed that women were stronger than men because they wielded the force of love, that war and evil were produced by men's violent quest for illusory power over women, and that secretly boys and men were "looking for an exciting, beautiful girl stronger than they are."

It was odd stuff for comics, but Marston was famously persuasive. His arguments were often based on crackpot science: "Woman's body contains twice as many love generating organs and endocrine mechanisms as the male. What woman lacks is the dominance or self assertive power to put over and enforce her love desires." And he knew how to pepper his speech with condescending chuckles and phrases like "The layman may think so, but as a psychologist . . ." In the end, Gaines offered Marston the chance to create his own superheroine. Marston said he'd do it only if he retained ownership of the character and royalties on sales in perpetuity. He even got Gaines to build a clause into the contract that the rights would revert to him or his heirs if the publisher ever failed to bring out an issue. The early comics publishers would give away a lot if they were pushed.

So William Moulton Marston, forty-eight-year-old maverick psychologist, joined the ranks of comic book writers. He used a pseudonym, "Charles Moulton" (a nod there to Charlie Gaines), although he never hesitated to tell the world who he was and use his comic book work to attract attention to his other writings. The heroine he created was an Amazon from Paradise Island who came to the world of men to put an end to war and exploitation. He called her "Suprema, the Wonder Woman." Sheldon Mayer nixed the "Suprema." He also tried to nix Marston's choice of artist, an elderly cartoonist named Harry G. Peter whose naive, antiquated style looked charming to the older academic but boring to the young comics editor. Marston liked the way Peter made his heroine look queenly and innocent, and dug in.

Knowledge of the story behind Wonder Woman's conception would not have inspired any reader to hope for much. The words of educational apologists for junk entertainment are always pallid compared to the fire and brimstone of their critics and the messy reality of the material itself. But something happened when Marston engaged with his fantasy heroine. He learned—as did Gaines, somewhat to his discomfort—that superheroes can come alive when a creator begins to work out his own dramas through the ritual of costumes, battles, victories, and defeats. They can impel a man to enter the dark and scary and heartfelt.

"Wonder Woman," Marston said, "is psychological propaganda for the new type of woman who should, I believe, rule the world." His core belief, his explanation of the world's ills (and perhaps his secret to happy polygamy), was that hatred and violence could be eliminated only by the surrender of male power to female. He gave Wonder Woman two main weapons. First, a pair of bullet-deflecting bracelets (based on the "Arab protective bracelets" worn by Olive Byrne). But there was more to them than prophylaxis—they were manacles as well, worn by the Amazons "to remind them of what happens to a girl when she lets a man conquer her. The Amazons once surrendered to the charm of some handsome Greeks [who] put them in chains of the Hitler type, beat them, and made them work like horses in the fields." The second weapon was a magic lasso that compelled whomever it ensnared to submit to her will. Marston intended it as a symbol of the real power of women, what he called "Love Allure." "Normal men retain their childish longing for a woman to mother them," he said. "At adolescence a new desire is added. They want a girl to allure them. When you put these two together, you have the typical male yearning that Wonder Woman satisfies . . . the subconscious, elaborately disguised desire of males to be mastered by a woman who loves them."

Every *Wonder Woman* story included at least one prominent scene— usually several—of someone bound. One story opens with a chained slave girl being berated by the god Mars, then proceeds to Dr. Psycho tying up a man and torturing him to death. Next Psycho suspends his fiancé, Marva, by her wrists, hypnotizes her, forces her to marry him, ties her to a chair, blindfolds her, and "uses her for occult experiments." He puts her on display in a glass box, still blindfolded; Wonder Woman arrives but is conned into tying her to the chair again ("Ow! Please don't tie me so tight!" "Why, that isn't half tight enough!") and then, two pages later, induced into tying her up yet *again* ("Oh, I hate to be bound—can't I please remain free?" "Certainly not, my dear! No woman can be trusted with freedom!"). Next the Amazon, in her secret identity as Diana Prince, helps manacle three office girls and strip them to their camisoles, panties, and garter belts. She discovers that her beloved Steve Trevor is locked in a cage, but in trying to rescue him, she's electrocuted and manacled to a wall—at ankles, wrists, arms, and throat. She escapes, frees Steve, and bursts into a vault to find poor Marva blindfold and shackled to a bed. In the end, a gang of sorority sisters echoes the "baby game" of Dr. Marston's early life as they chase Dr. Psycho to "give him a Lambda Beta treatment!" "Paddles up, sisters! Give 'im the works!"

The story is called "The Battle for Womanhood." The final panel squeezes the moral into Marva's lament and Wonder Woman's exhortation: "Submitting to a cruel husband's domination has ruined my life! But what can a weak girl do?" "Get strong! Earn your own living . . . fight for your country! Remember, the better you can fight the less you'll have to!" What the story leaves in us, however, is not the message to work for one's own living but images of bodies trussed and exposed.

Josette Frank, Marston's fellow member of DC's Editorial Advisory Board, warned Gaines that *Wonder Woman* "does lay you open to considerable criticism . . . partly on the basis of the woman's costume (or lack of it), and partly on the basis of sadistic bits showing women chained, tortured, etc." Marston's pat response was that "binding and chaining are the one harmless, painless way of subjecting the heroine to menace and making drama of it." But later in the same letter, he entered the thicket of the issues that his editors probably hoped he never would. "Women are exciting for this one reason—it is the secret of women's allure—women enjoy submission, being bound. This I bring out in the Paradise Island sequences where the girls beg for chains and enjoy wearing them." And that, he said, was "the one truly great contribution of my *Wonder Woman* strip to moral education of the young. The only hope for peace is to teach people who are full of pep and unbound force to enjoy being bound. . . . Only when the control of self by others is more pleasant than the unbound assertion of self in human relationships can we hope for a stable, peaceful human society."

Then he laid bare what no one else in that moment could or would have: "Giving to others, being controlled by them, submitting to other people cannot possibly be enjoyable without a strong erotic element." The eroticism of superheroes was not something a young man would ordinarily allow himself to see. But it was there, not only in the fetishism of Wonder Woman but in the crushing fists and twisting sinews of Jack Kirby, in the nocturnal masques of Bob Kane and Jerry Robinson, in the boyish smugness of Joe Shuster's great bodybuilder and the Charles Atlas ads across the page. The superhero comic book was about the body, the body in duress and supple joy, the body stripped down and made pure, the body discovered and glorified and also pushed away to a place unreal and unthreatening. It wasn't such a steep step from *Artists and Models* and *Pep Stories* to the comic books after all.

It turned out that Marston knew what he was doing. Despite its female protagonist, jumbled stories, and odd art, *Wonder Woman* was a huge and immediate success. Soon that erotic utopian polemic was appearing regularly in three comics, often outselling *Batman* and sometimes even *Superman*. And it sold mainly to preteen and teenage boys. A customer survey found that the Amazon's audience was 90 percent male; far more girls read *Superman* than *Wonder Woman*. That advertisers knew it is shown by the fact that *Wonder Woman*'s ads are mostly of the "Hey fellers, tell Dad to buy you a BB gun" genre. "By their comics tastes ye shall know them!" chortled Marston. "Tell me anybody's preference in story strips and I'll tell you his subconscious desires." Wonder Woman was less the model for girls that she's been made out to be than a way for boys to approach the most frightening mysteries.

After all those years of shilling and roaming and failing to grab the American imagination, Marston had found the themes he knew best and the passions he shared with millions of other males. And in the superhero comic book, he had found a field young enough, naive enough, unsupervised enough to let him bring those passions to the masses.

I⏀ HAD ALL happened so fast. Superman had appeared in an obscure corner of the newsstands in spring 1938 and begun to attract attention later that year. In January 1939 he appeared in the newspapers. Within six months new publishers and new superheroes were popping up on the newsstands. The next February Superman appeared on the radio and already had surging competition in the comics. By the middle of 1940, an industry was in full swing, shop bosses in their twenties were getting rich, and no-name rag publishers were getting richer. Newspaper columnists and clergy were already in an uproar. The very next year saw Plastic Man, Captain America, and Wonder Woman rewrite the genre that had just been born and the Superman cartoons secure it as the essential modern power fantasy. "Up, up, and away" and "Look, up in the sky" were catchphrases. Joe DiMaggio was being called "Superman." In just three years Jerry Siegel and Joe Shuster had gone from nobodies, to heroes, to the established old guard who had to be challenged, deposed, and outdone.

Fans and collectors would come to call those years the "Golden Age of Comics." Gradually the men who had lived them would adopt the phrase, too. For forty years after he got out of comic books, Jerry Robinson barely acknowledged his days with Batman and Daredevil, preferring to speak of his years in newspaper cartoons and his presidency of the National Cartoonists Society. But in his eighties, as he mounted a museum exhibition on Jewish comics artists, he found himself speaking casually of that "Golden Age."

It would glow especially golden through the clouds that came after. For suddenly there came the Japanese planes over Hawaii, and the long-awaited war, and the draft, and the camps and the sickness of heart and the leveling of popular culture and the end of the dreams.

Wars

THE WAR WAS good for the business of comics. Those fat, quick, colorful reads were perfect for the GI trying to kill time at the base or on ship. By the end of 1942, over 30 percent of the printed matter mailed to military bases was comic books. Sales that had been breathtaking went higher. *Superman* sold more than a million copies every issue, *Captain Marvel* sometimes two million. *Walt Disney's Comics and Stories* outsold them both combined.

The boom was best for the bigger publishers with the bigger paper allotments from the War Materials Board. Paper was restricted enough that the more marginal publishers found themselves unable to expand and were soon squeezed off the magazine racks. Before the war ended, comics had become less of a wildcat field and more of an established industry controlled by a handful of major players. The shops like Jerry Iger's and Jack Binder's began to fade, too, as they lost artist after artist to the draft and publishers found they could replace them with hacks of their own employ. The quality of the comics dropped even lower than it already had in prewar overproduction, but the medium had so seized the fancy of kids and soldiers that it didn't seem to matter.

Comics still weren't respected. The comic book, in fact, had become a byword for cultural stupidity to an extent that nothing—not dime novels, not pulps, not the funny pages, Hillbilly music, Mickey

Mouse, or even cowboy movies—had ever been before. When the press wanted to paint the murderous gangster Dukey Maffetore as mentally subnormal, they had only to report that he read *Superman* comics. Still, the furor about the comics' effect on the young had quieted, especially since so many superheroes were devoting themselves so vigorously to the war effort. Superheroes were also becoming better understood through the *Superman* cartoons and radio show, the *Mighty Mouse* parodies, the *Captain Marvel* and *Captain America* movie serials, and the *Batman* strip that now joined *Superman* in the newspapers. And the publishers' knowledge that their continued prosperity depended on the approval of military censors and PX masters also kept the material tamer for a while.

The war was generally pretty good for the men who made the comics. Writers and artists were usually able to get themselves assigned to propaganda or educational duties and stay out of combat. There were a few exceptions: Jack Kirby was too tough to ask for a break, so he was, in his own words, "handed a chocolate bar and an M-1 rifle and told to go kill Hitler." But most managed to spend the war painting posters or writing booklets on Jeep maintenance. Stan Lee made his mark with the classic "VD? Not me!" poster. He was also a master of featherbedding. His commander hated him for his cocky grin, his unshakable self-confidence, and the huge Buick Phaeton convertible he drove to and from camp every liberty. Once Stan connived to break into the camp post office after hours to get a plot summary Martin Goodman had mailed him. When he was caught, his commander told him with satisfaction that he'd be court-martialed and sent to Leavenworth. But Stan called Goodman, who called someone in the army and said that the writer of Captain America was being threatened with court-martial. The next day Stan was let out of the brig. His commander's hatred only grew hotter, but from that time on, it was a silent hatred.

For the best-known comic book writer of all, however, the war years were not so easy.

Jerry Siegel had lost his mother. The powerful Sarah Fine Siegel had been sliding into silence and lassitude since soon after her son's marriage to the girl across the street. She ceased to leave the Kimberly Avenue house, and her siblings, nieces, and children took turns looking after her. Always she brought the conversation around to that girl her son had married. Jerry tried to get her to give Bella a chance. He promised her a grandchild. But Sarah's darkness seemed unleavenable. "It wasn't just Jerry marrying Bella," said her nephew, Irv Fine. "It was everything that had happened to her, and she was sick. But she made it all about Jerry's marriage, and so did the rest of the family."

When Sarah died in August 1941, the matriarchs of the family decided that Jerry's marriage had killed his mother. "Are you happy now?" one of his aunts asked him. He went to the funeral, but Bella did not. Afterward he turned away from his family entirely, even the ones who didn't blame him. His cousin Jerry Fine wouldn't see him again for another forty years.

The marriage that the family hated so much was apparently not harmonious. Jerry still never spoke of his personal life, and neither he nor Bella would ever speak about their marriage even after decades passed; but he began to spend more time in New York, and the artists in his studio had the impression that he was getting away from the house in University Heights. His family's hostility couldn't have helped soothe whatever conflicts were building between them. Nor could his continuing arguments with Harry Donenfeld and Jack Liebowitz over the money he felt they owed him for Superman licensing. They were starting to send him checks for ancillary income now, but he always thought they were smaller than they should be. The artists who heard him talk about Bella's indifference to Superman gathered that she tolerated the Man of Tomorrow only because he was such a good provider. As much money as Jerry was making off the comic books and newspaper strip, the money he wasn't getting gnawed at him endlessly, and it must have gnawed at his wife, and their marriage, as well.

Harry's son, Irwin, had a strange memory from his adolescence that he insisted was true. Harry had moved Gea and the kids out of New York to a huge house in Woodmere, then on a ritzy stretch of the south shore of Long Island. Irwin was at home with Gea one Saturday morning when he looked out and saw Jerry and Bella Siegel marching back and forth in front of his house. And they were carrying signs: "Donenfeld Unfair to Jerry Siegel." Irwin asked his mother what was going on. Gea only shook her head and went back to what she was doing. Irwin watched the Siegels march up and down, up and down, on the sidewalk of a nearly empty new suburban development. Finally he got tired of watching, and when he looked again later, the Siegels were gone.

Could such a thing have happened? It has the quality of a Donenfeld family tale more than of reality. And yet there is, at least in caricature, a great deal of Jerry Siegel in it. It was always Siegel's way to express his anger through fantastic, slightly absurd vehicles that could not be taken seriously, that in fact nearly begged not to be taken seriously. His frustrations, defensive arrogance, and sense of alienation in high school he expressed through a geek's humor. His one social weapon was always the wisecrack. His lifelong hatred of criminals came out through the cartoon figure in tights who so often used his immense power to play the clown. Now he nagged for his share of licensing money with ineffectual letters and hesitant confrontations with Donenfeld in the halls of DC and, every time, nodded at the quick reassurance and swallowed his rage. It's true that his options were limited, since he'd sold away all his rights; but still, in those first few years of frustration he seems never to have demanded an audit, pushed to renegotiate his deal, threatened to take his talents elsewhere. He pestered and retreated at once, either not knowing what clout he had or afraid to wield it, hoping that presenting himself as the injured party would get justice done.

Perhaps it was true, as Irwin Donenfeld suggested, that his wife was pushing him to fight a battle that he didn't have the confidence for. Jerry was a fatherless boy from a Cleveland suburb, an outsider to New York and the world of business, who had no maps and no models to lead him. Bella, still only twenty years old and anything but worldly when the war began, no doubt wanted Jerry to be the successful adult he had played for her. How could he admit that he didn't know what to do and didn't believe in himself to get it done?

The first year of the war passed and the months of the second marched by, and still Jerry was not called by the draft. Joe Shuster would be declared 4F because of his vision, but Jerry had no such ailments. He'd told his family, "The government doesn't want me to go to war because Hitler promised to *kill* me if I do." His younger and more romantic cousins listened wide-eyed. They knew their oddball cousin had created something silly yet lucrative, but they never dreamed what a threat the Jewish Superman posed to the Nazis! The older and more cynical ones thought that maybe Hitler had other issues on his mind and wondered why men even more prominent than Jerry Siegel were being sent to war.

A persistent rumor in the comic book business was that Harry Donenfeld was arranging to keep Siegel out of uniform, which was the sort of thing Harry would and could do. And Jerry had reasons to ask not to be drafted, not only for the sake of his work and wife but for reasons of professional insecurity as well. He believed that DC was trying to ace him out of *Superman.*

"Joe and I had signed a deal giving us the exclusive contract to produce the comics," Siegel said, "but I was afraid when I went into the service that they would take advantage of the situation to assign stories to their own people. And I was afraid that even though Joe was still running the studio, that they'd use the situation to get around him too." His fears were not unfounded. From the moment Mort Weisinger arrived as editor in early 1941, he pushed Jerry to agree to let him hire writers and artists to help with *Superman.* He said the Shuster studio was overworked and didn't have enough strong draftsmen and that Jerry was too busy to do the best possible stories. To his superiors, Mort said that Siegel didn't know what do with his own creation as well as his editors did. Liebowitz already saw Siegel as immature and unrealistic and Weisinger as a proven master of juvenile pulps. Jerry's rejected "K-Metal" and Superboy ideas only supported Weisinger's arguments. Mort was drafted in late 1941, but he got DC to hire Jack Schiff, a friend and colleague from the Ned Pines pulp factory, to hold his job down until he came back; then by phone call, telegram, and letter he stayed on top of Schiff, keeping his hand on Superman's rudder from Fort Dix.

Disagreements about Superman's direction were brewing in 1942. Siegel and Shuster's work was growing more exuberant and more absurd. They did finally bring Superman into the war, although, by agreement with their editors, not as a combatant. They'd made such a superhuman being of him that the Axis armies couldn't have stood plausibly against him even for the length of a story, so the Man of Tomorrow decided that the war should be won by "the greatest of all heroes, the American fighting man," and contented himself with USO shows to boost morale and occasional forays against superscientists in the German camp. Mainly, Siegel and Shuster made Superman an escape from real-life conflict and tilted his adventures more and more toward humor. Having lost the battle over Superboy and his juvenile pranks, they filled their stories with absurd mischief makers: Mr. Mxyztplk, Topsy and Turvy, the Prankster, and Funny Face, who lives inside newspaper comic strips. They indulged in more and more self-referentiality too. In one story Clark takes Lois to the movies and finds a *Superman* cartoon appearing in front of him. ("As featured in *Action* and *Superman Comics*," read the credits. "I don't think I know those magazines," says Lois.) The whole story turns on his effort to keep Lois from seeing the scene where Clark Kent changes into Superman.

Weisinger and Schiff also loved twists, gimmicks, and humor but preferred them in settings of intricate plot and believable jeopardy. Their favorite writers included Bill Finger, who'd given Batman his emotional weight, and Alvin Schwartz and Don Cameron, who'd both started their careers as novelists and attacked their little superheroic dramas with uncommon earnestness. Siegel and Shuster flew through childlike fantasies with self-mocking brio. Weisinger and Schiff wanted *Superman* to do what their line of "Thrilling" pulps had done: cut straight to their young readers' appetites. Someone at DC even made a subtle but revealing change to the character's nickname. Their competitors at *Pep Comics* had a minor hero named Steel Sterling, "the Man of Steel." When his adventures were canceled, DC jumped on the name. "Man of Tomorrow," with its optimistic evocations of the pre-war world's fair, was replaced with a harder, more physical, more military descriptive.

Siegel fought every attempt to slip a story by another writer or artist past him. Bob Kane was much more amenable to DC farming out Batman stories, feeling that keeping his studio's quality high and his relationships smooth would ultimately be better for him. Kane had the advantage of a father in the printing business and daily experience with publishers, and he had an instinct for making himself liked that Siegel lacked. Jerry Siegel in the months before the war gives the impression of a man flailing against disaster he fears he cannot prevent. Such sudden, improbable success, coming so early and with so little preparation, can leave the ground underfoot feeling terribly insecure. Old losses and old inadequacies can rise from where they've been buried. Grandiosity turns to suspicion. To him, the prospect of two years on a military base looked like nothing so much as DC's chance to take away what he'd been promised.

Whatever kept Jerry Siegel out of the draft for all those months finally ended in the summer of 1943. The hand of Duke Ducovny and the DC public relations machine can be felt even then, however. Jerry was honored as a star inductee at a huge "Liberty Day" celebration in Cleveland on the Fourth of July. Walter Winchell got the scoop, and it played well in the Cleveland press. Jerry stood on a dais, he nodded, he took his papers, and then he was off to basic training.

By then Bella Siegel was nearly four months pregnant. The grandchild was coming at last, but too late for the family to welcome it. The Siegel family heard almost nothing about the baby who was born in January 1944. It got a small story in the *Plain Dealer:* "Son Born to Superman Writer." It said that Jerry had come home from maneuvers in West Virginia to attend the birth. But again the curtain is pulled around Jerry Siegel's life. In all the interviews he gave and all the conversations he had with fans over the next fifty years, he never mentioned his son. Michael Siegel would grow up with no memories of his father, only Bella's bitterness at how Jerry abandoned his family. "My father never paid a cent of child support," he said. "He acted like I didn't exist. I don't understand why he did that. Maybe he just couldn't handle being responsible for someone else." Unable to attend college, Michael would support himself and his mother with off-and-on plumbing work and odd jobs.

The next year, Bella bore a second son. This one died in infancy. Jerry began to withdraw completely from his wife. The army shipped him to Hawaii, to work on *Stars and Stripes*. Bella got fewer letters from him, but she did sometimes get receipts for jewelry he'd apparently bought for other women; prostitutes, she believed. For Jerry, the army may have been a comforting retreat, but it was also a lonely one. The men who served with him remembered him as pleasant but aloof, inclined to remind people often of who he was. One joke went that his name tag read "Cpl Siegel" because that's all the army had room for but that his full name was "Corporal Siegel the Creator of Superman." He would come out of the Army with only one close associate: a lawyer named Albert Zugsmith.

THE WAR WAS a grand time for Harry Donenfeld. Whether because of his connections or the morale-boosting value of his publications, he had no trouble getting paper and ink even during the tightest restrictions, leaving him better able to take advantage of the soaring popularity of comics than nearly any other publisher or distributor. Harry was not only getting richer but, as the man who owned Superman, was highly in demand for bond drives and patriotic campaigns. If the government wanted to get the word to kids about collecting scrap or saving rubber, it turned to Harry. If it wanted a cartoon hero to sell another bond issue, it turned to Harry. Only four years earlier he'd been facing the prospect of being driven to ruin for publishing *La Paree* and *Spicy Stories*. Then he'd stepped on a rocket, shot into the sky, and stepped off to find himself part of the establishment.

With Jerry Siegel in the army, Harry became the chosen spokesman for Superman to the magazines, newspapers, and radio. He even found himself on the *Baby Snooks Show*, doing shtick with the great Fanny

Brice herself. "The Man behind Superman" was the name of Harry's bit, and he milked the story of discovering the superhero with verve and volume. He clicked with Fanny; she was a Lower East Side girl, just a couple of years older than him, and they'd both conquered the world with childish fun and competitive aggression. When Fanny's foil, Frank Morgan, claimed that he was secretly Superman, Harry pounced on him with a flurry of almost believable outrage. Contrasted with Jerry Siegel's halting repartee with Fred Allen, the difference between the men's personalities is striking, the sense of Harry's greater power palpable. That episode of *Baby Snooks* was distributed to military bases by the Armed Forces Radio Service. It's likely that Jerry Siegel listened to it and likely that it deepened his resentment.

Harry was not reticent about advertising the success that Superman had brought him. He had a huge painting of Superman installed in the Detective Comics lobby and a big photograph of himself mounted in the boardroom. His fiftieth birthday was an occasion for a colossal party at the Waldorf. Ostensibly Jack and Rose Liebowitz threw it, but Harry's loud sense of humor shaped it. Jack had a mock newspaper published, with the banner headline "DONENFELD SPEECHLESS." Anyone whose ears had been bent by Harry must have laughed. There were excerpted telegrams from business associates all over the country and funny quotes from his friends. A cartoon had Adolf Hitler complaining to a beaming Harry, "I've been feeling awful since I turned fifty!" And an odd little comic strip showed Harry overpowering Superman and spanking his *tuchus*. The party was long, loud, drunken, triumphant. Afterward Harry said the only thing that made his heart heavy was that his wife could be there but not Sunny, the woman he loved.

Everything was a show to Harry. His son joined the army as soon as he turned eighteen and entered pilot training. He never saw combat but remained at Keesler Army Air Force Base to fight what he called "the battle of Mississippi." As a lightweight boxer Irwin soon became a camp celebrity, and he called his father to tell him he was going for the base championship. Harry said he was going to come down to see him, then added, "Tell whoever's in charge to arrange a dinner with the officers for me." "Dad, I can't do that," gasped Irwin. "I'm just another soldier here." Harry scoffed and hung up. A few days later, with the match approaching, Irwin looked up to see a lieutenant striding toward him. "Donenfeld," he said, "report to the colonel." Irwin went, "scared shitless," wondering what he'd done wrong. He was told to wait in the anteroom of the colonel's office. Suddenly the door flew open and in swept Harry Donenfeld. "There's my boy the boxer!" he crowed. Somehow he'd arranged not only a pass onto the base, not only a dinner with the colonel, but an officer's limousine to bring him in from the Biloxi train station. The colonel stepped out to meet the great Donenfeld. Within minutes, Irwin said, his father had established that the officer's wife and Gussie Donenfeld belonged to the same club, and he and the colonel walked off laughing, their arms around each other. Amazement still gleamed in Irwin's eyes nearly sixty years later. "He made *everybody* like him!"

Harry gave jobs to his friends and their relatives, staked others to new companies, tossed out loans. He'd funded his old gin rummy partner Ben Sangor in his own publishing company, the American Comics Group, and now he gave a young man named Fred Iger who worked on the *Superman* radio show the business manager's job. Iger married Harry's daughter, Peachy, when she was just eighteen, and Harry threw a huge wedding for them. The marriage went bad quickly and lasted barely a year, but Harry still liked Iger, let him buy his way out of the marriage and keep his job.

By the war years, Harry had reportedly pulled out of every illegal racket, as so many men who'd made their fortunes during Prohibition and hustled their way through the Depression did. He remained loyal to his old friends and enmeshed in enterprises built on dirty money, but his own funds now were all in publishing, distribution, and legitimate investments. That may have been largely due to Jack Liebowitz, who was doggedly making a clean, modern, presentable corporation out of Harry's murky and messy interests and, at the same time, making himself an increasingly powerful part of it.

All American Comics had been a huge success for Jack Liebowitz and his partner, Charlie Gaines. But Gaines wasn't happy. He and

Liebowitz fought constantly, and usually Harry weighed in to tip it in Jack's favor. Gaines saw the end of the superhero fad coming and wanted to get into something more durable, like children's books and magazines. And he still sincerely wanted to do something wholesome and worthwhile; even though All American's and DC's superheroes were among the most respectable in the business, he wasn't crazy about them. In 1944 he decided he'd had enough. He let Jack Liebowitz buy him out with a loan from Harry, keeping only his *Picture Stories from the Bible* as the foundation of his new company, Educational Comics.

Liebowitz promptly orchestrated the merger of All American Comics and Detective Comics into National Comics, of which he was the junior partner, vice president, and publisher. Next he took charge of organizing National Comics, Independent News, and their affiliated firms into a single corporate entity, National Periodical Publications. Liebowitz was the principal architect in making a legitimate distribution, publishing, and licensing contender out of all those hastily formed and quaintly named Donenfeld companies.

Always looking down the long road, Liebowitz knew that flexibility and coordination were going to matter as the publishing business changed. The pulp magazines, for one thing, were dying. The pulps had depended on a wide range of readers: kids and semiliterates seeking sensational adventures and illustrations on one end and, on the other, adults seeking decent fiction of the sort that wouldn't have seen print in *Colliers* or the *Post*. Comic books were stealing the first market, and another sensationally popular new form, paperback books, were stealing the second. Paperbacks had started with more highbrow publishers, but as the war began, some of the pulp and cheap magazine publishers who'd made money on comic books were jumping in with great success—among them Charlie Gaines's former partner, George Delacorte, and Harry Donenfeld's buddy Ned Pines with his Popular Library. Such frontiers would have seemed far beyond their reach just a few years before, when burlesque houses were still among their major outlets. But now they were in reach, and Jack Liebowitz wanted to be ready.

In the short term, the fading of the pulps benefited the comics. More people were following Mort Weisinger's example and leaving jobs in the pulps for spots at comics companies. Mort's old friend from science fiction fandom, Julius Schwartz, had to abandon his career as a literary agent in 1944 as the market for his clients' stories dried up. He was recommended to Sheldon Mayer at All American by one of his clients, Henry Kuttner (who had gotten into comics in the first place because of Mort Weisinger). Julie became an editor under Mayer; then, in the merger of the companies, he found himself working alongside Mort at National Comics.

But the comic book market was changing, too. Even by 1942, it was becoming apparent that the novelty was fading from superheroes. The established heroes were still selling phenomenally, but no new costumed characters were catching kids' fancy; *Wonder Woman* was the last big hit of the genre. At the same time William Marston's Amazon appeared, a very different but equally significant character had appeared in MLJ Publishing's *Pep Comics*. *Pep* sold mainly on the strength of the Shield, the first patriot-superhero, and the Hangman, a Batman imitation. But in late 1941 it featured the first episode, among its minor backup strips, of a series about a silly teenager named Archie Andrews. Kids liked Archie and the way he both reflected and mocked the adolescent culture they were growing into, and by early 1943 the editors were putting him on the cover. By late 1944 they'd dropped the superheroes from *Pep* entirely. Early the next year, MLJ changed its name to Archie Comics.

Every publisher was suddenly jumping into teen humor. The discovery that girls were buying *Archie* in huge numbers sparked a flurry of comics about young women: *Katy Keene, Nellie the Nurse, Millie the Model, Miss America*. Boys were going for comics about soldiers and aviators: *Blackhawk, Airboy, Boy Commandos*. Parents nudged their kids toward *Classic Comics* and *True Comics*, and the kids were cooperative enough to drive sales into the hundreds of thousands. George Delacorte outsold them all with his *Donald Duck* and *Mickey Mouse*. Soon he was licensing Bugs Bunny, Woody Woodpecker, Tarzan, Roy Rogers, and a slew of other pop culture fixtures and making Dell the biggest publisher in comics.

This was the evolving world Jerry Siegel nervously watched from the distance of Honolulu. Liebowitz was now a full partner in the company, and Harry Donenfeld, with his rosy promises, was no longer the court of last resort. The editors were turning against the Siegel and Shuster style. And Superman himself was becoming less central to National Comics's prosperity. Then, in late 1944, Superboy was rocketed into that world.

The success of Fawcett's Captain Marvel, Jr., and Mary Marvel showed that kids wanted juvenile spin-offs of their heroes. Whitney Ellsworth and Jack Schiff dusted off Jerry Siegel's Superboy idea from three years before—not a sidekick but Superman himself as a child—but made an essential change. The Boy of Steel wouldn't be a super-prankster but a wholesome young crime fighter. He would live with his farm-bred folks, Ma and Pa Kent, in a small town straight from the *Saturday Evening Post*; eventually it would be named "Smallville." The adventures would turn on grade-school secret-identity shenanigans and such cute revelations as "How Clark Kent first met Lois Lane." The editors understood that the idea would sell to eight-year-olds or not at all, and they pointed the series straight at them. Soon Superboy would even be given a superdog named Krypto.

For the first five-page story, the editors turned to the Siegel and Shuster studio. Years later Jerry Siegel would give the impression that he'd been surprised to find "Superboy" in *More Fun Comics* at the end of 1944. But that first story was unmistakably drawn by Joe Shuster and his assistants; and fans digging into National's files decades later discovered that Jerry Siegel was indeed the writer of record. It's possible that the story was executed within the studio and ghostwritten by someone Joe hired, without Jerry's awareness. But Jerry remained in touch with the studio throughout his tour of duty. He probably would have known. It's more likely that he banged out that first script without thinking about the implications—and only after the writing job was handed to

Don Cameron did he realize that National had just created a new character based on his idea without compensating him for it.

There may have been a pride issue involved, too. The stories bore the words "by Jerome Siegel and Joe Shuster" no matter who wrote them. No one would know that National had scrapped Jerry's original idea and replaced it with something calculatedly infantile. Jerry was thirty years old. He wanted the words "I'm Jerry Siegel, the creator of Superman" to make him bigger, not more ridiculous.

Jerry complained. Liebowitz dismissed him. They were still hiring his studio to draw the stories, weren't they? So Jerry was making money without having to work, wasn't he? Jerry had been here before: regretting his haste, watching his property slip away, and being treated like an ungrateful child by the publisher who got rich off his ideas. The drama of impotent rage he'd been acting for six years since the sale of Superman was starting to play all over again.

This time, though, he had a lawyer to talk to. He'd always resisted hiring lawyers, but it was different being in camp with one, shooting the breeze at night, finding Albert Zugsmith sympathetic to his complaints. In "Zuggy" Jerry could even see the kind of self-promoting savvy he'd always wanted in himself. He was four years older than Jerry and attacked the world with a bravado that made him seem still older. He was big, chunky, square cut, cigar munching, could have passed for forty instead of thirty-four. He'd grown up in Atlantic City, the huckster's paradise, and he knew how to sell himself. He had gotten his law degree because it seemed practical but discovered the newspaper game was more exciting and knocked around as a reporter for various papers and a press agent for local promoters. He started publishing advertising circulars and promotional magazines, and then, just before being drafted, he began producing radio shows in New Jersey. He decided he liked the entertainment business best of all. Some might have looked at him and seen an inexperienced lawyer, but Jerry Siegel saw a confident guy who knew showbiz, publishing, and the law. What Zugsmith saw was an insecure little man with a claim on one of the most lucrative properties in entertainment.

Jerry asked him if he thought he could sue for compensation on Superboy. Zuggy said he could do better than that. He could go for the big strike. He could get his rights to Superman back.

BY EARLY 1945 World War II was clearly coming to an end. Americans were looking ahead to the postwar world. What technological wonders would it bring, what social and economic shifts as millions of men came home? Jerry Siegel and Joe Shuster looked ahead to the final three years of their contract to produce *Superman* pages and saw reason to fear for their future. Mort Weisinger looked at the editorial post awaiting him at a burgeoning National Comics and saw opportunity.

Mort was another great self-promoter. He boasted about having edited a pulp magazine reviewed in *The New Yorker,* bulldozing past the fact that the review was S. J. Perelman's acidic "Captain Future, Block That Kick!" When he began selling fillers to *Readers Digest,* he pitched himself as an authority on the "legitimate magazine" market and launched an aggressive climb through the ranks of the Magazine Writers of America. Maybe Jack Schiff and Whit Ellsworth were more worldly and better educated than he, but they were also too modest. It was Mort who sold himself to Liebowitz as a big shot, a guy who could do a lot better than comic books if National didn't hang onto him.

Mort knew that the way to make himself most valuable at National was to take complete control of the Superman franchise. And he knew that the greatest obstacle to that goal was the Siegel and Shuster studio. He had begun his editorial career by usurping the job of Charles Hornig, one of his comrades in early science fiction fandom. To tear Superman from the grasp of his creators was just another career move for him—even if those creators were childhood friends from Gernsback fandom. When Mort and Jerry mustered out of the military in 1945, they both had their sights set on controlling Superman. But Mort held every advantage.

Jerry began to complain more openly that Jack Liebowitz and Harry Donenfeld hadn't lived up to the terms of their agreement. Liebowitz and Donenfeld responded with anger and dismissal. They believed they were fair, even generous, with their creative freelancers. They didn't consider writers and artists their equals: They didn't socialize with them or invite them to their birthday bashes. Jerry Robinson told the story of meeting Jack Liebowitz at a cocktail party and having Liebowitz ask him, with more than a trace of disgust, "What are *you* doing here?" To them the writers and artists were hired hands, what skilled cutters were to the rag trade. Donenfeld and Liebowitz paid higher page rates than most of the competition, invited freelancers to company parties, encouraged editors to take them out for lunch and drinks, gave credit to their best writers and artists in print, and offered "tokens of feeling" that they believed should buy them loyalty.

There is another Donenfeld family story, unprovable but clearly believed by the family and important to the battles that would follow. "My father paid for Joe Shuster's eye surgery," Irwin said. Joe's eyesight had been worsening under the strain of producing ever more pages of comics; that was part of the reason he'd needed the studio even before *Superman* added so much to his workload. According to the story told by Harry Donenfeld, a doctor told him surgery could help. Joe apparently never told Jerry Siegel this—but that would not be unlikely, as Joe always hid the severity of his vision problems, even after they finally prevented him from drawing at all. Word found its way to Harry Donenfeld, who immediately offered to pay for the surgery. It wouldn't have been unlike Harry to do it. But then, making up the story wouldn't have been, either.

True or not, the story stood in for Harry's conviction that he'd been generous with "the boys," more generous than another publisher in the same position would have been. And indeed, there were uglier companies in the field. Louis Silberkleit, John Goldwater, and Maurice Coyne of *Pep* offered even less to Vic Bloom and Bob Montana for their creation, Archie Andrews. Goldwater even claimed in print to have created Archie himself, and so he cut off Bloom and Montana's complaints in advance. Siegel and Shuster were certain they were being wronged by Donenfeld and Liebowitz when they manipulated profit statements and exploited their creations with other freelancers. But Harry and Jack were certain they were being wronged when Jerry and Joe complained.

There's a revealing moment in a skit Harry recorded for an Independent News distributors' conference in late 1940. As Bud Collyer, as Superman, addresses the distributors, Harry suddenly butts in: "Wait a minute, *wait* a minute, I've got something to say here!" "Who are you?" asks Superman. "Who am *I*?" cries Harry. "Do you ask who *I* am?! Why, I'm Harry Donenfeld! Your boss!" "I never heard of you." "Why, you . . . ! Look, I took you off a drawing board and made a *man* outta ya! I splashed your name from coast to coast! And you never heard of *me*? Step aside, Superman!" The skit proceeds to give Harry his comeuppance at Superman's hands, but there's no doubting the sincerity of Harry's assertion. In Harry's world the seller took the cash and the buyer owned. You could buy a suit from a tailor and wear it to a job interview and get a great job, and the tailor couldn't come around saying, "You owe me part of that job. I made that suit!" "Sure, Siegel and Shuster made him up," Irwin Donenfeld said irately, "but my father published him. He spent the money on him. He took the risk. Superman was a big success, and Siegel and Shuster made money off him, too. But if he'd bombed, who would have lost money? Not Siegel and Shuster. Only my father." Writers and artists believe in an ownership that transcends money and contracts, but salesmen and accountants don't. Donenfeld and Liebowitz didn't draw, didn't write, didn't make things up out of their pain and dreams. They bought and sold.

They also bent the ledgers the way the sellers of entertainment and other hard-to-track goods still do, making profits from one product disappear into losses from another. They waited until someone demanded an audit before acknowledging all their income. It was how they played their game. When they looked at Siegel and Shuster, they saw two odd kids who'd never have been successful and famous if not for their investments and their risks. They genuinely believed the boys should be grateful. The "boys" believed just as genuinely that they were being robbed.

Weisinger began to tell Liebowitz that Siegel and Shuster were more trouble than they were worth. Every writer in his stable was better than

Siegel, and there were others he could bring in, real pulp writers like Edmond Hamilton. Shuster's best ghosts, Wayne Boring and John Sikela, were already working directly for National. Letting Jerry get mad and stomp out the door could solve a lot of problems. When Jerry returned to civilian life, he wanted his old position back as the main supplier of *Superman* stories. Weisinger assigned him scripts, but he assigned more to Don Cameron and Alvin Schwartz. Just as he predicted, Jerry got angrier. Weisinger claimed Siegel had threatened him in his office, and he made the security guard frisk Jerry for weapons whenever he entered building. He said Siegel was trailing him, that when he left his house in the morning Jerry would be standing across the street staring at him. The angrier Jerry got, the more his old friend turned it against him.

Jerry told Joe that it was time for them to develop a new property, so they wouldn't need to depend on Superman, and then push Liebowitz and Donenfeld to a resolution of their conflicts. He moved almost full-time to New York, where he could be close to the center of power and close to his new friend Albert Zugsmith, who was moving actively into radio and exploring opportunities in television. In New York he was also further from his wife and baby son. He ceased to speak of his family anymore. Whatever had happened behind his curtain of privacy, his marriage had apparently died. He was devoting himself entirely now to his ride to disaster.

True Crime

No OTHER FAD in entertainment has ever paralleled real-life events as closely as the superheroes paralleled World War II. Superman first drew attention in the summer of 1938, as war fears grew out of the Czechoslovakia crisis, and it was after the war really began late the next summer that the superhero fad took flight. By 1941, as America moved inevitably into the war, the heroes grew rapidly in number, popularity, variety, and aggression, and some of the most popular were taking on the Nazis. The last new superhero to find a big audience, Wonder Woman, hit at the end of that year, as the war finally swept across the ocean. For the next three years, sales climbed. Superman and his imitators had captured a national emotional upwelling and turned it into a shared fantasy of escape. Their first and essential market was kids, but to enjoy the towering sales they did during the war, they had to be read by innumerable adults who pretended they were just indulging the "child in us all."

Superheroes turned anxiety into joy. As the world plunged into conflict and disaster almost too huge to comprehend, they grabbed their readers' darkest feelings and bounded into the sky with them. They made violence and wreckage exciting but at the same time small and containable. So flat, iconic, childlike, unreal, and absurd were those godlings in tights that no reader had to feel he was really engaging with his own angry fantasies. Superman was less a fantasy self than a god out of the machine—a sudden, flash-of-color resolution to conflicts too terrible to think about. The superheroes were slapstick comedians in a vaudeville of holocaust. Even in Captain America's angriest assault on the Nazis and Superman's darkest melodrama in Luthor's lab, every reader over the age of eight had to laugh at them. Superheroes served the purpose of slapstick comedians but on a global scale: They built fear and frustration in a containable fantasy world and then released them with a shock.

Superheroes allowed adolescents and adults to slip back to the confidence and inviolability of that last moment of childhood before the anxiety of pubescence. It had been a long, nerve-wearing run for twenty years, through Prohibition and sexual revolution and economic transformation and urbanization and Depression and the rumors of war, when a naive nation had to pretend to be adult and sophisticated. All through the 1920s and early 1930s, there had been childlike entertainment that had captured adults, but it nearly always had a cruel humor (*Our Gang*), strenuous melodrama (*King Kong*), or a melancholy sentimentality (Shirley Temple). Finally, at the end of the 1930s, in the moment of *The Wizard of Oz,* the American imagination retreated into the laughing, arrogant fun of the ten-year-old. Superman was the physical embodiment of that fantasy of wholeness, that wondrous sense of knowing who one is and believing one can do anything, that shatters in adolescence.

Superheroes were a latent-phase dream, embodying sex but invulnerable to it. They distilled that moment of swelling, big-kid pride in the new power and agility of the body, that last moment before the body begins to make its own scary demands and the world turns the mechanisms of shame against it. Superman in particular cartooned the cruelty of sex—Superman tricks Lois sadistically, but then as Clark he flings himself masochistically before her high heels—but with his famous wink at the reader, he let us know that he played every minute of it as a game. As the "Man of Tomorrow," he had supposedly evolved beyond sexual entanglements, but in fact he was the man of the day before yesterday, looking at the agonies of adolescence with the superior sneer of a little brother spying on his sister. After the frenzied sexual questioning of the Twenties and the cynicism of sex and economics in the early Depression, and with the draft now bringing on another huge dislocation, the superhero was a welcome island of prepubescence.

Superheroes were also an expression of a rising American thrill. All the queasiness of the Depression was about to be blown away in a great and terrible battle, and as much as most people shook their heads about the horror of war, there was a hunger for it, too. The war meant not survival and dirty compromise but utter triumph or utter disaster. It meant unity of purpose too, and the superheroes embodied that in their polychrome simplicity: Superman, Captain America, and Wonder Woman were the most distinct individuals imaginable, but at the same time, each of them was all of us. The rarely spoken hunger for war was especially sharp for the children of immigrants and of the polyglot cities. A nation dominated for a generation by isolationist, prohibitionist, and small-town Protestants was about to plunge into the world, led by its cockiest, most sophisticated progressives. America had won the last war. Since then it had only grown in size, influence, and industrial capacity. It had held itself back from world events as fascism spread, but Roosevelt's voters knew how powerful the country was. America was playing Clark Kent. It was time to rip off the suit.

The genius of Jerry Siegel and Joe Shuster was to combine movie slapstick with pulp adventure, make fun of their fantasies as they indulged them, retreat into childhood as they made themselves act like grownups, and laugh at the world that saw them as cowards as they held back their rage, just as America was skewered on the conflict between its wishfully innocent self-image and the most terrible necessities. The geek culture found its first moment of universal relevance as all those young men with their Depression smiles were yanked from their homes and sent to war.

But then the war spilled those exuberant energies. The long, draining realities of combat, self-denial, and labor ended in the huge relief of victory, but they ended also in horror. The bombs that ended the war with such breathtaking suddenness brought a new nausea. People began to think about what the next war would bring, and they knew America wouldn't be able to hold the secret of the bomb for long. And there was an enemy already. There would be no fifteen years of apparent peace after this war as there'd been after the last one. American and Russian tanks were squaring off against each other even before the Nazis had surrendered. The confetti had scarcely been swept up from the victory parades when conservatives in Congress were suggesting that Stalin had been our *real* enemy all along. Roosevelt was dead and Truman inspired no one's confidence at first. And there were the images trickling from the concentration camps, the numbers being slowly added up, the 9 million dead in the camps, the 50 million dead in the war. The monstrous capabilities of humanity forced their way into the American vision just as everyone was trying to celebrate the dawning of the age of democracy and decency.

From the beginning of 1945, with the end of the war finally in sight, superheroes' sales began to drop. By the end of 1946, they were only about two-thirds what they'd been at their peak. In 1947 publishers began scrambling for the next hot genre: humor, western, romance, crime, and horror comics poured out. By the end of 1948, most superhero comics had been canceled or converted to other genres. The survivors, mostly the big-name heroes, were being aimed more consciously at a juvenile audience.

The story Americans had told each other through the war was that G. I. Joe, through sheer humble, dogged effort, would triumph over evil and then go home to his old job while his bride returned to her kitchen and they'd raise a family and carve the nation up into a picket-fenced utopia. Most Americans struggled to make that very story come true. But there was so much that could not be spoken of if the story were to remain intact. What the men had had to do in combat and what they'd chosen to do in liberty. What the women had done in their absence and how thrilling that freedom and selfishness had been. What the old men and the 4Fs did to feather their nests when the workforce was at war.

Americans pulled a lid of tense harmony down on themselves, while a stew of fear and disgust bubbled under it.

The right wing, long pushed from power, climbed atop Roosevelt's grave to announce that it would enforce that false harmony in order to save us from the communists. The war was only six months past when the comic book industry felt the chill of their gaze. In early 1946 Lev Gleason, publisher of *Crime Does Not Pay* and *Daredevil*, was one of a group of sixteen men accused by the House Un-American Activities Committee of distributing pro-Soviet propaganda during the war. When he and his associates refused to turn over subpoenaed documents, they were arrested for intent to obstruct justice. It wasn't his comic books that had gotten him in trouble but the political books and magazines he distributed, and the case was eventually dropped. But the message was heard clearly by the men who published the comics, mostly immigrants, mostly marginalized, often experienced in troubles with the law and sometimes, as in Jack Liebowitz's case, with socialist ties in their pasts.

To American Jews the aftermath of the war brought especially poignant fears and hopes. Hitler was dead, racism pushed back on its heels, the world's sympathy extended to the victims of the Holocaust, the retaking of Zion about to come true. But at such a cost. The Jewish world of Europe had been obliterated, the world of shtetl and ghetto that had been the soil and the memory of the American immigrant, the world that gave history and definition and sound and smell to modern Jewishness. The old country that had turned its wounds into wails and bitter humor to nourish the Jewish soul was not wounded now. It was gone. Yiddish had been wiped from the earth.

In America, housing, educational, and job quotas were being dropped as Jews were accepted into the establishment as never before. But at the same time, so much that had defined American *Yiddishkeit*—leftist politics and noisy Jewish boosterism—were being discouraged. The Un-American Activities Committee wasn't just going after left-wing publishers and moviemakers, at least half of whom were Jewish, but also proposing that the post office deny second-class mailing rights to any foreign-language newspaper that didn't provide a full English translation. It was a petty gesture but a meaningful one, an obvious slap at the Yiddish press that had played such a vital part in disseminating left-wing ideas earlier in the century. After all, the driving force of that committee, the Honorable John Rankin of Mississippi, asserted that World War II had been the product of an "international Jewish plot" and that Walter Winchell was "a little slime-mongering kike."

To be an established American Jew now meant identifying fiercely with the survivors and the Israelis but, at the same time, embracing an ever narrower definition of Americanism; to be at once defensively observant but vigilantly conformist. For the comic book publishers who wanted social acceptance, that meant an aggressive pursuit of respectability. The trouble was, there was suddenly a great deal of money to be made in comics that were not so respectable.

With the fading of the superheroes and the return of the servicemen, comic book publishers and creators scrambled to find ways to keep their grown-up readers. Popular entertainment in the postwar years marked the gap between America's wishful self-image and its morbid fascinations in neon. In the movies, the big budgets and awards went to lumbering message pictures, but underneath them the real creative energy poured into superheated melodrama, tortured romance, and sordid crime. Popular music was either forcefully bland or jarringly iconoclastic. Paperback racks brought Shakespeare to the masses and put violent sleaze right next to him. The comic book industry had its overlay of *Superman*, *Archie*, *Donald Duck*, *Classics Illustrated*, and *Picture Stories from the Bible*, and now there was an exploding market for wholesome westerns, Roy Rogers and Gene Autry grinning off the newsstands to reassure us that America really hadn't changed at all. But the other new genres that popped up like mushroom growths in 1947 and 1948—steamy romance, realistic crime, and gory horror—were where the best work, the hottest creativity, and the fiercest audience enthusiasm could be found.

Joe Simon and Jack Kirby, having redefined superheroes with Captain America and then become solidly successful purveyors of kids' action comics for DC, took a chance on something they called *Young Ro-*

mance in 1947 and sold millions. Teenage girls and young women were hungry for stories that plunged grimly and juicily into the contradictions of desire, duty, freedom, and loneliness that postwar love and marriage entailed. Soon there were dozens of romance comics. Horror was pioneered by a sardonic writer named Leo Rosenbaum (who wrote as "Richard Hughes") at the American Comics Group, the company owned by Harry Donenfeld and his card-playing buddy Ben Sangor. Hughes's most successful theme was that behind the calm facade of the normal American home or business lurked a monster or a ghost or a devil eager to trick us into some Faustian bargain.

The most rapid and obvious success, however, belonged to Lev Gleason, Charlie Biro, and Bob Wood's *Crime Does Not Pay*. It had sold solidly all through the war, but not well enough to inspire imitations. Then, in 1947, as America's fascination with crime and corruption intensified, its sales soared. By the end of the year, it was outselling even *Captain Marvel* and *Superman*. It seems, in fact, to have stolen much of the superhero audience: Boys and young men who'd been able to enjoy cartoons of good guys smashing bad guys during the war suddenly wanted more ambivalent, more titillating stories of bad guys who lived it up at the expense of the good guys until they met a bloody end in the final panel. After years as the only crime comic on the stands, by late 1948 *Crime Does Not Pay* was just one of forty.

Buoyed by the new genres, more Americans than ever were reading comic books. By the end of the decade, there were about forty publishers selling three hundred titles—50 million comics a month. One study found that over half the readers were twenty or older, that adult readers averaged eleven comics a month, that nearly half the readers were female, and that white-collar workers read the most comics of all. The comic book looked as though it might become a mainstream American medium.

The crime comics spoke to their moment better than any others. There was pungency and narrative vigor in the best of them, but there was a sickness of spirit in them too. Comics had a freedom to indulge in gore and cruelty that the more closely watched media of movies, radio, and "slick" magazines didn't, and they tapped into American appetites that those other media hadn't revealed. The success of the material was unsettling to the very men who made and sold it—so much money for such seamy stories peddled under such smarmy, phony messages about the folly of crime. There was a viciousness in the crime comics that assumed a sadism in the reader and, in its exquisite intensity, revealed a sadism in the artist. Even Jack Cole, whose joyous *Plastic Man* was still running, threw himself into the pit with *True Crime*. His story "Murder, Morphine, and Me" would haunt him later—especially the image of a terrified young woman having her eyelids pulled apart by a drug dealer so he can thrust a needle into her bulging eye.

Public objections were inevitable. The publishers might argue that they were making these comics for adults, and to a great extent that was true, but it was just as true that kids were buying them by the millions. Boys at the brink of adolescence love to see how much evil and vileness they can stomach vicariously, and the more extreme the comics became, the more they gobbled them up. The exit holes from machine gun bullets spelling a bloody "RAT" on a mobster's body as he lurches in death agony with all the visual vigor Jack Cole could give him? Great stuff. A woman strangled to death in close-up as her killer gloats, "I've always wanted to kill like this! To squeeze . . . to feel the neck bones crack under my fingers!"? Heck, that was even better. The voices of teachers, preachers, and parents began to rise throughout the land.

The loudest and most persuasive voice came with a German accent. The March 1948 *Collier's* featured an interview entitled "Horror in the Nursery" with a psychiatrist named Fredric Wertham. He had superb credentials as both a researcher and a clinician and was then completing his third book, *The Show of Violence,* about the environmental factors that lead children to violent crime. In the interview, he asserted that comic books were the largest and most pernicious influence on American youth. It was not a new argument, but Wertham possessed what other outraged critics lacked: data and theory. He ran a psychiatric clinic in Harlem and claimed that he saw a frightening correlation between comic book reading and juvenile delinquency. He could cite specific cases of copycat crimes, in which children and adolescents had committed robberies, assaults, and even murders precisely as they had been portrayed in their favorite comics. And as the author of *The Brain as an Organ,* he could speak with authority about the ways in which comics "set off a chain of undesirable and harmful thinking," "supply the rationalization for a contemplated act," and "act as the precipitating factor of delinquency or emotional disorder." Wertham pushed anxieties about comics beyond taste and morals and into, at least at first glance, behavioral science and public policy.

That same month, Wertham ran a highly publicized symposium called "The Psychopathology of Comic Books." Two months later he published an article in *The Saturday Review* in which he reprinted that sickening Jack Cole drawing of the woman having her eye pierced. In a few more months he told the American Prison Association that comics were "a correspondence course in crime." He also cast his net far wider than merely the gory crime comics. *Superman,* he said, was just as great a threat, for it teaches children that physical force is the solution to their problems. "If I were asked to express in a single sentence what has happened mentally to many American children," he said, "I would say that they were conquered by Superman." When the *Collier's* interviewer asked him how parents could distinguish good comics from bad, he answered, "The number of 'good' comics is not worth discussing, but the great number that masquerade as 'good' certainly deserve close scrutiny." Nor was he simply warning parents about the dangerous comics. He said, "the time has come to legislate these books off the newsstands and out of the candy stores."

The public response was astonishing even to Wertham. Newspapers and magazines pounced on the danger of comics with an alarmism far beyond that of the flurry sparked by Sterling North eight years before. "Are Comic Books a National Hazard?" asked *Newsweek. Time* revealed that the police commissioner of Detroit had found comics "loaded with communist teachings, sex, and racial discrimination." Wertham had connected comics with sex and violence, but now they were being associated with political preachments offensive to the right and the left alike. Even people dismissed as pornographers were speaking out against comics: Gershon Legman—amateur psychologist, former assistant to Alfred Kinsey, collector of dirty jokes, and editor of the Freudian sex magazine *Neurotica*—wrote a book called *Love and Death* in which he claimed that comic book violence was a perverse result of our repression of sexuality and was the only *true* pornography on the stands. Along the way, he exposed Harry Donenfeld as a former pornographer and claimed that most of Martin Goodman's Marvel Comics staff was homosexual (a comment that Stan Lee, who prided himself on his success with women, found personally offensive).

The crime and horror comics were gruesome, and they did contain images no sane parent would want a young child to see. But they also became stand-ins for larger fears. No matter what anxieties one brought to the world—juvenile delinquents, atomic war, sexual license, sexual repression, the Reds, the Klan—they could find a match in comic books. In a society frightened of forces running out of control, the sheer unsupervised, irresponsible, uncontrolled information in the comic books was alarming in itself.

Churches organized boycotts of retailers who carried comics. Citizens' groups demanded action from police and lawmakers. The National Congress of Parents and Teachers declared that "freedom of the press . . . was never intended to protect indecency or the perversion of the child's mind." More than fifty cities passed legislation to curb comics sales. Detroit and Indianapolis each banned three dozen comic book titles to readers of any age within their city limits. Over half the state legislatures entertained bills to limit comics sales. One such bill was passed by both houses of the New York legislature before being vetoed by that old foe of the racketeers, Governor Thomas Dewey.

Then came the burnings. An impromptu crusade in Binghamton, New York, sent volunteers door-to-door to ask, "Are there any comic books in this house?" When the householders could be persuaded that doctors, police, and ministers were right about the dangers of comics, the volunteers gathered the offending publications and carried them to the local school yard, where they were piled high, doused with gasoline, and set afire. *Time* ran pictures of the comics blazing, children watching with some ambivalence from the background. Other cities followed suit. In Chicago a burning was organized by a Catholic diocese.

The publishers knew this had to be cooled off. The larger ones immediately began firing out press releases trumpeting their in-house codes of decency, and some who didn't have such a code, like Lev Gleason and Martin Goodman, quickly made one up. A group of publishers promptly formed an Association of Comic Magazine Publishers (ACMP), modeled on the Motion Picture Production Association with a comparable code of self-censorship. The result was based on the in-house code Fawcett had been using since 1941, which was based in turn on the DC code Jack Liebowitz had instituted the year before. The more respectable publishers quickly pulled out, however, because they didn't want to be associated with the sleaze merchants who shared the ACMP with them. Soon the best-known member was Gleason, progenitor of the crime comics and target of the House Un-American Activities Committee.

The effort to respond to their critics and establish a self-censoring body did seem to quiet the storm. But any publishers who thought they had solved the problem were going to be disappointed. They'd bought themselves time, but most of them used that time only to dig their own graves deeper.

Jack Liebowitz was one of those who withdrew from the ACMP and insisted his company's own editorial code was a reader's greatest guarantee of wholesome reading matter. Respectability meant more than ever to Liebowitz. He believed in long-term investments. Other publishers might be willing to chase every shift in the market and get ready to jump ship when the bottom cracked; but Liebowitz looked at the money he'd invested as a long-term commitment to his properties, and he was emphatic about using his best-known and most proven characters to expand the company's reach.

Superman was still popular on radio, and already Liebowitz was looking at the new medium of television. TV would be hungry for programming, and a familiar character from radio and the movies could sell itself. Radio and TV meant sponsors and Federal Communications Commission licenses, and those meant a need to be considered safe and respectable. Jack had learned that respectability paid much better long-term dividends than sleaze. In 1946 the *Superman* radio show featured a story line, developed in concert with the Anti-Defamation League, in which Superman battled a Ku Klux Klannish group in order to protect the rabbi and priest who ran an interfaith meeting place called "Unity House." *Newsweek* called it "the first children's program to develop a social consciousness." *Superman* won acclaim from institutions ranging from the National Conference on Christians and Jews to the Negro Press Association—and attracted enough attention to become the top-rated children's show on radio. That was the kind of publicity and community good will a company could build on.

Respectability mattered in Liebowitz's personal life too. He'd become a major contributor to charities and community organizations. He was a founding donor and trustee of the Long Island Jewish Hospital, a modern and superbly appointed new medical center in Great Neck. He'd come a long way from balancing the books for a pornographer, and he wasn't sliding back. So his company got no closer to crime than an adaptation of radio's *Mr. District Attorney*. He expanded the Editorial Advisory Board—he'd even gotten Pearl S. Buck, the dowager of respectable social novelists, to lend her name—and he ran educational pages in every comic book coordinated with the National Social Welfare Assembly. He wanted National Comics to stand as an accepted member of the children's entertainment establishment.

Superman was an essential part of that plan. Even if servicemen's fantasies had moved on, Liebowitz knew eight- and ten-year-olds could still be sold superheroes, and he knew he had the editorial staff, especially in Mort Weisinger, to keep delivering the readership. In 1947 and 1948 he was confronted with one more challenge to his designs. In the end, there was no longer any question of who understood the business of comics, the business of America, best of all.

BY THE END of the war, Jerry Siegel and Joe Shuster were looking ahead to the end of their ten-year deal to produce *Superman* material for National Comics. They were insecure about whether National would hire them again in 1948, or at least at the same price. Joe's eyes were bad and he needed the studio to survive. Some of his best ghosts had been hired away by National itself, and it was getting harder to sustain his quality. Jerry knew that National's editors, Weisinger and Schiff, preferred their stable of New York writers who could be told what to do. So Jerry decided that they should create something new, a series that would have all the punch and commercial potential of *Superman* but that they would own themselves. Then finally they would no longer depend on Jack Liebowitz to treat them fairly.

This had become standard practice for the big newspaper cartoonists. Hal Foster had made his name on *Tarzan,* then created a strip he owned, *Prince Valiant.* Joe Shuster's hero, Roy Crane, had left *Wash Tubbs* to create and own *Buz Sawyer.* In 1946 Milton Caniff left *Terry and the Pirates* for *Steve Canyon,* and Alex Raymond left *Flash Gordon* for *Rip Kirby.* To leave *Superman* and create something new was the logical next step for Siegel and Shuster. But how were they to carry their reputations and their audiences from *Superman* to a new property? Crane and Caniff stayed with the same genre and readership. Even Foster, leaping from ape man to Arthurian legends, and Raymond, trading space opera for spies, maintained a consistency of tone and visual style. Those cartoonists also boasted unmistakable personal styles and the best draftsmanship in their respective schools. Superman was a comic book superhero, now identified with a hundred others, and everyone agreed that the superhero fad was fading. Jerry and Joe themselves must have doubted that their names and studio-produced art could draw readers to yet another superhero. They needed something different, something very much their own and in keeping with the irreverent, conflicted postwar world.

Jerry went back to one of his favorite subjects: pranks. He'd loved Mr. Mxyztplk and his other prankster-villains for Superman, and the readers had loved them, too. He still believed his practical-joking Superboy would have been better than what National produced. Now he could create a whole hero around the idea of pranks. He could be a clown in big shoes and baggy pants who fights crime in the craziest ways. Boxing gloves pop out of his clothes. He throws juggling batons while riding on a unicycle. His squirting flower emits knockout gas. And he wisecracks the whole way, laughing "Yak! Yak!" Jerry could see it sweeping the nation. He *had* to see it sweeping the nation.

National's chief editor, Whitney Ellsworth, was interested in the idea, but he couldn't arrange to give Siegel and Shuster what they wanted: full ownership of the character, including the right to sell it themselves to a newspaper syndicate and licensors. National would agree to income participation, but it had to retain control of editorial content and subsidiary rights. The talks broke down in frustration. Just then a face from the past emerged: Vin Sullivan, first editor of *Detective* and *Action Comics,* the man who'd bought *Superman* for Harry Donenfeld, had recently found backers for a new publishing company, Magazine Enterprises. Hearing of Siegel and Shuster's growing frustrations with National, he said he'd be thrilled to work with them on any new project they wanted to bring him. He'd even be willing to give them the ownership deal they wanted, if it meant a shot at publishing the next *Superman.* It was a touchy situation. Siegel knew his editors at National wouldn't be happy with him taking his work elsewhere. But he was angry enough to take the chance. He and Joe started talking to Vin Sullivan about *Funnyman.*

Jerry's anger had been building through the war, and the latest disappointment with National only stoked it. Whenever Jerry got angry, he stewed for a long time, and then he popped. He fantasized and he exaggerated. Now Albert Zugsmith, the lawyer he'd met in the army, was there to encourage him. "Zuggy" was a radio station executive now, combining his background as attorney, producer, and promoter to build a career in broadcasting—but he was still happy to represent Superman's creators in their battle for a multimillion-dollar empire. He told Jerry that National Comics had no right to his character, that even if it had had some earlier claim, it had forfeited it by failing to pay him what it owed and creating Superboy without his permission. He said Jerry and Joe should sue.

The financial realities underlying the dispute remain unclear. Newspaper and magazine profiles of Siegel and Shuster from the 1940s typically claim they were making more than a $100,000 a year, a figure presumably provided by Jerry and Joe themselves. In the course of the lawsuit, Jerry Siegel insisted he and Joe had never made more than $30,000 in a year. Perhaps the disparity lay between the gross income of the studio and the take-home pay of the two partners, or perhaps Jerry Siegel just brought the number down to advance his cause. In any case they were not poor. Jerry kept his house, wife, and son in University Heights while he lived most of the time in a New York apartment. Joe supported his siblings and parents. Clearly, National was paying them some portion of what it owed them for licensing rights—although it probably wasn't as much as it could have been before the accountants worked their magic.

Then, in late 1946, came the moment when prior expectations and suspicions overwhelmed reality. During that year the checks arriving for Siegel and Shuster got smaller. Jerry complained. Liebowitz said Superman was generating less money than before. Jerry didn't believe him. But the fact is, sales of *Superman* and *Action Comics* dipped by over 20 percent from 1944 to 1946. Newspapers were dropping *Superman* and other juvenile adventure strips to make room for the new wave of postwar humor and melodrama strips. Superman licensing plummeted as kids preferred their pajamas to feature Roy Rogers. The drop in Siegel and Shuster's income was an inevitable reflection of slipping sales—but Jerry was waiting for the next act of violence against him. This, he believed, was it. He told Joe and Zugsmith that it was time to act.

First they sought allies. They knew they weren't the only ones who thought Donenfeld and Liebowitz were crooks. They quickly got Charlie Gaines onto their side. He'd broken with Donenfeld and Liebowitz on bad terms and was eager to believe the worst of them. Plus, his Educational Comics was $100,000 in debt while what would have been his share of National Comics was soaring. He offered Jerry and Joe moral and logistical support and said he'd be willing to testify on their behalf regarding their sale of Superman to Donenfeld. As they laid out their case, however, he began to back off. "As I get the story," his son Bill would later say, "a couple of sharp lawyers got ahold of these boys and got them malcontented. . . . [T]hey came down and gave a sob story to my father." But Charlie saw discrepancies and exaggerations in their story. "At which point," said Bill, "he dropped them like hot potatoes."

They also tried to form a united front with Bob Kane. They assumed he had a ten-year deal that would run out in 1949 and knew they'd have more clout if the creators of National's two biggest heroes challenged their ownership at once. No record was kept of their communication, but the result was that Kane went to Jack Liebowitz and told him that Siegel and Shuster were planning a legal challenge and that it would be better all around if he were willing to renegotiate Kane's original deal. Liebowitz apparently responded to the effect that National wasn't worried about anything, because its ownership of both Superman and Batman was indisputable. Then Kane pulled what may have been the most ingenious stunt of a career full of stunts. Didn't Liebowitz know, he asked, that National's income from Batman over the previous seven years was based on an invalid contract? Liebowitz asked how it could be invalid since Kane himself signed it. "Sure," said Kane, "but I was a *minor* at the time."

All the evidence was that Kane had been born in October 1916. There were even those who said he'd been born in 1915 and had first lied about his age to conceal the fact that he'd been held back in school. He graduated from high school the same year as Will Eisner, who was born in early 1917. Kane had to be twenty-two, if not twenty-three, when he signed the Batman deal. But there was no proof. There were no records to subpoena. In the tradition of Jewish immigrants, his father had made his birth certificate disappear early in his life. Who could prove that Kane wasn't born in 1919, as he was now claiming, and been precocious in school? Kane assured Liebowitz that his parents would be happy to testify to that effect.

With such a mess facing him, Liebowitz found it easier to buckle. He reportedly returned partial legal ownership of Batman to Kane, including rights of reversion and permission to veto its sale to any other company, then guaranteed him a certain number of pages per month at a staggering page rate and a percentage of subsidiary rights. The only condition was that Kane not tell anyone about the deal. He needn't have worried. Kane never talked about his deals, just as he never talked about his ghost writers and artists. He told Jerry Siegel that he wouldn't be joining him in a lawsuit.

Now Siegel and Shuster were on their own, but Zugsmith assured them they had the grounds to win. They'd get their character back along with all the money that was owed them. In April 1947 Albert Zugsmith filed a lawsuit on behalf of Jerry Siegel and Joe Shuster against National Comic Publications for $5 million and the return of all rights to Superman.

Harry Donenfeld and Jack Liebowitz were outraged. Liebowitz called Siegel and told him not to be ridiculous. He'd signed a contract selling the rights; he had no claim; he'd better withdraw this suit before it destroyed his career. But Jerry wasn't going to let himself be fooled by Jack Liebowitz anymore.

As the lawsuit moved forward, Jerry's spirits rose. *Funnyman* was coming along, with a first issue due on the stands at the end of 1947. He told himself it was good, this kind of wiseacre slapstick was what he always did best, and humor was the new trend in comics. He'd already gotten nibbles from newspaper syndicates just based on the fact that it was the new Siegel and Shuster creation, and he was confident he'd place it in the newspapers soon. Not even Liebowitz's immediate termination of their work with National seemed like much to worry about. After those years of feeling Superman slip away, the future suddenly looked bright: Superman and Funnyman in the comic books and the newspapers, at least one on the radio, both completely in his and Joe's hands, plus the millions from the lawsuit. Soon they'd be as big as Donenfeld and Liebowitz. Zugsmith was reassuring him about the trial, Vin Sullivan was reassuring him about *Funnyman*, he was reassuring Joe about everything; it wasn't hard to make himself believe it.

Then came the miracle that seemed to close the deal, that took him right back to the soaring dreams of 1936, when the comic book world had first opened its arms to him and he first thought they were going to place *Superman* with a newspaper syndicate. He and Joe were planning to attend a National Cartoonists Society costume ball at the Plaza Hotel in New York, and Joe had just learned that Joanne Carter, his old pen pal, the girl who had modeled for Lois Lane nearly twelve years before, was going to be in town. Joe invited her as his date. Joanne was thrilled to accept. She wanted to go as Lois Lane, but she'd heard that Joe and Jerry were having legal troubles with their publisher, so she changed herself into Dixie Dugan, a flirtatious actress from a comic strip known for its risqué lingerie shots. Joanne was never a classic beauty, but in her late twenties, experienced as an artists' model, she must have been a knock-out compared to the scrawny kid who used to visit Joe in Glenville. From the moment Joe brought her into the ball, Jerry Siegel was smitten.

Joanne stressed in her reminiscences that she hit it off well with both Joe and Jerry upon seeing them again for the first time after such a cataclysmic decade. But it was Jerry whose frenetic energy pushed through his shyness, Jerry who squired her around the ball introducing her to all the big cartoonists, Jerry who told her he was staying in New York for a while and would love to see her again.

Joe stepped aside. We don't know what he thought of Jerry and Joanne's budding romance, although the Siegel and Shuster studio wasn't shaken. Jerry and Joanne stayed in New York and spent nearly every day together. It must have been a dream for Joanne—coming off a bad marriage, struggling as an artists' model and a shop clerk, facing the end of her twenties without much in sight—to be suddenly back in that moment of adolescent hopes, suddenly within reach of fame and fortune. And it must have been a dream for Jerry, to have found this pretty young woman from his past, this incarnation of the comic book glamour girls he'd only been able to invent in his mind until then, to be making her his own at the moment his professional life would finally be his own, as well. He asked Joanne if she'd marry him if he were free of Bella. She said she would.

The lawsuit finally found its way to court. National Comics had engaged one of the nation's most respected copyright lawyers, Horace Manges, and he made it an exhausting battle. Siegel and Shuster had little going for them but their words, whereas National had all the documents. It was a grueling process of depositions and testimony. Zugsmith kept telling them they were fine. In the meantime, the case became more crucial to Jerry and Joe. The early reports on the *Funny-man* comic book were dismaying. The first issue had suffered big returns and the second looked headed for the same fate. Word from newsagents wasn't good. Mostly they said, "This is no Superman." Jerry and Joe needed a victory.

The decision came down in May 1948. The court ruled that Siegel and Shuster had sold all their rights to Detective Comics, Incorporated, and had no claim to Superman. It found no evidence of $5 million in damages. It did agree that their creation had been unfairly exploited with *Superboy* and called for the parties to reach a settlement. Zugsmith quickly came back to Jerry and Joe with an offer: If they surrendered all claims to *Superman* and *Superboy,* they'd get a settlement from National for $100,000.

Jerry was in agony. The settlement, one-fiftieth of what they'd asked, would go mostly to Zugsmith's fees. The money he and Joe would come away with wouldn't even equal a year's work for National—work they'd lost forever by suing. They had to appeal. They had to keep fighting. But Zugsmith told him there was no point. He and Joe had better take this settlement instead of pouring more money down the drain and maybe coming up with even less. Joe reportedly didn't want to keep going. Jerry finally agreed to cut his losses. He declined to file an appeal.

Things moved quickly now. Jerry went to Bella and asked for an immediate divorce. He offered to give her whatever she wanted if she would just set him free quickly. She filed on July 14, 1948, asserting that for two years he had been grossly negligent in his duties as a husband and father, disappearing for long periods of time without explanation and behaving with hostility and argumentativeness when he was around.

Jerry didn't contest it. The divorce decree was granted less than three months later, in early October. A minor scandal flared over it: The presiding judge, Samuel Silbert, had long been a vocal opponent of quickie divorces and pledged that his court would never issue a decree in less than six months. "Judge Sam" was also a venerable member of the Cleveland Jewish community and the local Democratic party apparatus. His official explanation was that the decree had been issued by a junior judge in his court and he'd been unaware of it; but his views on quick divorces were surely well known in his own court. Perhaps Jerry Siegel had one last bit of clout as a famous son of Glenville, and he used it to get free of Bella quickly.

Exactly one week after the divorce became final, Jerry married Joanne Carter, née Jolan Kovacs, at City Hall. Jerry asked the people at the license bureau to keep it quiet so that Walter Winchell could break the news. The bride and groom were living in a hotel: Jerry had no family to stay with.

Only five months after the disposition of the lawsuit, Jerry had divorced one wife and secured the next. Was he afraid of waiting, until everything, including Joanne, evaporated? That same spring had seen the final issues of *Action* and *Superman* with the Siegel and Shuster byline. Then came the *Superman* movie serial from Columbia Pictures, something Jerry and Joe would have made money on if not for the lawsuit. In September the *Superman* radio show began a new season, with no mention of its creators. The summer had seen the final *Funnyman* comic book; it had bombed so badly that it lasted only six issues. In October, the same month Jerry was divorced and remarried, *Funnyman* began running in newspapers through the Bell Syndicate. Not many papers picked it up.

It was, in fact, a dreadful comic strip. The humor was forced and the stories leaden. Funnyman himself was less playful than angrily obnoxious. Like some of Jerry Siegel's high school creations, he liked to make fun of people with "zero IQ." Joe's eyes were so weak that he drew only the broadest layouts, leaving all the subtleties and characterizations to newcomers whose work was too heavy-handed, too academic, ever to be funny. There was no joy or playfulness in *Funnyman,* only frustration and desperation to provoke a reaction.

By early 1949 the syndicate was suggesting that the writing and art had potential but that the lead character was too off-putting. Jerry and Joe made the transition to a new lead by bringing in a supporting character and building up his role. They returned to a character from their struggles to become newspaper cartoonists in the early 1930s, before Major Malcolm Wheeler-Nicholson turned them into comic book hands and action cartoonists: Reggie van Twerp, a musical-comedy twit with an omniscient butler. It was a strange decision, unless they were just shattered, just couldn't find it in themselves to come up with new material or trust themselves to make it work. *Reggie van Twerp* was better work than *Funnyman,* but it had no place in 1949. The syndicate dropped the strip.

Ten years after Superman had swept through the newspapers and leaped off the news racks, Jerry Siegel and Joe Shuster were out of work. They were thirty-five years old, with no ideas on the market and no prospects. They had no choice but to dissolve the studio. Jerry and Joanne gave up their apartment in University Circle, the place Joanne would later say they had been happiest, and moved back to New York. Jerry figured he could find jobs writing comics, but he didn't know if he could sell anything with a collaborator who could barely see and whose art style had been passed by. He told Joe he'd look for something they could do together. But if he looked, he didn't find anything. From the Glenville *Torch* to *Science Fiction* to *Jerry the Journalist* to *Slam Bradley* to *Superman,* there had always been a Siegel and Shuster. At the end of 1949 there no longer was.

WITHIN A YEAR, Whitney Ellsworth and Mort Weisinger were in Hollywood developing a *Superman* television show. They might have crossed paths with a man they'd heard of named Albert Zugsmith. In 1951 Zugsmith was producing a movie called *Invasion USA* for Howard Hughes. A few more cheap movies followed, then a deal with Universal that would find him producing dozens of movies, including some still remembered: *Touch of Evil, Written on the Wind, The Incredible Shrinking Man*. In an interview about his odd early career as lawyer, reporter, and small-time radio producer, he said he'd done whatever he had to do until "I had enough money to do what I pleased." How had he made enough money to become a movie producer?

Forty years later, off the record, Joe Shuster would voice the suspicion that had haunted him since 1948: that Albert Zugsmith had gone to Jack Liebowitz and said, "What will you give me to end this nuisance right now?"

Collision Course

CHARLIE GAINES NEVER was much of an outdoor guy. Zooming over the surface of Lake Placid in a Chris-Craft speedboat wasn't what his upbringing in Brooklyn had prepared him for. But it was the kind of thing a businessman did in the years after the war if he was doing OK. Everybody was camping, fishing, buying summer cabins if they could afford them. In truth, Charlie's comics business wasn't doing so well. *Picture Stories from the Bible* hadn't turned out to be the cornerstone of a publishing success story after all, and now he was trying something new, calling his company "Entertaining Comics" instead of "Educational Comics," hoping kids would buy the wholesome humor of *Tiny Tots, Fats & Slats,* or *Animal Fables,* starring Freddy Firefly and Konky Kangaroo. That wasn't working, either, and he was borrowing money to cover costs. But no businessman wanted to look like he was in trouble, so he kept the summer cabin and the Chris-Craft. When friends came to visit, as they did on that August afternoon in 1947, he liked to take them out cruising.

He apparently never saw the other boat coming. It hit his boat from the side, just behind the prow, and splintered it. His friend's young son survived—the Gaines family decided that Charlie must have hurled him to safety at the moment of impact—but both Charlie and his friend were killed where they sat. Charlie Gaines became the first of the comic book founders to die.

His son, Bill, came up from the city to take care of his widowed mother. Bill was twenty-five years old and just about to start the final year of an education that had been interrupted by the war. A wartime marriage he'd lunged into at twenty-two was coming apart. He was eager to put his past behind him and get on with becoming a high school chemistry teacher. But he was good to his mother. He took care of the funeral, endured the hollow condolences of men like Harry Donenfeld and Jack Liebowitz, helped straighten out his father's affairs, and packed up for the return to NYU.

But what, asked his mother, was he going to do about his father's business? Bill thought that was obvious: sell it. He knew nothing about business, wanted to know nothing; and he hated his memories of working for his father, being ridiculed and screamed at. "How the hell can I run a business when I couldn't even make it as the old man's stockroom boy?" he asked a friend.

But, said his mother, the business was all they had left of his father. And it was all she had to rely on in her old age. Bill agreed to talk to Sol Cohen, his father's circulation manager. Maybe he could look in on the business occasionally and let Sol run the show. When the comics line was more established, he could step away, let his mother take the income, and go on with his teaching career.

Then Cohen told him what a mess he'd walked into. Debts totaling $100,000. Nothing selling. Worthless properties. Charlie had tried to imitate *Wonder Woman* and ended up with a piece of fluff called *Moon Girl & the Prince*. He'd wanted to do a "celebrity comic," but the biggest celebrity he could afford was a second-rate Houdini named Blackstone the Magician. Charlie'd had noble ideals, wanting to give kids good, wholesome comics, but he didn't know what sold. Bill was young—he knew something about what kids wanted; he should stay until they got Entertaining Comics back on its feet. Cohen even knew a cartoonist, just twenty-two years old and still cheap, who was doing well with teen comics for Victor Fox. He'd send this Al Feldstein around to talk about getting Entertaining Comics into the teen market.

So Al Feldstein came by, a life-loving kid with a corny sense of humor who wrote and drew with appealing enthusiasm if not with much fluidity. Like Bill, he wanted to be a teacher and was drawing comics only because he'd gotten married in the service and had to support his wife. He and Bill hit it off instantly, and Al got started on *Going Steady with Peggy*. Bill also hit it off with Johnny Craig, who ran the art department—who *was* the art department—a self-taught artist who'd been mentored before the war by Bill's friend, Shelly Mayer. Johnny was only twenty-one and already married, another of those war kids who'd grabbed hold of domestic dreams to ease the pain of military service and figured out only later how they'd short-circuited their youths.

Johnny Craig was also something new in the industry: an artist who'd come of age on the comic books themselves, not just pulps or newspaper strips but *Superman* and *Batman*. When he was thirteen, in 1939, he'd hang around his local candy store flipping through comic books he couldn't afford, wishing he could draw like that. The store owner's son was an art student who knew a comics artist looking for an assistant—and so Johnny got into the business. The generation of comic book fans had arrived, only about a decade younger than Siegel, Shuster, and the other founders, but fundamentally different in their acceptance of the comic book as an established form and their desire to shake it up, refine it, and stretch it to fit their creative needs.

Bill, Al, and Johnny became a little gang, making fun of each other and the junk they were working on, laughing at their demanding wives and the old fools who ran the comics industry. Bill hated structured work and physical activity—he bragged about having danced and played softball once each in his life—but he discovered he loved to eat and drink and hold court with the younger guys who admired his zaniness. One day Al and Johnny gave Bill the flaming-rubber-cement treatment that Gil Kane got at *Pep*. Everywhere else, artists did stuff like that to teenage assistants. At EC they did it to the boss.

The big news in comics in 1947 was the sudden frenzy for *Crime Does Not Pay*, so Bill and his gang started joking that if they were going to sell *Moon Girl*, they were going to have to turn it into a crime comic. Then the joke became a desire. If he was going to save his father's ridiculous company, Bill knew, he was going to have to make it exactly what his father hadn't wanted. And how satisfying would that be after all the crap he'd taken from his old man? "I got the feeling that Bill went into the business as a joke," said Shelly Mayer, "to see if he could screw up things, change them for his private amusement, and still manage to make money doing it."

So *Moon Girl* really did become *Moon Girl Fights Crime*. *Blackstone the Magician* became *Blackstone the Magician Detective Fights Crime*. The other titles were scrapped in favor of *Saddle Justice, War against Crime, Modern Love*. Sales improved. Bill began to attract other talented, cynical young guys who'd gone straight from high school to the army to, for some, early marriage and precocious adulthood: Johnny Severin, Wally Wood, the clownishly dazzling Will Elder.

Bill was starting to enjoy himself. He got his BS in education, but he never did take a classroom job. He became a full-time comic book publisher, a caustic brat in a cigar-chewing fraternity of his father's old card buddies. And the deeper in he went, the more he wanted to kick those guys in the family jewels.

In early 1950 Bill decided to make a splash. He launched the "EC New Trend," a group of new titles aimed at adolescent and adult readers. Horror was catching on—Martin Goodman and Stan Lee's *Marvel Tales* had just ditched superheroes in favor of ghouls and zombies—so Bill led with *Haunt of Fear, Vault of Horror, Tales from the Crypt, Weird Science, Weird Fantasy*, and a crime comic with a spooky edge, *Crime SuspenStories*. Gaines and Feldstein imitated the radio suspense shows they liked; their horror comics were densely plotted, overnarrated, luridly descriptive, with cruelly funny twist endings. With a freedom to expose the nastiness of modern life that radio didn't allow, they devoted themselves with wicked chuckles to turning American sentimentality inside out: They unmasked respectable fathers who torture their children, big-eyed toddlers who plot their parents' deaths, young couples who seethe with homicidal venom, and most of all, sexy women who lure horny young blockheads to hideous doom. Bill's father's old adviser Sol Cohen was appalled and quit. But sales went up. Teenagers and adults began sending in passionate fan letters.

Encouraged, Bill and his gang dared to get political. He and Feldstein told stories about lynch mobs, racists, and small-town cops who frame innocents. It was another EC cartoonist, though, the fiercely funny Harvey Kurtzman, who really wanted to tell the truth about the world full of lying organization men he saw around him. "At the time," he said, "it was fashionable to do war comics in terms of fantasy and glamour, which I thought was a terrible immorality. They made war a happy event where American supermen go around beating up bucktooth yellow men. . . . The way war really is, you get killed suddenly for no reason." He edited, wrote, and did rough art for two comics, *Two-Fisted Tales* and *Frontline Combat.* The U.S. Army declared that it "considers these publications subversive because they tend to discredit the army and undermine troop morale." The FBI opened a file on Gaines and his company. That, of course, was just the kind of attention the EC gang loved.

As every boy learns, though, angry attention from grown-ups brings risks. In a time when public conformity and forced decorousness are given great meaning, the pursuit of bad taste becomes an especially effective and satisfying route to notoriety. From the beginning, crime and horror comics had tried to shock readers with violence and cruelty. The anti-comics furor kicked off by Fredric Wertham in 1948 and 1949 had scared the industry back briefly, but as the heat eased they began to test the edges again. Soon some of the smaller, newer publishers were trying to make their comics jump off the racks with increasingly grotesque covers: a close-up of an agonized man buried in an ant-hill, a man's face bloodily pierced by pixies with pins, vicious objects thrusting toward eyeballs.

Buoyed by impudence and confidence, Bill Gaines joined the game. Johnny Craig proved to have a special genius for the simple and brutal moment: the woman's head held under water as her last breath escapes her, the close-up of the hanged man with eyes rolled back and tongue protruding, and the one that would get his work on national television, the man holding a woman's severed head and a bloody hatchet, her eyes rolling up, saliva streaming from her open mouth—and on her body some feet away, her dress hiked high over her thighs. For Gaines and his gang it was as much about one-upmanship as about sales, but it put him on the front lines of the assault on American taste and set him on a collision course with cultural forces he never saw coming.

As BILL GAINES the school teacher became America's leading purveyor of sadistic gore, the company built on Harry Donenfeld's nudie magazines and bootleg business was thriving as the owner of America's most wholesome heroes.

The power was all Jack Liebowitz's now. The Fifties were his fifties, years of acquisition, consolidation, and long-term plans. His economic masterpiece was *The Adventures of Superman* television show. Everyone knew TV was going to hurt comic book sales, and by 1951 the market contraction was already showing, but no comics publisher except Liebowitz made any real effort to make the new medium work for him. Columbia Pictures's two movie serials had done extremely well, but Jack wasn't going to let Columbia collect the money when he conquered TV. Nor was he going to try to sell it to a network or a sponsor—no entity but National Comics would own the shows for syndication and resale. "I always wanted to do the films myself," he said. "I didn't want to send them out to subcontractors." In 1951 he sent Bob Maxwell, producer of the radio show, to Los Angeles to raid the talent from the serials and build a production company. He put Whitney Ellsworth, his comics' editorial director, in charge of the stories. The hour-long pilot was made to be released as a movie so as to recoup costs and demonstrate the size of the market. With a distribution deal in hand, they were able to capitalize a first season of episodes. Maxwell and his company cranked out twenty-four of them in ten weeks.

As cheap and fast as Maxwell was, he went over budget. For the second season, Liebowitz canned Maxwell and sent his inside boys, Whitney Ellsworth and Mort Weisinger, to run the show. Ellsworth had no experience with production, but he'd learned cost management from Jack Liebowitz. He and Weisinger would hole themselves up for weeks, plotting every episode with an eye on the budget, then assign writers to fill in the blanks. They'd have every script in hand before renting the studio, then they'd shoot every scene that required a particular locale for the entire season: all the *Daily Planet* scenes for twenty-six episodes, all of Clark's apartment scenes for twenty-six episodes, then all the abandoned warehouses and barns. The actors complained that they couldn't generate any feeling for the stories, but that was a price Jack Liebowitz was willing to pay to keep costs down. Jack spent money, though, when he saw long-term value. With the third season, in 1954, the show switched to color film, even though color TV broadcasting was still years away. The episodes were broadcast in black and white for nearly a decade, but ten years later, as Jack predicted, they became far more salable as reruns.

Superman was cheap but never sensational. George Reeves, the star and spokesman for the show, said, "We're all concerned with giving the kids the right kind of show. We don't go for too much violence. . . . Our writers and the sponsors have children, and they are all very careful about doing things on the show that will have no adverse effect on the young audience. We even try, in our scripts, to give gentle messages of tolerance and to stress that a man's color and race and religious beliefs should be respected."

Superman was a success. There were scarcely any superheroics or special effects on TV to compete with it, the cast was fun, the scripts were respectful of kids' sensibilities, parents approved, and the show had that mix of character comedy, inside jokes, and last-second rescues that Siegel and Shuster had long ago perfected. It even made Superman something of a national joke and a national pet again; not what he'd been in 1940, but enough to get the top-rated show on TV, *I Love Lucy,* to build an episode around him. Four seasons were produced, and all

four sold well in syndication. Even when George Reeves was found dead
of a gunshot wound and terrible rumors swirled around the show—
that playing Superman had typecast him so badly he'd fallen into despair, that he'd been murdered because of sexual escapades—it kept
selling to stations across America.

It kept selling the comics too. With Whitney Ellsworth decamping
permanently to Hollywood, editorial control of the comics was nomi-
nally handed to Harry Donenfeld's son, Irwin—who knew nothing of
storytelling, though, and happily surrendered control to the editors
under him. It was Weisinger, far more than Jack Schiff or Julie Schwartz
or the others, who had Liebowitz's ear. Liebowitz called him "a great
creative mind." The writers who worked with Weisinger would not
have agreed, but he was certainly a powerful political and marketing
mind. He took personal charge of the Superman line and threw his
weight around over his fellow editors. He had his old cohort Schiff particularly intimidated. Schiff was an outspoken liberal, and Weisinger
described him to Liebowitz as "the house Red" and "that crazy pinko."
Liebowitz didn't like reminders of socialism in the corridors of his
company. Schiff got the message that he had to keep his head down and
keep Mort on his side, and so Mort gained control of Schiff's Batman
franchise as well.

National became known for its hands-on editors who paid well for
the artists and writers they wanted but were less interested in individual visions than in a polished, easily accessible "house style." From *Superman* to *Young Romance* to *Pow Wow Smith, Indian Lawman,* all DC
comics looked and read about the same. With their even panel sizes,
reliable alternations of close-ups and two-shots, plots unpunctuated
by awkwardness or drama, well-schooled but passionless illustrations,
and careful inoffensiveness, they were perfect complements to Fifties
television.

Liebowitz's most important stroke, however, was based on a much
less wholesome superhero than Superman. Before the war, at the Funnies, Inc., shop where the *Sub-Mariner* and the *Human Torch* were being
produced for Martin Goodman's *Marvel Comics,* toiled a would-be pulp

writer named Franklin Michael "Mickey" Spillane. In between writing *Sub-Mariner* stories for Bill Everett and his ghosts to draw, Spillane developed a comic strip idea of his own, about a violent private eye named Mike Danger. It was too brutal for prewar comics, and he was able to sell only a watered-down version, *Mike Lancer*. But when Spillane came back from the war and needed a thousand bucks to build his new wife a house, he set up a studio with some other veterans of Funnies, Inc., to peddle *Mike Danger*. Crime comics were beginning to catch on, but the studio had no capital and couldn't land a distribution deal. So Spillane changed his hero's name to Mike Hammer and wrote the story as a novel. It took him nine days to pound out his comic book plot in frenzied, sweaty, crude, hostile prose.

"I reached up and smacked her across the mouth as hard as I could," says Mike Hammer. "Her head rocked, but she still stood there, and now her eyes were more vicious than ever. 'Still want me to make you?' 'Make me,' she said." Spillane's comic book partners told him the book would never sell. It was too mean, too crass. But Spillane had a friend who had a friend at a publisher, E. P. Dutton, and through an exchange of favors, he managed to place it. The novel came out in the summer of 1947. It didn't even sell 4,000 copies. Dutton unloaded the paperback rights on Signet, an imprint of the New American Library.

The paperback business was growing then, but it had yet to establish a personality distinct from hardbacks. The covers were more colorful and sometimes lurid, but the books that sold well in paper had usually been successful in cloth. Spillane's *I, the Jury,* blasted by critics and ignored by bookstore customers, stabbed straight to the fantasies of pissed-off, blue-collar ex-GIs who would never have spent two fifty on a hardcover novel or even gone in a bookstore but would glance at the paperbacks next to the crime comics, pulps, and girlie magazines at a newsstand or cigar store. The cover showed a blonde opening her blouse while a tough guy holds a gun on her. No brassiere. And the words didn't disappoint. The blonde is a double-crossing killer. She does her strip tease for Mike because she knows he'll want to make her, not kill her. But after she's stripped naked, he blows a hole in her stomach.

"'How c-could you?' she gasped. I only had a moment before I was talking to a corpse, but I got it in. 'It was easy,' I said."

I, the Jury was the ugly spirit of the meanest crime comics translated into prose, but for adult men it delivered a better punch than any comic book could. It sold 2 million copies in paperback, made Signet a major player in publishing, and sent out the signal that the men who read the grimiest comic books and men's magazines could be reached through the novel.

New American Library (NAL) was distributed by Fawcett Magazines, publishers of *Captain Marvel* comics, which had spent eight years fighting and appealing National's claim that they'd plagiarized *Superman.* The Fawcett brothers, in the grand cheap magazine tradition, instantly perceived that there was more money to be made by publishing their own paperbacks than just by distributing someone else's. Their deal with NAL barred them from setting up their own paperback reprint house, but they found a loophole: the contract didn't forbid them from bringing out brand new books in paperback. Within months of *I, the Jury*'s release, Fawcett created Gold Medal books and invented the "paperback original." Young writers unable to make headway with "legitimate" publishers were soon selling millions of Gold Medals. But Kurt Enoch, owner of NAL, was unhappy with the Fawcetts. In jumping through the loophole, he felt, they had violated the spirit of their agreement. As soon as their deal was up, he went looking for a new distributor.

In 1953 National Comics's lawsuit against Fawcett was finally settled in federal appellate court. Judge Learned Hand ruled that Captain Marvel was an infringement on Superman's copyright. Fawcett settled out of court for a few hundred thousand dollars and a promise to cancel the Marvel Family comics. With Gold Medal paperbacks selling millions a month, the Fawcetts decided it was time to fold up their comic book operations. Since Fawcett had modeled its comics line on National's in the first place, it was National that picked up the bulk of Fawcett's audience; its sister company, Independent News, picked up most of its news rack space and retail connections.

Jack Liebowitz learned that New American Library was looking for a distributor to replace Fawcett. Independent News had no experience with major magazines or large book publishers, but thanks to *Superman,* it was able to get product everywhere. Liebowitz outnegotiated bigger distributors and convinced Kurt Enoch that Independent could move books. Twenty years before, Harry Donenfeld had been glad-handing burlesque theater owners to get them to carry *La Paree.* Now Independent was distributing Signet books, including Mickey Spillane, coast to coast. The material may not have been any nobler, but in the eyes of the business world, it was a triumphant climb. Jack Liebowitz's combination of opportunism and consistency was unique in the cheap-magazine field, and it was paying huge dividends.

But a shadow lay over Liebowitz's victories. He lived with a private pain that may have fueled his ferocity to build and acquire: His wife was dying of cancer. Rose was still in her fifties, not close to enjoying the retirement she and Jack had talked about. Jack said little about his loss to anyone outside the family as Rose's life dwindled away at the Long Island Jewish Hospital that she and Jack had helped build. Their daughters, Joan and Linda, did most of the caretaking as Jack pushed himself to work and invest more relentlessly than ever.

When Rose died, Jack gave her a conservative funeral, accepted the condolences of his family and associates with dignity, made new contributions to the hospital in her name, and returned to work. His daughters took care of him when he stayed at the Great Neck mansion, but he spent more and more time at an apartment he'd bought on the Upper East Side in order to be closer to the office. The work, and the acquisitions, went on.

IN HEARING ALL the stories of Jack Liebowitz's maneuverings and conquests and corporate reconstruction, a question arises: Where was the man who built the company? Where was Harry Donenfeld?

Through the war, Harry had been the most visible party in Superman's world. But in the postwar years, he began to fade from the nightclubs and the distributors' conferences. When Jack Liebowitz became a partner in the business and its driving force, he pressed Harry to step down as figurehead. The new National Comics and its affiliates needed a more professional image. It was a firm now, not to be identified with any one man, especially a drunken, elfin rag salesman. The anti-comics furor of 1948 raised the stakes. Liebowitz wanted the old connections to *Spicy Detective* and *French Models* to stay buried.

In stepping out of the spotlight, something changed in Harry himself. When his son, Irwin, came home from Bates College in 1948 and showed up for his job in the family business, Liebowitz assigned him to take over his father's distribution work. Harry had given up the travel, saying he was too tired. He was in his late fifties and he'd been drinking hard for decades. The attention, the social whirl, and the gambling spirit of the early days had kept him flying, but in the new realities, he withdrew into a smaller and smaller social circle.

"It wasn't just the drinking, though," Irwin said. "After a while he just wouldn't *do* anything. I'd try to get him to go out and do something, even just dinner if he wasn't up to anything bigger, and he'd say he just wanted to stay in his hotel room." It was painful for Irwin to be finally an adult and a businessman in Manhattan, a man who might be able to enter his father's world, only to find his father removing himself from that world. Irwin became closer still to Jack Liebowitz. Liebowitz made no effort to draw Harry out. A Harry Donenfeld watching TV and playing cards with his mistress was a lot better than the alternatives.

With Irwin and Peachy out of the house, Harry no longer had any reason to pretend to be Gussie's husband or spend time at the Woodmere mansion. He lived with Sunny at the Waldorf in middle-aged marital comfort, seeing an ever smaller group of trusted friends, mostly fellow veterans of cheap-magazine distribution and their mistresses. Their marital placidity may have been more apparent than real, however. Sunny was over forty, unmarried, with no claim on the Donenfeld fortune. Gussie was hardheaded and combative and had the support of the law and Jack Liebowitz in her determination to remain Mrs. Donenfeld. But Sunny had proven she could be tough, too. As Harry lost the energy to play the games of finance and romance, he found himself surrounded by anger and demands.

Other forces, also, might have been driving Harry deeper into withdrawal. Old racketeers were trying to bury their pasts and move into America's booming corporate world. Meyer Lansky had taken the lead in lifting the Jewish mob into legal gambling in Nevada and Cuba and into other fields where a sympathetic business culture and a flow of concealable capital could be found. The harder rackets—heroin, extortion, brothels, illegal gambling—were being left more and more to the Sicilian gangs. A network of quietly interlocking businesses in a wide range of fields was being built on Jewish racket money. A couple of those would figure prominently in the future of National Comics: Seven Arts, a movie company founded by Lansky front men "Uncle Lou" Chesler and Elliot Hyman; and the Kinney Parking System, owned by Emmanuel Kimmel, a member of the gambling mob run by Lansky's most loyal New Jersey lieutenant, Abner "Longy" Zwillman. Although no direct links can be established among Seven Arts, Kinney, and National Periodicals in their early years, it's reasonable to assume that they were drawn together by relationships from the days of the rackets.

There were other parties, though, who saw opportunities in exposing those relationships. Estes Kefauver was a brilliant, publicity-minded politician who in 1948 had pulled off the miracle of winning election to the U.S. Senate from Tennessee as a pro–civil rights liberal. Immediately ostracized by the Senate's segregationist Southern bloc, he pulled a dazzling end run straight to the attention of the national electorate by advocating a committee to investigate organized crime. Gang busting had always been a Republican cause, and the Democrats had managed to keep it out of federal politics during their long hegemony under Roosevelt and Truman. Too many urban Democratic machines were soiled by mob ties for the party to welcome scrutiny. But when a Democratic senator who handled the press as ingeniously as Kefauver led the charge, the dodges and diversions became too embarrassing.

In June 1950, as chairman of the Senate Special Committee on Organized Crime in Interstate Commerce, Estes Kefauver became a TV star. The first politician to understand that television was the new power in America, he made sure that his interrogations of the nation's best-known racketeers, crooked politicians, and gang molls were televised live. Over the first nine months of intermittent hearings, he and his committee painted a picture of a vast Jewish and Italian conspiracy that owned whole industries, ran whole states, and raised itself above the law. The idea thrilled Americans, bringing together all the national fears of alien takeover and morbid fascination with corruption behind walls of respectability. When the hearing's road show made its last scheduled stop in March 1951 in New York City, home of everything most glorious and most evil about America, over 10 million viewers tuned in. The press was calling it the "Kefauver Show" and rated its performers as "a telegenic hit" (Longy Zwillman) and "an entertainment dud" (Lou Rothkopf). Wise guys in Jewish and Italian neighborhoods nationwide were gathering in bars to cheer on their favorite mobsters like baseball fans.

Until then, no gangsters had done much more than dance, deny, and take the Fifth. But Harry's old hero, Frank Costello, was too proud to play that game. Frank was a man who never appeared in public until he'd been perfectly groomed and manicured. He was a man who once rejected his lawyer's insistence that he wear a shabby gray suit in court instead of his customary powder blue elegance. "I'd rather blow the case," said Costello. Now he'd decided to look Kefauver in the eye, answer every question, and dare him to pin anything on him. His one demand was that the TV cameras not show his face. He wasn't going to be turned into cheap show business. The networks found a loophole: The cameras focused on his hands, gesticulating, drumming the table, wringing handkerchiefs, clenching and unclenching, fighting to be still when his anger rose. "Costello's hand ballet," the reporters called it, and in tandem with his growling voice parrying the committee's assaults, it was the most compelling show ever seen on TV. Viewership climbed over the week of Costello's testimony, breaking 30 million by the time Costello found himself trapped by questions about his income tax and finally had to invoke the Fifth Amendment. It was the biggest audience yet for any television show, and it delivered a TV finish. Kefauver had broken him.

Harry Donenfeld must have been watching. If his reactions were like those of Costello's other associates and admirers, they would have shifted from pride at the way the "Prime Minister" of the mob handled himself, to a laugh when the questions turned tough and he got up and walked out of the chamber, blaming it on laryngitis, and then to dismay as he began to contradict himself, as the Tammany Hall connections came out, as he became more evasive. When Costello was arrested for contempt of the Senate and the government promised to investigate his taxes, his superheroic status was gone. It would take a few years for the drama to play out, but that was the effective end of Frank Costello's power.

We can picture Harry greeting Costello at the Waldorf when it was all over, telling him he'd done great, thinking privately that maybe Frank wasn't the guy to be seen with anymore. Maybe Harry was glad that he'd gotten into a legal racket when he did and that his own connections were too small-time for anyone to investigate. What he didn't know, what no one in the comics business knew, was that Estes Kefauver had engaged a psychiatric consultant for the committee, a psychiatrist who knew how to use publicity nearly as well as Kefauver himself and wanted to call attention to his ideas that crime and violence were not simply the product of a few bad men but of a culture that legitimated and glamorized them. To fight crime effectively, insisted Fredric Wertham, the Senate must go after the industries that profit from crime not only directly but indirectly, through the seduction of America's children.

THE SWELLING OF the comic book market at the end of the 1940s lifted many boats. Jerry Siegel left Cleveland, Joe Shuster, and his dreams of owning his own comic strip and found himself with a deal that gave him one more shot at a real career. That's where Jerry had his collision—against his own limitations.

It was an odd sort of homecoming. The pulp publisher Ziff-Davis had bought the original *Amazing Stories,* the magazine that had made Jerry and his peers into science fiction fans. In 1946 its editor ran a letter from a paranoid reader who claimed he was being harassed by flying saucers from the subterranean civilization of Lemuria, thereby launching a national flying saucer mania and discovering a theretofore unexplored province of geekdom—those thousands of people who sincerely wanted to believe what had been just cheap fiction. By 1950 Ziff-Davis had money to spend and wanted in on the comic book boom. It hired Jerry Siegel to edit its line.

Siegel launched over forty new comics from 1950 to early 1952. He hit every genre and then some: *Romantic Marriage, Football Thrills, Kid Cowboy, G. I. Joe, Kiddie Karnival, Weird Thrillers, Space Busters, Wild Boy of the Congo, Famous Stars, Hot Rod King.* Except for superheroes. There was *He-Man,* with a cover very much like the first sketch Joe Shuster had done for Superman nearly twenty years before, a grinning muscleman lifting a crook over his head. But even *He-Man* featured only "iron men in deadly combat," no costumes or powers. Siegel wouldn't go back there.

He spent a lot of Ziff-Davis's money, but not to good effect. He hired Norman Saunders, a veteran of the pulps, to paint his covers. He bought the rights to *Ellery Queen* and paid Bob Feller and Red Grange to lend their names to sports comics. He also spent money on his writers and artists, more than other publishers, at or at least so the rumors said. But he never hired Joe Shuster. He wanted this to be a contemporary comics line and apparently didn't think Joe would help.

Which only made the end results more strange and sad. They were awkward, stodgy comics, comics that looked almost like parodies but seemed to take themselves too seriously. What is one to make of *Lars of Mars?* Or *Little Al of the FBI,* about a short federal agent? Or *Crime Clinic,* "starring Dr. Tom Rogers, Prison Psychologist"? Or the cretinous grin fixed to the hero's face on every *G.I. Joe*? Was it overwork, panic, or bitterness that made those comics so inept? Siegel wouldn't have been the first insecure writer to do bad work precisely because the pressure was so intense not to; nor would he have been the first one to tell himself that only garbage sells so he may as well give them what they want. In the end, he'd made his worst fears come true. In 1953 Ziff-Davis pulled the plug on its comics line.

Jerry was scrambling now. He and Joanne had had a daughter, Laura, and were trying to live a comfortable New York life during the Ziff-Davis stint. He found script work at several publishers, but nothing lasted. He complained that he'd been blackballed in the comics industry by Jack Liebowitz and Harry Donenfeld. That could have been true for the companies they distributed, but not across the industry. In that litigious, hostile little field, there were plenty of people happy to hire an enemy of Jack Liebowitz. It was Jerry Siegel they didn't want.

In 1955 he turned up at Charlton, a Connecticut printing company that produced and distributed its own sheet music, girlie magazines, and comics and paid only half as well as the Manhattan companies. They brought Jerry in to create a new superhero stable. He gave them Nature Boy, Nature Man, and Nature Girl; and Mr. Muscles, a professional wrestler who fights crime alongside Miss Muscles and Kid Muscles. "Bang-up Thrilling Displays of Physical Strength and Power," it promised. Like *He-Man,* it seemed to be one more return to the original idea for Superman, the carnival strongman who throws people around. It didn't work. The new series were canceled and Jerry Siegel was scrambling again.

WHEN ONE FOLLOWS the story of Joe Shuster through the 1950s, he seems to contract like the white dot of a television screen. For a year or two he apparently drew no comics at all. Sometime around 1951 or 1952 he seems to have found work with Charlton—not in its comics line but in its girlie magazines. There are some comic strips in low-rent titillation rags from Charlton and other publishers in the early Fifties, excuses for boob jokes mostly, that do look like a sloppy version of Joe Shuster's art. A trace of the buoyant anatomy is still there. But Joe never admitted to the work, and no one really knows if it's his. In 1954 he did his last real comic book work, a few issues of a Charlton crime comic. Then his confirmable credits disappear forever. There are more rumors, of girlie strips for Martin Goodman's sleazy men's magazines, of some sort of bottom-drawer gore rag called *Night of Horrors.* Then even the rumors stop.

His parents died. His sister married and moved to New Mexico. Joe and his brother moved into a smaller place in Forest Hills. Frank found work as an architectural draftsman and supported them both. Joe kept a scrapbook of his *Superman* days and listened to records in his room. His favorites were opera overtures, short and passionate and tragic.

ESTES KEFAUVER RAN for the Democratic presidential nomination in 1952. He won twelve primaries, enough to make himself a serious contender for next time. He needed a new platform to keep himself in the public eye and chose juvenile delinquency, a topic that touched on many of the same national anxieties as organized crime. He had already explored the issue in 1950 and had in fact already discussed it with the psychiatrist who had become a national figure by linking juvenile crime to comic books, Fredric Wertham.

Frustrated by the failure of any states to pass laws keeping objectionable comic books away from children, especially by Thomas Dewey's veto of the bill passed by the New York legislature, Wertham had begun writing a book called *Seduction of the Innocent,* laying out all his arguments against comics, illustrated with the most gruesome images he could cull from their pages. It was a smoothly written, alarmist, often smarmy book, rumored to have been ghostwritten by Gershon Legman, who had called Harry Donenfeld a pornographer in his own book, *Love and Death.* The chapters had titles like "I Want to Be a Sex Maniac," "The Devil's Allies," and "Homicide at Home." It was full of vast overstatements and mad leaps of causality—he cited the case of a ten-year-old girl who walked the docks at night selling sex acts and claimed crime comics were the cause—but whatever was lacking in its science and reason was more than compensated for by the sheer ugliness of the examples he chose. When the book came out in early 1954, shortly before Kevauver's subcommittee began its investigation of the comics, it shocked parents and terrified comic book publishers.

The tragedy of the conflict between Wertham and the comics is that Wertham was genuinely concerned about poor city kids, kids who'd come from the same world as the publishers and creators of comics. He was a left-wing Jew whose politics and social views overlapped with those of many of the men whose work he attacked. But he was of such a different background, such a different class, that he could not see comics the way their creators or readers did. He was born Friedrich Wertheimer in Germany in 1895, a year and a half after Harry Donenfeld but a world away from him. His family was well-to-do, educated, and nonreligious. He spent his youthful summers in London, where he discovered Fabian socialism, and moved there to study medicine at King's College. The First World War cut him off from his family and shattered the Europe he had known. He became concerned with the nature and causes of violence. "People like to be nonviolent," he said many times in his life. "There is no reason to believe that violence is indigenous to human behavior."

Wertheimer shone in the study of the brain and the physiological bases of behavior, and he served in the clinic of Emil Kraepelin, who led the world in the understanding of psychosis and its organic causes. The complexities of art, culture, and individual experience would never be Wertheimer's strong suit. He was intrigued, however, by a secondary idea of Kraepelin's, a "comparative psychiatry" that would consider the ethnic inflections of madness and look for the social and cultural forces that affect it. That idea, especially as it might relate to violence, was no doubt in his thoughts when he left Germany in the 1920s to take a position in that great, mad, violent social experiment across the sea called America.

Having been warned that Americans didn't like German names, he changed his to Fredric Wertham. He remained very German in his culture, however: he never lost his thick accent and never developed any fondness for American popular culture. His view of American society was surely colored by his work: During the 1930s, he established himself as a leading forensic psychiatrist in New York, consulting on some of the most sensational murder cases of the day and creating America's first clinic for the psychiatric screening of felons. He involved himself in the city's growing community of left-wing German intellectuals who had fled the Nazis, and he learned their ideas on modern culture and modern brutishness. The one who impressed him most was Theodor Adorno, a young musicologist and philosopher from Frankfurt.

Adorno was another cultured nonpracticing Jew. His father was a wine merchant named Wiesengrund; Theodor used the surname of his mother, an Italian opera singer. In Europe he had been part of a flourishing culture of radical artists and social philosophers of Jewish descent, an associate of Arnold Schoenberg, Alban Berg, Walter Benjamin, and Herbert Marcuse. They had all been driven from their homeland, and they all tried to make sense of the forces that could drive a civilized nation mad. When Fredric Wertham met him, Theodor Adorno was just unleashing his critique of the "culture industry." Mass-produced art and drama, Adorno said, is designed to excite passions and then provide a false, comforting resolution that leaves the consumer with a feeling of well-being inconsonant with the realities of life. This leads people away from true, individualized art that stirs uneasiness and provokes thought. Although profit may be the industry's only explicit goal, its effect was a mass deception that lulled people into political indifference and made them perfect victims of capitalism and fascism.

Adorno's ideas pointed Wertham's thoughts in a direction they had not gone, one that was not the best for a thinker of his background and inclinations. He began to consider the products of the "culture industry" as elements in the lives of the violent criminals he studied; but his understanding of movies and pulp magazines and comic strips was limited by the biases of the European culture elite from which he'd come and the scientific literalism at which he excelled. Since he viewed mass entertainments as mechanical products, he believed that their effects must be mechanistic: Violence in a comic book must trigger violence in the viewer. And, like Adorno, he believed that the masses were far more susceptible to such mechanical deception than the educated classes. This was the unfortunate condescension of the left-wing intellectual: Even a Marxist like Adorno and a compassionate doctor like Wertham believed that the multitude needed an educated elite to lead them free of the traps of mass culture. That belief led them into a certainty that their interpretations of mass entertainment were more valid than the interpretations of the people who actually made it and consumed it. It was a belief that distorted Wertham's reading of the comic books he studied, as it has distorted the academic study of media effects ever since.

The First World War had turned Wertham's thoughts toward violence. The Second turned him into an activist. He began to work with children in violent environments, especially those most brutally exploited by society. He studied the mental health of children in racially segregated schools; the data he provided to Thurgood Marshall and his partners played a part in the court cases that ended "separate but equal" education in America. With the support of New York's most important civil rights activists, he organized a free psychiatric clinic in Harlem that became a model for providing mental services for the poor. It was at that clinic that comic books became his personal cause.

"I began to notice," he said, "that every delinquent child I treated was a reader of these so-called 'comic books.'" As Wertham's critics have pointed out, since 90 percent of American children in the 1940s reported reading comics regularly and since those who didn't were more likely to be from more educated homes than the psychiatric patients at a free clinic, the coincidence of comic book reading and delinquent behavior was inevitable. But Wertham saw what he expected to see. When he found a comic book with a gruesome scene of a suicide by hanging, he immediately lined it up with the similar juvenile suicides he knew. When he saw Batman living with his young ward Robin, he saw an advertisement for homosexuality. And when he saw any hero using physical force he saw fascism.

"Superman (with the big S on his uniform—we should, I suppose, be thankful that it is not an S.S.) needs an endless stream of ever new submen, criminals and 'foreign-looking' people not only to justify his existence but even to make it possible," he said. "Superman has long been recognized as a symbol of violent race superiority. The television Superman, looking like a mixture of an operatic tenor without his armor and an amateur athlete out of a health-magazine advertisement, does not only have 'superhuman powers,' but explicitly belongs to a 'super-race.'"

No wonder no one in the comic book business was ever able to speak of Wertham with anything but rage and incredulity, that no one made even a token effort to acknowledge his good intentions. He was calling them Nazis: Jerry Siegel, Joe Shuster, Harry Donenfeld, Mort Weisinger, Jack Schiff, Alvin Schwartz, Jack Liebowitz, who used his *Superman* money to build a Jewish hospital and give thousands to Israel and B'nai B'rith—the men who created Superman or worked on him every day. And the hundreds of others in the industry who created the same kind of fantasy. Jack Kirby, who went to France to fight instead of drawing posters. Bernie Klein, Jerry Robinson's best friend, who died fighting Nazis at Anzio. Here was "Fredric Wertham," who'd told hardly anyone that he was a Jew, saying Superman should have an "S.S." on his chest. Wertham would have said that the Jews of comics were just playing at fascism for profit, but the men themselves knew: Theirs were the fantasies of *real* Jews, the daydreams of kids who'd been made to pay personally, by Russian pogroms and Irish fists, for their Jewishness.

In 1953 Wertham was appointed psychiatric adviser to the Senate Judiciary Committee's Subcommittee on Juvenile Delinquency. The subcommittee paid much more attention to narcotics, social agencies, parenting styles, and police procedures than to media influences, and it focused much more on television than on comic books. But for the comics industry, and for the fans who still say the names "Kefauver" and "Wertham" with venom, the whole investigation came down to the three days in May 1954 when the subcommittee came to New York to examine the comics. No publishers or creators of sleazy comic books were asked to appear. Wertham was to speak on the afternoon of the first day, to summarize what he'd just written in his book. The subcommittee's researcher was to describe the comic book industry and its readership. Friendly witnesses from the world of newspaper comics and Dell's wholesome comic books would appear to distance themselves from those dreadful crime and horror publishers. It might have been just a perfunctory stop-off for the subcommittee, barely meriting a newspaper article, if not for Bill Gaines.

Everyone else in the business knew not to testify. They were of a generation that stayed out of the spotlight. They'd seen what Kefauver did to Frank Costello. They knew their best hope was to keep doing what they did and hope for the storm to blow over. But Bill Gaines asked to testify.

By 1954 Bill was riding high. Not only were his horror comics the best and the most talked about in their genre, but he'd just scored a huge commercial success with a comic book called *Mad*. It was the brainchild of Harvey Kurtzman, the great satirist of Gaines's gang whose war comics had earned the army's censure. With the horror comics winning a passionate fandom thanks largely to the bad-taste humor of their editorial pages and fictional narrators (the cackling Crypt Keeper, Vault Keeper, and Old Witch), Kurtzman suggested a humor comic filled with parodies of other comic books, comic strips, and movies. *Mad* was the first full flowering of comic book geekdom, a comic that celebrated itself as "trash" produced by "the usual gang of idiots" that twisted and exaggerated and wallowed in every excess of the comics and the cheesy, overheated adolescent world that made them. It was funny and shockingly intense, crafted by young men who saw through their trash but still loved it, who were inventing something unimaginable and profoundly unacceptable to their parents' generation. Not "humorists" but savagely, chaotically aggressive clowns: Will Elder, Wally Wood, Jack Davis, and Kurtzman.

Mad started slowly, but in its fourth issue it delivered the parody that spoke to a generation of readers: a broad, cruel, sexually knowing send-up of *Superman*. One more time, and quite by accident, Jerry Siegel and Joe Shuster had changed the cultural landscape. *Mad* broke a million in sales, grabbed instantly by a generation that hadn't known how badly it had been craving just this kind of laugh. An entire style of funny, sleazy, pornographic, needling rebellion grew out of it. Among those who said *Mad* influenced them were Lenny Bruce, Hugh Hefner, and Robert Crumb.

So Bill Gaines became a hero to thousands of smart, stifled, wise-ass kids in the cities and small towns and suburbs of America who knew they were being sold a bill of goods but hadn't quite figured out how until it barked at them from the newsstands. "Hoo-hah!" they said, in Harvey Kurtzman's mangling of Yiddish English. "Enough already! Sheesh!" "Fan-Addicts" they called themselves. They formed the first comic book fan clubs, the first comic book conventions, the first back-issue mail-order businesses, and they joined loudly in denouncing the prudes and liars who attacked their comics.

Gaines thought he could win the fight against the handwringers and the censors. First he went to other publishers and suggested a united front. They could testify to the subcommittee, they could bring in experts to defend comics or puncture Wertham's arguments. They all told him to forget it. So Gaines took it on himself. He told the subcommittee he wanted to speak. Later he remembered, "I felt that I was really going to fix those bastards."

Wertham appeared right before Gaines. Most of what he said was familiar from his book, but one part of his testimony seemed aimed straight at Gaines's gut. *Crime SuspenStories* had run a story called "The Whipping" about a racist who gathers his friends to kill the Mexican boy his daughter is dating only to kill her by mistake. It was clearly meant as an anti-racist story, or at least a sensational twist-ending story in anti-racist garb. But Wertham pulled pieces out of context and harped on its use of the word "Spick." "Hitler was a beginner compared to the comic book industry," he said. "They teach them race hatred at the age of four before they can read."

Gaines sat fuming. He also sat fading. He was taking Benzedrine, ostensibly to lose weight, but probably also to increase his effectiveness. Bennies were a panacea drug in the early Fifties, prescribed to a huge number of middle-class men who complained of fatigue and overwork. Gaines had taken his pill in the morning, when he was scheduled to testify, but the morning witnesses had gone over, and he was rescheduled for late afternoon. He delivered his prepared statement well enough, a belligerent defense of the intelligence of young American readers. Then came the questioning.

One of the subcommittee's counsels asked him if there was any limit to what Gaines would publish. Gaines answered, "My only limits are bounds of good taste." At that Kefauver himself lifted a poster-sized replica of the Johnny Craig cover with the saliva-dripping severed head of a woman. "Do you think this is in good taste?" he asked. Gaines said, "Yes sir, I do, for the cover of a horror comic." And then he kept talking: "A cover in bad taste, for example, might be defined as holding the head a little higher so that blood could be seen dripping from it, and moving the body over a little further so that the neck of the body could be seen to be bloody."

It skidded downhill from there. There were questions about the messages in crime comics, about a dopey ad he'd run claiming that the opponents of comics were communists. Gaines was crashing. "I could feel myself fading away," he said. "They were pelting me with questions and I couldn't locate the answers." He walked out of the hearing room, where he'd thought he was going to "fix the bastards," in a daze.

The next day his testimony was on the front page of the *New York Times*. His defense of "good taste" made the evening news, with Craig's severed-head cover for all to see. Gaines lay in bed for two days with stomach pains. He knew that whatever Fredric Wertham had left undone he had just accomplished.

BY 1954 THE comic book business was slumping under the onslaughts of television and paperbacks. The rise of the supermarket and the fading of the small candy store and newsstand were hurting it, too, as the big stores gave little support to such low-profit items. The comics' hope of thriving as a prominent American medium depended on providing what TV could not, continuing to reach adults, and becoming "must haves" more than impulse purchases.

Seduction of the Innocent and the Senate hearings took care of that hope. Comics had a stink about them like never before. They'd always been junk reading. Now they were depraved junk reading. A new flurry of comics-controlling legislation was introduced in cities and states across America, citizens groups pressured retailers to return comics unsold, and wholesalers stopped ordering them. To save themselves, comics publishers knew they had to institute and enforce a strict self-censorship code that could win back the approval of civic groups. That meant comics could show even less than TV, and every one of them would have to be aimed at kids.

The Comics Magazine Association of America that was formed to create the new Comics Code Authority chose John Goldwater of Archie Comics as its president and Jack Liebowitz as vice president. Neither Archie nor National had to change much of anything since the code was based on the in-house codes they already used. Others were not so fortunate. The restrictions on the portrayal of crime would have throttled nearly every crime story ever published by Lev Gleason—not to mention the fact that the word "crime" could no longer appear prominently on a cover, killing *Crime Does Not Pay*. Gleason's company closed shop. A broad interpretation of the injunction that "romantic interest shall never be treated in such a way as to stimulate the lower and baser emotions" chased all the teenage girls and women out of the romance audience. Harvey Comics, which had pioneered romance and jumped on the horror and crime bandwagons, reduced its line to Casper the Friendly Ghost and his friendly friends. Martin Goodman cut the budgets on his comics and put more resources into his men's magazines, *Stag* and *Swank*. Smaller, sleazier companies just disappeared.

The rule against "crime" took care of Bill Gaines's *Crime SuspenStories* too, and bans on the words "horror," "terror," and nearly everything that made horror comics worth doing ("horror . . . gruesome crimes . . . lurid, unsavory, and gruesome illustrations . . . walking dead, torture, vampires and vampirism, ghouls, cannibalism and werewolfism") took care of most of the rest. Gaines fought the more restrictive aspects of the code fiercely, but all his dad's cronies saw him as the ungrateful brat who'd screwed them. "Jack Liebowitz hates my guts because he thinks I ruined the comics business," he complained. After a brief, disastrous experiment with code-approved adult comics like *Psychoanalysis,* Gaines threw in the towel. He turned *Mad* into a large-format, black-and-white magazine, sellable on the racks with the rest of the grown-up magazines, and shut down his comic book business. *Mad* sold better than ever in the new format, and Gaines was happy not to have to fight with the old guys anymore.

By 1956 the comics business had shrunk to half what it had been five years before. Writers and artists were heading for the exits. Early the next year the other shoe dropped. In a lawsuit brought by the Justice Department, the American News Company, once a virtual monopoly in magazine distribution and still the largest distributor in the business, had been found guilty of restraint of trade and ordered to divest itself of the newsstands it owned. Its biggest client, George Delacorte, announced he would seek a new distributor for his Dell Comics and paperbacks. The owners estimated the effect that would have on their income. Then they looked at the value of the New Jersey real estate where their headquarters sat. They liquidated the company and sold the land. The company that grew fat on the cheap magazine boom of the early century vanished without a trace in the suburban growth of the 1950s.

In a stroke, half the remaining comics publishers lost their distribution. Most of them went out of business. Martin Goodman was about to close the doors when Jack Liebowitz said Independent would be willing to carry him. Goodman had been famous for churning out comics wildly when the market was hot, until he overexpanded and had to fold up a few of his many companies. Liebowitz put him on a strict regimen of eight comics a month, plus his men's magazines. Liebowitz wanted industrial predictability and control. The Goodman comics stable was reduced to Stan Lee, his brother Larry, and a handful of freelance artists.

Liebowitz had two more acquisitions to make in the chaos of that moment. One was *Mad.* Gaines would have liked to have been distributed by anyone but Jack Liebowitz, but his alternative was going out of business. He expected to take grief from Liebowitz, but Jack was a businessman. Gaines said, "They gave me the nicest, cleanest contract you'll ever see, and nothing in the past was ever mentioned." *Mad* prospered, and Independent News added major magazine distribution to its comics and paperbacks.

Liebowitz's other acquisition was a men's magazine called *Playboy*. It was doing well, better than the rest of the girlie mags out there, although it was still confined to its limited market. Jack saw something, though, in Hugh Hefner's determination to keep making it bigger, slicker, more legitimate. Hefner was famous for stinting on his own income in order to pour money back into the magazine, an unheard-of practice among skin mag publishers. He believed in *Playboy* the way Henry Luce had believed in *Time* or the way Siegel and Shuster had believed in comics, and Liebowitz knew that such devotion was what made for long-term growth. He stretched the budget to buy the *Playboy* distribution contract.

Independent News was in the pornography business again, but in such a different way and such a different world that it only illuminated the vast distance between the America of 1936 and the America of 1956. Jack Liebowitz had learned how to survive among the hustlers of the Depression. Now he was becoming a master of the efficient, corporate culture industry of the richest nation in the world.

Silent Partners

WHEN THE COMICS collapsed, the cartoonists who'd been there from the beginning were entering their forties. They had wives, kids, and mortgages. Most of them left the business, including many of the best. A lot went to advertising, where they had less freedom and control of their work but discovered that the world gave a great deal more respect to men who drew car ads than those who made up superheroes. Jerry Robinson taught cartooning, illustrated books, and turned his energies to becoming a political cartoonist. Will Eisner packaged instructional magazines for the U.S. Army. Jack Cole sold cartoons to *Playboy*, and for a short while enjoyed the rewards of a real magazine before his lifelong depression overtook him and he ended his own life. When people asked what he'd done before, Cole would just say, "I spent eleven years in comic books," without ever mentioning that he'd created *Plastic Man*. With crime comics dead, Charlie Biro went into storyboarding for TV commercials. Stan Lee called him once to ask him what the comics business needed in order to rebound, and he said, "What comics needs is Charlie Biro, and I'm not coming back."

Biro's old friend and partner Bob Wood didn't cope as well with the collapse. He'd always been a violent drunk, but when he lost his regular stint, he descended into one binge after another. The last one ended when the police found him in a hotel room with the body of a woman.

After eleven days of drinking with her, an argument that he could no longer remember had led him to beat her to death with an iron. No one in the business visited him in prison. It was a time, a world, they wanted to put behind them.

Jack Kirby hung on in comics, but the pickings were so few that he and Joe Simon decided they'd have to dissolve their seventeen-year partnership to chase individual gigs. Kirby created a newspaper strip in collaboration with Jack Schiff, his editor at National—even career editors wanted off the comic book raft before it sank—but the project ended in a fight over rights and royalties, and Kirby came away feeling that National wouldn't hire him anymore. By 1959 the only reliable work he could get was from Stan Lee, who was presiding over the tattered remnants of the Marvel line. The rates were bad, and to keep supporting his wife and two kids, he had to produce more and more pages, planting himself in a chair for twelve or fourteen hours a day and drawing and drawing, eight or nine or ten pages a day.

Stan Lee himself put most of his time into writing men's magazine articles, books of golf jokes, and the occasional newspaper comic strip. Stan valued Kirby mainly for the fact that he could make up story bits on the fly. He had so little time that he'd feed his artists only rough plots and then hire his younger brother, Larry, to bang out dialogue to match the pages that came back. It was vapid, repetitive stuff, witless westerns and thrillers about monsters with names like Rommbu, Bombu, and Gomdulla. But it paid the bills, and Lee and Kirby hung on while they waited to find their separate ways out of comics.

JERRY SIEGEL TRIED to make the move into advertising. "Dear Mr. Frolick," began one letter to an ad executive: "Ever since I created Superman for the cartoons and comic strips I've believed in the potential for cartoon characters to advertise products. Now with the success of the charming Piel characters I believe that judgment has been borne out. If you see any usefulness I might provide to your agency, please contact me." The letter was hastily typed on a faded ribbon with type-overs and corrections in pen. It looked as if Jerry couldn't bring himself to put any effort into his pitch. The Mr. Frolick in question saved the letter as a souvenir for his kids but didn't bother to respond.

Jerry sold some gag scripts to *Mad* imitations like *Panic* and *Cracked*, but not nearly enough to support his wife and young daughter in New York and pay off his old debts. Joanne urged him to fight his way back into the comics business, even if it meant going back to National. Jerry said it was no use. But this wife wouldn't settle for hopelessness. She wasn't content to nurse pain and resentment like Bella or his mother. The former Jolan Kovacs had an angry Hungarian loyalty that fixed itself on an enemy and lashed out. She had already been nagging National off and on for years. When financial crises struck—the diaper service cut off, the rent on their one-bedroom apartment missed—she would call *Superman*'s publishers and demand that they help. She even told them that Jerry was writing letters to newspapers telling his side of the story. And the money came, a hundred here, two hundred there. This time, though, the situation was too dire for a hundred or two to bail them out. "This is Jack Liebowitz's fault," she insisted. "He owes you something." When Jerry refused to contact Liebowitz, Joanne said she'd do it for him.

Jack agreed to see her, but he wouldn't agree to give Jerry work. He'd done everything for Jerry he'd been legally bound to do and then some, he said, and Jerry had repaid him with an expensive and embarrassing lawsuit. In Jack's mind Jerry was out of the family.

"Listen," said Joanne. "Do you really want to see a newspaper head-line reading, 'Creator of Superman Starves to Death'?"

Liebowitz knew he couldn't afford to call her bluff. He told her he'd ask Mort Weisinger to assign Jerry a Superman script and see how it went.

Joanne had found a new weapon. Jerry had always wanted to come off as the nice guy or the know-it-all. But what finally worked was angry victimhood, playing on shame. Liebowitz did impose one condition:

that Jerry never claim publicly to be one of the creators of Superman. Joanne agreed. After twelve years Jerry Siegel was back on Superman.

JOE SHUSTER DISAPPEARS from the stories of the comic book industry but for a pair of anecdotes passed among men in the business. In one an artist sees him on a Central Park bench. He is so down and out that the artist buys him a sandwich, and Joe tells him how his life was ruined by the lawsuit against National. The artist asks if he can do anything for him, but Joe says no, thanks him for the sandwich, and hobbles off, using his cane like a blind man.

In the other, Joe is working as a delivery boy in Manhattan. One day he takes a package to National Periodicals' offices. A couple of editors recognize him and engage him in conversation. Just then Jack Liebowitz appears in the lobby and tells everyone to get back to work. When Joe has gone, Liebowitz calls the delivery service and tells them never to send that man to their offices again.

Were the stories true? Joe didn't like to relive the bad days, even during the later disputes with National, and avoided talking about whatever humiliations he may have suffered. But he did take odd jobs to ease his brother's financial burden, and he did spend most of his days in solitude. True or not, the stories had power because of what Joe had come to signify. There could be no clearer symbol of the heartlessness and ultimate hopelessness of the business than the descent of the artistic creator of Superman into poverty and anonymity. Telling stories about Joe Shuster was a way to say just how terrible the business and the owners were. It was also a way to tell yourself, "At least I didn't fall that far."

JERRY SIEGEL'S STORIES began appearing in *Superman* and *Action Comics* in late 1959. His tired work of the previous decade could not have prepared anyone for them. They were the freshest, most compelling, most alive Superman stories since Jerry and Joe's first few years. And they were utterly different from anything Jerry had done before.

Two years before, when the *Superman* TV show ended production, Mort Weisinger had set himself to revamping the comics. National's editors were beginning to emphasize superheroes again, seeking something to reach the boys' action market within the new editorial limits. Even though the code still allowed it to an extent, Liebowitz wanted violence—even fistfights—avoided. Superheroes had always been about fighting and mayhem, but now editors and writers were charged with devising plots that would get their characters flying, leaping, strutting their powers and facing life-or-death dilemmas without beating anyone up. Mort's old friend from science fiction fandom, Julie Schwartz, commissioned gimmicky, well-drawn stories with a space-age sheen for a revived Flash and Green Lantern, and they clicked with ten- and eleven-year-old readers enamored of outer space and rocket planes.

Weisinger took a different approach for Superman. He gave his hero a history and a family, providing kids a fictional world to enter and discover. In the process, he and Jerry Siegel discovered what had lain in plain view for twenty years but had never been explored: the pain at the heart of the orphan exile from another world.

The sheer volume of Superman stories was the greatest obstacle to keeping them entertaining. By the late 1950s, Superman and Superboy were supporting seven regular titles, most of them containing three stories each; Weisinger had to produce more than a hundred stories a year about the same hero. It didn't help that during the 1940s, Superman's writers had resorted to boosting his powers whenever they wanted to surprise the readers. The hero who had originally been able only to leap tall buildings and bend steel with his bare hands could now fly through the time barrier and juggle planets. Kryptonite, magic, and befuddling mysteries were almost the only ways to challenge him, and Weisinger's writers beat those devices to death.

Superman had ceased to be a metaphor for flying free and doing the impossible. In fact, he'd become his own opposite: a fantasy of being able to restore order by putting together clues and outsmarting the forces of chaos. Why has Jimmy Olsen gained superpowers and gone on a rampage? Superman deduces that he's been zapped by kryptonite and catapults it into space, after which the world settles back to dull calm. Superman had become a demonstration of what happens when the wild dreams of young men become the daily burdens of forty-year-olds. He'd become an essay on the constraining of the American imagination from the Thirties to the Fifties. He'd become the fantasy projection of an anxious editor with too much to juggle. But even Mort Weisinger could see that his hero needed new life.

Weisinger was a sharp editorial analyst, and he turned his disadvantages into strengths. Given a too familiar twenty-year-old character, too many stories, and no room for action, he recast his comics as an exploration of Superman's past and milieu. Siegel and Shuster had never used Superman's Kryptonian origin as more than an easy explanation of his powers, but now Weisinger saw that it was the one thing that made Superman unique.

In 1958 and 1959, in an explosion of ideas, Weisinger and his writers—particularly the inventive Otto Binder, who had once been Captain Marvel's main writer—turned Superman's predictable little world into a circus of surprises. They gave him a teenaged female cousin named Supergirl. They gave him a mermaid from an underwater city as a rival to Lois Lane. They gave him a monstrous opposite number, Bizarro, who matches his powers but is as ugly and stupid as he is handsome and bright. They invented a new form of kryptonite, Red K, that transforms the hero unpredictably—shrinks him, saps his powers, makes him old. They gave Superboy a group of friends from the far future, the Legion of Super-Heroes. From Doc Savage of the pulps, one of Superman's original models, they lifted the idea of a Fortress of Solitude in the Arctic where the hero can escape the petty anxieties of life as Clark Kent to study life on other worlds or explore records of his Kryptonian past.

If Superman could no longer embody fantasies of power and violence, he could at least embody the fantasy of being utterly unique, with unseen friends, a glorious hideout, and an astonishing secret. And he became more Jewish in the process, as Weisinger and Binder eased his Arctic solitude with a living relic of his home world: Kandor, a city shrunk into a bottle, where Kryptonians live their lives and yearn for the day Superman can restore them to their normal size. To those trapped in the ghetto of Kandor, Superman had become the Messiah.

When Jack Liebowitz asked Weisinger to find work for Jerry Siegel, Mort assigned Jerry mainly to fill in narrative blanks in Superman's past: how Clark was first hired by the *Daily Planet*, what baby Kal-El's life was like on Krypton before he was rocketed to earth. But Siegel soon began to bring an intensity to his dramatizations of the death of Krypton and the sundering of Superman's family that no other writers had tried to approach. The moment of Krypton's destruction had always been painted, even by the younger Jerry Siegel, with strokes of simple melodrama. But now Jerry took us straight to the weeping Kal-El as his puppy—the future Krypto the Superdog—is shot away in a test rocket. It was little kid stuff: "Me want my doggy! Waaa!" But it was *true* little kid stuff, the moments of powerlessness before adult tyranny and incomprehensible loss. When he wrote "The Ghost of Jor-El," in which Superboy is tricked into thinking he's encountered his father's spirit, Jerry stepped outside his intricate plot just long enough to let us feel Superboy's desperate need to believe it's true and his devastation as he learns his father is still lost to him.

Weisinger saw the power of those moments, and he began turning to Siegel for his most emotional stories. Siegel became the lead writer on *Supergirl*. He gave her a pet, Streaky the Supercat, put her through her first romance and a difficult adoption by an earth family, and sent her into the future to join Superboy's friends, the Legion of Super-Heroes—only to have her painfully rejected. Nine months later, though, they accept her, and she discovers that one of the Legionnaires has developed a crush on her. This was a new kind of intimate superhero drama. Jerry's attention to the roller coaster of little girls' feelings and fantasies suggested that he was well attuned to his daughter, Laura. At their best, though, his scripts were based on more than observation. Through the trite plots and the juvenile dialogue glint moments of surprising passion.

The moment Siegel realized his second Superman, the tragic Superman implicit in the first, came when he wrote "Superman's Return to Krypton" in 1960. The story was three times the normal length, filling the whole comic book, and it swept through months of Superman's life, revealing his highest hopes and deepest disappointment. In a desperate effort to save Krypton, he travels back in time and becomes his father's lab assistant. Concealing his true identity, he watches his parents in married bliss, watches them care tenderly for his own infant self; his "secret identity" had never been so poignant. He falls in love with a beautiful Kryptonian actress and plans a future with her, carrying the knowledge that her world, and their future, will die if he can't find a way to head off the building seismic cataclysm. Through it all he knows that if he saves his homeworld, there will never be a Superman on earth, all the good he did will never be done; but so deeply does he ache for the life that was taken from him that he cannot stop to think of that fate. When he realizes that Krypton cannot be saved, he decides to remain there, to die with his lover and parents.

Then it comes: The ground shakes, the Kryptonian towers begin to fall, the ground splits. But by a "strange twist of fate," he finds himself trapped in a second experimental rocket and shot away into space, watching helplessly as Krypton and his loved ones die. In the end, he resumes his life as Superman, the lonely alien who can save the earth a hundred times but never his own homeland.

Jerry Siegel had found the pain that had ached inside him since his father had been shot to death. He'd turned it into a comic book, but he had not trivialized it. There'd never been a comic book like this, broad and simple, almost primitive in its telling, but perfectly faithful to the love and pain it expressed. It had no villains, no plot tricks, and no simple morals. It was a superhero opera on unresolvable grief that a child could comprehend. This Superman was everything that Jerry and Joe's original version had not been. The first Superman was above caring that he had been sundered from his homeworld and his parents. His charm was his laughing invulnerability. Jerry's new Superman was a superhero because of his tragedy. His power was his superhuman grief.

Weisinger knew he had something. In the years to come, when he'd single Siegel out as "the most competent" of *Superman* writers, he'd mention "the classic 'Superman's Return to Krypton.'" Emotional tur-

moil became the baseline for Weisinger's comics for the next decade.
Most of the stories still turned on goofy shenanigans or evil schemes of
Luthor and Brainiac, but they were regularly punctuated by tear-jerking
returns to Krypton, "imaginary stories" in which Superman's loved ones
died, and churning melodramas of betrayal and loss. Siegel wrote the
best of them. He found every way there was to have Superman marry or
lose Lois, every way for Superboy to encounter his real parents or lose
his foster family. All the implicit but unexamined themes in Superman's
origin—orphanhood, immigration, lonely American boyhood, the passage of Moses—were laid bare on the page now.

Jerry had gone deeper into himself than he'd ever gone, and Mort
Weisinger had pushed him there with his insistence on doing something
new, his conviction that he knew what children craved, and his demand
that his writers bow to their tastes. It worked: *Superman* outsold every
comic book except Dell's Disneys and movie tie-ins and helped bring
superheroes back as the best-selling genre in the field. Jerry had his first
steady gig in years and was proving himself as a writer to the top-paying
publisher in comics. It should have been a good arrangement—except
that working for Mort Weisinger was a hell on earth.

Weisinger was notorious for his treatment of freelancers. He would
sit biliously behind his desk—Roy Thomas, his editorial assistant for
two weeks, described him as "looking like a malevolent toad"—and
swear and bellow and laugh at his writers and artists. Alvin Schwartz,
the poet who'd become the regular writer of the *Superman* newspaper
strip, left comics entirely because Weisinger wore him down. Don
Cameron, his other favorite writer, left him, too, but not before (or at
least so people said) grabbing him and holding him out an open window. "He'd pound on you until he found your weakness," said Curt
Swan, Weisinger's main artist in the 1960s. "Then he'd really go after
you." Swan, who was famous for his sweetness and affability, suffered
disabling stomach pains whenever he'd have to deal with his editor. He
found some relief only after he learned to yell back.

Jerry Siegel couldn't yell back, or at least didn't believe he could.
With Weisinger in front of him and the abyss behind him, he took

whatever his one-time friend dished out. Swan knew that Weisinger praised Siegel's work in public, "but whenever I went to the office and found Jerry there, Mort was berating him." Once, after reading a few pages of one of Siegel's stories, Weisinger stood up with the manuscript in his hand. "I have to go to the can," he said to Jerry. "Do you mind if I use your script to wipe my ass?"

Weisinger was a liar too. He had a trick to keep control in his hands. Jerry Siegel would come in and pitch a story about Lois Lane developing superpowers and realizing she doesn't need Superman anymore. Weisinger would say, "That's shit. I've got a better idea." He'd send Siegel off to write a story about Superman joining the Legion of Super-Heroes in the future. Then Otto Binder would come in and pitch a story. Weisinger would say, "That's shit. I've got a better idea." And he'd send him off to write his clever idea about Lois Lane developing superpowers and realizing she doesn't need Superman anymore. Later, of course, over gin rummy with Jack Liebowitz, he'd say, "Yeah, Siegel and Binder are giving me decent scripts, but I have to feed them all the fucking stories myself."

In later years Weisinger claimed to have been a tortured man. He became obsessed with Superman, he said. He'd have nightmares about him. Several times he tried to quit, but Liebowitz would raise his salary. A "golden cage" Weisinger called his job. Eventually Liebowitz insisted he see a psychiatrist and offered to pay for it as a business expense. Weisinger said his psychiatrist told him he was identifying with his Man of Steel. If Superman lagged in quality or sales, he'd feel his own sense of invulnerability unraveling. Superman always had to lead the company in sales and fan mail, and he always had to be Mort's. When Julie Schwartz scored a success with a new comic called *Justice League of America,* a team-up of all National's heroes, Mort cursed and threw tantrums and bitched to Irwin Donenfeld to keep Superman out of it. "It'll overexpose the character!" he yelled. Liebowitz finally intervened personally to talk Mort down.

No matter how Weisinger succeeded, he raged. He'd had nonfiction books published (probably ghostwritten), he'd appeared in *Readers Di-*

gest, he'd maneuvered his way to the presidency of the Magazine Writers of America, he ran *Superman,* he owned a huge house in Great Neck. His was a splendid résumé for a pulp hack, and he boasted about it endlessly, but with a defiant anger as if he were sure that the other guy was putting him down behind his back. He saw himself as superhuman in his accomplishments but utterly alone, tragically misunderstood, beset by enemies concealing emotional kryptonite. Maybe he did identify with his hero, but where his hero held it all together with physical power and condescending kindness, Mort held onto his power with cruelty.

Weisinger's hunger for control had given him an instinct for others' emotional twists. Who else but Jerry Siegel would have seen Superman as the personification of loss and futility? Weisinger didn't know about Jerry's loss of his father, but he knew Jerry had lost Superman in a hopeless struggle. Jerry was not a man who opened the door to his inner agonies easily. Weisinger drew those agonies out of him, but he pushed him into daily agony to do it.

Maybe Jerry could have endured even that, though, if he'd been able to keep ahead of his debts and take care of his wife and daughter as he wanted. But the cruelest thing of all about Weisinger, from the freelancer's most basic perspective, was that he demanded so many rewrites that Jerry couldn't produce enough scripts a month. Jerry had finally gotten his hero back, or a piece of him at least. But once again, trying to hang onto Superman was destroying him.

By THE END of the Fifties, Jack Liebowitz was turning his energies toward the biggest move of his career: taking his company public. National Periodical Publications was a perfect candidate for a stock offering. Now it included not only National Comics and Independent News Distribution but a new entity, the Licensing Corporation of America, which Jack had organized with a nephew named Jay Emmett. LCA was an outgrowth of Superman, Inc., that under Emmett, who had learned the ropes of showbiz as a publicist for the *Superman* TV show, was becoming a broker of merchandising licenses for a growing range of pop-culture properties. National Periodical was established, growing, diversifying, low in debt and rich in cash flow, and with Superman and his friends it owned unique properties exploitable in multiple markets. There was just one problem: One of its three owners was mixed up with the Costello and Lansky mobs. Investor confidence would not be encouraged by the threat of Justice Department or SEC investigations. Liebowitz wanted Harry's money moved into a Donenfeld family trust, and he wanted Harry off the board of directors.

Harry fought it. Jack pointed out he would make more money by getting out of the company's way and increasing the value of his own shares, but that wasn't enough for Harry. In his heyday what Harry had loved most was being known as the man who owned Superman. "My father wanted his picture on the wall of the boardroom," said Irwin Donenfeld. "Uncle Jack didn't care whose picture was where, as long as he made the money." Even after years of slow withdrawal, Harry couldn't stand his picture being taken off the wall or his name off the stationery. The fight was ugly.

Then the story took another turn. Gussie fell ill. Although we don't know what passed between her and Harry near the end, Irwin has hinted that she asked him to be practical for the sake of the kids and bow to Liebowitz's strategy. Harry finally conceded—partly out of duty to his dying wife, no doubt, but perhaps partly too because he saw a new life opening before him. For at least twenty years he had wished he could marry Sunny, the love of his life. Now the wish might become real.

Gussie Donenfeld died in 1961. Later that year National made its first public offering, with J. S. Liebowitz and Paul Sampliner on the board and Harry Donenfeld a silent partner. It proved to be a good investment, and Harry's children did well. After a suitable time of mourning, Harry announced that he and Sunny were going to be married.

The next several months of Harry's life—the last months of his full, waking life—would never be spoken of by his family. Business associates have said he seemed especially happy and sentimental as he prepared for his wedding and honeymoon cruise to Europe. But rumors also swirled of arguments with Liebowitz and with mob connections.

None of the rumors would ever come to rest on solid information; maybe there's truth to them, or maybe they were just efforts to give some narrative wholeness to what happened that night in 1962. Harry was, after all, a collection of stories. He needed a better story to go out on than the one his family told.

It happened a week before his wedding. Harry, said the family, got drunk alone one night in his suite. He passed out and hit his head on the corner of the TV set—or in some versions, a coffee table or the dining room table. Injured as he was, he managed to crawl into bed. The next day Irwin found him there. Irwin could see that he was breathing, but he couldn't wake him up. He called an ambulance. When Harry finally woke, he was blank. He seemed not to recognize his son. He didn't speak.

The story was inconceivable to the distributors and publishers who knew him: Harry Donenfeld without words, without stories, without a memory for faces. Questions arose. Was he really alone? Where was Sunny? How did Irwin know to go looking for him? Why did the details keep shifting? Who wanted him quiet? There are mundane answers, of course. Old men fall. Sons worry. But Harry had been so loud so long that it was hard to let him go quietly.

Harry lived for three more years. Irwin and Peachy found a good facility to care for him and visited him often. He became more functional with time, even speaking a few words, but he never regained his memory. Once Irwin brought him home for a visit when Irwin's son and a friend were playing on the porch. Harry looked at both little boys, then walked straight to his grandson and kissed him on the head. Irwin took his father inside and asked him, "You knew that was your grandson, didn't you, Papa?" Harry only looked at him. That moment would haunt Irwin for the rest of his life. He wanted to believe it was Harry's love, rising through his damaged brain for one last, brief visit to his family; but he would never be sure.

Harry Donenfeld died in silence in February 1965. No mention of his life or death was made in DC Comics.

New Owners

As NATIONAL PERIODICALS was offering its first stocks, a strange thing was happening a few blocks north in the little office in Martin Goodman's company, where Stan Lee juggled the tatty, nameless line of comics that had once been Marvel. National had scored its success with *Justice League of America,* and Goodman told Stan to crank out a superhero team in a hurry. Stan turned to Jack Kirby and through a process now eternally obscured by competing stories—both men claimed to have had all the basic ideas first—produced *Fantastic Four.*

These weren't typical superheroes, however, reputedly because Goodman's distributor, Jack Liebowitz, discouraged him from competing too directly with National. They had no costumes or secret identities. Kirby and Lee threw together a quartet of odd characters given strange powers by radiation: an obnoxious, teenaged Human Torch; a shy Invisible Girl; an angry muscleman called the Thing; and Mr. Fantastic, a scientist who stretched like Plastic Man and who would lead the group into bizarre adventures. Because Marvel's bread and butter then was its science-fiction monster stories, the Four were more like scientific freaks than heroes, and their adventures were ominous and dark. Because Jack Kirby was an angry man churning out pages in furious haste, the group was turbulent with bitter fights. Because Kirby was the man who brought poetic violence to comics through Captain America, the action was more liberating and intense than anything published since the Comics Code had been written six years before.

Little kids seem not to have taken much interest in *Fantastic Four*, but the twelve-, thirteen-, and fourteen-year-olds were intrigued. The adolescents who wanted a bit of darkness and angry drama had nearly abandoned comic books over the preceding years, but those who hadn't began to read *FF*. Kirby and Lee followed with another monster in vaguely heroic form, the incredible Hulk, then the Norse god Thor, then a scientist who shrinks to the size of an insect to become Ant Man. Goodman evidently persuaded Liebowitz to ease his restrictions on superheroes, because soon Lee was working with another artist—an odd young loner named Steve Ditko—on a character called Spider-Man.

Ditko was an unlikely match for a superhero series. Jerry Robinson, his cartooning teacher at the School of Visual Arts, once said, "From the beginning it was obvious that he was unlike anyone else." Ditko entered comics during the horror fad of the early 1950s and drew attention instantly with his mastery of psychological nuance, his figures contorted in rage and anguish, and the air of foreboding he gave to even the simplest images. He was too idiosyncratic an artist for National and the other big publishers, but Lee found him perfect for his more sophisticated suspense stories. Ditko boiled with emotion, but he didn't enjoy giving it free rein either in his work or his life; he was a fiercely private man who leashed himself with a steel rationalism, and who responded to the ethical relativism of the Sixties by devoting himself to the "Objectivism" of Ayn Rand. When he took on Spider-Man, he imbued even the most extravagant superhero fights with tension and pain.

Stan Lee was his temperamental opposite. His great talent, in both writing and life, was to win people's affection. He was raised to be lovable by a mother who worshipped him. "I used to come home from school," said Stan, "and she'd grab me and fuss over me and say, 'You're home already? I was sure today was the day a movie scout would discover you and take you away from me!'" She told Stan that he was the most handsome, most talented, most remarkable boy who'd ever lived. "And I believed her!" Stan said. "I didn't know any better!" Stan attacked the world with a crooked grin and a line of killer patter. No one else in comics ever wanted so badly to be liked or became so good at it. He was known as a soft touch on advances, deadlines, and extra assignments. Even people who didn't take him seriously as an editor or writer had to admit that Stan truly was a nice guy.

But that lovability had come at a price. Stan's father was a garment worker who consistently tried to support his family beyond his means but couldn't keep a job and disappeared into depression. Stan grew up with the sound of his parents' poisonous arguments in his ears. And as much as his mother cooed over him she criticized his little brother. "Larry grew up hearing his parents ask, 'Why can't you be more like your brother?'" Stan has said. "I've always felt bad that he had to go through that because of me." Stan made sure that Larry always had work as a writer or artist, but he could never dispel the guilt. All the maternal love that had made him so successful in the world had been stolen from his father and brother.

When Ditko and Lee turned their energies to creating an offbeat superhero, their passions and contradictions connected electrically. Spider-Man is a hero whose superpowers cause harm to his loved ones, whose anger and impulsiveness lead him into terrible mistakes, who is admired by teenagers but loathed by adults. Like Clark Kent, he is mocked in his human identity by the same people who idolize his costumed self, but he suffers more self-loathing as a superhero than he ever did as a scrawny outcast. Ditko and Lee had taken the idea of the tragic superhero a step beyond Jerry Siegel's Superman: They'd psychologized it, with a hero who did not simply weep for his inability to change fate but also questioned, every day, whether he was even doing the right thing by being a hero. Spider-Man spoke instantly to those guilt-ridden children of affluence and parental adoration who would become known as "baby boomers."

Now a new Stan Lee came into focus. His scripting had usually been pure formula, a hasty version of whatever else was out there. His best work was on teen humor comics, where he got to joke and flirt with his readers almost as he did in real life. Now, whipping out oddball superheroes with little expectation that they'd go anywhere, he took on a flippant, devil-may-care voice that could swing suddenly into hyperbolic, adolescent melodrama. The fans responded to Stan as a personality as they hadn't responded to any creator of comics since the heyday of Bill Gaines and his gang of idiots. Stan seized the moment, filling his comics with in-jokes, self-mockery, and nicknames for the heroes and their creators. "Stan the Man" united Jack Kirby's angry power and Steve Ditko's psychological intensity into the self-proclaimed "Marvel Manner." Soon "Marvel Maniacs" were beginning to evangelize in study halls across America.

During those same years, comic books were also being rediscovered by people who felt they were long past and far above their study hall days. A new American intelligentsia, shaped by the advertising-driven consumer culture and reacting against the phony sanctimony of the Cold War, began to make cheap commercial culture a subject of ironic exploration. Susan Sontag wrote her famous epigrammatic essay on "camp," turning a style of queenish, theatrical mockery into a badge of cultural knowingness. It was a relief, after the Fifties, to laugh at the earnest messages and cornball heroics of the past. The new movement called Pop Art brought a similar spirit to the making of symbols. Soup cans and collages of magazine ads were held up as objects of contemplation in a way that was both fetishistic and mocking and expressed a generation's ambivalence about a seductive but vacuous culture industry. As comic books began to assert themselves as shiny splotches on the pop culture landscape, a painter named Roy Lichtenstein turned them into icons. His big bright paintings of comic book people in moments of passion, built of hard, round color dots, were a perfect intellectual joke for self-conscious sophisticates in 1963 and 1964.

Lichtenstein's paintings also irritated comic book artists. The men who created the original images had sold them for ten or twenty dollars apiece, and here this "fine artist" was selling copies for thousands. One of the artists Lichtenstein copied often was Irv Novick, who had created the Shield, the first patriotic superhero, and gone on to become one of National's best war-comics artists. Novick recognized Lichtenstein's name: They'd been in the same army unit in World War II. They'd both wanted to be painters when they were young, but Lichtenstein came from an

Upper East Side family that could send him to college. Novick had had to work every day of his life. Now Lichtenstein was an art-world darling, and Novick was penciling furiously, anonymously, to pay the bills.

One comic book veteran who didn't just snort in annoyance at Pop and camp was Stan Lee. Stan had always wanted to be more than a pulp hack. He said he'd wanted to write the Great American Novel as a young man, but he'd liked making money too much to drop his comics work long enough to write it. His wife was a beautiful English model, his home an old carriage house on the Long Island shore. He wanted the attention of the bigger world. He called his comics "Marvel Pop-Art Productions" for a while. He encouraged his artists to be bolder, make their stories wilder. Steve Ditko put Spider-Man through an egghead's social agonies. Jack Kirby pitted the Fantastic Four against a planet-eating god and a "cosmic herald" who rides a surfboard through space. Sales climbed. Letters poured in, mostly from teenagers and adults. By 1965 Marvel comics were becoming a college fad.

At National, Julie Schwartz had already won over young science fiction fans with his *Flash, Green Lantern,* and *Justice League*. In 1964 he was assigned to revamp *Batman* and, not particularly liking the character, he gave it a self-mocking, almost intentionally campy tone. One issue caught the eye of a TV producer named Bill Dozier who was looking for a way to package the whole pop-camp-hip-cool style for the small screen. Comic books were about to be reborn in a new role at the front edge of popular culture.

THE FIRST ORGANIZED comic book fandom had formed around Bill Gaines's EC comics in the early 1950s. When Gaines abandoned all his comics except *Mad,* most of the "Fan-Addicts" moved on, but some continued to correspond, write newsletters, and even produce their own amateur imitations of the ECs they lamented. The best of the amateur comics were satirical, inspired by *Mad* and the new satire magazines *Humbug* and *Trump,* created by *Mad*'s founder, Harvey Kurtzman. *Foo,* by the brothers Robert and Charles Crumb, is still funny today.

In 1960 Kurtzman was approached by a young publisher named James Warren to create a new magazine, which they would call *Help*. Warren himself had been inspired to become a publisher by another *Mad* fan, Hugh Hefner. Warren's first success was *Famous Monsters of Filmland*, created and edited by Forrest Ackerman, who had been a pioneer of science fiction fandom along with Jerry Siegel and Mort Weisinger. Kurtzman agreed and got to work along with a brilliant and charming young editorial assistant named Gloria Steinem, who soon proved to have her own very strong ideas about what *Help* should contain. A new counterculture was developing around junk entertainment, science fiction, comics, politics, and sex. And as with the alternative culture of the 1920s, cheap magazines played a central role in it. Independent News, that descendant of Eastern News, played a role in this counterculture, too, although it was now at the top of the heap with *Playboy* and *Mad*. Independent was Warren's first choice to distribute him, but Jack Liebowitz told him, "Come back when you're bigger."

Help attracted the best-known humorists of its day: Mort Sahl, Ernie Kovacs, Woody Allen. It also attracted the young cartoonists who'd grown up loving Kurtzman and *Mad*. Among those who sent in cartoons were Robert Crumb and Art Spiegelman. Spiegelman stood out as one of the most artistically ambitious of the young cartoonists; he'd become fascinated by the potential of comics art when he discovered, among other comics, Will Eisner's *The Spirit*.

In 1965 *Help* folded. Kurtzman went to work for Hugh Hefner at *Playboy*. Warren assembled a group of former EC artists and young EC fans to create a group of magazines emulating the old Gaines-Feldstein-Kurtzman horror and war comics: *Creepy*, *Eerie*, and *Blazing Combat*. Like *Mad*, they were placed on magazine racks and ignored the Comics Code; they helped bring former EC fans and other adults into the comics fandom that was coalescing around Marvel Comics.

The young satirical cartoonists like Robert Crumb and Art Spiegelman began looking for new venues. Some contributed to small periodicals produced by the anti-war radical left, like *The Realist*, the brainchild of a former EC comics office boy, Paul Krassner. Some placed work in the "underground newspapers" that were popping up around the hippie culture: *The East Village Other, Yarrowstalks,* and *The Berkeley Barb.* Then some of them began to realize that they could create their own comic books, slicker versions of the fanzines of their youths, and distribute them through the same channels used by the lefty and underground press: alternative bookstores, hippie coffee shops, and those marijuana paraphernalia stores called "head shops" that were appearing in college neighborhoods across the country. The streets themselves became a distribution venue: Robert Crumb sold his *Zap Comics* out of a baby carriage on Haight Street in San Francisco.

By the end of the 1960s, the new "underground comix" were littering the crash pads and dorm rooms of America. The undergrounds synthesized political satire, drug humor, pornography, psychedelia, graphic experimentation, and indiosyncratic visions of life into an art form that shot straight to the imagination of millions of young Americans. Although alien and disturbing to the generation that had created the first comic books, they shared the qualities that had made comics such a vital form in the beginning: they were quick, they were cheap, they had no need of respectability or social approval, and they enabled cartoonists to get their visions straight to readers with a minimum of interference. The underground cartoonists knew their lineage too: One of the most popular features in the early issues of *Zap* was Gilbert Shelton's *Wonder Wart Hog,* a pornographic parody of *Superman.* Shelton owed a great deal to Harvey Kurtzman and Wally Wood's *Superduperman* from the fourth issue of *Mad,* but he also betrayed an unmistakable fondness for *Superman* itself. Jerry and Joe's fantasies of power and sexual cruelty still echoed, even for the generation that mocked them.

Scattered among copies of *Zap* and *The Fabulous Furry Freak Brothers* were *Spider-Man* and *Fantastic Four.* Stan Lee, Jack Kirby, and Steve Ditko had made superheroes relevant to a cultural moment very different from the one that had given them birth thirty years before. The Marvel superheroes were emotionally volatile, conflicted about who they wanted to be, and flamboyant in the use of their powers and the expression of their diverse personalities. They reveled in the ecstatic violence of their battles with supervillains even as they gnashed their teeth over the pain that their secretive, dangerous lifestyles inflicted on their loved ones. They suffered because their bizarre lives separated them from the women they loved even as their skintight costumes and rippling muscles advertised their sexual power.

Lee, Kirby, and Ditko dramatized what had been implicit in superheroes: the glory and torture of being unique, the divisions in modern identity, the ambivalence about the body that arises in an economy that makes physical labor less important as it makes body consciousness more so, the constant tension between self-indulgence and self-restraint demanded by a consumer culture. "Face front, true believers!" Stan yelled from his editorial pages. He knew Marvel had hit something. "'Nuff said."

Diverse readerships were overlapping and flowing together: superhero fans, Pop-fadsters, hippies, old EC Fan-Addicts. Comic book fandom was growing and finding its own complex identity. Fanzines proliferated, and some evolved into commercial magazines about comics. Back-issue dealers organized conventions where collectors could buy old comics and artists, writers, and editors could meet their fans. The most dedicated fans began to track down the creators of the comics and try to piece together the never recorded history of their field. The most talented began to badger editors to give them a shot at writing and drawing their favorite comics. Some, like Roy Thomas, were lifelong superhero lovers who wanted to flesh out their heroes' lives and milieus with novelistic detail. Others, like the young journalist Denny O'Neil, wanted to use superheroes to make social and political points. The geeks were starting to take themselves seriously.

THROUGH THE MID-SIXTIES, Jack Liebowitz continued to push his company to grow and acquire. In early 1964 Irwin Donenfeld signed a distribution deal with a fly-by-night publisher who'd bought the rights to do a fan magazine about a new musical group called the Beatles. Just before the magazine hit the stands, the Beatles appeared on *The Ed Sullivan Show* and became the biggest thing in pop culture. Independent

News made a killing on the magazine, and Irwin wanted to be sure Liebowitz knew that he was responsible. Liebowitz scowled at him. "You'd have made us a hell of a lot more money if you'd bought the guy's company too," he said.

But even Jack must have been pleasantly surprised by National's fortunes over the next three years. Bill Dozier sold ABC on the idea that a camp superhero show would bring in both the kids who dominated early-evening TV watching and the desirable demographics of hip young adults. With a hefty budget, Dozier's company built the *Batman* TV show on the stiff corniness of the Bob Kane studio and the sly silliness of Julie Schwartz and delivered a show so bright, preposterous, and smarmily derisive of old-style heroism that it became an instant craze. National Periodicals profited at every level. Comics sales soared, not just on *Batman* but across the line. Marvel Comics, being more innately hip, benefited even more than DC, but that meant more money for Independent News. The Licensing Corporation of America sold Batman's likeness everywhere.

And *Batman* was only part of the story. Independent News turned out to be perfectly placed for that overheated decade. *Mad* was more popular than ever, and *Mad* paperbacks became best sellers for Signet. *Playboy* rode the crest of the sexual revolution. Signet books had picked up a series of British espionage novels that performed moderately well for a few years, until suddenly James Bond, like *Mad*, *Playboy*, and *Batman*, became relevant to the mid-Sixties and Independent found itself with another cash cow. The merchandising rights to Bond were owned by the Licensing Corporation of America. That didn't look like much to most people in the business, but LCA's Jay Emmett was more than just a nephew of Jack Liebowitz: He was a natural promoter, young and charismatic, with an eye for pop culture trends. Emmett astonished the business by spinning a multimillion-dollar toy, trading card, and kids' clothing franchise out of an espionage series aimed at the *Playboy* man. He and LCA were becoming the stars of the licensing business just as that business was entering its most prosperous years.

Jack Liebowitz conducted his life by his own scrupulous code. Longer hair was becoming fashionable among businessmen, and Jack gave up his weekly haircuts; but he insisted upon paying his barber weekly nonetheless so that the man's livelihood would not suffer for Jack's vanity. In other arenas, however, that code could be harsh. As National's regular writers entered their fifties, they began to worry. Some tried to form a union and failed, but around 1966 a number of them—Gardner Fox, Bill Finger, Otto Binder, Bob Haney, Arnold Drake, and others, most of them loyal DC freelancers for more than twenty years—brought a set of demands to Liebowitz. They asked for compensation—royalties on sales, reprint fees, health benefits, retirement plans—that would make them less dependent on page rates. Liebowitz refused. The writers pointed out how much money National was making off their creations. *Batman* villains and plot gimmicks were being lifted wholesale from Bill Finger scripts, and Bill Dozier and Adam West and Jack Liebowitz were getting rich while Finger himself got nothing but the fee for last week's script.

"I know how you boys feel," said Liebowitz. "I was a socialist myself when I was a young man."

"The problem," snapped Arnold Drake afterward, "is that Jack Liebowitz had a youth of ten minutes." It was far longer than that, of course. It had been a long trip from fighting the law of the jungle to mastering it. But now he had become so completely the antithesis of what he'd been raised to be that the writers could see nothing across the desk but the perfect image of a Boss. He'd buried more than his wife and his former partner. He'd buried a whole America. He placated the writers with small page-rate increases and sent them on their way.

In the months to come, most of those writers found their assignments drying up. Some insisted it was punishment for their demands, but the change wasn't quick or consistent enough. More likely it was the arrival of a younger, hungrier, cheaper talent pool. The fans who'd grown up on Julie Schwartz and Stan Lee's superheroes were eager to try writing them. Editors knew those superhero-drenched kids would be able to reach the growing teen market better than the bitter old-timers, and they could do so for lower rates. In addition to the hard budgetary logic, there was an equally hard cultural logic: What were men in their fifties doing writing adolescent fantasies in 1967? So the men who had survived the collapse of comics in their forties found themselves out of work a decade older.

To Jack Liebowitz this was how it was done. People got what they worked for. If you want a job with health benefits, you find a job with health benefits. If you want to live as a freelancer, you die as a freelancer.

BOB KANE MADE a lot of money out of the *Batman* TV show, and not just from his piece of the licensing. The deal he'd struck with Liebowitz in 1946 allowed him to call himself Batman's creator, and he immediately publicized himself as such. Suddenly he was mentioned in *Life* and started appearing on talk shows. He headed for Los Angeles, drew a fee as consultant to the TV *Batman,* and started pitching himself to TV producers. He set up *Cool McCool,* a cartoon about a superspy that played off the Bond craze, with King Features Syndicate and NBC. It was shoddy stuff, but it lasted two years and made Kane a network TV series creator. The rumor, of course, was that he'd hired ghosts to write and draw his pitches.

In LA, Kane took to wearing yachting blazers and turtlenecks, topsiders and ascots and the occasional captain's cap. He kept a pipe clenched between his teeth and invited starlets and models to cruise in his convertible. But so deep was his hunger for recognition that he would stop to talk to teenage boys flipping through the comics in supermarkets. "You like comic books? Do you know who I am? I'm Bob Kane, creator of Batman." One of the boys he chatted up turned out to be a member of a comic book club, and Kane invited his whole club home to look at his original Batman art. He pulled out art boards and scribbled pictures of Batman for each of them as he bragged about his years drawing comics. Then one of the kids, Mark Evanier, asked him if it was true he'd used ghost artists for decades. Kane lost his avuncular chuckle and narrowed his eyes at Evanier. Then he flashed a different smile, the smirk of a gambler caught bluffing, and he said, "Let me tell you some things about comics, kid." And he told some of the real stories about the shell games and lies the comics business was built on.

His own shell game paid off even more richly than he could have expected. The fact that his great 1946 rights deal came up for renewal precisely when *Batman* hit the top of its meteor flight enabled him to increase his percentage of the take while freeing National of its obligation to buy pages from him. He could let the headache of the secret art studio go without worrying about his income. Then, in 1967, came a significant change in ownership at National. Because Kane owned partial rights to *Batman*, he could negotiate his own sale. He'd walk away with a million-dollar fee and an even bigger piece of subsidiary income.

After the *Batman* fad fizzled and *Cool McCool* was canceled, Kane remained in LA, taking meetings, talking about deals he was just about to make, and drawing sketches for all the movie brats who told him they'd grown up on comics. He invested in a waterbed and a hot tub and bragged about his liberated sexual philosophy with female receptionists and development assistants. He also announced that he'd evolved into a fine artist. At a gallery in Hollywood he unveiled his paintings of clowns. Wistful, poignant clowns in the artistic tradition of Red Skelton.

A few years later word went around the comics business that an artist was suing Kane for failing to compensate her as promised for paintings she'd executed anonymously for him to resell. Arnold Drake, that veteran DC writer, realized what the paintings must be. "The clowns," he said. "He even had a ghost for the fucking *clowns!*"

T HE *BATMAN* TV show brought little but pain to Bill Finger. For nearly thirty years he'd been writing comics for a page rate, almost always anonymously, and remaining strangely silent about his cocreation of Batman. He'd been a reliable scripter on dozens of series, but the wild acrobatic fights and death traps of *Batman* had always been what he'd done best. Serious fans could usually spot a Finger script by its odd conviction and clever use of sets and plots. Much of what made the TV *Batman* successful, from its earnest hyperbole to its giant deadly ice-making machines, came from Finger. When fans sought him out, he began to tell his story, but Kane blasted him in print for his "hallucinations of grandeur." "To the victor belong the spoils," Kane wrote to a fanzine. "I am assured that in the folklore of legendary comic history of our times, I know that Bob Kane will be remembered as the creator of 'Batman' and no one else."

Finger didn't press the issue much after that. The first generation of comic book creators felt a deep shame about what they did for a living, especially after the attacks on comics in the Fifties, especially as they entered middle age and associated with suburban neighbors and the fathers of their kids' friends. Joe Simon, who'd cocreated *Captain America* and brought the romance genre to comics, explained his odd working hours and the fact that he never commuted by spreading the rumor that he was a bookie. His son was a teenager before he quite figured out what his father did for a living. For Bill Finger, who had wanted to be a novelist, the shame of devoting his career to the Dynamic Duo was intense. The shame must only have been made more intense by the realization that he'd had a claim to that gold mine and never asserted it.

The decades of drinking were taking their toll on Finger. He missed more deadlines than ever, the wit evaporated from his scripts, his family came apart. The failure to get health or retirement benefits out of Liebowitz left him despondent. When the new generation of fan writers appeared, Finger was one of the first of the old guard who stopped getting assignments. He stopped talking to fans. Bob Kane told of meeting him after his career had ended. "He was a haunted man," said Kane. Finger was finished as a writer by his early fifties and dead at sixty. Only after his death would Kane begin to acknowledge what his friend had given him.

FOR JERRY SIEGEL the *Batman* TV show was by no means the most important event of 1966. That year marked the twenty-eighth anniversary of the sale of *Superman* to Harry Donenfeld—and the expiration of its first copyright term. National Periodicals would have to renew, and that meant the application could be challenged. It would be Jerry and Joe's last shot at staking a claim to their creation.

By 1963 Jerry had already contacted a lawyer and begun the process. He knew Liebowitz would fire him the instant he took him back into court, and even Joanne wouldn't be able to change his mind this time. But the pain and disgust of working with Mort Weisinger were wearing him down, and it showed in his work. He wondered if he'd be able to hang on at National much longer in any case. He asked Joe to join him, but his old partner said he couldn't do it. He couldn't afford the legal fees and he didn't have the heart to fight anymore. Jerry pressed on alone.

He pitched his services to other publishers so he'd have a place to land when Liebowitz cut him off. Stan Lee was the first to oblige. Jerry loved working for Stan, who was a great cheerleader and an easy editor. Stan found Jerry to be "the nicest guy in the world." He handed Jerry the Human Torch, a teenaged hero he thought had the potential to be another Spider-Man. Jerry worked anonymously, to put off his reckoning with National; he called himself "Joe Carter," after his one-time partner and the name his wife had used in her modeling days. He named the pleasant town where the Torch walked to high school along leafy sidewalks "Glenville." For a moment Jerry was back among the hopes of thirty years before, back at the Glenville High *Torch* with his artist friend and the would-be model who cheered them on.

Marvel's readers, unfortunately, found Jerry's style too corny, his supervillains too pat and gimmicky. They wanted Lee and Kirby's startling plots and gaudy action. Stan cast around for other writers who could keep the Torch closer to the heart of the Fantastic Four. In the end, he wouldn't find anyone who could give him what he wanted, until he turned to the young fans who were asking him for a chance to write. Stan had taken superhero writing where no one else in his generation could follow.

In 1964, however, Jerry found a publisher that thrived on corn: Archie Comics. He worked on an updated version of Street and Smith's Shadow, the pulp character who'd first inspired Jerry to think about superheroes, and a pair of Marvel imitations called *Fly Man* and *Mighty Crusaders.* He'd found Archie just in time, for in early 1965 his challenge went to court, and once again he was fired from *Superman*—this time with less drama and more resignation all around. At first the Archie superheroes sold fairly well, and Jerry was able to keep paying his legal bills through the first round of delays. One painful new reminder of his plight arrived in the spring of 1966: a Broadway musical called *It's a Bird, It's a Plane, It's Superman*. But it didn't survive long, and it served as a spur to keep fighting.

Then the bottom dropped out of the *Batman* craze. The comics business suffered a sharp contraction. The superhero comics that appealed to the hipper fans still did well, but the campy and the corny suffered. Archie folded up its superhero line. Jerry couldn't get the editors to give him work on its bread-and-butter teen humor comics. He turned to Stan Lee again. All Stan could offer him was a proofreading job. Jerry took it.

He tried to sell articles and short stories to magazines, but he never had been a prose writer. Jerry was ashamed to tell many people, but word got around that he was out of work. Someone told Jim Warren, publisher of *Help* and *Creepy*, that the creator of Superman needed help. Warren called him immediately. "I told him who I was," he said, "and that I was sending a car to pick him up at his home and take him right to our office—so that we could load him up on writing assignments." Jerry arrived with four or five scripts in hand. "He was somewhere in his fifties, looking awful, wearing a shabby raincoat in the dead of winter," said Warren. "My heart sunk." Warren read the scripts. "They were not publishable." He sent Jerry home with a stack of his magazines and told him to write something in keeping with the Warren line.

Jerry came back in a week with two stories. Warren's editor, Archie Goodwin, was waiting eagerly with him this time, and the men took turns reading the scripts. "They were both awful," said Warren. "I glanced over at Archie, who was trying to hide his disappointment. One of us had to tell Jerry his work was unacceptable. Archie couldn't. Neither could I. Finally I said, 'Jerry, the scripts are good! We're going to use them. We'll buy them.'" Archie Goodwin rewrote them both completely. "I don't know if Jerry knew the difference," said Warren. "He was that beat."

Jerry's challenge to National's copyright was denied in court. With pro bono legal help he filed an appeal. The process would drag on for years, but his hopes were flagging. In 1968 he began to take leave of his friends in New York. He told some that his doctor had said he had to move to the West Coast for his health, others that he and Joanne wanted to establish residency in California so their daughter could attend UCLA, still others that he had a chance at some writing work out there. In the end, it may have been that he was just finished. Finished with the comic book business, finished with Jack Liebowitz's city.

When he said goodbye to Joe Shuster, he left Joe with hardly anyone in his life but for the brother who supported him. Occasionally Joe heard from his old friend Jerry Robinson, but their different life courses had pulled them far apart. Robinson had become a successful political cartoonist. While Joe was selling off his record collection to help his brother pay the rent, Robinson and his wife were staying with Lyndon Johnson on his Texas ranch. In 1967 Robinson had been elected president of the National Cartoonists Society, and he helped Joe get some financial help from the society's charity fund. But after Joe had expressed his gratitude, he didn't have much else to say.

ONCE THE YOUNG writer on the upswing and the not-so-old accountant working to keep a small publishing firm together had not been so far apart in wealth or position. But now, as Jerry Siegel drove out of New York and away from the publishing world, Jack Liebowitz prepared to step to the top of the mountain. American capital was booming. The 1960s were the golden age of mergers and acquisitions. The old entertainment and publishing establishments were breaking down; everything was up for grabs. And National Periodicals fit the plans of the man who would soon become the acknowledged master of the modern media conglomerate.

Money loomed large in Steve Ross's childhood. His father, Max Rechnitz, had made a lot of it in the building trades during the 1920s, then lost it all in the Depression. Max changed the family name to "Ross" hoping it would help him professionally, but it didn't. Little Steve hustled for every way to make money he could. When he was eleven, he sold magazines on the streets of Brooklyn; the early issues of *Action Comics* may have passed through his hands. Jerry Siegel and Joe Shuster, thirteen years his senior, would have seemed like distant big shots to him then.

Max Ross got a job in the plumbing supply business during World War II, and the family was able to move up to the Manhattan middle class. Steve earned a scholarship to a private school and began to mingle with Upper East Side money. He learned to ski, to dress well, to chat up the rich and carry himself with class. By 1950, when he turned twenty-three, he'd become a successful salesman in the garment industry. As a math whiz and a master gamesman he loved gin rummy. He loved to win, and he usually did. At twenty-seven he won a nineteen-year-old bride named Carol Rosenthal whose family owned a chain of funeral homes. Soon he was making a name for himself as a tireless and popular funeral director.

The Rosenthals didn't own just funeral homes. They owned racehorses too, and they shared interests with Caesar Kimmel, son of a New Jersey gambler who was part of Longy Zwillman's mob. Kimmel also owned the Kinney System parking garages. Edward Rosenthal brought his favorite son-in-law into his negotiations with Kinney to invest jointly in a car rental company. By 1960 Steve Ross had developed a plan to merge the two companies and take them public. The funeral home people would dominate the board, and the financial interests of the Kimmel and Zwillman families would be buried deep. Ross negotiated the deal and was named president of Kinney Service, Inc., when it moved into its new headquarters at Rockefeller Center.

Ross quickly proved to be a master not just of gamesmanship and persuasion but of the mechanics of business as well. He learned corporate law and accounting on the job. He also learned mob business. The parking and rent-a-car branches of the company sustained a million-dollar secret fund by skimming from garages and expense accounts for the payments that couldn't show up on the books: payments to union bosses, city inspectors, police. Ross's biographer, Connie Bruck, quotes a Kinney executive as saying, "I once saw $100,000 in a brown paper bag, left on someone's desk to solve a problem."

Now, in that time of big mergers, Ross discovered that his great love was acquisition. In his first five years as president he swallowed car leasing, funeral home, cleaning, painting, plumbing, and electronics companies. Then, in 1967, he turned to National Periodical Publications. Rumors swirled that it was hidden connections that had drawn Kinney to it: Donenfeld, Costello, Zwillman, Kimmel. But such rumors will arise when companies with bootlegging and numbers rackets in their heritage meet. Ross may just have been looking at likely growth industries and seen *Mad*, *Playboy*, James Bond, and *Batman*.

Ross acquired National for $60 million. The Donenfeld and Sampliner families were mostly content to collect their earnings and move on. Irwin Donenfeld wanted to keep his editorial position, but Ross's people didn't want him. Irwin bought a wharf and a maritime supply business in Westport, Connecticut, launched a boating magazine, and settled into small-town life with his wife and kids. Only the Liebowitz family continued to be involved in the company. Jack himself reinvested his earnings in the conglomerate and took a place on the Kinney board. His nephew Jay Emmett continued to run the Licensing Corporation of America, where his boundless energy and sense of adventure shone brighter than ever—and soon caught the eye of Steve Ross himself.

That was the end of the old DC Comics. The new management gave control to loyal insiders who wouldn't cost too much: An old production hand, Sol Harrison, was made publisher, an artist named Carmine Infantino editorial director. Mort Weisinger was let go with a golden parachute and promptly announced he'd sold a novel: *The Contest*, an exposé of the sex and corruption in the dressing rooms of the Miss America pageant. It would be the crowning moment in Mort Weisinger's career as a writer; it would also turn out to have been ghostwritten by an alcoholic comic book writer named Dave Vern. Mort's old pal Julie Schwartz was made the editor of *Superman*. He promptly swept away all the messy, prepubescent madness and angst of the Mort years and remade it into just another sleek, efficient comic book.

Steve Ross quickly acquired a talent agency, Ashley Famous, and then went after his prize: Warner Brothers–Seven Arts. Elliot Hyman, owner of Seven Arts and a Meyer Lansky associate, had bought Jack Warner's shares of his movie studio and record company. Now he was selling the company and started a bidding war. Ross couldn't top the competition's numbers, which meant he had to win on charm and skill. The big money men in Seven Arts had come up from the Lansky mob. They were unreconstructed racketeers, old casino builders and race fixers from the wild years. Ross knew how to talk to them. They wanted to make the deal, but there was one obstacle. A part owner of Warner-Reprise Records had veto power over any sale and needed to be convinced separately. But that part owner was Frank Sinatra, and Ross knew how to talk to him too. They signed the deal over dinner at Sinatra's mother's house in New Jersey. It was old-style business, neighborhood gang business, and Ross had worked it perfectly to create Warner Communications.

The remnants of National Periodicals became integral parts of the conglomerate. Independent News formed the foundation of Warner Books and Warner Publisher Services. Comic book sales were slumping, but the Licensing Corporation of America kept selling DC properties, spinning *Wonder Woman* onto prime time and *Superman* and *Batman* into cartoons. Jay Emmett became a Warner vice president.

Liebowitz took a place on the Warner board. Through aggressive stock acquisition he increased his share in the firm until he became one of the largest individual shareholders in Warner Communications. He'd remarried, to an attractive socialite named Phyllis many years his junior. She wasn't liked by Jack's daughters or the rest of the Liebowitz and Donenfeld clans, but she doted on him and he was loyal to her. Jack and Phyllis lived mostly in Manhattan, on the Upper East Side. Jack kept an office high in Warner's headquarters building in Rockefeller Center and reported regularly to work. Steve Ross came to respect him as a dignified elder of corporate America.

THE SIEGELS FOUND a small apartment in Westwood, near UCLA. They were a close family, Jerry, Joanne and their daughter, Laura. Laura blossomed in LA. She wanted a career in movies or television, and she was soon being encouraged in both her acting and writing by teachers and fellow students.

Jerry started writing for Western Printing and Lithography, which published Disney and TV tie-in comics under its Gold Key imprint and had decided to take a stab at superheroes. *Owl Man* and *Tiger Girl* died quickly, but this time someone was willing to help Jerry land on his feet: Western passed him on to Disney's European line. The men who ran American comics may have had little sentiment and even less regard for history, but the editors of *Topolino*, the Italian *Mickey Mouse*, were pleased to have the creator of Superman writing for them. So he wrote scripts for *Donald Duck* and *Uncle Scrooge* that were translated into Italian. He found new fans too, as he filled his stories with broad action and slapstick that was a refreshing change to the usual Disney restraint.

He was still a freelancer, though, without health benefits or a retirement fund. He couldn't get enough work from Disney to buy the security he needed. He was almost sixty years old, and he needed a real job. So, with resignation, he followed the path that so many of his cousins had pursued, so many of the men he'd broken with and left behind: the path of civil service. The California Public Utilities Commission needed clerks to type and sort the mail. It paid $7,000 a year with decent benefits. Just the job for an aging man with no other prospects.

In 1972 a reporter for the *Cleveland Plain Dealer* named Tom Brazaitis stumbled upon an account of Superman's creation, based on Jerry's erroneous reminiscences of long ago, that assigned it to a summer night in 1932. He wanted to write a piece on the fortieth anniversary of Cleveland's most famous fictional native and set out to contact the creators. He hit two dead ends. Joe Shuster, he wrote, "could not be located in New York, where, one source said, he has gone into seclusion. He is said to be going blind." Jerry Siegel "was traced to Los Angeles, where he is employed with the Public Utilities Commission. He refused to grant an interview."

For three more years the world would not hear a word from Jerry or Joe.

Continuity

MARIO PUZO WAS a man's writer. He'd grown up in Hell's Kitchen in the Depression, made his mark with a couple of literary novels, and then, in 1965, taken a hard look at himself: "I was forty-five years old and tired of being an artist. Besides, I owed $20,000 to relatives, finance companies, banks and assorted bookmakers and shylocks." So he wrote a novel about the Mafia to make money. To pay the bills during the writing, he cranked out three stories a month for Martin Goodman's sweaty men's magazines. While Stan Lee was scripting his Marvel Comics, his coworkers in the next office were pasting up tough-guy stories by Mario Puzo. Then *The Godfather* made Puzo rich and famous. His name attached to a movie made people sit up and notice. It worked for *Earthquake*. And Alexander Salkind was counting on it to work for *Superman*.

Salkind didn't want his *Superman* movie to be a piece of fluff like the *Batman* TV show. As a producer he'd just scored huge successes with his *Three Musketeers* and *Four Musketeers* and saw in the Man of Steel the foundation of a big-budget adventure franchise. He wanted it to have the gloss, the special effects, and the star power of *The Towering Inferno* and *Airport 1975*. He wanted it talked about too, so he spent a quarter of a million dollars to hire Puzo to write the first two drafts. Puzo's script was unfilmable, but his name brought *Superman* instant mainstream credibility. Suddenly the rumors that Francis Ford Coppola had been asked to direct—or was it William Friedkin or Arthur Hiller or Norman Jewison?—had weight. Suddenly dads who'd have sneered at their nerdy sons for still liking comics were trying to picture Al Pacino or Paul Newman as the Man of Steel.

Jerry Siegel might have dreamed once of being such a writer, but reality had not been so kind. He didn't know how to beat the system, didn't know how to make money, didn't know how to bring credibility to himself, let alone a movie. During the very years Puzo was writing *The Godfather*, Jerry was vainly challenging the *Superman* copyright and sliding into oblivion. The years of Puzo's glory were Jerry's years of despair. A federal court denied his appeal. His last hope, a faint one, was to ask the U.S. Supreme Court to hear the case. He suffered a heart attack. His doctor told him he shouldn't travel or strain himself. He wondered if he could go on fighting.

Then, in April 1975, came the call from his lawyer. Jay Emmett of Warner Communications was trying to clear the decks for the *Superman* movie and wanted to get Siegel's decade-long lawsuit out of the way. Warner, he said, could see its way to offering Jerry and Joe some sort of annual stipend if Jerry would just drop the suit. Jerry couldn't see why he should trust Emmett—he was Jack Liebowitz's nephew, after all—but he didn't know what else to do. He agreed to close the door on his last legal hope.

Jerry waited for Warner's people to live up to their word. They did nothing. He wrote, and he wrote again. No one responded. He began to fear that it would all end right there, and he'd leave nothing for Joanne and Laura. Then a series of small but remarkable events occurred. The tendrils of comic-book fandom that had been growing slowly for over a decade finally found their way to the creator of the superhero.

A couple of fanzine publishers named Alan Light and Murray Bishoff stumbled upon a newspaper mention of Jerry's last court decision, tracked him down, and started writing editorials on his behalf. Intrigued by this new fandom, Jerry mail-ordered the favorite fan book of the moment, The *Steranko History of Comics*. The parcel was delivered to the wrong apartment, to a comics collector named Chuck McCleary. He brought the parcel to Jerry's door and asked him if he was *the* Jerry Siegel. Then he invited him to speak at a comic book convention in San Diego. Jerry went, long enough to unload his grievances on a small roomful of adult fans. They were outraged. They told Jerry he should make his story known, and they offered to help. He rode home and simmered in the pale heat of Southern California summer. That's when Mario Puzo turned in his epic, three-hundred-page script about the hero Jerry Siegel had created. That's when the story appeared in *Variety* about the $3 million that had been transferred from Warner Studios to National Periodicals for the rights to Jerry's dreams.

In September 1975 Jerry wrote his press release. For ten single-spaced pages he told of how he and Joe had been cast into want as they made other men rich. He told of Jack Liebowitz's promises and lies, of Joe's blindness and his own bad health, of his years of court battles. His words were frantic and repetitive. He tortured logic to explain away the fact that he really had sold all his rights. His voice rang clear, however, when he made his plea: "I can't flex super-human muscles and rip apart the massive buildings in which these greedy people count the immense profits from the misery they have inflicted on Joe and me and our families. I wish I could. But I can write this letter and ask my fellow Americans to please help us by refusing to buy comic books, refusing to patronize the new Superman movie, or watch Superman on TV until this great injustice against Joe and me is remedied by the callous men who pocket the profits from OUR creation."

Jerry made a thousand copies. He mailed them to every national news program, every big-city newspaper, every LA-area media outlet from the *Times* down to weekly giveaways. Then he sat back and waited for calls from reporters.

The calls didn't come. Weeks passed, and slowly the reality sank in: Even in his first searing moment of self-exposure Jerry had been unable to get himself taken seriously.

He'd nearly given up when the first response came. Phil Yeh was the twenty-one-year-old publisher of a free arts newspaper called *Cobblestone* and the creator of a comic strip for the Long Beach State school paper. He was part of the local "underground" comics community—a genial bunch of shaggy-haired, dope-blowing kids who drew funny cartoons about sex and politics and California boredom—and cared nothing for superheroes. But when he found Jerry's letter on a stack of unread mail, he knew he had a story that needed telling. He called Jerry, hoping he could be squeezed in for some quick questions among the major-media interviews he must have lined up. Jerry was thrilled to have gotten a call. Phil drove up to Jerry's apartment in West Los Angeles, and they sat down together, the battered, sixty-one-year-old Jewish writer from Cleveland and the bushy, fiery-eyed, Filipino hippie artist from Southern California. They found a commonality that crossed the vast gap between them. They were both immigrants' sons who'd grown up on the edge of American prosperity and found meaning in disposable but strangely inspired bits of popular culture: science fiction, Douglas Fairbanks, the Fabulous Furry Freak Brothers. They'd both wanted to forge their own version of that culture, to find a way to live in their dream-worlds, "to avoid," as Yeh put it, "looking for a job." They were both geeks.

With Joanne sitting beside him, voicing the anger that he held back, Jerry told his whole story, for the first time, to someone outside the circle of family and lawyers. Phil turned it into a passionate story for *Cobblestone*. Jerry discovered that for a new generation, he wasn't a loser but a hero.

At last, in late October, the break came. The press release Jerry had sent to the *Washington Star* had slowly found its way to a feature writer named John Sherwood. Sherwood called Jerry for the story, then called National Periodicals, where no one would comment. Los Angeles was too far for the *Star* to send him, but Sherwood took the train to New York, where Joe Shuster gave his first press interview since the days of Superman's early glory. The story appeared on the front page of the *Star*, and it touched a nerve in that moment of popular disgust with the American corporate system. It hit the wire services and other papers began to call.

Still no one at National Periodical or Warner Communications would comment. Apparently the company strategy was to wait out the flurry of news items until people forgot and business could go on as usual. It might have worked, too, had not the producers of a late-night talk show, *The Tomorrow Show* with Tom Snyder, thought the story would make an interesting short piece. Jerry was about to tell his tale on national TV.

JERRY ROBINSON ALWAYS worked with the TV on. The background noise made it easier to relax into the semiconscious flow of brush on paper, and sometimes he picked up a tidbit of news that sparked a political cartoon. He was working late that night in his apartment on Riverside Drive, past the evening news, past Johnny Carson, and into the intimate, smoke-filled domain of Tom Snyder. He heard the name "Jerry Siegel" and put down his brush.

Robinson was shocked to hear Jerry's story. A few years before, he'd heard that Jerry was fighting National in court, and then Jerry and Joe had gone silent. "I was under the impression they'd reach some sort of settlement with the new owners," Robinson has said. "I had no idea they'd still been fighting and suffering all those years." He immediately tracked down Jerry's phone number and asked what he could do for him. Jerry didn't know what could be done, but he'd be grateful if Robinson could think of anything. Maybe he could call Neal Adams, a comic book artist who was already advocating for him. Robinson knew Adams and called him the next day. They agreed to launch a campaign to pressure Warner Communications into doing its duty.

The National Cartoonists Society's annual board meeting happened to be convening the next week and Robinson took the cause to it. He came out with a unanimous statement of support for Siegel and Shuster. With that in hand he secured the support of the Screen Cartoonists Guild, then the Writers Guild of America. He knew that cartoonists didn't matter much to Warner Communications, but the TV and movie communities did. Robinson owned a weekend cottage on Cape Cod, and he called up two of his neighbors, Norman Mailer and Kurt Vonnegut, to ask if he could add their names to the campaign. They not only let him use their names but also began lining up support from the literary and journalistic communities. The media took note. The *CBS Evening News* covered the dispute, and Jerry was flown to New York to appear with Joe on *The Today Show*.

Neal Adams, meanwhile, roused the comic book community. He packed significant clout at National Periodicals. He'd been the fans' favorite superhero artist since his expressive, naturalistic style had first burst into DC Comics in the late 1960s. National's publisher, Carmine Infantino, personally admired his work. In the past few years, Adams had been drawing fewer comics, finding advertising a far more lucrative field; but when he returned to draw the occasional *Batman* story, it was an event. When Adams called on his fans and peers to push National to do what was right, the executives felt the pressure. Nor did the pressure come only from the outside: More and more editorial seats were filled by young men who'd come up through fandom. The most respected young editor at National was Adams's friend and frequent collaborator, Denny O'Neil.

The pressure worked. In early December Warner Communications announced it was ready to settle: It would pay Jerry and Joe each $10,000 annually for life. Jerry Robinson told the two not to take it and made a counteroffer on their behalf. On Tuesday, December 9, Warner increased its offer to $15,000 and gave Jerry and Joe two days to accept it. Robinson stalled with a provisional acceptance but demanded that Warner cover Siegel and Shuster's legal debts and pay for full medical insurance besides. By Friday the two sides were close to a monetary agreement. They planned for Jerry to fly in from LA, and on Monday, the 15th, all the parties would sit down in the Warner offices in Rockefeller Center for a final negotiation.

On Monday morning the *New York Times* reported that Siegel and Shuster were "expected to accept an offer of $15,000 a year for life." Robinson thought the financial offer was far too low, but Jerry and Joe wanted to close the deal before it could fall apart. The end of their long battle was in sight—except for one issue on which neither side would budge. Every Superman product, Robinson insisted, must bear the words, "Superman created by Jerry Siegel and Joe Shuster." Warner said no.

Robinson understood how much it meant to Jerry and Joe that the world knew who'd invented the Man of Steel. He also understood that he was fighting for principles much greater than Jerry and Joe's feelings. "In Europe," Robinson has said, "one of the fundamental rights in art and entertainment is the creator's right to be credited for his work. In some countries it's in the law. This was an area in which American law and business practice badly needed change." To Warner's attorneys, however, credit threatened to open the door to legal challenges. If someone other than the corporation could claim to have created an intellectual property, authorship and ownership could be called into question. And if Siegel and Shuster were given credit as creators, who would be making the same demand next? What other properties would be disputed?

The negotiations went nowhere Monday and resumed Tuesday morning. Now Jay Emmett took personal command of Warner's forces. Emmett had become a major player in the conglomerate, one of the four men closest to Steve Ross in power. He was also Ross's best friend—some said "soul mate" or "consort"—and was once called "the glue that held everything together under Steve." Temperamentally, he was as different from his uncle Jack Liebowitz as he could be: ebullient, funny, immensely likable, and accustomed to winning most battles on charm alone. Robinson made a point of resisting his charm, but he did notice another Emmett trait: "He was the sanest businessman there."

By Wednesday the meetings were nearing the breaking point. Emmett had increased the offer to $20,000 a year with built-in cost-of-living increases and provisions for Siegel and Shuster's heirs, but he couldn't give creators' credit. Robinson said credit was a deal breaker. On Thursday the Warner group hinted they might pull the offer off the table if an agreement couldn't be reached soon.

On the way out of the building that evening, Jerry Siegel told Robinson that he couldn't take it anymore. He was physically ill and worrying about his heart. He could live without the credit; he just needed it over with. Robinson said he believed they could win this. "I'll give it one more day," said Jerry. "Whatever their lawyers agree to by tomorrow is what I'll live with. I'm sorry."

Emmett had given Robinson his home number in the course of the negotiations. That night, Robinson called him. "Look, Jay," he said, "we've got to bring this to a close somehow. You want the bad publicity to stop. Give them 'created by' credit and Warner's looks like the good guy." Emmett said he'd call his lawyers and get back to him. About an hour later he called back to say they could put the credit in the comic books, but not on toys or in the movie—it was too hard to put text on plastic toys, and the movie credits were already designed. Robinson scoffed. "I'll grant you the toys," he said, "but I've been involved with enough movies to know that the credits are the *last* thing you do." Emmett laughed. "I'll call you back," he said. A little after midnight, Robinson's phone rang again. "Okay," said Emmett. "Credit on all printed matter, TV, and movies. But no toys." It was done.

The next day, Friday, December 19, the parties shook hands. The signing of the contracts was scheduled for the following Wednesday. Robinson promised an exclusive on the story to CBS News. Joanne and Laura Siegel joined Jerry and Joe at 75 Rockefeller Center for the signing. Afterward, Robinson flagged a cab in the freezing wind and took Jerry and Joe to his apartment on the Upper West Side. He and his wife had arranged a party in their honor, starting early enough that everyone could see the signing announced on the evening news. The apartment was filled with people who'd helped with the campaign. Neal Adams was among them, and Jules Feiffer and Norman Mailer and Kurt Vonnegut. Robinson's neighbors, Anne Jackson and Eli Wallach, dropped in. Jerry and Joe were given seats of honor in front of the television set as the news came on. Segment after segment rolled by, and no mention was made of Jerry and Joe. Other news, it seemed, had pushed them aside.

And then, in the broadcast's final moments, Walter Cronkite began to speak of the boys from Cleveland who had created a hero and then lost him. He told of their fall into poverty and their struggle to wring some recognition from their publisher. As he announced the signing of the settlement, an image of Superman in flight appeared on the screen. "Today, at least," Cronkite said, "truth, justice, and the American way have triumphed."

Jerry and Joe couldn't hear anything above the cheers that filled the room, but for a few more seconds, they stared at the TV, as though they still had to make sure it was all true. They watched Walter Cronkite mouth his final words: "And that's the way it is, December 24, 1975."

THE SETTLEMENT WITH Siegel and Shuster was only part of a more sweeping change of image brought by Warner Communications to its comic book subsidiary. Just weeks after the settlement, National Periodicals' publisher—the gravel-voiced, cigar-chomping Carmine Infantino—was let go. His replacement was an executive unlike any ever seen in the industry: Jenette Kahn, a children's magazine publisher in her early thirties, a Reform rabbi's daughter from the Upper East Side, a complete outsider to the old-boy comics network. Under Kahn the company would even shed the name Jack Liebowitz had given it, becoming DC Comics, Incorporated. That same year a young editor, Paul Levitz, was promoted to editorial coordinator. Paul was a die-hard comics fan who'd taken a job at National when he was fourteen years old and never let go. His passion was the *Legion of Super Heroes,* a series first written by Jerry Siegel in the early 1960s, and even as he rose in the company, he seized every opportunity to write *Legion* stories himself. With Paul's ascendancy, there could no longer be any doubt that the fans were taking over the industry.

In February 1976 DC presented its smiling new face to the world by sponsoring a comic book convention in New York. Paul Levitz, who handled the programming, brought in not only the fan favorites of the moment but some of the most important figures from DC's past: Bob

Kane, Sheldon Mayer, Jack Schiff, and the creators of Superman. Jerry and Joe met fans they'd never realized they had and reacquainted themselves with men they hadn't spoken to for decades.

One old coworker chose not to appear at the convention because of his health but made a point of coming into the city to see Jerry. Mort Weisinger was still bilious and sour, more obese than ever and battling high blood pressure. When he saw Jerry, though, he acted as though they'd always been only the best of friends. He reminisced about the old days in science fiction fandom and the crazy things that had happened in the early comic book industry. He told Jerry he should pitch a story idea to their old pal Julie Schwartz, who was still editing *Superman*. Jerry couldn't hold the past against him. As much resentment as Jerry could pack away, he never could sustain it in the face of friendliness; he wanted too badly to be liked. When Mort died two years later, Jerry was one of the few people in the comics industry who spoke kindly of him.

Another old associate was less eager to mend fences. One day Jerry Robinson saw Jack Liebowitz eating alone in a restaurant. Wanting to be gracious, Robinson stopped to say hello. He had a copy of his latest book, *The Comics*, with him and showed it to Liebowitz. Liebowitz flipped through it perfunctorily until he came to a passage about Superman. He looked up at Robinson and growled, "What do you mean by defending Siegel and Shuster?" Robinson snapped, "What did *you* mean by *screwing* them?" He took his book back and left.

A new world opened for Jerry and Joe in 1976. With his $20,000 per year, Joe could at last escape the cold of New York and the cramped bedroom of his brother's apartment. He moved to Southern California to be closer to Jerry and Joanne. No sooner had he arrived than he and Jerry were invited to be guests of honor at the San Diego Comics Convention. After their years of invisibility they could not quite believe the reception they got: the "Inkpot" awards for lifetime contributions to comics, the standing ovation when they spoke, the young men who grasped their hands and thanked them for making comic books and superheroes possible. Fandom was still a fairly small community—the San Diego convention consisted of a few hundred dealers and collectors in a ballroom at the El Cortez hotel—but it was loyal and passionate. Jerry especially enjoyed the fans' attention. They looked different from the fans he'd grown up with, with their overstretched T-shirts, long hair, and splotches of beard and sideburn, but he felt immediately at home with their myopic zeal, their obsessive knowledge of the objects of their devotion, their social awkwardness and lunging enthusiasm. The geek culture that Jerry had helped pioneer in the 1920s had endured and thrived, and now it welcomed him back.

Jerry and Joe enjoyed the convention circuit over the next two years, signing autographs and looking through comics brought to them by fans, comics they'd cranked out in their youth and were now preserved in plastic and sold for hundreds of dollars. For both of them, though, the true moment of triumph came in December 1978, when they were brought by limousine to the Hollywood premiere of *Superman: The Movie*. They met the stars and talked to reporters. They heard the audience cheer when the name "Superman" appeared on screen. Then they saw their own screen credit: "Based on the comic book created by Jerry Siegel and Joe Shuster." The movie rolled, and Jerry and Joe saw Marlon Brando playing Jor-El, Superman's father, the character they had named and drawn so long ago.

The Superman on screen was a synthesis of many versions, but it was truer to Jerry and Joe's flamboyant, sanguine, self-satisfied hero of the early Forties than to any other. And he was as refreshing to audiences of the weary late Seventies as he'd been to readers at the frazzled end of the Depression, exactly forty years before. "You'll believe a man can fly," promised the ads, and the movie delivered on the promise, not only with modern special effects but with a cornball élan from an earlier age of moviemaking. Many cues in the script and the cinematography specifically pointed viewers back to the 1940s, casting Superman as a figure who'd come from a confident youth to reinvigorate us in our tired middle age. The Man of Tomorrow had come back to life as the Man of Yesterday, and as such he became the pop culture event of the end of the 1970s. Jerry and Joe had become relevant one more time.

They did complain about their lack of financial participation: "I think it's fine that Marlon Brando was paid $3 million for twelve days' work," said Jerry, "and that Mario Puzo received $250,000 for just being one of the screenwriters. But it would be nice if Joe and I weren't out in the cold." They also, however, thanked Warner Communications and praised the movie.

"I even got to meet producer Alexander Salkind," Jerry bubbled to a reporter. "And I told him I'd like to be hired as a consultant on sequels to the film. If he had hired me for this movie, I could have pointed out errors they made, and I could have come up with suggestions that would have made it more of a blockbuster."

He was still the hustler. Still the geek.

SUPERMAN: THE MOVIE was an early bellwether of a change that was to sweep through entertainment and popular culture in the 1980s: What had once been kid stuff and nerd stuff was becoming mainstream. *Star Wars* got there first and helped nurture the market for *Superman*. Over the next few years, *Star Trek, Alien, Raiders of the Lost Ark, Conan the Barbarian, E.T. the Extraterrestrial,* and their many sequels and imitators established the "comic book movie"—the high-speed, expensively upholstered, wish-fulfilling romp about superheroes and monsters—as the highest-grossing genre in the movie business. Decades later, trend after trend, it remains just that.

Other media discovered the same change in what their audiences wanted. Once science fiction and fantasy novels had been sustained by small audiences of oddball adolescents and hard-core adult fans who identified themselves by their genre tastes and shunned what was trendiest and most popular in the larger culture. But suddenly "cyberpunk" was a hip literary movement, and the comic book horror of Stephen King was outselling everyone else. The animation industry came back to life when movie studios and TV programmers realized that twenty-somethings comprised as much of their audience as kids and began funding smartly written, self-referential, wise-ass, graphically arresting cartoons. Beginning in 1987, *Star Trek*—that holy grail of the pudgy, undersexed male dweeb—sneaked up on the TV industry and became one of the favorite shows of twenty-five-to-fifty-year-old women with its *Next Generation*.

There were new media too, and old media that had never been components of a grown-up entertainment industry until the mainstreaming of fantasy in the 1980s. The video game exploded into the home market with *Space Invaders* from Atari—a Warner Communications subsidiary. Plastic toys based on movie characters had been kicking around America's toy boxes for decades, and small numbers of grown-up fans had hung on to those that represented their favorite characters. But with *Star Wars* the "action figure" became a "collectible," and suddenly millions of teenage and adult accumulators were scouring toy stores to complete their sets.

In the days of the computer, the global village, the ascendant consumer industry, suburbia, the celebration of diversity, and cultural, moral, and philosophical relativism, the preoccupations of geekdom had become the culture's preoccupations. The geeks knew the joy and power of organizing useless information before anyone. They knew before anyone else the joy of bonding over manufactured totems, the inadequacy of old gender types, the desire to glorify and caricature the body, the need to throttle aggression and diffuse it into flights of cartoony fancy. The 1980s marked the triumph of the geeks.

In the same years, the comic book industry exploded. The "comics specialty shops" that had provided loci for the growing fandom of the 1970s hit a critical mass at the end of the decade that enabled them to demand a change in the way the publishers did business. In place of the decades-old consignment system, in which retailers carried no financial risk and nearly half of every print run was expected to be returned for credit, the specialty shops began buying comics outright from the publishers on a nonreturnable basis. That shifted the risk from the publishers and distributors to the retailers, but in exchange the retailers got their comics a month before the newsstands and in better physical condition (not an insignificant matter when collectors were becoming a significant part of the market). The result was that comics could survive on much smaller print runs, allowing for more esoteric and fan-focused material; per-issue production costs could be raised, enabling comics to become slicker, more collectible products; and publishers could afford to take more risks, could even step outside the Comics Code, to see just what the older fans were willing to support.

By the early 1980s, a comic book revolution was under way. Marvel and DC expanded their lines, and new publishers sprang out of the retail shops and the new distribution companies created to handle the "direct sales market." New York was still the center of the business, but publishers popped up in Chicago, Los Angeles, San Diego, and sleepy Forestville, California. With the new publishers offering unprecedented creator-ownership and profit-sharing plans, Marvel and DC were forced to offer royalties and incentives to keep their talent. Established writers and artists, long frustrated by the old market restrictions, began to tell stories of a range and complexity they'd never dared before. A new generation of fans jumped into print with their private fantasies of what the medium could be.

Teenagers raised on superheroes found themselves in the same venues and the same subculture as the old hippies who'd created the "underground comix." They created comics like the Hernandez Brothers' *Love and Rockets,* in which Mexican American car mechanics and punk guitarists met superpowered Amazons and Jack Kirby monsters. They welcomed comics like *Maus: A Survivor's Tale,* in which Art Spiegelman used the form of the "funny animal" comic to tell a searing story of the Holocaust. Spiegelman had followed a path all his own, from admiring Will Eisner's *Spirit,* to drawing cartoons for Harvey Kurtzman's *Help* and the undergrounds, and finally, in the 1980s, to publishing his own graphic art magazine, *Raw.* In *Maus* he wove together the threads of junk culture, satire, fine art, and Jewish history to create the first comic book that fans and literary critics alike agreed was a significant work of art.

The new comics found a market far outside hard-core geekdom. There were comics that spoke to punk rockers, art students, middle-school girls, young Republicans, and pallid middle-aged men who spent their nights organizing and reorganizing their vast collections of old superhero comics. Comics were hip and comics were geeky, in a confluence of the ultracool and the ultradorky that could not have happened before the Eighties.

This new comics fandom had a sense of history too. Jack Kirby, having left Marvel Comics in frustration at not being able to own or control his own characters, created a new line of comics for National in the 1970s, only to have most of them canceled; after that he left comics for TV animation. But the independent publishers brought him back into comics in the 1980s. When Kirby found himself in an ugly dispute with Marvel Comics over its failure to return his original artwork and to grant him proper credit for his cocreations—the Hulk, the X-Men, the Fantastic Four, and most of the rest of its superhero line—the fans rallied to his support. Fund-raisers were held, petitions signed, the mainstream press alerted, Marvel executives shamed, until Kirby got a chunk of his artwork back and gained recognition as a seminal figure in American popular art. He became such a symbol of the brilliance, anger, and suffering of the comic book artist that he, more than any other figure, inspired Michael Chabon to write *The Amazing Adventures of Kavalier and Clay.*

When the comic book industry introduced its first major awards for excellence in 1985, they were called the Kirby Awards. When the group presenting the awards split in two a few years later, one faction established the Harveys, named after Harvey Kurtzman of *Mad* and the EC war comics; the other established the Eisners. For Will Eisner had come back to comics, too.

In 1975, after decades producing instructional comics for the U.S. Army, he had made a deal with the publisher Jim Warren to reprint his old *Spirit* comics. The new fandom greeted them ecstatically. Two years later, when Eisner was about to turn sixty, he decided it was time to act on an old dream and create a "graphic novel," one of the first books of its kind, a work of naturalistic fiction in comics form. *A Contract with God* consisted of four novellas about the Jewish residents of a Lower

East Side tenement in the early century and marked Eisner's first narrative entry into the *Yiddishkeit* from which he, and so many of his peers, had come. It didn't do well in the general book trade, but the smarter comics fans embraced it as an embodiment of what their beloved field could and should be.

Fandom provided the core audience that supported Eisner's graphic novels over the years to come. A veteran underground comix publisher, Denis Kitchen, brought out the *Will Eisner Quarterly*, the first regular magazine devoted to anthologizing a single comics artist. By the end of the 1980s, Eisner had been generally recognized by fans as the elder statesman of the comic book. He would appear at the Eisner Awards at the San Diego Comics Convention every year, tall and straight in suit and tie, decades removed from the assembly-line shop boss but still in charge of the room. By that time the convention had far outgrown its hotel ballroom. It took over the San Diego Convention Center, drawing 30,000 attendees a year. The auditorium where the Eisner Awards were presented was as big as the rooms that contained whole conventions a decade before.

Although the new comics supported stories of every genre and every style, the commercial heart of the business and the driving fascination of the great majority of comics geeks remained the superhero. The fashion of the 1980s was the revamping of old heroes in a hard-edged, self-examining style that appealed to longtime fans outgrowing the stories of their childhoods. A young cartoonist named Frank Miller turned *Daredevil* into a violent suspense series owing a great deal to old films noir. Then, in 1986, in an expensive, glossy, four-volume graphic novel called *Batman: The Dark Knight Returns,* he imagined the Caped Crusader as a bitter, over-the-hill vigilante fighting a quixotic battle for old-time order against a fascistic Superman in a Gotham City gone to hell. Its boldness, its nastiness, and its blocky, jagged, expressionistic cartooning made it a sensation among comics fans, a best seller in the general book trade, and a litmus test of pop-cult hip among twenty-five-year-olds nationwide. Its astonishing commercial success and media coverage helped push Warner Brothers to make a *Batman* movie a reality.

DC immediately set loose another young cartoonist, John Byrne, to revamp Superman. Byrne started the story over the from the beginning, throwing out Superboy, Supergirl, Krypto the Super-Dog, the bottle city of Kandor, and nearly every other accretion of the previous four decades. He reduced the hero's powers to the level Jerry and Joe had left them at in the 1940s and restored the exhilarating, big-graphic fun of the early days. But he also undid the central emotional tangle of Jerry and Joe's idea: Byrne's Clark Kent was a confident hunk and a worthy competitor to his own alter ego for Lois Lane's affections. This was a new kind of secret identity for a new kind of pop culture kid. Byrne himself was a confident, even arrogant star of a booming industry, loved and hated and envied by tens of thousands of fans. With the new Clark Kent, he showed the world how geeks were beginning to see themselves now.

The superhero was enshrined as an essential element of the mass-market imagination in 1989, when the *Batman* movie broke every box-office record. Unlike the *Superman* of eleven years before, Tim Burton's *Batman* didn't look back to lost dreams of childhood or past decades but placed its vengeful crime fighter squarely in the consciousness of the young, the hip, the cynical, and the freaky. Bill Finger and Bob Kane had created a character so elemental and so true that he could be easily turned into an embodiment of the doubt, anger, and yearning for explosive freedom inside a generation fifty years distant from their own.

A new superhero boom followed the *Batman* movie. Just like the boom at the eve of World War II, it made small fortunes for the men who could move quickly to exploit it. The money was big enough to lure Wall Street opportunists Ron Perelman and Carl Icahn into a war for control of Marvel Comics that nearly ruined the company. In this boom, though, writers and artists were among those making the fortunes. A group of hot Marvel artists formed their own company, Image Comics, and sold millions of copies of their first issues. Old-timers benefited, too. Bob Kane got a piece of all the Bat-marketing and sold his ghost-painted portraits of Michael Keaton and Jack Nicholson for thousands. Stan Lee quit Marvel and formed Stan Lee Media, producing superheroes for the World Wide Web. Unfortunately his business partners ripped off their investors and ended up in prison, leaving Stan to pick up the pieces—the comics business hadn't changed completely after all.

The year of *Batman* also marked the apotheosis of the company that owned it. Steve Ross orchestrated a merger of Warner Communications with the Time-Life Company that created one of the biggest publishing and entertainment firms in the world. The wheel of fortune would turn against Ross from that moment on. The government would investigate him for his old mob ties and for skimming and money-laundering operations. His friend Jay Emmett would take the fall for him and keep him out of prison; but by then the cancer was eating at Ross's body. He died in 1993, but the conglomerate he'd forged kept on growing. And it kept on profiting from superheroes.

EARLY IN THE rise of the new comic book market, Jerry Siegel tried one last time to bring his writing career back to life. He sent proposals for series to most of the small publishers jumping into the field. Eclipse Comics published a few of his stories, but the rest regretfully turned him down. He entered negotiations with DC to write a few special issues of *Superman*, but the contracts never satisfied him; he was very careful about what he signed now.

In 1986 Tom Hall of Elite Comics learned the Siegel story in an unpleasantly vivid way. "I couldn't believe I'd actually gotten a submission from the creator of Superman," he said. "I tore open the envelope and pulled out the scripts. There was one for something called 'Future Cop' and one that seemed to be a reworking of *Slam Bradley*, and there were two versions of each—one PG-rated and one R- or X-rated. But I never got to read all of them. As I began to read them, I was beginning to itch. Then I noticed fleas jumping right off the scripts. I jumped up and took the scripts outside so my furniture wouldn't become infested. I had to get rid of the scripts and the envelope, since it was full of fleas, too. And all I could think was that here was someone we owe our industry to, and he's living in a small apartment in LA with fleas."

But as Superman kept making money, Jerry finally found himself able to end the hustle for work that had devoured him for over thirty-five years. Three sequels followed *Superman: The Movie,* then *Supergirl,* then a Saturday morning cartoon series, and then, in 1988, a *Superboy* TV show that ran for four years. Interest in *Superman* comics was boosted by the revamp in 1986, and soon the Man of Steel's four titles were accounting for sales of nearly a million a month. Superman's image was licensed for a vast array of products, not only kid stuff but note cards and clothing for pop culture–steeped adult hipsters, too. The Six Flags theme park chain signed a deal with Warner that made Superman, Batman, and the Looney Toons menagerie its mascots. Time-Warner insiders, including Paul Levitz of DC Comics, pushed the company to share some of its largesse with Siegel and Shuster. Although the numbers would remain undisclosed, it was reported that Jerry and Joe's annual pensions had each surpassed a $100,000 by the ends of their lives and that their heirs would continue to receive the same.

It was a tiny sum compared to what Time-Warner made off *Superman,* but it supported them in some comfort. Jerry, Joanne, and Joe came to trust Levitz to take care of them as best he could within the limits Time-Warner imposed. "We now have a very good relationship with DC Comics," Jerry said in the 1980s. "They've been really good to us," said Joe.

Joe Shuster lived in quiet comfort in a one-bedroom apartment and spent his money on audio equipment. He upgraded his sound system sometimes twice in a year and donated his old equipment to the blind. Although he continued to socialize with Jerry and Joanne, he withdrew from the worlds of fans and publicity. Then, in April 1992, he agreed to give one last interview, to the paper he had sold on the streets at the age of nine, the *Toronto Star.* The accompanying photo showed an old man, barely able to hold the comic books the photographer had handed him, but the words revealed that his memories of life from his boyhood in Toronto all the way to the present were sharp and mostly pleasant. He seemed at peace with the course of his life. "There aren't many people who can say they're leaving behind something as important as Superman," he said. "But Jerry and I can, and that's a good feeling." Three months later, on July 30, 1992, Joe Shuster's heart failed, and he died at the age of seventy-eight.

Jerry and Joanne Siegel were able to escape the fleas and the traffic noises of their little apartment in LA and buy a condominium in Marina Del Rey that looked out at the Pacific Ocean. Jerry stopped trying to sell comics scripts and, in his seventies, finally settled into a life of retirement. His daughter, Laura, had built a career writing and producing in television; she'd married and given him two grandchildren. When Jerry Fine, the cousin from Cleveland who'd introduced Jerry Siegel and Joe Shuster in the first place, went to visit him, he found Siegel upbeat, eager to show him around his town. He said that even more than the money he was finally receiving, his greatest satisfaction was simply knowing that every comic book, every movie, and every TV episode featuring Superman bore his name.

Jerry lived to see his hero attain one more peak of national attention. In 1991 DC had run a story line in which Superman revealed his secret identity to Lois Lane and asked her to marry him. Fifty years before, Siegel had pitched the same idea to his editors without success. Now the editor, Mike Carlin, thought it would be a good way to keep public attention focused on an aging franchise. The announcement drew media coverage and pushed sales higher, but the follow-through was never to see print. For no sooner had the wedding been announced than DC's publisher, Jenette Kahn, closed a deal with ABC and Lorimar Productions to launch a prime-time TV series called *Lois and Clark: The Adventures of Superman*. That in itself was a sign of the depth of Superman's penetration into the popular psyche: The show was aimed at adult women and used the hero and his secret identity as an object of romantic fantasies and an embodiment of the complexities of sex and gender in the modern world. Superman had bounded far beyond nostalgia and boyish power fantasies to become a national dream self, a universal reference point.

The first impact of *Lois and Clark,* however, was to put the Superman-Lois marriage indefinitely on hold, since the show was to center on their unrelieved erotic tension. Mike Carlin suddenly needed a different "publishing event." He fell back on one of the standbys of the modern comic book, the apparent death of the hero. The fans would know that his "death" would be followed by his miraculous return, but their boundless capacity to suspend their disbelief might make it a successful bit of melodrama nonetheless. Carlin checked with Jerry Siegel to see if he had any objections to Superman's temporary death. Jerry was flattered to be asked and said it sounded fine to him, "a good way to shake things up." All the writers and artists involved felt better about the story line, said Carlin, "knowing that 'Daddy' approved." So they went ahead with the story, planned to culminate in the November 1992 issues, and began dropping hints to the fan press of what was coming.

Then an odd thing happened. Word found its way to the mainstream press, and people took it seriously. Stories began to appear that Superman, after fifty-four years as the world's best-known hero, was about to die. *Newsday* put the headline on its front page: "The Death of Superman." Editorial writers moaned and fretted about what this meant about America, its heroes, and its soul.

No one in comics could figure it out. True, most of the world didn't realize that Superman was a very profitable franchise and in no danger of cancellation, but still—how could so many smart journalists think that a major corporation would bury one of its best-known trademarks? Maybe it was just because the *Superman* movie franchise had ended so dismally. Or maybe the collapse of the Iron Curtain had something to do with it, or anxieties about video games and the Internet, or dismay over the new, mean entertainment of gangster rap and Quentin Tarantino, or even the first ripple of fin de siècle resignation. For whatever reason, Americans were willing to believe that the Man of Tomorrow was about to die, and they would not let him go easily.

Advance orders for the death issue topped 5 million before it hit the stores. When it finally came out, people lined up to buy it. Stores that had laid in hundreds of copies imposed one-to-a-customer limits to avoid mob scenes. Millions of people wanted to own the final issue of *Superman,* either because it meant something to them or because they believed it would be worth even more to future generations. "The Death of Superman" became one of the most famous and most profitable comic books of all time.

Superman returned after a few months, of course, just as everyone in comics knew he would. His resurrection drew a bit more media and another sales blip. Jerry Siegel enjoyed it all. He knew the artificiality of the death didn't take away what the public reaction had proven: that in Superman he and Joe had created far more than a bit of four-color ephemera or a fantasy self for kids and geeks. In Glenville, in the Depression, in the desperation to succeed, in Sarah Siegel's dark house and the crowded apartment of the Shusters, they had created a national symbol.

Jerry Siegel died quietly at his home on a Monday morning, January 28, 1996. He was eighty-one years old. DC Comics ran a fine obituary for him in which they thanked him for helping create the comic book industry. Among the many comic book veterans who spoke at his memorial, Jerry Robinson said the words that would be best remembered: "For too many years Jerry was lost in the wilderness. But he came home at last."

The next year, Joanne Siegel took a step that Jerry had been reluctant to, fearing that it would shatter his good relations with Time-Warner. Under new copyright laws she was entitled to terminate Jerry's original grant of copyright transfer to DC and claim half ownership of the title and characters. And so she did. This time, there would be no ill will with the publishers. Paul Levitz and his fellow employees of Time-Warner understood that Joanne was just doing what the law allowed and let the process take its course. In 1999 she won the first round: A court declared that the Siegel family owned half the copyright to Superman's first appearance in *Action Comics.* Five years later the case continues to be alternately disputed and negotiated, a never ending battle for truth, justice, and a resolution to the unresolvable question of who owns the make-believe.

THEY WERE FADING now, the generation that created the comics. Sheldon Mayer, the editor who first advocated for Superman, died in 1991. His old friend Bill Gaines followed the next year. Jack Kirby died in 1994, Bob Kane in 1998. Vin Sullivan, Superman and Batman's first editor, followed in 1999. Will Eisner, Jerry Robinson, and Stan Lee, but few others, would continue into the new century, still vital and still working. "If you have any questions for the guys who started it all," said Stan to one interviewer, "you'd better ask them quick!"

The generation before them, the generation of publishers, was already long gone. The last survivor of them all was Jack Liebowitz.

When Time-Warner was created, Liebowitz took a place on the new board and continued to increase his holdings. In the days of *Spicy Adventure*, *Time* and *Life* had existed in a rarefied realm high above his head. Now he found himself a decision maker in the company that produced not only those but *People* and *Entertainment Weekly* as well—and the magazine industry was one of its lesser holdings. He continued to keep an office in the Time-Warner Building and attend board meetings into his nineties. He saw his company launch its own television network in 1995 and, the following year, become a cable TV giant by acquiring Turner Broadcasting.

As Jack finally stepped down from the summits of American business, he did something no one would have predicted: He granted an interview to a comic book fan. Mike Catron was a fanzine publisher, an amateur historian, and a great proponent of Siegel and Shuster who expected no response when he asked the very old and very rich Jack Liebowitz for an interview. But Liebowitz let Catron come into his office and videotape his answers to questions about his life, career, and purchase of Superman. The answers were guarded and politic, a dignified businessman's summary of a dignified career. But the mere fact that he wanted his side heard by such a small, odd world as comic book fandom indicated a great deal. Somehow, despite all he'd achieved, Superman and the messy facts surrounding him were more central to Jack's view of his own life than anyone would have guessed.

In January 2000 Time-Warner merged with AOL in the biggest business deal in history. It created the fourth largest corporation in the United States, worth a third of a trillion dollars, employing over 80,000 people. It transformed the mass-media industry and consolidated the Internet into the world of global conglomerates. A series of strokes had by then impaired Liebowitz's speech and thought, but Irwin Donenfeld, who still checked in occasionally on his Uncle Jack, said he seemed to understand what was happening. He understood, at least, that his company had achieved a place of wealth and power he could never have imagined as he hawked newspapers and dreamed of the socialist utopia to come on the cobblestones of Allen Street in a world long gone.

Jack died on December 14, 2000. He was one hundred years old. He had spanned the century that he had come to understand so well. He left a fortune that has been estimated in the hundreds of millions of dollars. He left Superman and Batman and their peers as famous and endlessly profitable pieces of a media empire. No one balanced the books better than Jack Liebowitz.

THE MEN ARE gone, but the art form and the characters they created are as alive as ever. The comic book industry stumbled into another serious bust after the boom of the early 1990s. Once again retailers and publishers went out of business, and cartoonists found other ways to make a living. But once again the core of the industry survived, once again sales began to nose up, and new writers and artists rushed in. No one speaks of the imminent end of comics anymore.

New comic books continue to be created and find enthusiastic readers, while *Superman, Batman, Wonder Woman,* and *Captain America* continue to be revamped to tap into each new generation's kid fantasies and geek dreams. Once the field of first entrance and last resort for men who wished they could do something better, superhero comics now possess a mystique all their own. Kevin Smith, after making his name as a filmmaker with *Clerks* and *Chasing Amy,* took time away from the movies to write *Daredevil* for Marvel. When Joss Whedon retired from producing *Buffy the Vampire Slayer* he started writing *X-Men.*

No characters have survived the shifting mass-culture sands like the superheroes. Mickey Mouse and Donald Duck live on as company mascots. Bugs Bunny and Daffy Duck are still good for the occasional revival, but they've never been successfully reinvented for the present. Blondie Bumstead hangs on in the newspapers by habit and nostalgia. The pulp heroes, the Shadow and Doc Savage, are just gone. But after nearly seventy years, the comic book superheroes are still flying through the movie theaters, TV screens, video game consoles, and toy stores of the world. They may be more popular and more culturally relevant now than when they were new.

Comic books have become reference points in the most popular and the most esoteric fiction and art. Everyone understands a Superman allusion or a Batman joke. The pop-cult literati bring a constellation of associations to the name "Jack Kirby." Those who prefer the grungy underbelly of American culture still embrace Bill Gaines and Harvey Kurtzman, and the ones who dig deeper still know Charlie Biro. In the book *Jack Cole and Plastic Man: Forms Stretched to Their Limits*, Art Spiegelman and graphic designer Chip Kidd demanded that superhero cartooning be viewed as art. Anyone who cares about the exploitation of popular artists feels a quickening heartbeat at the mention of Jerry Siegel and Joe Shuster.

The critics, teachers, philanthropists, and religious leaders who once denounced comic books as a national disgrace have embraced them. In 2003 *Reform Judaism* magazine ran Arie Kaplan's "How the Jews Created the Comic Book Industry," reclaiming a part of an ethnic heritage that any respectable Jew of the 1940s or 1950s would have vehemently denied. The next year, Jerry Robinson mounted an exhibit on superhero comics for the William Breman Jewish Heritage Museum in Atlanta. In 2001 Michael Chabon's novel about the "golden age" of the superheroes, animated with references to Will Eisner and Jack Kirby and Jerry Siegel and Joe Shuster, won the Pulitzer Prize. A few years later he turned Kavalier and Clay's creation, *The Escapist*, into a comic book. So the superheroes loop from junk to literature and back to junk again. Nothing has tested or proven or forced the fluidity of contemporary arts like comic book superheroes.

No gangster or geek, no Harry Donenfeld or Jerry Siegel, could have imagined what would come of his work and his daydreams. Harry and his peers were just trying to make some money, have some fun, and print some pictures of naked girls. But they assembled a machine out of cheap paper and crooked distribution and young men's hunger that could deliver dreams no one had dreamed before. Jerry and his fellow geeks just wanted to see their fantasies out in the world and make a living without having to work a real job. But they distilled the passions of children and outsiders to such pure, glowing symbols that they can be passed from generation to generation without dimming. They are constantly remade and reshaped, but they always find their way to the same hidden yearnings.

These men were pulled in childhood from an ancient world and plunged into the life stream of America in its most joyous, brutal, corrupt, and boundless years. They responded with the wildest desires and the most improbable fantasies, and throughout their lives they worked to sell those fantasies to an America that existed half in hard-learned fact and half in their own imaginations. In the collision of desire and possibility, they made a new reality. In the strange alchemy of their long pasts and the indefinable present of a mongrel nation, they glimpsed and created a future.

NOTES ON SOURCES

PROLOGUE

This telling of the events leading up to Jerry Siegel's decision to write his press release is a pastiche of details culled from people who knew him then and in later years, particularly Jerry Robinson, Mike Catron, Tom Andrae, and Mark Evanier. Because of the ongoing litigation and negotiations concerning the Superman copyright, many of Siegel's friends and family members felt unable to speak on the record for this book, but some parties provided information anonymously that helped flesh out the events. Quotes from the press release are thanks to Mike Catron.

CHAPTER 1

Most of the material about Harry Donenfeld's family and early childhood comes from interviews with Irwin Donenfeld and other members of the Donenfeld family, conducted in 2003 and 2004. Some of Harry's more boastful stories he told to his family, but many he told instead to his cronies in the publishing and distribution fields; among those to whom he told his Roosevelt stories, for example, was Jack Adams, formerly of Independent News, who in turn passed them on to Michael Feldman. Some stories became legends of the comic book industry and found their way into this book by way of Jack Schiff, Murray Boltinoff, and others. "He usually said he was born. . . ." In the 1930 U.S. Census, Harry is listed as having been born in 1892. He always celebrated his milestone birthdays, however, as if he'd been born in 1893.

The material on the Romanian Jews comes mainly from Irving Howe, *World of Our Fathers* (New York: Harcourt Brace Jovanovich, 1976), and Carol Iancu, *Jews in Romania, 1866–1919: From Exclusion to Emancipation* (New York: Columbia University Press, 1996). The description of the Lower East Side was constructed from many sources, among them Howe, *World of Our Fathers*; Moses Rischen, *The*

Promised City: New York's Jews, 1870–1914 (Cambridge, MA: Harvard University Press, 1962); and those two powerful (if often patronizing) works of social advocacy, Jacob Riis, *The Battle with the Slum* (New York: MacMillan, 1912), and Lincoln Steffens, *The Autobiography of Lincoln Steffens* (New York: Harcourt Brace & Co., 1931). Indispensible to any study of the East Side are those two sharply observed novels, Michael Gold, *Jews without Money* (New York: Liveright, 1938), and Abraham Cahan, *The Rise of David Levinsky* (New York: Harper & Bros., 1917), the latter providing especially vivid glimpses of the workings of the garment industry. "Alter, Alter . . ." is from Arthur Goldhaft, *The Golden Egg*, quoted in Howe, *World of Our Fathers.* "abyss of generations" is from Steffens, *Autobiography.*

Lower East Side youth gangs are examined in Albert Fried, *The Rise and Fall of the Jewish Gangster in America* (New York: Columbia University Press, 1993), and Jenna Weismann Joselit, *Our Gang: Jewish Crime and the New York Jewish Community, 1900–1940* (Bloomington: Indiana University Press, 1983). "Jews. . . why do you just stand . . ." From Uri Dan's interview with Meyer Lansky, quoted in Rich Cohen, *Tough Jews: Fathers, Sons, and Gangster Dreams* (New York: Simon & Schuster, 1993). The popular views of Jewish "delinquency" are from Howe, *World of Our Fathers.* "Some of my friends became . . ." Kurtzberg quoted in an interview with Jack Kirby (Jake Kurtzberg) in *Comics Journal,* no. 134 (Feb. 1990). Harry's Eddie Cantor stories were fleshed out with help from Herbert G. Goldman, *Banjo Eyes: Eddie Cantor and the Birth of Modern Stardom* (New York: Oxford University Press, 1997).

Throughout this book, details of Jack Liebowitz's family background and personal life have been sketched with the help of members of the Stillman, Levy, and Donenfeld families. Many dates and other specifics were provided by Mike Catron's obituary of Liebowitz, published in *Comics Journal,* no. 230 (Dec. 2000).

On socialism and the pogroms, see Hans-Dietrich Lowe, *The Tsars and the Jews: Reform, Reaction and Anti-Semitism in Imperial Russia, 1772–1917* (Reading, UK: Harwood, 1992). On the culture and politics of labor on the Lower East Side, see Nan Enstad, *Ladies of Labor, Girls of Adventure: Working Women, Popular Culture, and Labor Politics at the Turn of the Century* (New York: Columbia University Press, 1999), and Annelise Orleck, *Common Sense and a Little Fire: Women and Working-Class Politics in the United States, 1900–1965* (Chapel Hill: University of North Carolina Press, 1995). The details of gang involvement in the labor movement and politics are taken from Fried, *Rise and Fall.* The newspaper circulation wars and Moe Annenberg's involvement in them are explored in Christopher Ogden, *Legacy: A Biography of Moses and Walter Annenberg* (New York: Little, Brown, 1999). "stumbled over gauntlets . . ." Gold, *Jews without Money.* For the sexual culture of young people on the East Side, see also Enstad, *Ladies of Labor,* and Charlotte Baum, Paula Hyman, and Sonya Michel, *The Jewish Woman in America* (New York: Dial Press, 1976).

In the 1930 census Harry's "age when first married" is reported as twenty-three, Gussie's as twenty, although their ages are listed as being five years apart. Either Harry had a first marriage of which nothing is known, or whoever in the household gave information to the census taker was too hasty. Such discrepancies suggest the difficulty of piecing together these long-ago life stories.

CHAPTER 2

Throughout the book the information on the Siegel family and Jerry Siegel's private life comes mainly from interviews with Irv Fine and Jerry Fine in October 2003 and subsequent correspondence, and from conversations with a few other members of the family who have requested to remain anonymous. Exceptions will be noted.

For Cleveland history, see William Ganson Rose, *Cleveland: Making of a City* (Kent, OH: Kent State University Press, 1990), and Carol Poh Miller and Robert A. Wheeler, *Cleveland: A Concise History, 1796–1996* (Bloomington: Indiana University Press, 1997). The portrait of the Jewish community of Cleveland has been built mainly from Lloyd P. Gartner, *History of the Jews of Cleveland* (Cleveland: Western Reserve Historical Society, 1987); Sidney Z. Vincent and Judah Rubenstein, *Merging Traditions: Jewish Life in Cleveland* (Cleveland: Western Reserve Historical Society, 1978); and Cleveland Jewish Centennial Committee, *Jewish Community of Cleveland Historical Digest, 1837–1937* (Cleveland: CJCC, 1937). Some of the details about the 105th Street neighborhood are drawn from back issues of the Glenville High School *Torch*. "Almost every block . . ." Vincent and Rubenstein, *Merging Traditions*. "The long streets were always . . ." Violet Spevack, quoted in Vincent and Rubenstein, *Merging Traditions*. "Judaism is less a dogma . . ." Herbert Adolphus Miller, *School and the Immigrant*, quoted in CJCC, *Jewish Community of Cleveland Historical Digest, 1837–1937*. The exploits of Benny Friedman's Tar-Blooders were chronicled in many issues of the Glenville High *Torch* in 1921 and 1922.

Jerry Siegel's childhood experiences with movies and other entertainment are discussed in many articles in comic book–fan publications. The most extensive is the superb interview with Jerry Siegel, Joe Shuster, and Joanne Siegel, "Of Supermen and Kids with Dreams," conducted by Tom Andrae, Geoffrey Blum, and Gary Coddington, in *Nemo: The Classic Comics Library*, no. 2 (Aug. 1983). Some material here, especially Siegel's memories of his first discovery of Douglas Fairbanks and his first sight of *Amazing Stories*, came from the author's own conversations with Siegel in the 1980s.

"the age of hero worship . . ." Richard A. Martinson quoted in Will Murray, *Wordslingers: How the Pulp Western Was Won and Lost* (not yet published). Unless otherwise noted, all quotes from and stories about Will Eisner come from the author's interview with Eisner, October 2003. Hugo Gernsback's career and early science fiction are thoroughly explored in Mike Ashley and Robert A. W. Lowndes, *The Gernsback Days* (Holicong, PA: Wildside Press, 2004). The early history of fandom is covered in sometimes excruciating detail in Harry Warner Jr., *All Our Yesterdays* (Chicago: Advent, 1969), and Sam Moskowitz's dramatic but biased *The Immortal Storm* (Westport, CT: Hyperion Press, reissued 1974). "I weighed my life up to that time . . ." Francis T. Laney quoted in Warner, *All Our Yesterdays.* "He sent me a manuscript . . ." Author's interview with Jack Williamson, October 2003.

The date of Mitchell Siegel's death is disputed by various oral sources, and no documents have yet been found to settle the matter; some place it in Jerry's early teens or even before. The present chronology seems to be the most reasonable, based on Fine family stories. If the dates of Jerry's schooling are confusing, note that junior high extended through the ninth grade in the Cleveland system.

CHAPTER 3

The impact of Prohibition on the New York Jewish community and the subsequent rise of the liquor gangs is explored in Fried, *Rise and Fall,* and Joselit, *Our Gang.* "now we have delicatessen . . ." Fiorello H. LaGuardia, testimony before the Committee on the Judiciary, U.S. Senate, 69th Congress, archived on the Schaffer Library of Drug Policy, http://www.druglibrary.org/schaffer/alcohol/laguardi.htm.

Stories of Harry Donenfeld's family life throughout this book come, unless otherwise noted, from the author's interviews with Irwin Donenfeld and other surviving family members. The stories of Donny Press and Eastern News are known as well as they are thanks to the long, diligent research of Michael Feldman, passed along to the author in interviews and correspondence from December 2003 to June 2004. Additional pieces were filled in by Will Murray in his "DC's Tangled Roots," *Comic Book Marketplace,* no. 53 (Nov. 1997), and in interviews with this author, 2003.

"Let me put it to you . . ." This anecdote comes from Bob Beerbohm. The portrait of Costello and his associates draws mainly upon Cohen, *Tough Jews,* and George Wolf and Joseph DiMona, *Frank Costello: Prime Minister of the Underworld* (New York: William Morrow, 1974). "I used to think of the *Mirror.* . . " Quoted in Martin A. Gosch and Richard Hammer, *The Last Testament of Lucky Luciano* (Boston: Little, Brown, 1975). "Gangsters who never graduated . . ." Quoted in Cohen, *Tough Jews.* The version of the "FDR Brain Trust" story suggested here was pieced together by Michael Feldman.

The 1926 ILGWU strike and the gangs' involvement is discussed in Fried, *Rise and Fall,* and David Dubinsky and A. H. Raskin, *A Life with Labor* (New York: Simon & Schuster, 1977). "A Jew could make a lot of money . . ." Quoted in Neal Gabler, *An Empire of Their Own: How the Jews Invented Hollywood* (New York: Random House, 1988). On the Jewish presence in American popular culture of the 1920s, see Paul Buhle, *From the Lower East Side to Hollywood: Jews in American*

Popular Culture (New York: W. W. Norton, 2004). On the magazine boom of the 1920s, see John Tebbel and Mary Ellen Zuckerman, *The Magazine in America, 1741–1990* (New York: Oxford University Press, 1991). The information on Bernarr MacFadden is drawn mainly from Robert Ernst, *Weakness Is a Crime: The Life of Bernarr MacFadden* (Syracuse: Syracuse University Press, 1999). On Hugo Gernsback, see Ashley and Lowndes, *Gernsback Days*.

Margaret Sanger's involvement with Harold Hersey is revealed in Hersey's *Margaret Sanger: The Biography of the Birth Control Pioneer* (unpublished, 1938; in the collection of the New York Public Library). Her position in the larger context of American politics and popular culture is interestingly considered in Geoffrey Perrett, *America in the Twenties* (New York: Simon & Schuster, 1982). Hersey describes his own career in *Pulpwood Editor* (Silver Spring, MD: Adventure House, reprint 2002). Michael Feldman collected the material on Hersey's unofficial "consulting."

The story of Frank Armer and the "smooshes" depends heavily on Douglas Ellis, *Uncovered: The Hidden Art of the Girlie Pulp* (Silver Spring, MD: Adventure House, 2003). Other material, especially that concerning Harry's involvement, comes from Michael Feldman and Will Murray. "The Art of Alfred Barnard" is from *Artists & Models,* no. 6 (Sept. 1925). "Mimi L'Enclos . . ." Quoted in Ellis, *Uncovered.* "All right, you have won . . ." John Dos Passos, *The Big Money* (New York: Harcourt Brace, 1936).

CHAPTER 4

The descriptions of Glenville High School and the *Torch* staff are drawn from the yearbooks and back issues of the *Torch* carefully preserved by Carolyn Johnson in the Glenville High library. Much material is also taken from Dennis Dooley and Gary Engle, *Superman at Fifty: The Persistence of a Legend* (Cleveland: Octavia Press, 1987). "I had certain inhibitions . . ." and other Siegel quotes, from the interview in *Nemo,* no. 2.

Joe Shuster's family background and early life is taken from interviews with Jerry Fine and relatives of the Shuster family in 2003; from *Nemo,* no. 2; and from Dooley and Engle, *Superman at Fifty.* The history of comic strips in the 1920s and 1930s is splendidly covered in Jerry Robinson, *The Comics: An Illustrated History of Comic Strip Art* (New York: G. P. Putnam's Sons, 1974), and Bill Blackbeard and Martin Williams, *The Smithsonian Collection of Newspaper Comics* (Washington, DC: Smithsonian Institution, and New York: Harry N. Abrams, 1977). On *Tarzan* and *Buck Rogers,* see Bill Blackbeard's introduction to Hal Foster, *Tarzan in Color* (New York: NBM, 1993), and Robert C. Dille, *The Collected Works of Buck Rogers in the 25th Century* (New York: Bonanza Books, 1969). "I'd try to get him to come out . . ." Quoted in the *Toronto Star,* April 26, 1992. The material on Bernarr MacFadden and bodybuilding culture is drawn mainly from Ernst, *Weakness Is a Crime.*

The history of *The Shadow* was provided by Anthony Tollin. Insights into the pulp and comic strip origins of the "superhero" were assisted by interviews with Tollin, James Van Hise, and Will Murray in 2003. "He was cloaked entirely . . ." Walter B. Gibson, writing as "Maxwell Grant," "The Living Shadow," *Shadow Magazine*, no. 1 (Mar. 1931). On *The Time Traveller*, see Moskowitz, *Immortal Storm*, and Julius Schwartz, *Man of Two Worlds: My Life in Science Fiction and Comics* (New York: Harper Collins, 2000). Jerry Siegel's *Science Fiction* is discussed in the Glenville High School *Torch*; Dooley and Engle, *Superman at Fifty*; and *Nemo*, no. 2.

"Great deeds were always . . ." This and the quotes to follow are from Philip Wylie, *Gladiator* (New York: Alfred A. Knopf, 1930). For Wylie's place in the literary scene of the 1920s, see Roger Matuz (ed.), *Contemporary Literary Criticism,* Vol. 43 (Detroit: Gale Research Corp., 1987). The Joseph Pirincin anecdote is courtesy of Denis Kitchen. "The Reign of the Superman" was reprinted in *Nemo,* no. 2. The material on Doc Savage benefited from the author's interviews with Anthony Tollin and James Van Hise. On *Detective Dan* and Humor Publishing, see Bob Hughes's biography of Joe Shuster on the wonderful "Superman Artists" Website, http://www.supermanartists.comics.org/superart.

In *Gladiator* we find a clue to much that is mysterious about the shifting tales of Superman's creation. Siegel flatly denied that Wylie's novel had influenced him in any way, despite the timing and the striking similarities that would seem to leave no doubt of *Gladiator*'s role. His denial seems to date from Wylie's threat to sue him for plagiarism in 1940—Siegel reportedly even signed an affidavit attesting to it—and appears to have been a self-protective act. Siegel's stories of having conceived Superman full-blown as early as 1932 make much more sense when they're examined in the light of the many plagiarism suits and challenges to his claim of authorship that might have followed; he had to place his idea before the other heroes with capes and superstrength who proliferated in the 1930s. This also helps explain Siegel's odd assertion that he declined the syndication interest mentioned by Major Wheeler-Nicholson in 1935 (chapter 6). In his 1947 lawsuit against National Comics, Siegel claimed that he had sold Superman to National *only* because of Jack Liebowitz's assurances that he and Joe Shuster would be given an unusually good deal. To support his argument, he claimed he had spurned earlier interest in Superman—the major's—because the terms weren't good enough. When one considers the complexity of balancing genuine recollection with legal strategy over a course of decades, the inconsistencies in Siegel's retellings becomes quite understandable.

CHAPTER 5

Harry Donenfeld's publishing history in the 1930s is related in Ellis, *Uncovered,* and Murray, "Tangled Roots." Many details also come from Irwin Donenfeld. "It may not be a coincidence . . ." Author's interview with Michael Feldman, February

2004. Feldman provided much of the information about Independent News's early distribution system and growth. "Boy meets girl . . ." For Jack Woodford's incomparable wisdom about the craft of writing, see *Trial and Error* (Seattle: Woodford Memorial Editions, 1980). "The thin silk of the dress . . ." Quoted in Ellis, *Uncovered*. Ellis's book covers Harry's battles with the censors in some detail. "We are going to give . . ." quoted in the *Los Angeles Times*, July 20, 1933. New York's social climate, politics, and racket activities during Repeal are discussed in Cohen, *Tough Jews*; Fried, *Rise and Fall*; and Robert A. Rockaway, *But He Was Good to His Mother: The Lives and Crimes of Jewish Gangsters* (Jerusalem: Gefen, 1993). The Herbie Siegel story has been told by dozens of people who worked in the comics industry from the 1930s to the 1950s. This version owes most to the author's conversations with Julius Schwartz and Murray Boltinoff in the 1980s.

"I jammed the roscoe . . ." Here the author cheats a bit. This is not, as far as can be verified, an actual Bellem line, but a pastiche of Bellem phrases concocted by a fan; it seemed the quickest way to suggest his style and vocabulary. For the man's actual lines ("It sounded like a roscoe sneezing 'ka-chow'. . . "), see Robert Leslie Bellem, *Dan Turner, Hollywood Detective* (Madison: University of Wisconsin Press, 1983). The Perelman quote is from *The New Yorker*, Oct. 15, 1938.

This reconstruction of the roles of Eastern Color Printing, Charlie Gaines, and George Delacorte in developing the comic book is built on many sources, including Mike Benton, *The Comic Book in America: An Illustrated History* (Dallas: Taylor Publishing, 1989); Jamie Coville's "Collector Times" Website, http://www.collectortimes.com/~comichistory/index.html; and Robert Beerbohm's exhaustive but as yet unpublished history of comic book distribution and retailing, *Comic Book Store Wars*. Portions of the latter can be viewed at http://members.aol.com/comicbknet/reality.htm. Further information about Charlie Gaines comes from Frank Jacobs, *The Mad World of William M. Gaines* (Secaucus, NJ: Lyle Stuart, 1972), and Maria Reidelbach, *Completely Mad: A History of the Comic Book and Magazine* (New York: Little, Brown, 1991). Douglas Nicholson and Will Murray were the author's principal source of information on Major Malcolm Wheeler-Nicholson. "I see these magazines . . ." Letter to Jerry Siegel, quoted in Les Daniels, *Superman: The Complete History* (San Francisco: Chronicle Books, 1998).

What is known about Sunny Paley comes by way of Michael Feldman from Jack Adams and other former associates of Harry Donenfeld's who have asked to remain anonymous. Obviously, much more remains to be discovered. Feldman has also reconstructed Harry's business activities in the South. "I really admire Mr. Donenfeld . . ." From a mock newspaper prepared for Harry's fiftieth birthday by Jack Liebowitz and other associates, October 1943; courtesy of Irwin Donenfeld.

The role of the lumber industry and William Randolph Hearst in the illegalization of marijuana is a subject tangled in the politics of hemp, and much overstatement surrounds it; no doubt this telling is too simple, as well. However, to this author's mind, the evidence remains compelling and reasonable even when one works to tease it free of political screed. It stands as one of many illuminating examples of the ways in which Hearst, like so many newspaper and magazine publishers of his time, used his position to advance the most venal private schemes. See Mike Gray, *Drug Crazy* (New York: Random House, 2001).

CHAPTER 6

The prepublication history of Superman, including Siegel's collaboration with artists other than Shuster, may be the most exhaustively studied subject in comic book–fan research, and the list of people, Websites, magazine articles, and books consulted in piecing it together would be dauntingly long. Much of the material in this chapter derives from the author's interviews with Will Murray, Tom Andrae, Mike Catron, Michael Feldman, and Denis Kitchen.

"I hop out of bed . . ." This and the remainder of the first version of Superman's origin appear in James Steranko, *The Steranko History of Comics* (Reading, PA: Supergraphics, 1972). "I'm a perfectionist . . ." This and other quotes and details from the later telling of Superman's origin appear in Siegel and Shuster's interview in *Nemo,* no. 2, and Daniels, *Superman;* the latter contains Siegel and Shuster's early contributions to *New Fun,* the major's letter about the "pending" syndication deal, and the brainstorming sketches for the "sensation of 1936." The quotes from and about *Popular Comics* come from *Siegel and Shuster: Dateline 1930s* (Forestville, CA: Eclipse Comics, 1984). Joanne Carter's story is from *Nemo,* no. 2. Michael Siegel believes this story was fabricated later by Siegel, Shuster, and Carter. Gaines's place in Superman's history has been reconstructed by Will Murray, Tom Andrae, and others; Worth Carnahan's story comes through Michael Feldman. "His thundering fists. . . " *Detective Comics,* no. 1 (Mar. 1937).

Superman's sale to Vin Sullivan is another of the most often told and most often debated of the legends of the comics subculture. This telling is based primarily on David Siegel's interview of Vin Sullivan at the San Diego Comic Con, August 1998, and the author's subsequent conversation with Sullivan, checked and balanced with insights from Mike Catron, Tom Andrae, and Will Murray. Sheldon Mayer's background was drawn in part from Lambiek's online "comiclopedia," http//www.lambiek.net/artists/index.html. Throughout the writing of this book, this Website was a valuable source of thumbnail biographies of comics writers and artists. The first Superman story appears in two parts, in *Action Comics,* no. 1 (June 1938), and *Superman,* no. 1 (Summer 1939).

CHAPTER 7

"It is summer . . ." William Manchester, *The Glory and the Dream: A Narrative History of America, 1932–1972* (Boston: Little, Brown, 1974). "a lot of Jews will lose . . ." Quoted in Gabler, *Empire of Their Own.* The New York Jewish experience in the 1930s is explored in Beth S. Wenger, *New York Jews and the Great Depression: Uncertain Promise* (New Haven: Yale University Press, 1996). On the role of popular entertainment and mass communications in the culture of that moment, see also Alice Goldfarb Marquis, *Hopes and Ashes: The Birth of Modern Times, 1929–1939* (New York: Free Press, 1986), and Michael Denning, *The Cultural Front* (New York: Verso, 1997). "working out routes . . ." Author's interview with Alex Singer, May 2003. Mort Weisinger and Julius Schwartz's stories were constructed mainly from the author's interviews with Schwartz and Jack Schiff in 1984 and 1985, with information from Sam Moskowitz, *Seekers of Tomorrow: Makers of Modern Science Fiction* (Cleveland: World, 1966); Warner, *All Our Yesterdays*; and Schwartz, *Man of Two Worlds.*

Bob Kane's story is a fascinating one to reconstruct, due to his lifelong habit of fictionalizing his own life. His autobiography (with Tom Andrae), *Batman and Me* (Forestville, CA: Eclipse Books, 1989), provides a sort of hand-scrawled treasure map to the truth of the story, but finding that truth requires collecting anecdotes from those who knew him and sifting for common, plausible, and verifying threads. Fortunately, the number of people who worked with Kane and are eager to talk about him is legion. The author has drawn mainly on his interviews with Will Eisner, Jerry Robinson, Sheldon Moldoff, Jack Schiff, Julius Schwartz, Michael Uslan, Tom Andrae, and Mark Evanier.

"If your father wasn't such . . ." Will Eisner, *To the Heart of the Storm* (Princeton, WI: Kitchen Sink Press, 1991). "It's difficult to put into words . . ." Kane, *Batman and Me.* The story about Will Eisner and the "eight pagers" comes from Art Spiegelman's introduction to Bob Adelman, *Tijuana Bibles: Art and Wit in America's Forbidden Funnies, 1930s–1950s* (New York: Simon & Schuster, 1997). Jerry Iger was described as "a promoter and operator" by Pierce Rice in an interview in *Comics Journal,* no. 219 (Mar. 2000). "I was hungry . . ." Most of the Eisner quotes here come from the author's interview, but this anecdote is taken from an interview in *Comics Journal,* no. 249 (Sept. 2001). The descriptions of the working methods of the Eisner & Iger studio have been mainly taken from articles and interviews in *Will Eisner Quarterly* (1984–1985). Bill Finger's story has been pulled together from Kane's *Batman and Me* and the author's interviews with Jerry Robinson and Jack Schiff.

Superman dialogue from *Action Comics,* no. 5 (Oct. 1938). Details of the Superman newspaper strip and the initial Superman fad are pulled from Daniels, *Superman,* and Jerry Siegel and Joe Shuster, *Superman: The Dailies* (Northampton, MA: Kitchen Sink Press, 1999). Victor Fox is described amusingly in Joe Simon, *The Comic Book Makers* (New York: Crestwood, 1990); the truth behind the "bookkeeper" story, however, was uncovered by Michael Feldman. The origin of Batman is discussed, in different ways, in Les Daniels, *Batman: The Complete History* (San Francisco: Chronicle Books, 2000), and Kane, *Batman and Me.* The reconstruction of Bill Finger's original contribution is due mainly to Jerry Bails, among whose many articles on the subject the most important was "If the Truth Be Known; Or, a Finger in Every Plot" in the seminal fanzine *CAPA-Alpha*, no. 12 (Sept. 1965). The author's interview with Michael Uslan in September 2003 contributed greatly to the synthesis attempted by this book. Much of the analysis of Batman's later development derives from the author's interview with Jerry Robinson in April 2004. Lines and events from the stories are taken from *Detective Comics*, no. 27 (May 1939) and no. 29 (July 1939).

With Batman's origin story, *Detective Comics*, no. 33 (Nov. 1939), we encounter another intriguing puzzle of comic book history. The origin first appears within a Batman adventure generally attributed to Gardner Fox. (See Daniels, *Batman*.) However, comics historians (including Jerry Bails, Craig Delich, and Michael Uslan) generally agree that the origin sequence itself was Finger's work. It certainly reads more like Finger's writing style to this author.

Mort Weisinger's development of *Captain Future* and awareness of Superman is based on the author's interview with Jack Schiff and on Moskowitz, *Seekers of Tomorrow*.

CHAPTER 8

The story of the Superman radio show is told by Anthony Tollin in his booklet for Smithsonian Historical Performances' *Superman on Radio* CD. Tollin's article has been archived on two highly informative and entertaining Web shrines devoted to the Man of Steel, "Superman Homepage," http://supermanhomepage.com, and "Superman through the Ages," http://theAges.superman.ws/welcome.php.

On the Waldorf-Astoria and the mob, see Wolf and DiMona, *Frank Costello*. Material on Ben Sangor comes from the author's interview with Michael Feldman and from Michael Vance, *Forbidden Adventures: The History of the American Comics Group* (Westport, CT: Greenwood Press, 1996). The Dubinsky story is from Irwin Donenfeld. Jack Schiff and Vin Sullivan contributed to the author's understanding of the corporate development of All American and Detective Comics, Liebowitz's response to the war, and the Captain Marvel lawsuit. "golf courses, yacht clubs . . ." Great Neck description from Arthur F. Rausch, *A Look Ahead,* courtesy of Steven Morgan Friedman. Thanks also to the Great Neck Historical Society.

Sterling North, "A National Disgrace," *Chicago Daily News,* May 8, 1940. Thanks also to the Sterling North Society of Edgerton, Wisconsin. On the public reaction to the comic book scare and publishers' responses, see Amy Kiste Nyberg, *Seal of Approval: The History of the Comics Code* (Jackson: University Press of Mississippi, 1998). George Orwell, "Boys' Weeklies," reprinted in *A Collection of Essays* (New York: Doubleday, 1953). "would seem to offer the same . . ." Lauretta Bender quoted in Nyberg, *Seal of Approval.* Josette Frank paraphrased from her introduction to George Lowther, *The Adventures of Su-*

perman (New York: Random House, 1942). "speak to the innermost ears . . ." Quoted in Les Daniels, *Wonder Woman: The Complete History* (San Francisco: Chronicle Books, 2000).

"Frankly, when I got through . . ." Liebowitz quoted in Jerry Siegel's press release from 1975. Siegel's resistance to using a lawyer has been discussed by Vin Sullivan and Jerry Fine. "besides affording entertainment . . ." Slater Brown, "The Coming of Superman," *New Republic,* Sept. 2, 1940, courtesy of Will Murray. The Spectre first appeared in *More Fun Comics,* no. 52 (Feb. 1940). See also Don Markstein's helpful "Toonopedia," http://www.toonopedia.com. Thanks to Mike Sangiacomo for information on Joe Shuster's life in Cleveland, and to Jerry Robinson and Mike Catron for information on his move to New York. "brown manila paper . . ." Eileen Freeman quoted in *Cleveland Plain Dealer,* Dec. 12, 2000.

Siegel's appearance on Fred Allen's radio show can be downloaded from the "Superman through the Ages" Website; the same MP3 file includes Harry Donenfeld's comedy routine with Bud Collyer described in chapter 10, and it is recommended to all interested readers, as the author's powers are inadequate to draw the contrast between the social styles and levels of confidence of the two men half as well as do the sounds of their own voices. "Jerry, being undersized. . . " *Liberty,* July 1941. The "K-metal" story and much of the context for it are courtesy of Mark Waid. Mort Weisinger's tenure at DC has been reconstructed mainly from interviews with Jack Schiff and Julius Schwartz.

According to recent discoveries passed on by comics historian Roy Thomas, *Superboy* was developed in tandem with a proposed *Superwoman,* and among the ideas entertained for the latter was a superpowered Lois Lane. Both ideas were deferred when Fawcett hit the stands first with Captain Marvel Jr. and Mary Marvel. After the Fawcett titles proved themselves successful, *Superboy* was revived.

"Get behind your work . . ." and "show that we lost money . . ." From correspondence that Siegel quoted often, including, in part, his 1975 press release.

CHAPTER 9

For comics publishing history and sales figures, here and in subsequent chapters, see Benton, *Comic Book in America,* and another thorough Benton book, *Superhero Comics of the Golden Age: The Illustrated History* (Dallas: Taylor Publishing, 1992).

The story of the *Daredevil* weekend is taken mainly from the author's interview with Jerry Robinson. Robinson wasn't certain that the man who drew the short straw was Bernie Klein, but a slightly different version of the story passed down by way of George Roussos suggests that it was.

"The work was relentless . . ." Jules Feiffer, *The Great Comic Book Heroes* (New York: Dial Press, 1965). "They would take rubber cement . . ." Interview with Gil

Kane by Gary Groth, *Comics Journal,* no. 186 (Apr. 1996). "introspective, imaginative . . ." and "Cole's world teems . . ." Art Spiegelman and Chip Kidd, *Jack Cole and Plastic Man: Forms Stretched to Their Limits* (San Francisco: Chronicle Books, 2001). "He had enormous vitality . . ." Gil Kane, *Comics Journal,* no. 186. Other material on Biro and Bob Wood comes from Nicky Wright, "Seducers of the Innocent," *Comic Book Marketplace,* no. 65 (Nov. 1998); the Lev Gleason Website at http://www.angelfire.com/mn/blaklion; and Mike Benton, *Crime Comics: The Illustrated History* (Dallas: Taylor Publishing, 1993).

"I think anger will save . . ." Quoted in an interview in *Will Eisner's Spirit Magazine,* no. 39 (Feb. 1982). "Each street had its own . . ." Jon B. Cooke, "Kirby's Mean Streets: The Lower East Side of Jacob Kurtzberg," *The Jack Kirby Collector,* no. 16 (June 1997). "made me so fearful . . ." and "They threw me out . . ." Quoted in *Will Eisner's Spirit Magazine,* no. 39. "In my neighborhood . . ." Quoted in Ray Wyman Jr., *The Art of Jack Kirby* (Orange, CA: Blue Rose Press, 1992). The towel anecdote is taken from an interview with Will Eisner in *The Jack Kirby Collector,* no. 16. The brown betty story is from Simon, *Comic Book Makers.* Other information is drawn from the author's interview with Mark Evanier, who is currently writing what will no doubt be the definitive Kirby biography. The story of Martin Goodman is based mainly on the diligent research of "Doc V," Dr. Michael J. Vassallo.

Gardner Fox's biography is from Vin Sullivan. Alvin Schwartz's is drawn from his own reminiscences; see "Alvin's Round Table" at http://www.comicscommunity. com.

The descriptions of All American Comics, Charlie Gaines, and Sheldon Mayer owe a great deal to the Merrily Mayer Harris interview in *Comic Book Artist,* no. 11 (Jan. 2001), and to Jacobs, *Mad World.* William Moulton Marston's story was pieced together largely by Geoffrey C. Bunn, whose article on Marston in *History of the Human Sciences* 10, no. 1 (1997), contains many of the quotes used here. Material is also drawn from Daniels, *Wonder Woman,* and the reissue of Marston's *The Emotions of Normal People* (Minneapolis: Persona Press, 1979), including John G. Geier's introduction. The story described appears in *Wonder Woman,* no. 5 (June–July 1943).

The circumstances of Gaines and Marston's meeting are another area calling for more investigation. Stories handed down through comics fandom, reputedly derived from Gil Kane or Robert Kanigher, maintain that Marston had some sort of self-promotional scheme going at the 1939–1940 World's Fair, where he and Gaines met and began talking about comic strip ideas. As Michael Feldman has pointed out, Marston's article about comics in *Family Circle* in October 1940 certainly reads as if he were already promoting a comic book idea in tandem with Gaines: He singles Charlie out as the most enlightened of publishers, even though Gaines had very few publications on the stands yet.

CHAPTER 10

Dukey Maffetore's love of comic books comes from Cohen, *Tough Jews*. "Handed a chocolate bar . . ." From *New Gods*, no. 1 (March 1971). The Stan Lee story is from the author's interview with Lee, October 2003. "Joe and I had signed a deal. . . " *Nemo*, no. 2. Much insight into the internal politics of DC has been provided by Jack Schiff and Alvin Schwartz. Siegel's induction is described in "Half of Superman Drafted," *Cleveland Plain Dealer*, June 30, 1943. "Son Born to Superman Writer," *Cleveland Plain Dealer*, Jan. 14, 1944. The material on Michael Siegel comes from the author's email correspondence with him, November 2004.

The story of Siegel and Superboy, from rejection to revision to conflict, is drawn from many sources in fandom. Mark Waid, Michael Uslan, and the late Rich Morrissey were especially helpful to this telling. Some researchers, including Les Daniels (*Superman*), attribute the first "Superboy" script to Don Cameron; but no one doubts that the Shuster Studio illustrated it. Zugsmith's life is described in C. Jerry Kuttner, "Albert Zugsmith's Opium Dreams," *Bright Lights Film Journal*, no. 20 (Nov. 1997); further information is courtesy of the University of Iowa Special Collections Department. Harry's appearance on the Fanny Brice program is courtesy of the J. David Goldin collection. The source of Harry's Superman skit is described in the notes for chapter 8.

CHAPTER 11

Bradford W. Wright, *Comic Book Nation: The Transformation of Youth Culture in America* (Baltimore: Johns Hopkins University Press, 2001), includes a fine discussion of the medium's place in postwar American politics and culture. See also William W. Savage, *Cowboys, Commies, and Jungle Queens: Comic Books and America, 1945–1954* (Middletown, CT: Wesleyan University Press, 1998). Lev Gleason's encounter with HUAC has been discussed by Paul Buhle and Michael Feldman.

On the horror genre, see Mike Benton, *Horror Comics: The Illustrated History* (Dallas: Taylor Publications, 1991). On Leo Rosenbaum, see Vance, *Forbidden Adventures*. On the crime genre, see Benton, *Crime Comics*. Fredric Wertham and the anti-comics campaign are discussed in Nyberg, *Seal of Approval*, and Wright, *Comic Book Nation*. The campaign is effectively placed in a larger cultural context by James B. Gilbert, *Cycle of Outrage: America's Reaction to the Juvenile Delinquent in the 1950s* (Oxford: Oxford University Press, 1988). Martin Barker's *Comics: Ideology, Power, and the Critics* (Basingstoke, UK: Palgrave MacMillan, 1989) focuses mainly on the comic book scare in the United Kingdom but is a valuable look at the cultural meaning of the debate in both the United Kingdom and the United States. "set off a chain of . . ." Quoted in Judith

Crist, "Horror in the Nursery," *Collier's*, Mar. 27, 1948. *Newsweek* and *Time* quoted in Nyberg, *Seal of Approval*. Gerson Legman, *Love and Death: A Study in Censorship* (New York: Breaking Point, 1949). "freedom of the press . . ." Quoted in Nyberg, *Seal of Approval*.

On the "Unity House" story line see Anthony Tollin, "Superman on Radio," archived on "Superman Homepage." The story of Siegel and Shuster's lawsuit is a composite of information from their many interviews in later years, particularly in *Nemo*, no. 2, Siegel's 1975 press release, the original court documents, Daniels's *Superman*, the author's conversations with Siegel and Shuster in the 1980s, and the author's interviews with Michael Uslan, Mike Catron, and Jerry Robinson. "As I get the story . . ." Quoted in Daniels, *Superman*. Details related to Bob Kane are mostly from Michael Uslan and Mark Evanier. Funnyman's history comes in part from Vin Sullivan. The story of Joanne Carter's return to Jerry's life is taken from *Nemo*, no. 2. Some details of Siegel's divorce and remarriage, and the minor scandal surrounding Judge Silbert, are taken from articles in the *Cleveland Plain Dealer* from July to November 1948. "I had enough money . . ." Quoted in C. Jerry Kuttner, "Albert Zugsmith's Opium Dreams."

CHAPTER 12

"How the hell can I run . . ." and "I got the feeling that Bill went . . ." Quoted in Jacobs, *Mad World*, which chronicles Charlie Gaines's demise and Bill's assumption of control of EC. The most thorough treatment of the formative days of EC, however, is Grant Geissman and Fred von Bernewitz, *Tales of Terror: The EC Companion* (Seattle: Fantagraphics Books, 2002). "At the time it was fashionable . . ." Kurtzman quoted in Mike Benton, *Masters of Imagination: The Comic Book Artists Hall of Fame* (Dallas: Taylor Publications, 1994). "considers these publications subversive . . ." The FBI and military files on EC are archived on the "Mad Magazine Collector Resource Center" Website, http://www.collect-mad.com/fbi/fbi-mad-bufiles.htm.

"I always wanted to do the films . . ." and "we're all concerned with giving . . ." Quoted in Daniels, *Superman*, which contains a good overview of the *Superman* TV show. Other material can be found online at http://www.supermantv.net. National Periodicals' internal history is drawn from interviews with Jack Schiff, Julius Schwartz, and Murray Boltinoff conducted in 1984 and 1985 and with Irwin Donenfeld twenty years later. Thanks also to Mark Evanier and Mark Waid. On Mickey Spillane, see Max Allan Collins and James L. Traylor, *One Lonely Knight: Mickey Spillane's Mike Hammer* (Bowling Green, OH: Bowling Green Popular Press, 1984.) "I reached up and smacked her . . ." Mickey Spillane, *I, the Jury* (New York: Signet, 1948). On the history of paperbacks, including Fawcett and NAL, see Kenneth C. Davis, *Two-Bit Culture: The Paperbacking of America* (Boston:

Houghton Mifflin, 1984), and the publisher-by-publisher essays compiled by Russell Barns at http://www.paperbarn.www150megs.com.

The Jewish racketeers' movement toward legitimacy is explored in Fried, *Rise and Fall,* and Rockaway, *But He Was Good to His Mother.* On Estes Kefauver and the organized crime hearings, see Joseph Bruce Gorman, *Kefauver: A Political Biography* (New York: Oxford University Press, 1971), and William Howard Moore, *The Kefauver Committee and the Politics of Crime, 1950–1952* (Columbia: University of Missouri Press, 1974). "telegenic hit" and "entertainment dud . . ." Quoted by Allan May in "Refusing to Refuse: The Kleinman/Rothkopf Testimony," one of his columns for "American Mafia," http://www.americanmafia.com. On Frank Costello's testimony, see Wolf and DiMona, *Frank Costello.* The strange story of Ziff-Davis and the flying saucers is told in Ron Goulart, *Cheap Thrills: An Informal History of the Pulp Industry* (New York: Arlington House, 1972). Jerry Siegel's stint there was reconstructed with help from Michael Feldman. Feldman also assisted with the last years of Joe Shuster's art career, as did Tom Andrae and Jerry Robinson.

Fredric Wertham's biography and education are described in essays by Peter Nisbet and James E. Reibman in *The Fredric Wertham Collection* (Cambridge, MA: Harvard University Press, 1990) and considered in the context of comic books in Nyberg, *Seal of Approval.* His ideological debt to Adorno is discussed in Gilbert, *Cycle of Outrage.* The latter's ideas on the culture industry as a mechanism for mass deception are developed in Theodor Adorno and Max Horkheimer, *Dialectic of Enlightenment* (London: Verso, reissue 1979). Some critics have questioned the extent of Wertham's familiarity with Adorno; although Wertham claimed to know Adorno, Adorno apparently never mentioned Wertham, a fact that may reflect as much on the intellectual pecking order of the high-culture industry as the acquaintanceship of the men.

"I began to notice . . ." Quoted in Nyberg. "Superman (with the big S. . .)." Fredric Wertham, *Seduction of the Innocent* (New York: Rinehart, 1954). On Gaines's appearance before the subcommittee, see Jacobs, *Mad World,* and Geissman and von Bernewitz, *Tales of Terror.* "I felt that I was really going to . . ." and "I could feel myself fading . . ." Gaines's personal comments are quoted in Jacobs. The testimony and questioning are transcribed in Geissman and von Bernewitz. The author was able to view films of Wertham's and Gaines's appearances before the subcommittee through the courtesy of Mark Evanier, which contributed some of the details and "stage directions" in this telling.

On the history and effects of the Comics Code Authority, see Nyberg, *Seal of Approval,* and Wright, *Comic Book Nation.* On the folding of the American News Company, see Davis, *Two-Bit Culture,* and Tebbel and Zuckerman, *The Magazine in America.* "They gave me the nicest, cleanest . . ." Quoted in Jacobs, *Mad World.* Help with piecing together the expansion of Independent News was provided by Michael Feldman.

CHAPTER 13

"I spent eleven years . . ." From Donald Swan, "Jack Cole: A Life in Four Colors," *Once upon a Dime* (Winter 1991). "What comics needs is . . ." Author's interview with Stan Lee. Bob Wood's story is told in Simon, *Comic Book Makers*. Jack Kirby and Stan Lee's experiences are taken from an interview with Mark Evanier and from Stan Lee and George Mair, *Excelsior! The Amazing Life of Stan Lee* (New York: Fireside, 2002).

Letter to "Mr. Frolick," courtesy of Billy Frolick. Joanne Siegel's confrontation with Jack Liebowitz is composited from many sources, including *Nemo*, no. 2, Mike Catron, Tom Andrae, and Mark Evanier. Material on Mort Weisinger's editorship comes from the author's interviews with E. Nelson Bridwell and Jack Schiff, from many interviews and conversations with Mark Evanier over the years, from Alvin Schwartz's online reflections, and from Guy H. Lillian III's interview with Weisinger himself in *Amazing World of DC Comics*, no. 7 (Aug. 1975). Stories referenced are "Life on Krypton," *Superboy*, no. 79 (Mar. 1960); "The Ghost of Jor-El," *Superboy*, no. 78 (Jan. 1960); *Supergirl* series in *Action Comics*, nos. 261–291 (Feb. 1960–Aug. 1962); and "Superman's Return to Krypton," *Superman*, no. 141 (Nov. 1960). Thanks to the Grand Comics Database, http://www.comics.org, for help verifying writing credits.

Stories of Mort Weisinger's treatment of freelancers are so ubiquitous among veterans of National Periodicals that a list of sources would be virtually identical to a *Superman* credits list. A good clearinghouse for the best of them has been Mark Evanier. Some anecdotes about Weisinger at his worst—not always verifiable—can be found in Steve Duin and Mike Richardson, *Comics: Between the Panels* (Milwaukie, OR: Dark Horse, 1998). The Don Cameron story comes from Alvin Schwartz; other versions of the story assign the role of the defenestrator to different freelancers, but Schwartz's general reliability and closeness to the Weisinger stable make his seem the most likely. On the other hand, a different Schwartz, Julius, once insisted that the story could not be true because the windows of National's offices at the time didn't open. The story is true, at least, in the heart of everyone who ever worked for the man.

"looking like a malevolent toad . . ." Quoted in Bill Schelly, *The Golden Age of Comic Fandom* (Seattle: Hamster Press, 1995). For Swan's experiences, see Eddy Zeno, *Curt Swan: A Life in Comics* (New York: Watson-Guptill, 2002). Weisinger's claims to have been a tortured soul come mainly from Lillian's interview in *Amazing World of DC*.

The circumstances of Harry Donenfeld's death are only now being explored by comics historians, and much remains murky. This attempt at a telling puts details garnered from Irwin Donenfeld alongside rumors passed from Murray Boltinoff and Jack Adams to Michael Feldman. Feldman states that some former associates of Harry's are certain that Harry was the victim of a contract killing, but until more material is gathered, this must be classified as another of those speculations that grow spontaneously around men with mob affiliations.

CHAPTER 14

The genesis of the Marvel superheroes in the early 1960s is another of the most thoroughly discussed subjects in comic book history, and it was such a prominent subject in the author's own years in the business that it becomes almost impossible to speak of sources; these stories were such a part of the general conversation of a whole community that the author draws upon them as if they were personal memories. "From the beginning . . ." Author's interview with Jerry Robinson. "I used to come home . . ." Author's interview with Stan Lee. See also Lee and Mair, *Excelsior,* and Jordan Raphael and Tom Spurgeon, *Stan Lee and the Rise and Fall of the American Comic Book* (Chicago: Chicago Review Press, 2003).

The reader interested in Pop, camp, and the comics is strongly advised to read Peter Benchley's astonishing report, "The Story of Pop! What It Is and How It Came to Be," *Newsweek,* Apr. 26, 1966, which is archived on the Roy Lichtenstein Foundation's Website, http://lichtensteinfoundation.org/newsweekapr66.htm. In only 3,700 words Benchley throws together Roy Lichtenstein, Andy Warhol, Marshall MacLuhan, Marcel Duchamp, Batman, Susan Sontag, Rudi Gernreich, Humphrey Bogart, Edie Sedgwick, the Gemini space program, Jay Emmett, a used comic book dealer named Burt Blum, and, yes, Jack Liebowitz into one loud wall splatter of an essay on the momentary unity of commerce, irony, joy, and despair in mid-Sixties America. Soon afterward Benchley would go on to write speeches for Lyndon Johnson, then would become his own sort of pop icon with *Jaws,* the novel that helped create the comic book movie of the late 1970s.

The Irv Novick material comes in part from his son, Kim Novick. On Kurtzman, *Help,* and the underground comix, see Mark James Estren, *A History of Underground Comics* (Berkeley: Ronin, 1989). Thanks to Art Spiegelman for corrections of some finer points. The growth of superhero fandom is covered splendidly in Schelly, *Golden Age.* On the TV *Batman* and related phenomena, see Daniels, *Batman.* On Jay Emmett and LCA, see *Look Magazine,* May 1965. The haircut anecdote is courtesy of Charlie Goldberg. The story of the writers' confrontation with Liebowitz is taken from Mike Barr, "The Madame and the Girls," *WaP!* (1988), and the author's subsequent conversations with Barr. The material on Bob Kane and Bill Finger is from Mark Evanier and Michael Uslan; thanks also to Jerry Bails. "To the victor belong the spoils . . ." From Kane's letter to the *Batmania* fanzine, Sept. 14, 1965, reprinted in *Alter Ego* 2, no. 3 (Winter 1999). The bizarre phrasing is typical of Kane's writing when he didn't hire a rewriter. The Joe Simon detail is from Jim Simon's introduction to Simon, *Comic Book Makers.* "He was a haunted man . . ." Kane, *Batman and Me.*

Jerry Siegel is credited on paper (as "Joe Carter") for only two *Human Torch* scripts, appearing a year into the series' run, but anecdote and internal evidence both argue for Siegel as a contributor to the series from the beginning. (The Torch, for example, lives in Glenville from the first episode.) The chronology of Siegel's challenge to the Superman copyright is courtesy of Mike Catron. "I told him who I was . . ." From an interview with James Warren by Jon B. Cooke, in *Comic Book Artist,* no. 4 (Spring 1999). Siegel's move to California has been variously explained and speculated upon by Mike Catron, Tom Andrae, Stan Lee, and Jerry Robinson.

Most of the Steve Ross passage is drawn from Connie Bruck, *Master of the Game: Steve Ross and the Creation of Time-Warner* (New York: Simon & Schuster, 1994). Some material on his acquisition of National Periodicals is from the Carmine Infantino interview in *Comic Book Artist,* no. 1 (Spring 1998). Other insights were provided by Irwin Donenfeld, Michael Feldman, and Paul Levitz.

CHAPTER 15

"I was forty-five . . ." Mario Puzo, *The Godfather Papers and Other Confessions* (New York: G. P. Putnam's Sons, 1972). See also Bruce Jay Friedman's introduction to Adam Parfrey, *It's a Man's World: Mens' Adventure Magazines, the Postwar Pulps* (Los Angeles: Feral House, 2003). Friedman spent over a decade as Martin Goodman's editor on skin magazines and violent pulps, hiring Puzo as his assistant for a time, while he wrote his own viciously funny novels about the suburbanization of New York Jews. Later, Friedman became a prosperous screenwriter while his sons, Drew and Josh Alan Friedman, emerged as a prominent artist and a writer, respectively, in the alternative comics scene of the 1980s. Comic books, pornography, sweaty men's entertainment, movies, underground culture, and immigrant assimilation reveal new connections every time we look.

The development of the *Superman* movie is tracked at http://www.supermancinema.net/superman1/general/scripts/index.shtml. The circumstances of Siegel's press release and early response were conveyed by Mike Catron and Phil Yeh. This telling of the campaign for Siegel and Shuster's settlement depends mainly on Jerry Robinson's telling, with help from Mike Catron, Paul Levitz, and Mark Evanier. "I think it's fine . . ." Quotes from the *Cleveland Plain Dealer,* Jan. 7, 1979.

Once we enter the 1980s, the description of the comic book industry and fandom is drawn largely from the author's own experience. Details are included from the author's interviews or correspondence with Art Spiegelman, Michael Chabon, Will Eisner, Michael Uslan, and Paul Levitz. The Tom Hall story ("I tore open the envelope. . . ") came to the author courtesy of Carla Seal-Wanner. "We now have a very good relationship . . ." Interviewed in *Nemo,* no. 2. "There aren't many people . . ." Quoted in the *Toronto Star,* Apr. 26, 1992.

Mike Catron's obituaries for Joe Shuster and Jerry Siegel in *Comics Journal,* no. 153 (Oct. 1992), and no. 184 (Feb. 1996), respectively, provide much information about their later years. Mike Carlin's comments on Jerry Siegel's reaction to Superman's "death" are quoted in Jerry's Reuters obituary, Jan. 31, 1996. Thanks to Mike Catron for the information on Jack Liebowitz's final videotape interview, and to Irwin Donenfeld for his comments on the last years of his "Uncle Jack."

INDEX

CPSIA information can be obtained at www.ICGtesting.com
Printed in the USA
LVOW04s0848161015

458550LV00007B/11/P